THE MAKING OF THE SCOTTISH COUNTRYSIDE

The Making of the Scottish Countryside

Edited by
M. L. PARRY and T. R. SLATER

CROOM HELM LONDON

McGILL-QUEEN'S UNIVERSITY PRESS
MONTREAL

Croom Helm Ltd, 2-10 St John's Road, London SW11

British Library Cataloguing in Publication Data

The making of the Scottish countryside. —
    (Croom Helm historical geography series).
    1. Scotland — Historical geography
    I. Parry, M L II. Slater, T R
    911'. 411   DA867

    ISBN 0-85664-646-6

McGill-Queen's University Press
1020 Pine Avenue West, Montreal H3A 1AZ

ISBN 0-7735-0523-7

Legal deposit 2nd quarter 1980
Bibliothèque Nationale du Québec

Printed and bound in Great Britain

CONTENTS

TABLES

FIGURES

PLATES

PREFACE

This is the first collection of essays on the Scottish rural landscape. It brings together thirteen original papers, all based on primary sources, as an integrated report on the present state of knowledge in the subject. As such it illustrates both the salients of research and the enclaves that mark the incompleteness of our knowledge. We hope that it will serve both to consolidate the gains already made and act as a platform for research in the future.

The framework in which these essays have been written and presented serves to illustrate the authors' belief that the Scottish landscape is the product of a continuum of development that has been punctuated by phases of accelerated change. The emerging landscape can successfully be understood only in the context of the forces of those changes and their antecedents.

M. L. Parry and T. R. Slater

ACKNOWLEDGEMENTS

The editors wish to thank David Thomas, Paul Temple and the late Harry Thorpe, both for their encouragement and for access to the reprographic facilities of the Department of Geography, University of Birmingham. We acknowledge the considerable help offered by the secretarial, cartographic and photographic staff of the Department. We are also grateful to our colleagues Peter Jarvis, Denis Shaw and Rowland Moss, and to Hugh Prince for their informed comments on parts of the manuscript. The contributors to this volume acknowledge their debt to the archivists and staffs of the Scottish Record Office, the National Library of Scotland, and the Map Room of the Royal Scottish Geographic Society. Miss M. Wilkes of the National Library of Scotland and B. S. Benediks of the University of Birmingham Library (Special Collections) gave particular assistance in the preparation of photographic material. We are grateful to the Royal Scottish Geographical Society and Dr W. P. L. Thompson for permission to reproduce Figure 4.2; the School of Scottish Studies and Dr R. Miller for Figure 4.1; and the late Professor K. Walton for material incorporated in Figure 8.1.

Acknowledgement is given to the Trustees of the National Library of Scotland for Plates 1, 2, 3 and 4; to the Trustees of the British Library for Plate 6; to the Librarian of the University of Birmingham Library for Plates 8, 14 and 21; the Controller of Her Majesty's Stationery Office for Plates 10, 11 and 12 (Crown Copyright Reserved); John Dewar and the Royal Society for the Protection of Birds for Plate 13; John Dewar Studios for Plates 16, 17 and 19; Aberdeen University Library (G. W. Wilson Collection) for Plate 18; Dr M. L. Parry for Plates 7 and 9; Dr J. M. Lindsay for Plate 22 and J. P. Shaw for Plate 23.

INTRODUCTION: THE COURSE OF RURAL CHANGE IN SCOTLAND

M. L. Parry

It is a measure of the rate of recent progress in research on the Scottish landscape that when, in 1973, I first considered a collection of papers to take stock of progress in this field, there was hardly sufficient material to warrant the task. Now, six years on, not only is there sufficient material but there is a pressing need to consolidate the achievements of the last decade.

The progress that has been made can be credited largely to a change in approach. In particular there has been a move from a descriptive to a more analytical study of the past, with greater emphasis on function than on form, and with the explanation of landscape change being sought in changes in under-lying technological or institutional processes. The concern to understand these processes has inevitably drawn the historian and geographer more firmly to the study of contemporary documents and has confirmed what was long suspected — that an excessive reliance on retrospective, printed sources of the late eighteenth and nineteenth centuries has painted a misleading picture of the Scottish rural economy of earlier times.[1] Thus the essays collected in this volume employ contemporary sources to focus on process and in this respect are somewhat different from other studies.[2]

The form of the landscape can be considered as the visible expression of a number of interacting forces. In addition to environmental factors, which are not likely to change to any great extent or with any rapidity, there are structural and technical factors. For example, agricultural land use (and its infrastructure of farmsteads, fields, shelter-belts etc.) is the visible expression of the interaction between the structural base of agriculture (the framework of estates and hold-ings) and the farming 'system' (the blend of farming capital, labour and techno-logy — and the farming knowledge that arranges this blend). Changes in landscape can therefore best be comprehended by analysis of underlying structural change. For example, in Chapter 5, Whyte makes the point that structural changes in Scottish agriculture in the seventeenth century enabled landowners to maximise the benefits of subsequent changes in farming technology during the Improving Movement. This has important implications for any discussion of the origins of the Improvement, which we shall return to later, but also emphasises the special role of the landowner in the Scottish countryside. It will be seen that in almost every sphere of rural endeavour, and certainly in every phase of Scottish history, the large landowner played a crucial role. In Chapter 7 Adams makes a strong case for the special part enacted by a few landowners as agents of landscape change in the eighteenth century, and the argument is given some credence by Timperley's calculation (Chapter 6) that the great landlords controlled just over one-half of the total agrarian wealth of Scotland in 1770. The role of the landowners and the organisation of their estates are themes which are threaded through all these essays.

In addition to changes of structure, technological changes lie at the root of landscape development. In the past these have been given greater weight than they might be given today,[3] but it is certainly true that advances in crop ecology, horticulture, silviculture and veterinary science opened up new horizons in eighteenth-century farming that fostered major modifications to the traditional farming landscape. Some advances initiated a chain of subsequent innovations and deserve specific mention. An example of these was the introduction of Small's swing-plough first in east Berwickshire in about 1763, subsequently throughout south-east Scotland by about 1780, and elsewhere in the Lowlands by 1790 (Plate 8). Since the new plough was lighter and less sturdy than the 'old Scotch' plough it could less easily break up the unploughed balks and was damaged by the 'sit-fast' stones in the furrows. Moreover, its advantages of a reduced need for draught power, obviation of a need for a driver, and the ease with which it could turn a straight furrow were lost in the tillage of the traditional crooked and uneven ridges. Thus the levelling and straightening of ridges quickly followed the adoption of the swing-plough, and the increases in productivity resulting from the cultivation of previously unploughed furrows amounted to as much as 13 per cent.[4] In a similar fashion, many technological innovations that underlie the Improving Movement in Scottish agriculture were closely interconnected with others and required their simultaneous adoption. While some technical changes worked their way slowly into the farming system others, therefore, were rapidly and extensively adopted and appear to have had a quite sudden impact on the face of the Scottish countryside.

A further advantage of the new focus on underlying landscape processes is that it allows a developmental view of landscape change instead of the occasional cross-section that was the feature of orthodox historical inquiry. Its benefits are several but two, in particular, deserve a special mention because they recur through these essays. First, it has pointed to the origins and antecedents of important landscape features and has generated lively debate on a number of issues. For example, Dodgshon discusses in Chapter 3 the evidence for the connection between the expansion of ferm-touns and the creation of outfield, and thus links the origin of the Scottish infield-outfield system to the growth of farming communities in the late Middle Ages. This is in contrast to Whittington, who has seen the origins of extensive rotating outfield cultivation in Scottish prehistory and has pointed to the subsequent development of perennial infield cultivation as a result of increasing pressure on the land in the Middle Ages.[5] Given the importance of the infield-outfield system both to the reconstruction of past landscapes and to the composition of the modern one, the outcome of this debate is of especial interest; for example, it touches directly upon the question of the antiquity of cultivation of a very large proportion of Scottish farmland and influences any discussion of the importance in the Scottish landscape of the head-dyke, the dyke which divides the outfield from extensively grazed moorland.[6]

Second, the developmental approach has also encouraged discussion of the rate or pace of landscape change, and in particular of the question: is the Scottish landscape the product more of a few, brief phases of quite rapid development separated by longer periods of diminished activity than of a continuum of development? The view espoused by Lebon in the 1940s was of a surprisingly enduring landscape not radically different today from that in the seventeenth century.[7] This was countered by Caird in 1964 with the argument that 'Scotland's rural landscape is in fact a landscape of revolution rather than of evolution.'[8] It is an argument that has been supported by Adams,[9] and is further developed by these two authors in Chapters 7 and 9 of this volume. It has, however, been criticised by Whittington and Whyte, who have emphasised the important changes that occurred in the seventeenth century far in advance of the period around 1750 to 1820 normally noted for its 'agricultural revolution';[10] and in Chapter 5, Whyte has expanded upon his thesis of seventeenth-century agrarian change which, he argues, formed an essential foundation for the more spectacular achievements of the eighteenth century. The notion of landscape change as a continual rather than as a step-wise process is an extension of the arguments developed by Whittington, Dodgshon and Fenton in Chapters 1 to 3.

The debate is an important one and the arguments appear and reappear in relation to several different issues in this collection of essays. It is possible, by a clear definition of the relevant terms, to reconcile the contending viewpoints. First, we should distinguish the process of changes in the farming system from the effects that they wrought on the farming landscape and, second, we should distinguish between the rate of development of new farming systems in progressive (or 'hearth') areas of Scotland and their diffusion elsewhere in the country. The orthodox view of the Improving Movement as a phase of structural and technological change in agriculture has been one of dramatically accelerated development over 1750-1820 based on an important prelude in the seventeenth century.[11] Whittington and Whyte have lent support to this argument while giving greater emphasis to the prelude.

On the other hand, the orthodox view of the Improving Movement as a force for reshaping the rural landscape hinges on the limited areal extent to which the technological changes (not only the structural changes) had been widely effected. The argument has been that these were limited to the mains farm and to hearth areas and were not implemented on a national scale until after 1750. Thus Adams has argued that while nearly all the innovations were well tried, 'the revolution lay in their simultaneous use across the face of the country.'[12] The new policies and planned villages discussed by Slater and Lockhart, and the new woodlands and rural industries examined by Lindsay and Shaw, are facets of this 'emerging landscape'. Thus an important distinction is being drawn between the *evolution* of the idea, the organisational framework and the technology, and the *revolution* of their implementation on a large scale, albeit with substantial regional variations in timing and in form.

The regional variation of landscape change is itself an important issue to emerge from this debate. Up to now there has been a tendency for historical studies of rural Scotland to focus either on specific regions or on particular themes regardless of important regional differences. In either case the regional linkages were ignored; yet there are signs in these essays that the authors have a new and sufficient confidence in their interpretation of the past to draw conclusions about the diffusion of ideas between regions, groups and individuals. This development, in addition to the several others already mentioned, promises well for the future of Scottish landscape studies.

Notes

1. Whyte, I. D. (1978), 'Scottish historical geography – a review', *Scottish Geographical Magazine* (hereafter SGM), *94*, 2-26

2. For example, Millman, R. N. (1975), *The making of the Scottish landscape* (London)

3. See for example: Handley, J. E. (1953), *Scottish farming in the eighteenth century* (London); Handley, J. E. (1963), *The agricultural revolution in Scotland* (Glasgow)

4. Parry, M. L. (1976), 'A typology of cultivation ridges in southern Scotland', *Tools and Tillage*, *3*, 3-19

5. Whittington, G. (1973), 'The field systems of Scotland', pp. 512-79 in Baker, A. R. H. and Butlin, R. A. (eds.), *Studies of field systems in the British Isles* (Cambridge)

6. Robertson, I. M. L. (1949), 'The head-dyke: a fundamental line in Scottish geography', *SGM*, *65*, 6-19

7. Lebon, J. H. G. (1952), 'Old maps and rural change in Ayrshire', *SGM*, *68*, 104-9

8. Caird, J. B. (1964), 'The making of the Scottish rural landscape', *SGM*, *80*, 72-80

9. Adams, I. H. (1968), 'The land surveyor and his influence on the Scottish rural landscape', *SGM*, 84, 248-55

10. Whittington, G. (1975), 'Was there a Scottish agricultural revolution?', *Area*, 7, 204-6; Whyte, I. (1978), 'Agricultural revolution in Scotland: contributions to the debate', *Area*, *10*, 203-5

11. Parry, M. L. (1976), 'A Scottish agricultural revolution?', *Area*, *8*, 238-9

12. Adams, I. H. (1977), 'The agricultural revolution in Scotland: contributions to the debate', *Area*, *10*, 198-203

THE EARLY COUNTRYSIDE

1 PREHISTORIC ACTIVITY AND ITS EFFECT ON THE SCOTTISH LANDSCAPE

G. Whittington

Any attempt to discuss the debt which the present Scottish landscape owes to events in prehistory is fraught with problems. To provide a comprehensive view of prehistoric human activity presupposes an encyclopaedic knowledge and almost certainly demands at the very least an acquaintance with the subject-matter and findings of a large number of academic disciplines, each of which has its own methodology and aim. However, if our understanding of the appearance of Scotland's early landscapes is to be furthered, an attempt to bring together evidence from many disparate sources should be attempted. The only existing synthetic views are the partial ones pioneered by Stuart Piggott,[1] and since they were written new evidence has begun to accumulate quite rapidly. Many fundamental characteristics of the evidence, however, have not changed. By the very nature of the investigations carried out and the number of workers involved, the evidence used in this chapter will inevitably be fragmentary, discontinuous in space and time, and its interpretation will doubtless be no less contentious than similar attempts at explanation in the past.

The Available Evidence

In writing about prehistoric landscape there must be a total reliance on evidence derived from other than literary sources. Paramount among the sources will be the records produced by the archaeologist. Where careful stratigraphic excavation has taken place, a variety of artefacts is often revealed; these are of vital importance in unravelling the economic history of the people who by their efforts to obtain a living must have affected the Scottish landscape. Prime among these artefacts are tools and farming equipment, bones from slaughtered cattle, grain (either carbonised or its impression on pottery), and that vital piece of equipment in seed-eating communities, the quern. With this class of evidence the problems of fragmentary and discontinuous knowledge have to be borne carefully in mind.

Another class of evidence has a dual importance: the relict feature. Where physical remains of past activities are still extant in the landscape, we are provided not only with present landscape features but also with evidence that can be used to suggest both the areas in which previous activity took place and the sort of effect their creators would have had on the contemporary landscape.

Into this category, and especially important in this task, fall the surface expression of long-decayed domestic structures and also those remains which were associated with farming activities, both pastoral and arable. The major problem associated with this evidence is that of its time or origin. Without stratified artefactual material or the existence of radio-carbon dates, there are great dangers in using this type of evidence and especially in attempting to date it by its close spatial relationship with relict features of a known date. Much of the dating evidence here must come from excavation and unfortunately much more interest has been shown in funerary remains than in those associated with livelihood gaining or domestic structures.

Perhaps the most drastic changes that have occurred in the Scottish landscape have been to the vegetation cover and, perhaps concomitantly, to the soils which supported that vegetation. The part played by man in the removal of woodland and the date at which that occurred are topics of considerable debate. Furthermore, whether much of Scotland's present moorland cover is due to past anthropogenic interference or whether it has a climatic origin is of great interest; certainly the extent of this vegetation complex is so great that it cannot be ignored. Evidence for past changes to Scotland's plant cover comes from palynological studies and as yet these are few and far between.[2] Most pollen studies that have taken place have been in a Highland context and are frequently more concerned with events of the later Post-Glacial, rather than with those of early prehistoric times. However, some pollen studies are of outstanding importance and these provide much of the evidence used in this chapter. Just as the other evidence reviewed presents problems of interpretation, so too does that to be derived from fossil pollen records. The rate at which plants produce pollen, the ways in which it is dispersed, its survival rate and variations in the rate of accumulation of the sediment in which it is preserved all present difficulties for the palynologist. Furthermore, without radio-carbon dating fossil pollen studies are of strictly limited value. Nevertheless, it will be seen that the fossil pollen record can contribute much important information.

Although much can be done in the way of chemical and organic additions to soils, the basic characteristics of our soils are fundamental to farming practice and hence to the present landscape appearance. The evolution of a soil from its raw mineral beginnings to a mature state is of long duration, but a change to the mature structure can be achieved over a much shorter time. We need to know whether soils in Scotland, especially those which are podsolised or peaty, are in that state due to natural environmental conditions and change, or whether man has brought about differences as a result of his farming activities, some of which may have been really damaging when viewed in the long term. To answer such questions, the fossil pollen evidence is important, but the occurrence of fossil soils, fortuitously preserved, is a vital factor.

The fusion of these distinct but intertwined pieces of evidence should allow the evolution of the Scottish landscape to be traced from its early state to the time when the written record begins to throw more light on the social and economic behaviour of the inhabitants of Scotland who were to continue to modify the landscape by their changing attitudes to farming and settlement location. But without an understanding of the modification made in the pre-historic period, much confusion could occur in interpreting later landscapes and in assessing the contribution made by successive generations.

The Boreal Period

In setting the scene in our investigation of change, it is vital to understand that we are concerned with a period in which the climate was still subject to change as a result of the last ice age. By about 7600 BC, Britain was being subjected to a continental type of climate; summers were short, but warm, while winters were long and severe, especially in upland areas. Rainfall was less than is received at present in Britain. During this so-called Boreal period, which lasted until about 6000 BC, the vegetation cover changed considerably. Trees which had been completely absent since before the Pleistocene recolonised, and as a response to warmer conditions began to clothe Scotland again: first birch and pine (Pre-Boreal, 8000 BC to 6800 BC), then hazel (Boreal, 6800 BC to 5000 BC), and finally, towards the end of the Boreal, the thermophilous oak, lime and elm, though these only became dominant in the later Atlantic period. The rate at which the trees re-established themselves had an effect upon the development of soils. In areas where mixed deciduous trees became established, soils developed profiles which were in equilibrium with the climate and with the vegetation: thus in the east and south of Scotland brown forest soils developed. In the west and south-west, areas where acid soils had come into existence, the development of a forest cover meant that strong podsolisation did not occur. The north-west, however, presented a somewhat different picture, in that the recolonisation by trees was a slower process, thus allowing a long period in which podsolisation could take place; this was mainly the result of a lack of humus derived from leaf litter and the recycling of nutrients by trees. The development of tree species in this area therefore appears to have been confined to pine and birch, except in areas where rocks rich in base elements provided exceptionally favourable vegetation habitats.

At some stage towards the end of the Boreal, Mesolithic man made his first appearance in Scotland. The evidence from fossil pollen diagrams and stratigraphic analyses is somewhat equivocal as to the possible effect that the Mesolithic peoples may have had upon forest cover. For their subsistence they were dependent upon hunting and gathering, but there is argument as to whether they deliberately removed forest cover to encourage the growth of herbaceous species and thus attract herbivores, or whether they merely destroyed woodland in their hunting campaigns. To these ends they could have made use of both the axe and fire, and evidence is forthcoming from both north-west and south-west Scotland to suggest that people culturally akin to the Obanian or Banchory groups[3] did engage in forest clearance. In the north-west, McVean[4] has found charcoal, which points to considerable forest-burning, while Nicholls[5] believed that there had been modification of the vegetation in the neighbourhood of Aros Moss in Kintyre. But in both cases there is doubt as to whether anthropogenic causes are involved; certainly McVean considers lightning to be the fire instigator in the north-west, while Nicholls is uncertain as to whether rises in grasses, sorrel and bracken representation and a decline in the pollen of many tree species is due to man's activities or to local variations in the ecology of the moss. Until much more detailed work has been done on the fossil pollen assemblages of the time when Mesolithic man was active, it is safest to retain an open mind on this period. In any case, any effects which Mesolithic man did have would probably have been short-lived due to natural plant regeneration.

The Atlantic Period

During the sixth millenium BC the Scottish climate underwent a fundamental change. The continental conditions which had prevailed hitherto gave way to a maritime climate in which there were increasing rainfall totals and a high incidence of westerly winds. While winters were very wet, the summers were still dominated by warm anticyclonic conditions. During this Atlantic period the so-called Post-Glacial Climatic Optimum occurred, allowing a progressive colonisation of Scotland by the more thermophilous tree species. Apart from the north-west, most areas had a deciduous forest cover in which oak was frequently dominant but lime was also present and an important additional constituent was elm. Soils were in 'equilibrium' with this forest cover and podsolisation, which many pedologists consider to be the naturally dominant soil process in Scotland, was delayed by the copious leaf litter and nutrient cycling by the trees. The tree-line certainly reached up to 800 m O.D. in the mountains but peat growth, which had been occurring since the Boreal, was also taking place as low as 250 m O.D. in the Grampians and 380 m O.D. in the Cheviots.

The initial development of agriculture in Scotland is generally considered to have taken place somewhere between 3500 and 3000 BC. Thus the effect of the Neolithic peoples perhaps began in the Atlantic period, but the evidence suggests that it became most important in the years following 3000 BC and thus mostly occurred during the Sub-Boreal period.

The Sub-Boreal Period

In relation to man's effect upon the landscape the Sub-Boreal period (3000 BC to 500 BC) is perhaps the most crucial, and is certainly one which raises many contentious issues. It saw a reversal of Scotland's climate to conditions more similar to those of the earlier Boreal period, for the Azores high-pressure system became a dominant feature producing long warm summers and short hard winters. This encouraged a further development of thermophilous vegetation species and allowed ash to become a woodland component. It is from the study of fossil pollen that most evidence for events in this period comes. Artefactual evidence is very limited and non-sepulchral relict features are unusual, being largely restricted to the northern isles where rather different conditions seem to have obtained from the Sub-Boreal onwards.[6]

Many pollen diagrams from north-west Europe show that at the beginning of this period a definite difference in floristic composition was occurring. Several arboreal components declined, while birch and hazel increased, and some herbaceous taxa, including grasses, ruderals and cereals made an appearance.

This change was also accompanied by a marked reduction in elm pollen. This so-called elm decline was at first considered to be a result of climatic change but, following the work of Iversen[7] in Denmark, it has become recognised that elm decline, the reduction of pollen from many other tree species and the increase in the pollen of grasses and weeds can be related to the activities of man. There is evidence of elm decline from sites widely spread over Scotland, but it is not always associated with unambiguous evidence of human activity. Interpretation of the effect man was having on the woodlands and thus on the landscape in the early parts of the Sub-Boreal is difficult. The amount of elm in the woodlands may have been small and so to detect the true effect of the elm decline may be difficult. Furthermore, signs of anthropogenic activity are usually considered to exist where the pollen of ribwort plantain suddenly increases. But this could be a dangerous interpretation, for that plant will grow wherever soil is disturbed and where there is no closed woodland canopy. Man need not have been the agent of disturbance, and unless cereal pollen is also present, arable farming should never be inferred from such evidence alone.

However, as a result of Iversen's work, it can be shown that distinct phases of vegetation change are recognisable in the Sub-Boreal and that they were due to man's agricultural activities. The decline in tree pollen was seen as an episode of forest clearance and where an increase in grass was accompanied by an appearance of cereal pollen, arable agriculture was held to be taking place; where the tree pollen was replaced by herbaceous pollen not including cereals, then pastoralism only was involved. A third stage in vegetation change took place when pollen totals returned to their earlier percentages; this would be explained by the abandonment of the agricultural clearing and the regeneration of woodland.

As far as Scotland is concerned, the clearing of the primary forest may well have had a fundamental and long-lasting effect on the landscape, but this is a subject of some contention. If a widespread elm decline did take place, and there is evidence of a primary elm decline before major clearances in Kirkcudbrightshire, in the Great Glen, in Fife and in Aberdeenshire, then Neolithic pastoralism, which could have involved the feeding of elm leaves to stalled cattle, may have been the first process to affect the woodland cover. The effect of deliberate clearances, either by the use of fire, or axe, or ring barking or a combination of these, is even more difficult to assess. In Iversen's original clearance scheme he considered that the openings in the woodland canopy would have been of a temporary nature involving nomadic or semi-nomadic groups of people. He termed the clearances 'landnam' phases in which agriculture would have been of short duration, probably for only two years, after which soil exhaustion would have made crop returns very poor; after abandonment the clearance would have taken at least 50 or 60 years to regenerate a tree cover.

To ascertain the length of the clearances is, however, difficult. Unless pollen analysis is undertaken by the absolute method, so that pollen influx can be related to sedimentation rates, which in turn are obtained by close-dating of the pollen-containing matrix by radio-carbon dating, there can be no accurate assessment of the length of time over which clearances existed. At present, a major stumbling-block in discussing the effects of the Neolithic farmer is caused by the very few suitable pollen sites investigated. But at two sites where absolute pollen counts have been undertaken and radio-carbon dates are frequent, primary clearance and its effects seem to have been of long duration. At Loch Clair in north-west Scotland an arboreal decline over 150 years was followed by pastoral activity for 200 years and the regeneration of woodland for a further 100 years.[8] At Loch Davan in Aberdeenshire there is a clearance associated with the elm decline of about 1,000 years;[9] this includes an initial tree decline over 400 years and a farming period of about 300 years. This length of clearance is also attested to from the nearby Braeroddach Loch. Such lengthy periods of anthropogenic effect on woodland make it apparent that the term 'landnam', with its short-length connotations, is not applicable in such areas. Indeed it leads to the question as to whether the 'landnam' suggestion of Iversen can now be fully supported. Did such short periods of clearances as he postulated really exist? Where primary clearance did occur we know that the effect on elm was sometimes drastic. In some areas it recovered (Loch Davan and at Black Loch in Fife[10]), but in others it never regenerated. This was probably due to the impoverishment of soils by leaching so that sites previously occupied by elm were no longer suitable for that tree. This could have occurred in areas where the soils were already poor, that is those where the slow primary development of vegetation on acid soils had allowed a high degree of podsolisation. But in many areas, especially those with brown forest soils, for leaching to have been the main reason for the lack of elm recolonisation the period of clearance must have been longer than that postulated by Iversen.

We must, furthermore, consider the people involved in this early modification of woodland cover. If, as Iversen thought, cultivation only took place for two years before soil exhaustion occurred, then even with a minimal population density very large areas of woodland must have been cleared. What evidence can be produced from the archaeological record to help shed light on this problem? Unfortunately, known habitation sites from the Neolithic are few in number and it is to the funerary monuments that we need to turn for help. Perhaps the two most important sites in this respect occur near Fettercairn, in Kincardineshire,[11] and at Pitnacree in Perthshire.[12] At both of these sites there are Neolithic long barrows in which large amounts of turf were used for construction. The excavation of Dalladies barrow at Fettercairn showed that the barrow was built almost immediately after the forest clearance of its site, for some of the turf used in the construction seems to have come into existence following clearance by a slash and burn technique. The interesting feature of this excavation is that the turf used in the barrow would have necessitated the cutting over of an area of at least 0.73 ha. That would have rendered the area useless for arable agriculture as the topsoil was removed with the grass, although some low-level pastoralism might have been possible within a short time span. But in fact the area lost would only have supported one individual, for it is thought that a group of 20 people would have needed about 15 to 20 ha of arable land alone.[13] The additional pastoral area also needed means that the extent of Neolithic clearance must have been considerable. It is true that this suggestion is based on the supposition of arable farming, but there is evidence that it did occur at sites like Dalladies. At Pitnacree, existing vegetation conditions were not discovered, but the nature and content of the contemporary land surface provided important evidence. Arable agriculture is strongly suggested here by the angled position of pottery sherds and stone fragments in the soil, positions gained during the process of preparation of the soil for cultivation.

If clearances on the scale suggested for Dalladies were usual, then the combined effect of arable and pastoral activities must have led to very large areas of Scotland having their woodland cover modified. Contemporary and earlier activities of farming groups would have caused separate modifications in plant cover, and therefore of pollen production, which would have had overlapping effects in the pollen record and thus it is perhaps too much to expect unambiguous evidence for discrete, short-lived periods of clearance. With that in mind, it is not at all surprising to find that the evidence from Lochs Clair and Davan points to very long periods of clearance and its effect.

No mention has as yet been made of the interesting work undertaken by Turner[14] at several sites which include Bloak Moss, a site in an area of extensive peat coverage lying at about 70 m O.D. in the Ayrshire lowlands north-east of Kilmarnock. Here there appears to be very little evidence for forest clearance at all in the Neolithic, and thus a contradictory situation to that postulated above seems to exist. However, the prominence given to the situation at Bloak Moss in the Neolithic and perhaps too for the following periods in other writings is perhaps unfortunate. Due to the relatively few pollen investigations undertaken so far in Scotland in which anthropogenic activity has been the main motivating force behind the investigation, sites with such evidence have been used for generalised statements about Scotland as a whole. It may very well be that the evidence from Bloak Moss is atypical. The site is at a very low altitude and in a zone where peat moss covers large areas so that it could well be an area not favoured by the early farmer. Certainly there does seem to be a conflict with the evidence from other sites and this points to the need for much more pollen work in areas where known Neolithic activity existed. At present all that it is possible to suggest is that there could have been two different kinds of economy existing contemporaneously in different parts of Scotland. Unless, that is, an evolutionary line is pursued in the development of agriculture. Then an early primary phase might be seen as at Bloak Moss, when hunting and gathering were still important, to be followed in time by more sophisticated agriculture as represented in the longer clearance phases at Lochs Clair and Davan. At that time mixed farming involving the keeping of large numbers of cattle, sheep and pigs would have been in existence; the involvement of pigs would have hastened the clearance process by preventing the regeneration of trees. If we see such variants as being possible, then it must not be suggested that this was an eastern-western or a Highland-Lowland contrast in agricultural practice; there is at present no evidence for this. The need for many more radio-carbon-dated clearance phases is vital, for this will allow correlation of sites and a comparison of their probable agricultural practices.

As the Sub-Boreal period continued, modification of the environment by man became more profound. Evidence for increased activity over a wide area comes from a variety of sources and can also be obtained from a wider spectrum of material than was available for the Neolithic period. The convention that there was a cultural break in terms of economic activity between the Neolithic and the Bronze Age is becoming harder to maintain and, indeed, it appears that much that in the past has been considered to be late Neolithic should now be regarded as of Bronze Age date.[15] We are still faced, however, with the problem of how sedentary the Bronze Age farmer was and what his main agricultural activity could have been. It is perhaps best to look at the farming activity of the later Sub-Boreal in relation to the classes of evidence available.

The evidence for this period, which comes largely from palynological work on the Ayrshire mosses, suggests that on several occasions after about 2300 BC clearance activity occurred and regeneration of woodland took place. Such statements must be treated with caution because some of the radio-carbon dates used to calibrate the profile investigated are statistically inseparable, while the fact that active peat growth was occurring during this time makes any assessment of the duration of clearance and regeneration phases very difficult.

Before returning to the area of mixed woodland to see the effect of Bronze Age clearance we might turn to the zone of pine forest of the north and north-west. Pollen analyses undertaken at Loch Garten on Speyside[16] show clearances dated to 2090 BC after which the vegetation was dominated by heathland taxa. In the north-west the pine-birch woodland was destroyed between 2000 and 1500 BC, probably resulting from the combination of lower temperatures, higher rainfall totals and burning initiated by man. Thereafter, birch and pine grew in small areas on well-drained slopes and on areas of poor soil, while peat growth covered very large areas.

The tree cover of the north-east, from the pollen evidence at present available, appears to have been affected variably; analyses by Durno on the coast of Aberdeenshire and in the hills to the south have shown that tree pollen remained at between 50 and 70 per cent from the Boreal until the Sub-Boreal.[17] However, the activities of Bronze Age farmers, and probably Neolithic farmers as well, then caused a drop in arboreal pollen totals. The areas investigated showed a differential response, however. The coastal sites reveal a reduction in arboreal pollen of 32 per cent while those inland drop by only 14 per cent. This contrasts strongly with the evidence from the Howe of Cromar, an upland basin in southern Aberdeenshire.[18] At 1870 BC there was a clearance which is believed to be associated with pastoralism and which lasted for about 300 years. Chemical tests of lake deposits have shown that soil as well as vegetation disturbance was occurring. Later in the Sub-Boreal, around 1390 BC, an even greater change occurred with tree pollen dropping to very low levels and herbaceous pollen, especially that of plantains, grasses and compositae, as well as spores of bracken, rising to very high values. Furthermore, that arable and pastoral farming was responsible for this strong vegetation modification is shown by the presence of cereal pollen (barley) in the pollen spectrum. That the soil disturbance was of some magnitude is suggested by the inwash of soil into Braeroddach Loch from its catchment area; erosion of the soil was removing material from the lower parts of the soil profile as well as the topsoil. The suggested increase in wetness which occurred in the later part of the Sub-Boreal was an added encouragement to peat growth and this is indicated here by the high frequencies of sphagnum spores.

A major element of landscape evolution was the appearance of the widespread moorlands which today are so much a part of Scotland's scenery. While discussing the effect of Bronze Age farming this topic must be aired. On some sites in Britain it has been shown that early agricultural activity caused soil changes of considerable extent.[19] The existing brown forest soils with their deciduous woodland cover were converted to strongly podsolised soils supporting a heathland plant complex. Much argument has ensued following these discoveries as to whether Scotland's moorland has an anthropogenic origin. The opposite argument to this is that the heathlands are climatic in origin. What is not in doubt, however, is that towards the end of the Sub-Boreal and beyond, the pollen of heathland components does rise spectacularly in many pollen diagrams. This rise is probably related to an increase in podsolisation of soils brought about by the removal of the tree cover. That podsolisation was occurring in the Bronze Age is not in doubt; it is attested by the increase in pine pollen which accompanies the rise in that of heathland species. In contradistinction, many pedologists would suggest that the natural continuing tendency towards podsolisation in Scotland, a climatically induced feature, is responsible for the soil change.[20] What is more probable, however, is that the natural tendency for soil change was compounded by the farming activities. The rate of natural podsolisation was increased by leaching of minerals induced by long periods of primitive agriculture. Once farming ceased, natural regeneration of the previous woodland components did not take place.

From the pollen evidence it becomes apparent that alteration of the woodland cover did occur and that, in association with changes in climate, caused great landscape modification. In the Bronze Age we have other evidence which can be used to look at areas in which human activity was taking place. Unfortunately little is known about the domestic sites of the period; indeed as late as 1967 it was concluded that no Bronze Age settlements had been identified in Peeblesshire although more than 100 round cairns and barrows are recorded.[21] There have been attempts since that date to show that domestic features can be pushed back in origin to the sixth or seventh century BC but such dates must be treated with caution. In this context the most important site is at Hownam, in Roxburghshire,[22] where the earliest sequence of superimposed structures has revealed what could be the tradition of late Bronze Age settlement. Palisaded settlements with timber housing appear to have been the main domestic form of the Bronze Age; support for this idea also comes from another site at West Plean.[23] Certainly relict and artefactual evidence is not strong from the southern part of Scotland and this has led to two main suggestions: first, that timber was the sole construction medium for housing, this being a further factor in the destruction of woodland already deduced from the pollen evidence; and second, that agriculture was mainly of a pastoral nature and involved a nomadic people who, by their continual movement, left no lasting impress in terms of field boundaries on the landscape.

Evidence for an arable component in their farming does, however, exist. Cereal pollen grains have been discovered at many sites. Furthermore, at two locations, the preservation of elements from Bronze Age landscapes are of considerable interest. At Black Crofts, on the northern shore of Loch Etive in Argyllshire, a system of fossil boundaries has been found under the peat of the Moss of Achnacree. Radio-carbon dating of the base of the peat, and of the soil beneath the boundary walls, shows that the latter must have come into existence between 1650 and 1200 BC.[24] Further work has revealed the boundary system to be quite extensive and the suggestion has been made that the whole system is related to Bronze Age arable activity.[25]

A very interesting and complex site at Rosinish, on Benbecula,[26] in the Outer Hebrides, also attests to arable activity at this time. It is always considered that arable farming would have been undertaken in Scotland during this period by means of hoe cultivation. This is purely supposition in that plough marks and plough or ard parts have not been found in Bronze Age contexts on the mainland, and, indeed, later fields do in many instances have shapes and an overall organisation which appears to be incompatible with the use of a plough. Until recently, however, it is doubtful whether fossil plough marks would have been recognised and indeed so few excavations of domestic sites have taken place that the possibility of revealing plough activity is very small. Excavations at Rosinish have revealed plough marks, in the form now so familiar from Gwithian in Cornwall, in a Bronze Age context. Furthermore, carbonised grain from this site shows that barley was not the only cereal grown at this period, for emmer was also recovered at this level; the report that oats were also found has since proved to be incorrect.

Evidence from the Scottish islands has not been widely utilised before this point because what occurred there seems, from the present state of knowledge, to have been quite different from events on the mainland. But evidence for farming, and especially for cultivation, is very strong. Suggestions for the differences are due to the lack of woodland from an early date, a fact attested by extensive pollen analyses from Orkney.[27]

Stone work dominated the construction of housing and tools from an early period. Thus it is possible that the survival of early cultivation methods and relics is only reflecting what occurred at the same time on the mainland but there in an environment in which wood was readily available. Such a suggestion would of course negate the apparent uniqueness of the evidence from Rosinish. Important in this context was the discovery of large numbers of stone bars in Shetland and Orkney.[28] These bars are pointed at one end and show wear on one side of the tip only. That they are shares for ards is now readily accepted, the bars being mounted in a mortise in the end of the plough beam. That field systems in which grain was grown also occurred in the northern isles is also well attested. Curvilinear fields covering an area of about 1 ha and with an individual long axis measurement between 20 and 80 m occur at Scord of Brouster on Shetland.[29] Recent work on the main house at this site has revealed both carbonised barley and oats in a deposit with the early date of 2220 ± 80 BC. (HAR-2413). The oats will probably prove to be the wild variety (*Avena fatua*) which still leaves the first known occurrence of cultivated oats as being of Roman origin.[30]

Grain impressions are also known; one of naked barley was found in a chambered cairn on the Calf of Eday and one of hulled barley from a cairn at Unstan, both sites on Orkney. While the grain belongs to this period, it is not certain that the plough bars and the fields are of Bronze Age date, but that that is a distinct probability is suggested by clearly datable artefacts and relics from Jarlshof in Shetland.[31] Here under 1.5m of wind-blown sand, and overlain by Iron Age fields, is a Bronze Age field system contemporary with stone-walled houses of a date similar to that for Rosinish and Gwithian.

The occurrence of grain at Bronze Age sites on the mainland should also be considered. In their survey of cereals in prehistoric Britain, Jessen and Helbaek[32] listed a number of sites at which barley, both naked and hulled, and some wheats were discovered. They are recorded from Dumfriesshire, Berwickshire, Ayrshire, Fife, Stirlingshire, Lanarkshire, Aberdeenshire and Midlothian. While it is true that those workers were dependent upon dates provided, in many cases, by early archaeologists who have been shown to be wrong, not all of the Bronze Age occurrences have been discredited and it is clear that Bronze Age farmers were not purely pastorally oriented. Whether they did use traction or relied purely upon hoes for cultivation is a question still to be answered, but that Bronze Age activity was considerable and affected large areas of Scotland is in no doubt.

The Sub-Atlantic Period

During the later part of the Sub-Boreal Britain's climate was again changing − to a more maritime regime. Summers become cooler, winters were raw and experienced, with the summers, an increase in the number and frequency of Atlantic depressions. The peat growth which had occurred during the Sub-Boreal now developed at greater speed and over a more extensive area, pod-solisation increased and, where peaty soils developed, iron pan usually formed and in turn enhanced the peat growth. With the greater moisture availability and occurrence of westerly winds, the west coast and the upland areas suffered increasingly from exposure. The combination of this climatic deterioration and man's activities on the land, both in the further clearances of woodland and in the cultivation of soils, was likely to increase the modification and replacement of vegetation complexes.

The period of transition between the Sub-Boreal and Sub-Atlantic as well as the early period of the full development of the Sub-Atlantic climate is one for which much more evidence is available as to man's activities in Scotland. Settlement locations, patterns and types are revealed in abundant relict sites and artefactual evidence becomes more prolific. With the added examination of the fossil pollen record, a more coherent statement on the economic and even the social organisation of Scotland can be made.

The close of the Sub-Boreal period cannot be defined with any great assurance. Indeed, it is probable that there was a period of transition and modification over several centuries; certainly recurrence surfaces are frequent and complex in bog stratigraphies suggesting that there were alternating periods favouring and retarding the growth of peat. Evidence exists from about 900 BC for a considerable increase in peat growth[33] and it was still invading settlement areas as late as 400 BC.[34] Thus the Iron Age peoples experienced a climate which was less pleasant than that of the second millennium BC and they were operating on a land surface in which peat-forming and podsolisation processes were occurring with renewed vigour.

Pollen analyses, especially those by Turner and Durno, indicate that it was during this period that Scotland began to resemble England in that it was undergoing widespread woodland clearance. At Bloak Moss, Iron Age clearance was more frequent and, indeed, in the post-Roman period became permanent; the same thing has been demonstrated from the area around Flanders Moss in

Stirlingshire.[35] In his work on Aberdeenshire Durno[36] has shown the marked effect Iron Age activity had on the still-existing woodland. During this period, however, it was the turn of the inland areas to suffer greater deforestation. While arboreal pollen totals fall by 6 per cent at the coastal sites, inland totals decrease by up to 20 per cent. The expansion of ericaceous species in the coastal area during this period was particularly marked, showing that, where a conjunction of man's activities and climatic deterioration occurred, a strong development of heathland took place. The clearest evidence for Iron Age clearance comes from analyses undertaken for Lochs Davan and Braeroddach in Aberdeenshire.[37] At the latter site the major clearance initiated in the Bronze Age continued until after 205 BC. At Loch Davan the arboreal pollen content declines progressively to a level similar to that for the present from about 1680 BC. In this clearance activity, which lasted for over one thousand years, it is most probable that fire was used judging by the large amounts of charcoal in the stratigraphic column. Arable agriculture is attested by the appearance of cereal pollen at about 600 BC. In accord with the evidence from north-east Aberdeenshire that ericaceous heath with peaty soils developed widely during the Iron Age, there also occurs at Loch Davan an increase in the pollen of sphagnum, sedges and heather. The deterioration of climate leading to the spread of heathland, podsolised soils and peat brought irreversible changes to large areas of Scotland and it is those areas today which support moorland. These changes need to be supported by an examination of the settlement pattern and agricultural system for which more evidence exists for the Iron Age than for any earlier period.

The Iron Age has perhaps been more fully studied and is better understood than any previous period and perhaps any succeeding period until the eighteenth century. A whole variety of house forms and groupings and associated field systems occur as relict features. In some instances several types are superimposed, allowing suggestions to be made as to the development of society and economy. Variations on a regional basis can be seen and for the first time it is possible to suggest that the origins of a difference in the way of life between upland and lowland occupants was coming into existence; a factor perpetuated into history and brought about in the first instance by a deteriorating upland environment in terms of both climate and soils. The amount of evidence which has accumulated from excavation is much greater than for any preceding period and artefactual material is so much richer.

The area which has been most carefully investigated lies in the south. In that area the comprehensive surveys undertaken by the Royal Commission on the Ancient and Historical Monuments of Scotland over a long period have revealed by painstaking field-work an enormous range of relict features. Excavations by some of the field surveyors have also thrown light on the evolution of settlement forms and patterns. The fact that so much of southern Scotland lay in the zone of Roman frontier activity has concentrated attention and archaeological activity there. The earliest type of settlement in the south would seem to be the so-called unenclosed platform settlement. It occurs widely in Peeblesshire while examples are known in adjacent parts of Lanarkshire. These settlements, presumably involving timber buildings, were built on platforms which had been constructed by cutting into the upper part of a slope and using the material removed to level the lower part of the site. These settlements were totally unenclosed and are, in that, probably direct descendants from the settlement forms of the later Bronze Age.

Settlement forms which had a much wider distribution in the south-east of Scotland can profitably be studied from a site at Hownam Rings in Roxburghshire. Here, an important excavation by C. M. Piggott[38] has established a sequence of events which can be used as a model for settlement evolution during the Iron Age for much of the southern region; indeed it is possible that much of the Tyne-Forth region was epitomised by this sequence. At Hownam the earliest signs of settlement are provided by palisaded settlements which Jobey thinks might be as early as the sixth or seventh century BC[39]. This would place them in a Bronze Age context, especially as this type of settlement bears a strong resemblance to that known from the same period for areas outside Scotland. Within this palisade were timber-framed houses. In some instances, as at Gray Coat in Roxburghshire[40], there was a single house (referred to by archaeologists as a homestead) occupied by one family. At Hayhope Knowe in the same county there were eleven hut sites arranged in two lines with an access way between them. Such sites as these would have a considerable effect on the area in which they were located for they obviously contained a small community. On Hayhope Knowe there could well have been a population of up to 100 people and there are sites where up to 16 huts are discernible. These hut sites, too, were frequently on sloping ground and scooped platforms had been constructed for them; thus they may have been continuing earlier constructional ideas, but at a time when cattle-keeping was more frequent, thus demanding the development of the palisade, or, perhaps, when social strife was appearing.

The simple palisade was at some stage in the Iron Age converted from timber to a stone wall about 3 m thick and then this presumed defence was reorganised by creating three ramparts with external ditches. The existence of this defended settlement was probably a response to the troubled times associated with Roman activity to the south. Once more stable conditions returned, the need for defence disappeared and the banks and ditches were all allowed to fall into disrepair and some were built over. It was at this time, during the third century AD, that the stone-based hut made its first appearance in south-east Scotland. Unlike the 'street-like' form of some of the platform settlements, the groups of stone hut circles are only loosely and formlessly agglomerated. In terms of societal organisation they seem to be a direct continuation of the earlier timber-framed houses. Society at this time also appears to have allowed for single homesteads as well as those of a grouped nature, for at Crock Cleuch and other sites only one stone hut circle exists.[41] The original building of these stone huts varies;

that at Crock Cleuch seems to have been lived in from the second to the sixth or seventh centuries AD; those at Hownam Rings have an origin late in the Roman period.

In terms of a possible hierarchy of habitations it is possible to consider the homestead at the base and the settlement at a higher stage. In the territory of the Votadini a higher echelon is also conceivable. Until about 79 AD, Eildon Hill North, in Roxburghshire, supported an enclosed hill-town which at its maximum extent covered over 15 ha and involved up to 300 platforms. Perhaps more important is the *oppidum* on Traprain Law in East Lothian, which not only covered a similar large area but also seems to have been occupied virtually continuously from the middle of the first millennium BC to the arrival of the first Saxon incomers. A habitation centre of this size and the appearance of stone-walled houses in the south at the comparatively late date of the second century AD would seem to set the area apart from the rest of Scotland where the huts are known from much earlier periods. But in cultural terms alone it is doubtful whether any great significance should be placed on this. The hut foundations in the south related to the unenclosed sites are similar in form to those which occur in Fife, at Dalrulzion and other sites in Perthshire, at many sites in Aberdeenshire, including Sands of Forvie and in the northern counties, as exemplified by Kilphedir, Sutherland. The earlier construction in wood in the south could either reflect a greater length of time over which building timber was generally available, with all the implications that would have for differential woodland clearance rates in earlier periods, or to the greater ease with which stone was suggested as the basic building material due to the different surface conditions in the north. As yet, no totally acceptable explanation can be given and the reason for this interesting difference in constructional material must be left as an open question. Local variations in the actual layout and building styles of the huts did occur. Thus in Caithness and Sutherland the habitation known as the 'wag' had an oblong chamber attached to it.[42] In the western and northern islands the round house and the wheelhouse were distinct variants. In the Perthshire examples there are also varied forms; some of the double-skinned houses have small D-shaped enclosures attached to them, as at Blackhall in Glenshee.

In the earlier discussion of house sites it was pointed out that phases of enclosed and unenclosed building took place. Throughout the east and south there are hill-forts and it is possible that the distinction between these and the other habitation sites in terms of their basic purpose was slight; they were all basically just agglomerations of habitations. It was also considered earlier that by the Iron Age it was possible to suggest the appearance of distinct regions in Scotland. The Tyne-Forth region with its myriads of settlements and such distinct features as the Traprain-Eildon complexes stands out quite clearly. There were other distinctive features among the habitations which suggest that three other regions at least should be discerned, not because their basic subsistence forms were different, but purely on building styles and conventions.

In the area between the Tay and the Dornoch Firth, the hill-forts commonly met in the Tyne-Forth area take on distinctive characteristics and provide the so-called vitrified forts. In the west and north, including the outer isles, the large communal site suggested by the hill-fort is missing and habitation seems to be on a homestead basis. These homesteads take the form of brochs, enclosures provided with walls of considerable but varying heights. The date, provenance and development of the form is controversial, but they do distinguish the Atlantic province from the rest of Scotland.[43]

The remaining province of Scotland, the Solway-Clyde, is much less well-studied than the other areas, but in addition to the platform sites of the Tyne-Forth region and some vitrified forts which were intrusions from the north-east region, there are also two distinctive habitation forms. The first is the dun, a circular or oval homestead, with a stone perimeter occurring frequently on a promontory and in some instances with attached gardens; this, however, is a class of building not well studied. The same might be said for the other form, the crannog. This was an artificial island on which a circular timber thatched house was constructed. The Scottish examples which date from the end of the first millennium BC into the first century AD are restricted to the south-western area.

Habitation sites in the Iron Age are widespread, but what evidence exists as to the way in which a livelihood was gained? There would be a continuation of agriculture, but is there any evidence as to its type and whether it was pre-dominantly arable or pastoral or of a mixed nature? Excavations at Iron Age sites in northern Scotland have shown that the remains of domesticated animals are frequent — sheep, cattle, horse, pig and goat bones have been recovered from brochs and barley, of one kind or another, is frequently evidenced either by actual grains or spikelets. That grain was grown widely is shown by the wide distribution of querns; saddle and rotary querns occur over the whole of Scotland. The actual importance of their degree of sophistication will be considered later.

Of considerable importance in this question are the tools that were available and used in the Iron Age. Comment has been made which considers there to have been no plough agriculture in Scotland before Roman times. But much depends upon what is meant by the word plough. Certainly the ard, which is a type of plough, was in use at Rosinish in the Bronze Age. Was that just an isolated instance? Apart from the bar shares of the northern isles, which again point to ploughing in a non-Roman context, until recently the only surviving plough parts were thought to come from southern Scotland. An ard beam of possible first or second century AD date was found in a peat bog at Loch Maben, in Dumfriesshire, and a plough-head and stilt was discovered during the important excavation at Milton Loch crannog,[44] while an ard point, assigned to the Iron Age, has been obtained from a crannog in Loch Gorm on the Isle of Islay.[45] Whether these ards were in use in pre-Roman times or not, it is quite certain that the Romano-British period of the south of Scotland saw iron ploughshares being used. Finds of iron parts from Traprain Law, Eckford, Falla Farm and Blackburn Mill show that iron-shod ards, asymmetric ploughs and spades were in use.[46]

If arable agriculture was of considerable importance and if, as much evidence suggests, the population in many areas showed considerable continuity, then it might be expected that field systems would occur in close proximity to the habitation sites. A search of the Ordnance Survey's archaeological site cards[47] has shown that throughout the Tyne-Forth and north-east regions and over much of the Atlantic region as well, hut sites are frequently in association with small ruined stone walls, lynchets and boundary banks. That the fields and the huts are contemporary has not yet been proved, but their intimate physical relation and similarity in walling style are highly suggestive. The plots vary greatly in size and areal coverage, but areas of 20 m square for individual plots are quite common and the area occupied by such plots varies from 1 ha to 15 ha. Also to be found on many of these fields, frequently where no field boundaries are to be seen, are large numbers of stone cairns which are commonly 3 to 4 m in diameter with a height usually less than 1 m.[48] There has been considerable controversy over these cairns as to whether they represent the results of field clearance to allow unimpeded cultivation or whether they are cemeteries. Very little investigatory work has been undertaken on this problem; cairns which have been taken apart have usually shown no sign of internment, but unless phosphate analysis is made of the underlying soil, the absence of bones alone is not conclusive evidence against the burial theory. It is conceivable that these cairns filled a dual purpose, but from their close proximity to field systems the idea that none of them originate from field clearance seems difficult to support.

In an assessment of the Iron Age economy in northern Britain, S. Piggott[49] put forward vigorous views that an agriculture dominated by corn-growing, such as existed in the south of England, did not occur in Scotland before the Roman entry. He felt that north of the Jurassic ridge, stock-raising would have been the dominant feature throughout the Iron Age. His argument is based on the lack of grain storage pits, squarish fields, evidence of corn parching and the use of pre-Roman types of rotary querns in Scotland. In fact he sums up pre-Roman agriculture in south Scotland as being of the Stanwick type involving a heavy reliance on cattle, hoe cultivation and a considerable element of nomadism with little or no grain surplus from the small plots derived ultimately from a Bronze Age husbandry.

A critical review of Piggott's ideas suggests that he over-stated his case. It is true that there is little evidence for a Woodbury type of agriculture in the Scottish Iron Age, but the absence of features that were distinctive to it does not automatically mean that the Iron Age saw a continuity of the nomadic pastoralism which he believed characterised the Bronze Age. Pits are not the only method of storing grain. They are well suited to chalk and Oolitic limestone areas and just because they did not exist on the Yorkshire Wolds, which are of chalk, it is not possible to extrapolate from that an absence of corn-growing on any scale north of the Jurassic ridge. As Mackie has recently shown, it is probable that rotary querns with fixed handles were in use in Scotland well before the Romans had any impact there.[50] The lack of widespread corn-growing is also deduced by Piggott from the fact that all carbonised grain from Brigantia and further north is of Roman or later times. That surely is a comment which is far from having been proved.

In order to examine this situation, the actual field remains must be considered. In his survey of prehistoric agriculture in western Europe, Fowler comments on the field plots associated with settlements like those at Scord of Brouster in Shetland.[51] His view is that they should not be called field systems, for they are unlikely to have been cultivated with a dragged implement and perhaps only had a short history of cultivation. With such comments it is necessary to agree and with them in mind, evidence from the cultivation plots around the Iron Age habitations of the Scottish mainland seems to support Piggott's argument for a non-Wessex type of economy. But it is also true to say that very little is known about the field systems; few are surveyed and excavation is virtually unknown. It was for this reason that Feachem, in his survey of ancient fields, was unable to do any more than make some very generalised speculations.[52]

What is very clear from the field evidence still extant is that cultivation did take place at considerable altitudes. Throughout the eastern part of the country, fields are commonly found at and above 300 m O.D., an altitude at which today only plantations or some improved pasture intrude into a general sea of moorland. It is from this consideration that the suggestion is made that from the early centuries AD, with increasing annual rainfall and lower temperatures, the Highland-Lowland division in Scottish agriculture first came into existence. From then on the Highlands became concerned with stock-raising while the Lowlands were able to indulge in a mixed agriculture in which cereal-growing played a large part.

Conclusion

The base upon which the settlement pattern and agricultural system of Scotland's historic period was built is almost totally unknown. Whether there was continuity from the organisation of the Iron Age, or whether new systems were imposed by fresh colonists or new ruling classes is not as yet finally determined. Unfortunately our archaeological knowledge of the Dark Ages is still virtually blank, a situation not very different from that outlined in 1953 by Clarke,[53] and thus for any idea of the appearance of Scotland's landscape between about 500 and 1100 AD it is necessary to enter into the realms of conjecture. Certain strands of evidence do exist, however, most of them coming from an interpretation of place-names.

By the end of the first millennium AD the landscape had undergone radical changes from its Boreal state. Most of the tree cover had at least been modified and in many areas it had been totally removed, being replaced by heath. Soils had become increasingly podsolised even in the climatically more favourable east. This meant that developments in the settlement pattern were restricted to the lowland areas and the straths which penetrated the major hill masses. It appears that in these areas there was continuity of settlement even if that meant continuity of population within a small area rather than continuous occupation of one site. Certainly there is evidence that many of the Iron Age dwelling sites were re-occupied,[54] but that of course may have been a purely local phenomenon. The strongest evidence for continued occupation of the most naturally favoured areas, that is those with the best soils and most equable climate, comes from a study of the location of the early place-names which have a direct relationship with the apportionment of land. Thus the place-name elements *pit*, associated with the Pictish period in eastern Scotland, and *bal*, belonging to the Q-Celtic-speaking people who colonised Scotland from the fifth century AD, pay for careful study. The first element in particular shows how the best soils, usually freely draining brown forest earths and podsols, were favoured, and how crowded the settlements were in certain areas.[55]

The agriculture of these settlements is unknown, but there seems to be little reason for thinking that the mixed farming of the Iron Age communities would have been greatly changed. Certainly if we work back from documentary evidence, which starts about 1100 AD, the agricultural pattern of Scotland seems to have been basically stable for a long time. Again, as Barrow[56] has pointed out, place-names come to our aid here. Old estate names like Goatmilk and Cash (from *cais*, Gaelic for cheese), both in Fife, and evidence from rents paid in cattle and cheese point to the continuation of a strong pastoral element in farming. Arable agriculture was also strong, for there is continual reference to mills and mill-based taxes. As Barrow concludes, 'by the twelfth century and probably long before, the pattern of rural settlement was chiefly determined by the amount of ground that could be ploughed and sown, and of the crops that could be harvested.'[57] Thus it is obvious that in a country where the climate was dominated by westerly air streams and where the largest continuous stretches of favourable soils lay in the east, it is to this latter area that we need to look for the densest settlement and where we would expect to find evidence for its social organisation. The manner of this organisation is still unknown. For many parts of England and Wales, Jones[58] has proposed a hierarchy of settlements, originating in the prehistoric period and being embroidered upon in succeeding centuries. As with our knowledge of agriculture in Scotland, so in the realm of social organisation we are forced to rely on place-names for any understanding of this feature. Pre-eminent in the work done on this problem is that undertaken by Barrow,[59] who has demonstrated convincingly that an early system of social organisation in small units not only existed in Scotland in the earliest historic period, but probably much earlier. He has shown how the thanages or shires were located in areas which have P-Celtic names, that is belonging to the period before Gaelic was commonly spoken. Within these shires were settlements which contained in their place-names the *pit* element which again indicates their origin in Pictish and pre-Gaelic times.

Thus it appears that long before the historic period a system of settlements organised in social (fiscal?) units had come into being. Furthermore, in trying to trace the origin of the shire in Scotland, Barrow has provided a suggestion which would intimately relate early social organisation there to the hypothesis put forward by Jones for its origins in England. In his discussions Jones points to the continuing importance of the Iron Age fortified centres in social organisation. Barrow believes that the term shire, which was borrowed from England, could well have been preceded in Scotland by 'a word cognate with, or ancestral to, Old Irish *cathir*, "a city" . . . or Primitive Welsh *caer*, fortified centre'.[60] If this can be proved, then we have a very early origin for, and a convincing demonstration of, continuity of the system of social and fiscal organisation found in Scotland in the medieval period. Furthermore, it appears to be a system which not only existed over Britain as a whole, but which was able to survive in Scotland despite the other changes wrought by the post-Iron Age colonisations by Q-Celtic-speaking peoples from Ireland and Norse speakers from Scandinavia.[61]

While it is true to say that we are left with many problems as to the way of life up to and including the Iron Age, they are as nothing when viewed against the almost totally blank nature of our knowledge of the Scottish Dark Ages. And yet we are provided, especially by place-name evidence, with tantalising glimpses of Dark Age life. In terms of viewing the development of Scotland's landscape as a slowly evolving process, rather than one in which sudden change occurred, it is the Dark Ages which hold the important key. Until such times as more detailed palynological study for the period from the early sub-Atlantic until *c*.1100 AD is undertaken and until the archaeology of the Dark Ages is more fully investigated, we will be left with a gap in our knowledge as to the evolution of settlement and agriculture and thus in the development of the countryside's appearance.

Notes

1. Piggott, S. and Henderson, K. (1958), *Scotland before history* (Edinburgh); and Piggott, S. (1958), 'Native economies and the Roman occupation of north Britain', pp. 1-27 in Richmond, I.A. (ed.), *Roman and native in north Britain* (London)
2. Pennington, W. (1974), *The history of British vegetation* (London). This book gives an excellent account of palynological studies in Britain and is illustrated with many pollen diagrams
3. Lacaille, A. D. (1954), *The Stone Age in Scotland* (Oxford)
4. McVean, D. N. (1964), 'Pre-history and ecological history', p. 563 in Burnett, J. H. (ed.), *The vegetation of Scotland* (Edinburgh)
5. Nicholls, H. (1966-7), 'Vegetational change, shoreline development and the human factor in the later quaternary history of south-west Scotland', *Transactions of the Royal*

Society of Edinburgh, *67*, 145-87

6. Davidson, D. A., Jones, R. L. and Renfrew, C. (1976) 'Palaeoenvironmental reconstruction and evaluation: a case study from Orkney', *Transactions of the Institute of British Geographers*, NS *1*, 346-61

7. Iversen, J. (1941), 'Landnam i Danmarks Stenalder', *Danmarks Geologiske Undersøgelse II Rk Nr 66*, 1-68

8. Pennington, W., Haworth, E. Y., Bonny, A. P. and Lishman, J. P. (1972-3), 'Lake sediments in north Scotland', *Philosophical Transactions of the Royal Society of London*, 264, Series B, 191-294

9. Edwards, K. J. (1976), 'Clearance phases in pollen diagrams from the north of Britain', paper read to a symposium in Edinburgh University

10. Whittington, G., from unpublished work undertaken on sediments from Black Loch in north Fife

11. Piggott, S. (1971-2), 'Excavation of the Dalladies long barrow, Fettercairn, Kincardineshire', *Proceedings of the Society of Antiquaries of Scotland* (hereafter *Proc. Soc. Antiq. Scot.*), *104*, 23-47

12. Coles, J. M. and Simpson, D. D. A. (1965), 'The excavation of a neolithic barrow at Pitnacree, Perthshire, Scotland', *Proceedings of the Prehistoric Society* (hereafter *Proc. Prehist. Soc.*), *31*, 34-57

13. Piggott, (1971-2), 'Excavation of the Dalladies long barrow', 46

14. Turner, J. (1965), 'A contribution to the history of forest clearance', *Proceedings of the Royal Society of London* (herafter *Proc. Roy. Soc. Lond.*), *161*, Series B, 343-53

15. Burgess, C. (1976), 'Britain and Ireland in the third and second millennia BC; a preface', *British Archaeological Reports* (hereafter *Brit. Archaeol. Rep.*), *33*, i-ii

16. O'Sullivan, P. E. (1974), 'Radiocarbon-dating and prehistoric forest clearing on Speyside (East-central Highlands of Scotland)', *Proc. Prehist. Soc.*, *40*, 206-8

17. Durno, S. E. (1957), 'Certain aspects of vegetational history in north-east Scotland', *Scottish Geographical Magazine*, *73*, 176-84

18. Edwards, K. J. (1975), 'Aspects of the prehistoric archaeology of the Howe of Cromar', pp. 82-7 in Gemmell, A. M. D. (ed.), *Quaternary studies in north east Scotland* (Aberdeen)

19. Dimbleby, G. W. (1965), 'Post-glacial changes in soil profiles', *Proc. Roy. Soc. Lond.*, *161*, Series B, 355-61

20. Ball, D. F. (1975), 'Processes of soil degradation: a pedological point of view', pp. 20-7 in Evans, J. G., Limbrey, S. and Cleere, H. (eds.), *The effect of man on the landscape: the highland zone*, Council for British Archaeology, Research Report 11 (London)

21. Royal Commission on the Ancient and Historic Monuments of Scotland (1967), *Peeblesshire I*, p. 13

22. Piggott, C. M. (1947-8), 'Excavation at Hownam Rings, Roxburghshire', *Proc. Soc. Antiq. Scot.*, *82*, 216

23. Steer, K. (1955-6), 'The early iron age homestead at West Plean', *Proc. Soc. Antiq. Scot.*, *89*, 227-52

24. Ritchie, A., Ritchie, G., Whittington, G. and Soulsby, J. (1974), 'A prehistoric field boundary from the Black Crofts, North Connel, Argyllshire', *Glasgow Archaeological Journal*, *3*, 66-70

25. Barrett, J., Hill, P. and Stevenson, J. B. (1976), 'Second millennium BC banks in the Black Moss of Achnacree: some problems of prehistoric land use', *Brit. Archaeol. Rep.*, *33*, 283-7

26. Shepherd, I. A. (1976), 'Preliminary results from the beaker settlement at Rosinish, Benbecula', *Brit. Archaeol. Rep.*, *33*, 209-16

27. Davidson, D. A. *et al.* (1976), 'Palaeoenvironmental reconstruction and evaluation'

28. Fenton, A. (1962-3), 'Early cultivating implements in Scotland', *Proc. Soc. Antiq. Scot.*, *96*, 264-317

29. Calder, C. S. T. (1955-6), 'Report on the discovery of numerous stone age house-sites in Shetland', *Proc. Soc. Antiq. Scot.*, *89*, 358

30. I am indebted for this pre-publication information on Scord of Brouster to Dr A. Whittle; the cereal identification so far carried out is by J. R. B. Arthur.

31. Hamilton, J. R. C. (1956), *Jarlshof* (London)

32. Jessen, K. and Helbaek, H. (1944), 'Cereals in Great Britain and Ireland in prehistoric and early historic times', *Det Kongelige Danske Videnskabernes Selskab Biologische Skrifter Bind III*, 1-68

33. Piggott, S. (1972), 'A note on climatic deterioration in the first millennium BC in Britain', *Scottish Archaeological Forum* (hereafter *Scot. Archaeol. Forum*), *4*, 109-13

34. Fairhurst, H. and Taylor, D. B. (1970-1), 'A hut-circle settlement at Kilphedir, Sutherland', *Proc. Soc. Antiq. Scot.*, *103*, 65-99

35. Turner, (1965), 'A contribution to the history of forest clearance', 344

36. Durno, (1957), 'Certain aspects of vegetational history', 178

37. Edwards, (1976), 'Aspects of the prehistoric archaeology of the Howe of Cromar'

38. Piggott, (1947-8), 'Excavation at Hownam Rings'

39. Jobey, G. (1966), 'Homesteads and settlements of the frontier area', pp. 1-14 in Thomas, C. (ed.), *Rural settlement in Roman Britain*, Council for British Archaeology, Research Report 7 (London)

40. Royal Commission on the Ancient and Historical Monuments of Scotland (1956), *Inventory for Roxburghshire* (Edinburgh)

41. Steer, J. K. (1946-7), 'Excavations in two homesteads at Crock Cleuch, Roxburghshire', *Proc. Soc. Antiq. Scot.*, *81*, 138-57

42. Curle, A. O. (1944-5), 'The excavation of the "wag" or prehistoric cattle-fold at Forse, Caithness', *Proc. Soc. Antiq. Scot.*, *80*, 11-24

43. For a discussion of the brochs see Mackie, E. W. (1970), 'The Scottish iron age', *Scottish Historical Review*, *49*, 1-32

44. Piggott, C. M. (1952-3), 'Milton Loch crannog I', *Proc. Soc. Antiq. Scot.*, *87*, 134-53

45. The exact dating and recovery of this ard point is still to be clarified, but an Iron Age date is probable, indeed it may well prove not to be an ard point at all

46. Fenton, (1962-3), 'Early cultivating implements in Scotland'

47. Grateful thanks are recorded here to Mr J. Davidson of the Archaeological Division of the Ordnance Survey, Edinburgh

48. Graham, A. (1956-7), 'Cairnfields in Scotland', *Proc. Soc. Antiq. Scot.*, *90*, 7-23

49. Piggott (1958), 'Native economies and the Roman occupation of north Britain'

50. Mackie, E. W. (1971-2), 'Some new quernstones from brochs and duns', *Proc. Soc. Antiq. Scot.*, *104*, 137-46

51. Fowler, P. J. (1971), 'Early prehistoric agriculture in western Europe', pp. 153-82 in Simpson, D. D. A. (ed.), *Economy and settlement in neolithic and early bronze age Britain and Europe* (London)

52. Feachem, R. W. (1973), 'Ancient agriculture in the highland of Britain', *Proc. Prehist. Soc.*, *39*, 332-53

53. Clarke, J. (1956), 'The archaeology of dark-age Scotland', *Transactions of the Glasgow Archaeological Society*, new series, *14*, 121-42

54. Morrison, A. (1974), 'Some prehistoric sites in Scotland with medieval occupation', *Scot. Archaeol. Forum*, *6*, 66-74

55. Whittington, G. (1974-5), 'Placenames and the settlement pattern of dark age Scotland', *Proc. Soc. Antiq. Scot.*, *106*, 99-110

56. Barrow, G. W. S. (1973), 'Rural settlement in central and eastern Scotland', pp. 257-78 in *The Kingdom of the Scots* (London)

57. Ibid., p. 278

58. Jones, G. R. J. (1976), 'Multiple estates and early settlement', pp. 15-40 in Sawyer, P. H. (ed.), *Medieval settlement* (London)

59. Barrow, G. W. S. (1973), 'Pre-feudal Scotland: shires and thanes', pp. 7-68 in *The Kingdom of the Scots* (London)

60. Ibid., p. 65

61. Small, A. (1968), 'The historical geography of the Norse Viking colonisation of the Scottish Highlands', *Norsk Geografisk Tidsskrift*, *22*, 1-16

2 MEDIEVAL SETTLEMENT AND COLONISATION

R. A. Dodgshon

The colonisation of waste and the foundation of new settlements are complementary processes in any expanding rural society. Their reactive and creative association in medieval Scotland, 1100-1650, can be assumed almost without question. However, their exact history and phasing are still uncharted, at least compared with what is known about their history in other parts of north-west Europe over the same period. The explanation usually offered for this shortfall in understanding centres on the supposed lacuna in documentary evidence that overarches the period. It is implicitly assumed that the layout of the most basic settlement unit, the clachan or fermtoun, appears to us only at the eleventh hour in its history through the window of eighteenth-century estate plans or surveys. Thereafter, estate reorganisation brought about its rapid transformation. Seen clearly only at the point of their extinction, the clachan and fermtoun have been instated in the literature as elusive institutions, lacking an exact genealogy or historical perspective.

Whatever their deficiencies, it must be conceded that eighteenth-century estate plans and surveys do at least impart form and definition to the problem before us. In plan after plan, we are confronted with a landscape that can only be classed as fully settled. Even in the Highlands and Islands, the extensive areas of waste and hill pasture recorded by them does not detract from the fact that every pocket of suitable soil, and many that were unsuitable, had been pressed into service to sustain a large and growing population. No other source could summarise so vividly the amount of colonising activity that had gone on in the preceding centuries. Such plans also have the unique advantage of depicting the morphological character of early farming touns as a small clustered settlement form, one that commonly lacked any semblance of order. Only in the more completely settled areas of the south and east is there a hint of touns having a more structured layout.

Of course, to define a problem is not to understand it. There are many outstanding questions about medieval colonisation and settlement which estate plans alone could not possibly answer. For instance, there is the straightforward question of chronology. When were the main phases of land colonisation and settlement formation? Did they always proceed step by step with each other? If not, why not? Can we identify phases of decolonisation? Separate from these are questions concerning the processes involved. We need to know how land was colonised and the manner in which settlement developed. By way of being a prolegomenon to such questions, it will be helpful if we try to structure the wider context of colonisation and settlement history by reviewing, however imperfectly, the prevailing social and economic conditions of the period together with the factors that affected the supply of land. But first, there is the problem of source material to contend with.

The Problem of Source Material

Once we seek answers to the kinds of question posed in the previous paragraph, we stretch the problem beyond the limits of eighteenth-century estate plans and confront what some would see as the endemic scarcity of early evidence for this sort of detailed, topographically based problem. However, it could be argued that the deficiencies of early sources have been over-stressed. Without wishing to denigrate the role of the antiquarian, the problems we face have been compounded or accentuated by an over-concentration on place rather than process. Too often, the starting-point for settlement studies has been the selection of a particular place or area as the study problem. Invariably, the success of this approach is subject to all the vagaries of chance documentation. Little progress is made until someone fortuitously selects a place or area for which adequate material happens to be available. Under the circumstances, a more efficient method is surely to let the potential and opportunities inherent in particular sources determine the approach. What is urgently needed is a greater concern for the way certain types of source material shed light on the general processes of colonisation and settlement history irrespective of place.

Early land charters and rentals form an obvious source of evidence. The former are available from the twelfth century onwards. Scattered examples of the latter exist for the thirteenth and fourteenth centuries, but it is not until the fifteenth and sixteenth centuries that they become available in quantity. The very fine sets of sixteenth-century Crown and monastic estate rentals provide excellent bench-marks in the settlement history of many areas. Where land charters or rentals are available in sequence, like those for Ettrick, Islay and Shetland, a serial view of the local settlement pattern can be constructed. Not only can this reveal changes in the total number of touns, but it can also highlight the structural reorganisation of individual touns. Some of the finer points of settlement history, such as why growth took the particular forms it did, or how touns adjusted the boundaries between each other, can be gleaned from the plethora of legal papers and processes that are to be found amongst estate, baron's court and sheriff court records.

Arguably, the documentation of colonisation demands as much of ourselves as of our sources, for much appears to hinge on how we interpret what is available. It cannot be assumed that colonisation was a conveniently labelled process that surfaced in manuscripts as so many acres of *assart* here or a formal grant of waste there. It may have shown itself only as an augmentation to customary rents or, if no breach of existing rights was involved, as an increased amount of land being cropped with neither writ nor ceremony to proclaim the event. In short, it is imperative that the nature of colonisation be clarified so that we know what to expect in the way of documentation. As will be shown below, once this is done, then readily available sources like charters of conveyance, rentals and tacks can be used to give scale and chronology to the process of colonisation. Even the structural configuration of touns as it appears in eighteenth-century plans can be shown to have meaning for the history of colonisation, once the processes involved are understood.

Medieval Colonisation and Settlement: a Background

Reduced to its basics, the progress of colonisation and the creation of new settlement expresses the relationship between, on the one hand, rural population and, on the other hand, the supply of land.

Table 2.1: Estimates of Scottish Medieval Population

Late 11th century	250,000
Late 14th century	c. 400,000/470,000
Late 16th century	c. 550,000/800,000
c. 1700	800,000/1,000,000

Based on figures cited in Lythe, S.G.E. and Butt, J. (1975), *An economic history of Scotland 1100-1939* (Glasgow and London), pp. 3-4. Their main source was Cooper, Lord (1947), 'The numbers and distribution of the population of medieval Scotland', *Scottish Historical Review*, *26*, 2-6.

Regrettably, the study of Scottish population during the period 1100-1650 is an exercise in speculation since, as yet, there is no documentary basis for an exact estimate. Those estimates which have been made are given in Table 2.1. Whatever reservations might be entered about the precise level of population at particular points, few scholars would disagree with the overall trend these figures disclose of a gross increase in the six centuries or so prior to Dr Webster's census of 1755. Needless to say, the study of colonisation and settlement needs a more detailed analysis of population trends than this. Unfortunately, it can only be assumed from comparison with countries elsewhere that this overall trend of increase can be broken down into phases of rapid increase during (a) the twelfth and thirteenth centuries and (b) the sixteenth and seventeenth centuries, with an intervening phase (c) of standstill or stagnation. What is clear is that in addition to these phases of increase or stagnation, there were moments of decrease brought on by 'hunger and pestilence, two buddes of the same tre'.[1] The most serious outbreak of pestilence was the so-called Black Death in the mid-fourteenth century. According to Andrew of Wyntoun's *Orygynale Cronykil:*

> A thowsand thre hundreyre fourty and nyne
> Fra lychtane wes the suet ryrgyne,
> In Scotland the fyrst Pestilens
> Begouth, off sa gret wyolens,
> That, it was sayd, off lyward men
> the thyrd part it destroy'd them.[2]

Fordun's *Chronicle* documents another serious outbreak in 1362, which he likened to that of 1349 'both in the nature of the disease and the number of those who died'.[3] Other outbreaks continued to occur right up until the mid-seventeenth century. There were also recurrent famines. Observers were impressed by the poverty of Scotland from as early as the thirteenth century onwards.[4] With so many living on the edge of subsistence during an average year, it is hardly surprising that a poor harvest invariably meant a famine. For instance, a 'great mortality' was said to have followed the poor harvest of 1602, when a mildew affected the barley crop and caused 'dearth and famin all the North and Highlands over . . . This was called by the vulgar *Blaen in Chaa*, the sidd yeares, becaus the corn yelded no meale, but seeds (sidds).'[5] At times, famine and pestilence followed each other so quickly in succession that it was almost as if they worked in harness. The sixteenth century was such a period. As one writer remarked, 'reading the domestic history of Scotland in the 16th century, every third year seems to bring a famine, and every sixth the pestilence.'[6]

The supply of land is another vital parameter whose trends are obscured by lack of comprehensive data. In a sense, the record of colonisation itself is the only real commentary we have on how much land was available. The basic problem to be resolved is whether there was any period when the supply of land became exhausted. The obvious temptation is to draw the comparison with England, where writers like Postan have argued for a condition of acute land hunger by the late thirteenth century. The evidence for Scotland, though, is not so clear-cut. Gilbert has referred to how Alexander II disafforested Gala and Leader in the Southern Uplands during the early thirteenth century 'as a result of economic pressure', and how hunting forests generally began to shrink towards the close of the century.[7] However, Alexander II's very first piece of legislation (1214) was one compelling bondmen and more substantial land-holders to cultivate their land: the impression it gives is that whilst there may have been a food supply problem, it was not necessarily a land supply problem.[8] In fact, a Crown ruling issued five years earlier, in 1209, provides the key to this particular Malthusian crisis. It accused 'erlis baronis and frehaldaris' of 'wastand thair landis and the cuntre with multitud of scheip and bestis thairby trubilland godis peopill with skarsnes poverte and utter herschip'.[9]

Whatever the demand for land at the time of the Black Death, the latter must have eased it substantially. Even if population did not stagnate for a century or so afterwards, it is unlikely this period saw much new colonisation. Any growth would simply have taken up the slack caused by the Black Death. Moving into the sixteenth and seventeenth centuries, conditions alter. References to outsets, outfields, the division of commonties and the creation of new settlements suggest there was both a steady demand and supply in land. An interesting comment on the opportunities still present in sixteenth-century Scotland is provided by Estienne Perlin, a clergyman, who estimated that the amount of arable land in the country had recently been doubled, partly on the encouragement of the then Dowager of Scotland, who had campaigned for an increase.[10] But the opportunities were not unlimited. There are signs that in some areas the land supply had started to run out by the seventeenth century. For example, it was during the seventeenth century that writers become more impressed by the excess of cultivation in the Highlands and Islands than the lack of it. On a tour of the region in 1689, Thomas Morer expressed his surprise with the words that 'their arable ground is very considerable; and 'tis almost increadible how much some of the mountains they plough'.[11] It is also over the seventeenth century that some touns began cultivating their shieling ground or settling moss.[12] Most revealing of all, reports of over-population, such as that for Orkney in 1627, start to appear.[13]

Even if the trends of population and land supply could be plotted with greater exactness, it would not be a sufficient background for understanding colonisation and settlement history. This is because the impact of population growth was channelled through particular social and economic institutions which could advance or retard the demand for land. Thus, in Orkney and Shetland, a key factor was udal tenure. This was an allodial tenure which gave many peasants absolute rights of possession. Linked to it was the practice of partible inheritance, a custom whereby property was divided equally between coheirs. Court records for the Northern Isles provide instances of these divisions, or *schones*, taking place.[14] The outcome was that population growth was quickly translated into smaller holdings and a demand for land, a feature of the system that did not pass unobserved by early writers. It also had a formative influence on the history of settlement. This role has been made clear by Clouston. The growth of particular townships in Orkney, he argued, could be linked with the growth of particular family groups. As each family group expanded over a period of generations, the township associated with it became progressively subdivided into a complex of different farms. The original farmstead of the township's settlement pattern, or what formed the original patrimony of the family group, was often identified by the place-name element *bus*. Amongst the townships which Clouston cites as having this exclusive relationship with a single family group, such that the settlement history of the one mirrored the genealogical history of the other, were those of Eg and Linklater.[15]

Elsewhere in Scotland, the demand for land was channelled through the landlord-tenant or lord-vassal relationship. These relationships were measured and finite, at least during the period under review. Holdings and touns were computed in terms of defined units like ploughgates, husbandlands, merklands, pennylands and davachs. These units had a varied background and not all began life as measures of land *sensu stricto*, but they certainly all had this meaning by *c*. 1100, or soon after. They created a structured framework within which settlement and arable developed. Initially, they acted as a restraint on the amount of land that could be colonised by a toun. Instead of a system in which a toun expanded responsively according to its need, there existed one in which touns had bounds, bounds that were laid out and perambulated at the time of its foundation or assessment.

Usually, there existed an area of waste, or non-assessed land, around the toun that was used for pasture. Subsequent growth into this non-assessed waste was an interaction between the legal restraints implicit in the assessed bounds of a toun and its needs. To sum up, the entire process of growth in such touns was a regulated process. It had built-in checks capable of holding up growth or giving it a distinctive character.

The landowner-tenant relationship had other dimensions to it which are relevant to the problem of colonisation. For instance, it was commonplace throughout this period, 1100-1650, for tenants to pay part or all their rent in kind. In the Lowlands, this consisted largely of grain or meal plus fowls.[16] However, in the Highlands and Islands, there could be a more diverse composition to rent, with stock, cheese, fish and cloth often specified in addition to grain and fowls.[17] The nature of these rents in kind meant that most touns, even those in marginal areas, had some pressures on them to crop a certain amount of land. Brand's reference to rents in Orkney *c*. 1700 is worth repeating here. He wrote:

> Rents when collected, whether payed in Money, Meal, Oats, Barley or Butter are ordinarily sent South, which causeth great grudge among the People, some of them thereby being redacted to great straits, not getting Meal, Barley or the like sometimes to buy as in the late dearth.[18]

Other references to rents in kind being excessive can be found for parts of mainland Scotland.[19] They leave little doubt that rents in kind were part of the pressures acting on Scottish rural society in its relationship to land.

Yet another factor in the situation was estate policy as regards the size of both holdings and touns. If a fermtoun carried large numbers of tenants, then the pressure for expansion was obviously greater than in the case of a toun where tenant numbers had been limited. As yet, there is no reason for seeing this as a critical distinction during the early part of the period 1100-1650, but it seems to have become crucial towards the end. As the Lowlands were drawn slowly into a system of production for the market, there are signs that in areas like the Southern Uplands, tenant numbers were reduced.[20] Quite apart from the fact that there were fewer tenants to support, this reduction in tenant numbers was widely associated with a shift from grain to stock production, so that in such touns, arable acreages fell. To the north and west of the country, opposite trends prevailed, with tenant numbers increasing and holding size shrinking. In the Highlands and Islands especially, these trends were manifest not only through the overloading of touns with cottars and tenants, but also, in the cultivation of poor, difficult soils, whether upland shielings or lowland mosses. Set in contrast to the falling tenant numbers of the gerss or pastoral touns in the Southern Uplands, such smallholdings help demonstrate the importance of estate policy in regulating the relationship between society and land.

Colonisation 1100-1650

Documented instances of colonisation in progress appear with the earliest land charters. Some leave no doubt they are foundation charters, carving a new holding or toun out of waste. For example, in the late twelfth century, Arbroath abbey was granted by the King 'one ploughgate or arable in Mondynes [in Fordoun], Mearns, on the Bervie Water, measured at his command'.[21] Others are less explicit. In a few cases, their pioneering nature can be inferred from their environmental context, such as with the grant of the poorly drained Airthmuir and Edirpolles areas to Cupar abbey, areas which were reclaimed by the abbey over the period 1170-1230.[22] Surprisingly, there are few references to *assarts* in early charters, despite the spread of Norman influences into Scotland over the twelfth and thirteenth centuries. In fact, some grants seem concerned to restrict the practice. Thus, a twelfth-century grant of a clearing at Blainslie (Roxburghshire) to Melrose abbey mentioned how it was 'to be ploughed and cultivated without making an *assart*'.[23] This lack of reference to assarted land cannot be ascribed to any lack of detail in these early charters, for as the Blainslie charter demonstrates, it was not a matter to be overlooked. In all probability, the reason lies in the nature of the colonising process at this stage. As the Arbroath and Blainslie charters together illustrate, colonisation was still regulated through land units and the finite limits these placed on what could be occupied as arable. The term *assart*, meanwhile, like the term more commonly used in Scotland — outset — was reserved for non-assessed land. The ongoing creation of land units after 1100 is of course apparent from charters like that granting land to Arbroath abbey. In a wider context, Duncan has argued that in those areas north of the Forth where the davach and ploughgate existed beside each other, the latter can be seen as land newly assessed (and therefore, newly colonised) from the twelfth century onwards, when the ploughgate was introduced into the area as the preferred unit of measurement.[24]

In the case of a large unit like the ploughgate, the majority of the examples we see being measured and perambulated in early charters probably formed separate touns. More difficult to detect are those instances where early colonisation involved the outward expansion of existing touns by the addition of extra land units. Faced with an absence of examples, it is tempting to place the blame on the inadequacy of early sources for this sort of micro-analysis of touns. However, it is worth keeping in mind that in the Northern Isles, where the problem of assessments has received more scrutiny than in other parts of the country, the basic pattern of merklands has been dated to the early phases of the Norse period and is commonly assumed to have undergone no change thereafter.[25] In fact, what may well have happened with many Scottish touns is that they expanded by revaluing the acreage of their land units, rather than by adding extra ones to their overall assessment. McKerral, for instance, has focused on the broad contrast that can be drawn between the davachs of the western Highlands and those of the North-East, the latter being much larger than the former. He explained the discrepancy by suggesting that the latter were an expanded version of the former, an expansion designed to accommodate new land.[26] If this was the case, then the fact that the enlarged davachs of the north-east were based on four ploughs of 104 acres, a unit equal in size to the ploughgate, may be a clue as to when this uprating of the north-eastern davach took place. A similar argument can be advanced with regard to land units in the extreme south-east. Early sources suggest the size of land units in the region to have been either around eight acres or thirteen acres.[27] What raises suspicion over a possible link between these two seemingly distinct types of land unit is the way terms like bovate, merkland and husbandland were used on occasion to describe either. One way of rationalising this confusion of terms and sizes is by seeing one as an expansion of the other. Support for this notion is provided by the toun of Newstead (Roxburghshire). Eighteenth-century sources show this was a toun of 24 husbandlands. When considered in relation to its assessed area, or infield, these husbandlands appear to have averaged 12.9 acres.[28] Yet sixteenth-century manuscripts talk of Newstead being divided into 'aucht aiker cavills'. What is more, when grossed, these 'aucht aiker cavills' equalled 196 acres, meaning they were 24 in number.[29] The explanation for this dual system of assessment becomes evident when it is disclosed that the infield of Newstead consisted of two portions, one totalling 196 acres and the other 115 acres. It can be inferred that the toun initially equalled 24 × 'aucht aiker cavills', but that at some point it was revalued or reassessed to produce 24 × 13-acre husbandlands, with the addition of a new portion of infield adding 5 acres to each 8-acre cavill.

Following the Black Death and the slackening of demand, the pioneering of new land probably ceased for a time. However, by the late fifteenth century, there are indications that a new phase of colonisation was beginning, a phase that continued over both the sixteenth and seventeenth centuries. This new impetus to colonisation could be dismissed as a function of the more abundant documentation for these centuries. Much harder to dismiss as a sign of renewed activity is the distinct way in which land now colonised was being treated. Its distinction was embodied in the use of novel terms like outsets and outfield, in the fact that it formed an arrented supplement to customary rents, and in the fact that it was measured in acres rather than incorporated into land units.

Of all these indicators, the most revealing are the references to outsets. These occur from the late fifteenth century onwards, becoming especially numerous during the sixteenth century.[30] Typical are the references to outsets at Burlie (Perthshire) in 1525[31] and Sanquhar (Dumfriesshire) in 1539.[32] As its name implies, an outset was a portion of land which lay outside the main set of a toun. Most were cultivated as appendages to a toun, but some became established as separate touns in their own right. For example, a grant of half of the toun of Kindrocht (Aberdeenshire) in 1542 referred to 'lie outset vocato the Dene-End'.[33] In the far north, the terminological structure of touns differed. Three sectors eventually emerged: tumals, tounland and quoys. Tumals were toft areas held in severalty whilst tounland was 'rendallit' or runrig.[34] Together they formed the assessed area of touns. Any ground cultivated outside this assessed area was quoyland. The equivalence of quoyland to outsets is made clear in A. Peterkin's comment that 'ane quoy land or Outbrek is ane peece of land newly win without the dykis.'[35] The significance of these references to outsets and quoylands may go beyond their value as signs of colonisation in progress. As will be explained at greater length in Chapter 3, it has been argued that they formed the basis for outfield cropping systems. Seen in this way, it means that the extent of colonisation during this phase can be gauged from the outfield cropping systems which surrounded most Scottish touns by the end of the seventeenth century.

Yet another way in which this phase of colonisation over the sixteenth and seventeenth centuries manifests itself is through certain subtle changes of rent. In quite a number of cases, new land appears as a cash supplement to customary rent. The significance of this can only be appreciated when it is grasped that customary rents related to the assessed area of a toun. The cultivation of non-assessed land went beyond this stable nexus and paved the way for the exaction of new and higher forms of rent. Examples are fairly common. For instance, Shetland rentals sometimes specify the food rent of a toun and then the cash payment which it made for quoys or 'conquiest land'.[36] A grant in 1588 of lands in the Ross of Mull and on Islay continually refers to what it calls 'Eik in money' payed by each toun in addition to rent in kind. It means 'the augmentation added or eiked to the rental by the present grant'.[37] An interesting source of information is the *Report on the State of Certain Parishes* drawn up in 1627. It is clear from its entries that the rent of many Lowland touns, but especially those in the Lothians, had undergone substantial increases in the decades prior to its compilation.[38] Since most of the customary rents, as well as their increases, were paid in kind, it follows that the latter constituted real increases and not just inflationary adjustments. A number of entries ascribe the cause of the increases to the 'extraordinary labouring' of the land, a phrase which probably covered increases in the amount of land cultivated. One entry, that for Espertoun (Midlothian), says as much.[39]

Most of the land affected by this phase of colonisation was common pasture or commonty, waste land which lay beyond a toun's framework of assessed land. Some documents state this quite clearly. Thus, a 1595 charter permitted the toun of Easter Dalgarrog (Aberdeenshire) to cultivate 'mure' as its 'proper landis'.[40] In some cases, the expansion into waste involved commonty land shared with other touns and landowners. Formal divisions were necessary. Such divisions were possible long before the 1695 *Act, concerning the Dividing of Commonties* which only mattered in those cases where one or more heritors objected to a division. In fact, a search through estate papers soon brings examples of these early commonty divisions to light. For instance, in 1594, commonty land was divided between the touns of Cullow, Lethnott and Corsmilne in Angus.[41] A few years later, in 1604, commonty land at Hedderwick in Angus was divided.[42]

Settlement 1100-1650

The discussion of settlement over the period 1100-1650 has been broken down into six different themes. First, there is the amount of settlement that existed by 1100. Second, there is the question of how much settlement was created during the early part of the period under review, that is 1100 to 1350. Third, there is the question of how much was created after 1350. Fourth, the problem of toun splitting needs to be considered. Fifth, the extent and phasing of settlement desertion before 1650 will be discussed. And lastly, the section will be concluded with a brief review of settlement morphology and house types.

Scottish Rural Settlement c. 1100

The question of how much settlement already existed in about 1100 is not one that can be answered confidently. Yet no matter how provisional the answer, it is a question that has to be faced for it is prejudicial to what can be said about the growth of settlement thereafter.

As the previous chapter made clear, work on early place-name elements affords a way of approaching this problem, for place-names incorporating an element like Pit- are unquestionably of pre-1100 origin. Another approach is through the earliest land charters. In a study of settlement in south-east Scotland over the twelfth and thirteenth centuries using such manuscripts, Barrow concluded that even by about 1100 AD 'the social agrarian pattern of Scotland both south and north of the Forth appears to be of very long standing.'[43] This conclusion was based on a variety of features from the fiscal assessment of touns to the existence of early forms of territorial order like the shire system, all of which appear about 1100 as part of a mature system. The same sorts of reasoning might be used of other parts of Scotland. For instance, it is probable that the davach was part of a mature system of land assessment by the time we begin to perceive it in early documents like the *Book of Deer*.[44] There is no extant charter which shows a davach being established for the first time. Indeed, as Duncan has reminded us, we do not even see one being perambulated.[45] Of course, the davach usually comprised a cluster of touns,

Figure 2.1: Daugh of Taminlienen (Banffshire), 1761

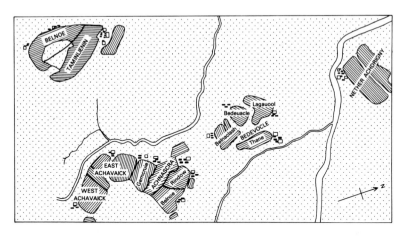

Line shading = arable, stipple = pasture

not just one. To cite an example, the *Daugh of Taminlienin* (Banffshire) consisted of thirteen separate touns when surveyed in 1761 (see Figure 2.1).[46]
Given the size of davach, this multiple-toun character may have been present
from its inception. In other words, when we read of areas like Assynt equalling
four davachs − or the davachs of Ard-assynt, Edra-isk, Rowst Rowstore and
Slish-a-chilish − or an area like Durness equalling fifteen,[47] it does not follow
that they contained four and fifteen touns at the point when they were first
assessed. All that can be assumed is that they contained a number of settlements.
We cannot say how many.

The problem of shires and thanages is especially important. In character,
these were territorial units, or multiple estates, that embraced a number of
settlements. Their constituent character is well brought out by Skene's description of the thanage of Kintore (Aberdeenshire). He wrote:

> The extensive Thanage of Kintore, with its Church of Kinkell, and its
> tenandria, and its foresta, its liberetenentes, its bondi, bondagii, nativi et
> eorum segueli, its burdens of *Can* and *Ferchane*, was probably a fair
> representative of what had been an Ardmendat or chief tribe residence,
> with its Ardcell or chief church.[48]

Shires were similar in composition. Together, they represent for us early units
of kingship or lordship, and as such, were already old by the time we glimpse
them for the first time in twelfth-century documents.[49] A recent review of their
nature by Barrow has shown that they were to be found throughout eastern
Scotland, the thanage to the north of the Forth, the shire to the south.[50]
Although the majority are lowland in distribution, there were some, like the

thanages of Fortingall and Glentilt, that were sited in upland areas. If we bear in mind that each shire or thanage represented a system of settlements, then the seventy or so examples to be found in eastern Scotland clearly have a bearing on where and how much settlement existed *c.* 1100. In fact, Barrow's paper tries to reconstruct the constituent parts or touns of quite a number of examples (see Figure 2.2). In a pioneer paper written in 1872, Robertson approached this aspect of their character in a more abstract fashion, by discussing their notional composition. He reasoned that they both comprised at the outset twelve townships and total assessments of 48 carucates (shires) or davachs (thanages). In support of this, he cites the fact that Coldingham consisted of twelve townships when the shire was first granted to the monks of Durham and the fact that Huntly is traditionally regarded as equalling 48 davachs.[51] But without ruling

Figure 2.2: Reconstruction of the Shire of Kinghorn (Fife)

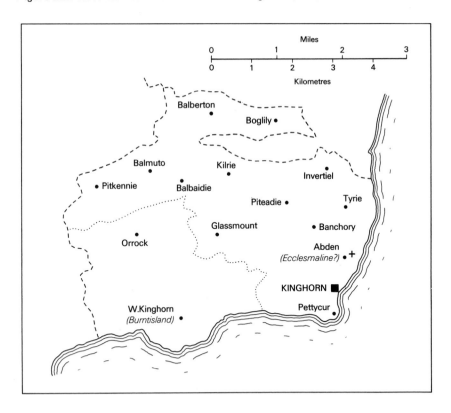

Source: after G.W.S. Barrow (1972)

out the possibility that such units did once have a fixed and uniform structure, it would be optimistic to believe this structure can be gleaned from the information available to us at present. For the time being, we must be content with the conclusion that thanages and shires were multiple estates that appear in early sources to have had a varying number of touns within their bounds.

Considered together then, place-names and early documents suggest no lack of settlement by about 1100. However, it is important that the amount which existed be weighted correctly. In all probability, there simply existed *a well-spaced but still elemental pattern* based on touns that appear later as key settlements. In terms of residual opportunity, there was still sufficient scope for the outward growth and intense subdivision of these touns, for the infilling of the surrounding waste with new touns, and for the settlement of whole new areas previously avoided by settlement.

Settlement Formation 1100-1350

The section on colonisation has already given instances of land being granted over the twelfth and thirteenth centuries which led to the foundation of a new toun. Like the grant in 1179 of land in Ashkirk Forest (Selkirkshire) to Glasgow Cathedral Church which allowed it to 'plough, sow and cultivate everywhere within the fence which was erected on the day this charter was made',[52] there are definite signs of something new being created. Unfortunately, the bulk of other charters are less explicit, making it impossible to discern whether a pre-existing toun was being regranted or a new one established. For example, when Thomas de Galweia, Earl of Athole, granted Cupar abbey his land of Tholaw *per suas rectas diusas* in 1211 × 1231[53] or when David I granted Robert Avenel the land of Eskdale in 1124 × 1153,[54] we can only guess from their phrasing that they were already settled blocks of landholding rather than holdings being pioneered from the waste, whose settlement is given a *terminus post quem* by these grants.

Special problems are posed by many of the early charters relating to the estates of the abbeys, for quite a number have the form of a perambulation. At first sight, they give the impression of touns being newly carved out of the waste, replete with boundaries or marches. In view of the image of monastic orders like the Cistercians as communities that deliberately sought isolation, this would be a plausible conclusion. In fact, the position is more complex. Many of these perambulation charters are concerned with fixing the boundaries between two adjacent touns or holdings, not with determining the full boundaries of one. An agreement drawn up in 1223-4, for example, perambulated and fixed the boundary between Clenkatyn (Scone abbey) and Drumyn (Cupar abbey).[55] Such charters must be handled cautiously. Much more so than the ordinary peasant, the abbeys were keen to establish exclusive control over their pasture resources. After all, commercial wool production was an important part of their estate economy during the twelfth and thirteenth centuries.[56] When scrutinised closely, many of these early perambulations were not concerned with peram-bulating arable land, but with securing for the abbeys their exclusive or several control of the pasture around it.[57] Some of the areas involved did, in fact, have long histories. For instance, the upland area behind Yetholm, on the edge of the Cheviots, was one where a number of abbeys jostled each other with peram-bulation agreements, yet it was an area which had previously formed a shire centred on Yetholm and must already have possessed an elemental pattern of landholding and settlement.[58] In short, what many of these perambulations signify is the start of the long and vital process by which all touns extended their exclusive control from assessed arable to the pasture around it. At first, such an extension may only have given them more defined rights of grazing, but it obviously facilitated the absorption of such land as full property when it became possible to do so.[59]

Where early charters granted a fairly substantial block of landholding, it sometimes forms a basis for a long-term comparison. Only rarely, though, do they allow a comparison to be made within, or largely within, the early phase of the period 1100-1350. For instance, between the time it became part of the Morton lordship in the thirteenth century and the time of a Morton estate rental in 1376, the *Foresta* of the Liddel acquired a number of stedes or touns, like Laslawhope, Sougden and Hardenleys.[60] Other land charters, like the very detailed grant of the thanage of Birse (Aberdeenshire), in 1172, need to be set in a longer time perspective. However, when the Birse grant is compared with a mid-sixteenth-century rental, it too shows an expansion of settlement. In place of the 16 touns present in 1172, the 1511 rental records 24 touns. A number of these new touns had developed in what was known as the Forest of Birse, an area devoid of settlement in 1172.[61]

Settlement Formation 1350-1650

The period after 1350 provides the student of settlement history with a much wider range of documentation. It now becomes possible to trace the developing settlement pattern of many areas. Overall it is remarkable how much settlement seems to have been formed over this period from 1350 up to 1650.

A handful of examples must suffice. In 1390, the lordship of Morvern was granted to Lachlan Makgilleone. Altogether, 7 touns or units of landholding were listed. By the late fifteenth century, the number had grown to 20. An early sixteenth-century listing records 28. By the mid-eighteenth century, there were 53.[62] Rentals for Islay also reveal a progressive increase in the number of touns. In 1509, there existed around 150 separate landholding units on the island. By 1614, the total had grown to 165 and by 1722, to 192.[63] In a study of North Uist covering roughly the same period, Crawford discovered a similar increase.[64] That part of Glenisla held by Cupar abbey is also instructive on how settlement formation continued on after 1350. First granted in free forest to the abbey in the late twelfth century, it already had settlements established in it by 1233, such as Bellaty and Freuchie. By the time of a 1542 estate rental, the number of separate touns had risen to 29. Some of this growth, like Auchinleck and Cambok, represent new gifts to the abbey of old established touns. But others represent newly established touns. Altogether, approximately a quarter might be dated to the period after 1350.[65]

The more elaborate documentation of the post-1350 period allows the nature of settlement formation to be researched more thoroughly. For instance, it is clear that some new settlement represented an offshoot of existing settlement, an attempt to settle the surrounding waste with something more independent than an outfield cropping system. Thus, a charter of 1600 talks of the 'terras de Knokreauche cum illa pendicula et lie outset . . . appellata Newtoun de Knokreache alias Wrak'.[66] Quoyland in Orkney and Shetland could also break free from existing settlement and become separate settlement, like the quoys of Smoogro and Orakirk in Orphir parish (Orkney).[67] In other cases, new settlement took the form of a deeper penetration into what had been a waste area. A good example of this has been published by Mather.[68] It concerns Glen Strathfarrar in Ross and Cromarty. During the medieval period, Glen Strathfarrar was devoid of settlement except for Culligan at its mouth. Most of it, in fact, formed the Forest of Affarick. From the late sixteenth century onwards, though, references to new touns in the Glen occur. By the late seventeenth century, a considerable population existed as far into the Glen as Glentilt. Although some were entirely new foundations, Mather believes some of the new settlements began life as shielings or grazing areas for touns to the east. This would be consistent with the work of Gaffney and Miller, both of whom have shown how many Highland touns began to crop their shieling areas over the seventeenth century and how some were eventually constituted as separate touns.[69] In so far as Mather's study shows forest area being opened up for settlement, then it compares with Ettrick in southern Scotland.

Prior to the fifteenth century, Ettrick was a hunting forest with little settlement except for the scattered lodges and stedes of the rangers and foresters who managed the different wards. In effect, it was sealed off from the normal colonising process. For Ettrick, the main change came after the mid-fifteenth century, when it passed into the hands of the Crown. The number of stedes was greatly increased and their character altered towards commercial sheep-farming. This shift from forest to commercial sheep-farming was assisted by the substitution of feuing for short-term leasing from the early sixteenth century onwards. An outline of these various changes can be constructed through a fine sequence of Crown rentals for the area.[70]

The Process of Toun Splitting

A neglected aspect of Scottish settlement history is the nature and origin of toun splitting. The extent of splitting is shown by the many pairs or groups of farms which carry a common surname but are distinguished from each other by prefixes like East, West, Nether and Upper (see Figures 2.3 and 2.4). There is hardly a corner of the Scottish landscape whose settlement pattern is not deve-

Figure 2.3: Easter and
Wester Delavorar
(Banffshire), 1773

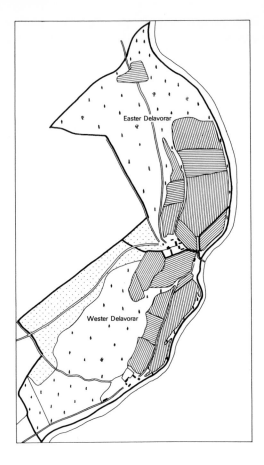

Line shading = arable,
stipple = pasture,
tree symbols = woodland

Figure 2.4: Daugh of
Deskie (Banffshire),
1761

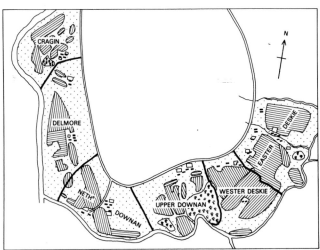

loped around such groups. Although once interpreted as a by-product of the eighteenth-century Improvers' Movement, many are much older, dating back to before 1650. A simple measure of their early importance can be derived from the many land charters printed in the *Register of the Great Seal of Scotland*. The volume for the period 1593-1608 contains 978 references to touns bearing the prefixes East, West, Over, Nether, Little, Meikle or their variants.[71]

Some split touns may have been laid out as such from their very beginnings as settlements. but the balance of evidence favours the view that most were formed by the splitting of an established, single toun into two or more separate touns.[72] Circumstantial support for this process can be pieced together from rentals. It is relatively easy to find touns which appear in one rental as a single toun, but in a later rental as a split toun. The fine run of rentals for Islay covering the period from the sixteenth to the seventeenth century is a good source of examples.[73] So too are the Crown rentals for Ettrick.[74] Crawford refers to other examples in his study of rentals for North Uist.[75] Clouston was also appreciative of how a single settlement would undergo fission to become a pair or group of settlements. Amongst those he published for Orkney was that of Linklater in Sandwick. Initially a single toun, it appears in seventeenth-century records as Nether, Over and West Linklater.[76] Estate records sometimes yield direct documentary evidence for splitting, such as when Easter Moniack (Inverness-shire) was split into Easter and Wester halves in 1609.[77]

Easter Moniack also illustrates a point that is crucial to the history of Scottish rural settlement, that is, that splitting could affect a toun or touns on more than one occasion. As a result, a single toun could develop over time into a complex of touns. Indeed, this formed one of the key ways in which rural settlement developed after 1100, by fission rather than procreation. There are many eighteenth-century estate plans which bear the imprint of such development. The Daugh of Taminlienin is one (see Figure 2.1). These complexes contain a vital lesson concerning the relationship between early settlement and its modern counterparts. It is not sufficient to take early references to settlement in an area and to argue from them that settlement was well established early on. Often all that was present was the main settlement in what was to become a complex. In short, to ignore the way a particular place-name and its associated toun became elaborated into East and West portions, etc., may well be to strip Scottish rural settlement after 1100 of its essential *élan vital*.

The process of splitting was rooted in a number of causes. One which may explain many early examples is the practice of partible inheritance. Given what was said earlier, this may have been especially potent in the Northern Isles. A related cause was the proprietary break-up of a toun through sales or feuing. Once divided between two or three different estates, there clearly existed strong pressure for the splitting of a toun. Many split touns, though, lay within the bounds of a single estate and cannot be explained by either of the foregoing causes. The reason for the splitting of these touns can only have been to combat their growing size and complexity. It was a response to their growth problems, enabling smaller, more manageable units to be created as more land was absorbed.[78]   Seen in this way, splitting was a means by which the overall size of touns could be regulated. Arguably, had it not been for splitting, many more Scottish touns would have had the village-like character of touns in the south-east.

Deserted Settlement 1100-1650

The problem of deserted medieval settlements has been touched on in a number of recent studies. Those by Laing and Fairhurst mention sites deserted before 1650, such as Galtway and Dunrod in Kirkcudbrightshire, but both go on to argue that the majority of deserted sites in both the Lowlands and Highlands date from the eighteenth century and later.[79] That by Parry concentrated on a particular region, Lammermuir, and was more systematic in its approach. Altogether, he discovered 15 settlements that had been abandoned during the period 1300-1600. Most were situated high up on Lammermuir. Parry saw their abandonment as influenced by, amongst other things, climatic deterioration during the late Middle Ages.[80] No doubt if similar studies using air photographs in conjunction with documentary material were carried out for other parts of Scotland, they would reveal a similar retreat from marginal sites during this period.

Until such work is carried out, the student of settlement history must be content with trying to establish the historical context of settlement desertion. In addition to climatic deterioration, there are other reasons why we can expect desertions over the period 1100-1650. Splitting is one. The structural reorganisation of a toun into two or more touns may have meant a change of site for the dwellings. Some split toun groups, therefore, may contain an older abandoned site within them. Interestingly, one of the more important excavations of a deserted rural settlement, that of Lix (Perthshire), involved a split toun. The report of the excavation stressed that no building or structure could be dated to before the eighteenth century. This was put down to the use before then of perishable building materials.[81] An alternative possibility is that the splitting of Lix into East, Mid and West portions altered the disposition of settlement so that dwelling sites excavated at Lix may not have coincided with the old focus of the toun when it was a single, integral settlement. Pillaging and wars could also affect settlement. Reports of settlements being destroyed by the armies of the 'auld enemy' or by internecine fighting between clans are commonplace. Most settlements affected in this way would have been subsequently rebuilt, but not necessarily on the same site or with the same alignment.

Settlement Morphology 1100-1650

The morphology of early settlement is not easily researched. Indeed, with reference to this aspect, Fairhurst has written that 'for the medieval period strictly speaking, the dearth of information is almost complete.'[82] However, the dearth is not so complete that the main issues cannot be outlined.

A problem that demands immediate attention is the extent to which settlement in the Highlands and Lowlands differed. The description of settlement in the former as clachans and in the latter as fermtouns implies differences of type. In actuality, their differences, both as regards terminology and morphology, were not so clear-cut. Historically, the term clachan was used in the Lowlands as well as the Highlands.[83] Likewise, the term toun if not fermtoun was widely used of settlement in the Highlands.[84]

As if to underline this catholicity of terms, the main morphological types of settlement do not coincide with this broad topographic distinction either. In terms of scale, large and small touns can be found in both the Highlands and Lowlands, albeit in different proportions. As regards morphology, a loose distinction can be drawn between a minority of settlements which possessed a semblance of order and the majority which did not. The latter formed the typical toun in both the Highlands and Lowlands. In it, dwellings, byres and kailyards were disposed as irregularly shaped clusters. If eighteenth-century estate plans can be read literally, their dwellings had no preferred orientation, despite the old Highland adage that houses should be back to the wind, face to the sun. As Burt remarked specifically of Highland touns, they were 'all irregularly placed, some one way, some another'[85] (see Figure 2.5). Touns laid out in an orderly fashion were to be found in the more fertile parts of the Lowlands, and consisted of simple one- or two-row alignments (see Figure 2.5). Given our dependence on eighteenth-century plans, it is possible that some of these settlements acquired their order after 1650. However, some unquestionably date back to the medieval period, like Midlem (Roxburghshire).

An added feature of many irregular touns, and one that contributed much to their irregularity, was the constant flux in their layout. This was especially true of touns whose dwellings were constructed of mud, wattle or turf and which, in consequence, had a fairly limited life. Just how temporary such dwellings might be is underlined by those Highland touns in which timber was scarce, yet essential as roof supports. It was common in such touns for the roof couples and even the doors to be removed by tenants at the end of their tack. Early court records sometimes document this process through the friction it caused.[86] It was a process that encouraged a continual abandonment and renewal of dwellings. Burt has an interesting comment to make on the same process as it affected the edge of towns. Their outskirts, he wrote,

were nothing but the Ruins of little Houses . . . Of this I asked the Reason, and was told, that when one of these Houses was grown old and decayed, they often did not repair it, but, taking out the Timber, they let the Walls stand as a Fit Enclosure for a Kale-Yard . . . and that they build anew upon another Spot![87]

Figure 2.5: Pre-enclosure Toun Plans

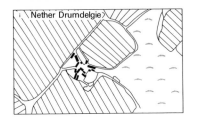

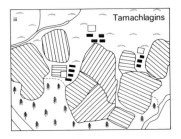

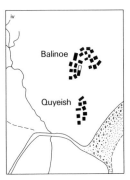

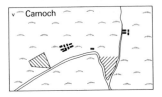

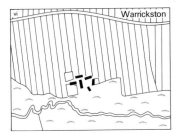

Line shading = arable, stipple = pasture

(i) Nether Drumdelgie (Aberdeenshire), 1779
(ii) Belvattan (Inverness-shire), 1770
(iii) Tamachlagins (Banffshire), 1762
(iv) Balinoe and Quyeish on Tiree (Argyllshire), 1767
(v) Carnoch in Barrisdale (Inverness-shire), 1771
(vi) Warwickston (Aberdeenshire), 1779
(vii) Nether Pleugh of Old Flinders
    (Aberdeenshire), 1762
(viii) Auchencraw (Berwickshire), 1713

Herein also lies the reason for the changing shape of many rural touns. In a sense, the layout which these touns display in eighteenth-century estate plans must be seen as a mere snapshot of a potentially fluid situation. Not all touns, though, were built of such perishable materials. Some had dwellings built of stone. Thus, contemporary descriptions, as well as excavations at sites like Lour (Peebles-shire), affirm that simple stone dwellings were to be found in parts of the Lowlands before 1650.[88] It is also known that stone was used in the Northern and Western Isles during the medieval period. Thanks to excavations at Udal in North Uist by Crawford, the Hebridean black house can be taken back into the medieval period, but not, it seems, back in an unbroken lineage to the Norse stone dwellings of the area, despite their undoubted similarities.[89] Whether such stone-built touns had equally fluid layouts compared with those discussed above remains to be seen.

Conclusions

The foregoing review of colonisation and rural settlement 1100-1650 has, of necessity, been exploratory in nature. There are too few studies on these critical themes for it to be otherwise. However, it is possible to draw some tentative conclusions about overall trends. The most important is that the unfolding pattern of colonisation and rural settlement needs to be seen as a chronologically elongated process rather than a compressed one. Not only was there a well-established settlement pattern by 1100, but the process of colonisation and settlement formation continued on into the early modern period, or the sixteenth and seventeenth centuries. An urgent task for future work must be to calibrate their phasing more exactly. Another conclusion that can be tentatively advanced is that, with the possible exception of the major hunting forests, the history of colonisation and rural settlement, 1100-1650, was not a case of settled regions expanding into uninhabited regions, the two separated by a moving frontier of pioneer activity. Most regions and most environments already had some human presence by 1100, their settlement history thereafter being largely one of intensification, by extensive infilling and fission, with early settlement emerging later as key nodes in complex systems of settlement.

Notes

1. *An exhortation to the Scottes by James Harryson, Scottesheman*, printed as Appendix to Murray, J. A. H. (ed.) (1872), *The complaynt of Scotlande* (English Text Society, extra series, XVII, p. 208
2. Laing, D. (ed.) (1872), *The orygynale cronykil of Scotland by Andrew of Wyntoune* (Edinburgh), Vol. II, p. 482
3. Skene, W. F. (ed.) (1873), *John of Fordun's chronicle of the Scottish nation* (Edinburgh), p. 369
4. See, for example, the anonymous poem in Scott, T. (ed.) (1970), *The Penguin book of Scottish verse* (London), p. 59

5. Mackay, W. (ed.) (1905), *Chronicles of the Frasers, The Wardlaw manuscripts* (Publications of the Scottish History Society) (hereafter Pubs. SHS), 1st series, *47*

6. Murray (1872), *The complaynt of Scotlande*, p. lxiv

7. Gilbert, J. M. (1975), 'Hunting reserves', pp. 33-4 in McNeill, P. and Nicholson, R. (eds.), *An historical atlas of Scotland c. 400-c.600* (St Andrews)

8. *Acts of Parliament of Scotland*, *I*, p. 397

9. Ibid., p. 382

10. Brown, P. H. (1973 edition), *Early travellers in Scotland* (Edinburgh), p. 74

11. Ibid., p. 267

12. See, for example, Gaffney, V. (ed.) (1960), *The Lordship of Strathavon* (Third Spalding Club, Aberdeen), pp. 28-9

13. Peterkin, A. (1820), *Rentals of the ancient earldom and bishopric of Orkney* (Edinburgh), section III, p. 72

14. See, for example, Donaldson, G. (ed.) (1958), *The court book of Shetland 1602-1604* (Scottish Record Society, Edinburgh), pp. 36 and 95

15. Storer Clouston, J. (ed.) (1914), *Records of the earldom of Orkney 1299-1614* (Pubs. SHS), 2nd series, *7*, lxi; *idem* (1920), 'The Orkney township' *Scottish Historical Review*, *17*, 16-45

16. See, for example, Miller, A. (ed.) (1890), *The Glamis book of record* (Pubs. SHS), 1st series, *9*, 48-9

17. A good example is the 'Rentaill of the lordschipe of Huntlye alias Strauthbogye 1600' in (1849) *The Miscellany of the Spalding Club*, *4*, 261-319

18. Brand, J. (1883), *A brief description of Orkney, Zetland, Pightland-Firth & Caithness* (Edinburgh), reprinted from 1701 edition (ed. Brown, W.), pp. 39-40

19. See, for instance, (1885) *Reports on the state of certain parishes in Scotland 1627* (Maitland Club, Edinburgh), pp. 78-9, 171 and 205

20. Dodgshon, R. A. (1972), 'The removal of runrig in Roxburghshire and Berwickshire 1680-1766', *Scottish Studies*, *16*, 121-7

21. Barrow, G. W. S. (ed.), with collaboration of Scott, W. W. (1971), *The Acts of William I King of Scots, 1165-1214, Regesta Regum Scottorum II* (Edinburgh), p. 303

22. Duncan, A. A. A. (1975), *Scotland: the making of the kingdom* (Edinburgh), pp.320-1

23. Barrow, G. W. S. (ed.) (1971), *Acts of William I*, p. 318

24. Duncan (1975), *Scotland*, pp. 319-20

25. See, for example, Balfour, D. (ed.) (1859), *Oppressions of the sixteenth century in the islands of Orkney and Zetland* (Maitland Club, Edinburgh), Appendix II, III

26. McKerral, A. (1943), 'Ancient denominations of agricultural land in Scotland', *Proc. Society of Antiquaries of Scotland*, *78*, 52

27. Dodgshon, R. A. (1975), 'Towards an understanding and definition of runrig: the evidence for Roxburghshire and Berwickshire', *Transactions of the Institute of British Geographers*, *64*, 21-2

28. Based on Roxburgh Sheriff Court, Jedburgh, Decreet of Division of Newstead, 1752

29. Romanes, J. H. (1939), 'The kindly tenants of the abbey of Melrose', *Juridical Review*, *51*, 211

30. The growing frequency of its use can be monitored through the *Register of the Great Seal of Scotland*; see, for example, Paul, J. B. and Thomson, J. M. (eds.) (1883), *Register of the Great Seal of Scotland 1513-1546* (Edinburgh)

31. Ibid., pp. 66-7

32. Ibid., p. 440

33. Ibid., p. 593

34. The best summary is Storer Clouston, J. (1919), *Records of the earldom of Orkney*, pp. 16-45

35. Peterkin (1820), *Rentals of the ancient earldom and bishopric of Orkney*, Part II, p. 2

36. Ibid., p. 6

37. (1847) *Collectanea de rebus albanicis, consisting of original papers and documents relating to the history of the Highlands and Islands of Scotland* (Iona Club, Edinburgh), pp. 172-9

38. *Report on the state of certain parishes*, pp. 72 and 78-80

39. Ibid., p. 41

40. Thomson, J. M. (ed.) (1890), *Register of the Great Seal of Scotland 1593-1608* (Edinburgh)

41. Scottish Record Office (hereafter SRO), GD16/section 4/24, Airlie MSS., Division of commonty of Cullow etc., 1594

42. SRO GD4/262, Division of Hedderwick commonty, 1602

43. Barrow, G. W. S. (1973), *The kingdom of the Scots* (London), p. 277

44. Jackson, D. (1972), *The Gaelic notes in the book of Deer* (Cambridge), pp. 116-17

45. Duncan (1975), *Scotland*, p. 318

46. Based on SRO, RHP2487, survey of Glenlivet, 1761

47. (1855) *Origines Parochiales Scotiae* (Bannatyne Club, Edinburgh), *2*, 692 and 704

48. Skene, W. F. (1873), *John of Fordun's chronicle*, Appendix 4, p. 449

49. The antiquity of the multiple estate is explored in Jones, G. R. J. (1976), 'Multiple Estates', pp. 15-40 in Sawyer, P. H. (ed.), *Medieval Settlement* (London)

50. See the chapter on 'Pre-feudal Scotland: shires and thanages', pp. 7-68 in Barrow (1973), *The kingdom of the Scots*

51. Robertson, E. W. (1872), *Historical essays in connexion with the land, the church &c.* (Edinburgh), pp. 125-8

52. Barrow (1971), *The Acts of William I*, p. 263

53. Easson, D. E. (ed.) (1947), *Charters of the abbey of Coupar Angus* (Pubs. SHS), 3rd series, *40*, 48-9

54. (1837) *Liber Sancte Marie de Melros* (Bannatyne Club, Edinburgh), *I*, xvi

55. Easson (1947), *Charters of the abbey of Coupar Angus*, pp. 78-9

56. See Franklin, T. B. (1952), *A history of Scottish farming* (London), pp. 77-85

57. Abbeys with property in areas like the Cheviots generally had rights to graze a specific number of sheep on the surrounding pasture. Inevitably, with a stock-orientated economy, this would have been a vital part of their land grant. See *Originales Parochiales*, 410 *et seq.*

58. Examples of perambulations can be found in *Liber Sancte Marie de Melros*, vol. I. An attempted reconstruction of Yetholm shire can be found in Barrow (1973), *The kingdom of the Scots*, p. 33

59. A fuller discussion of this aspect is contained in Dodgshon, R. A. (1979), 'Law and landscape in early Scotland: a study of the relationship between tenure and landholding', in Harding, A. (ed.), *Lawmaking and lawmakers in British history* (Studies in History, no. 14) (London), pp. 127-45

60. (1853) *Registrum Honoris de Morton* (Bannatyne Club, Edinburgh), Vol. I, p. xlvii *et seq.*

61. The 1172 grant, which Barrow redates to 1180 x 1184, is printed in Barrow (1971), *The Acts of William I*, p. 286. The 1511 rental is cited in Browne, G. F. (ed.) (1923), *Echt-Forbes family charters 1345-1727: records of the Forest of Birse, 926-1781* (Edinburgh), pp. 192-7

62. *Origines Parochiales*, vol. 2, p. 190; McNeill, G. P. (ed.) (1897), *The exchequer rolls of Scotland*, Vol. XVII *A.D. 1537-1542* (Edinburgh), p. 645

63. Smith, G. G. (1895), *The book of Islay* (Edinburgh), appendices

64. Crawford, I. A. (1966), 'Contributions to a history of domestic settlement in North Uist', *Scottish Studies*, *9*, 36-41

65. Easson (1947), *Charters of the abbey of Coupar Angus*, pp. 52-7 and 93-8; the charters in the latter should be compared with the rental in Rogers, C. (ed.) (1880), *Rental book of the Cistercian abbey of Coupar Angus* (London), Vol. 2, pp. 195-201

66. Robertson, J. (ed.) (1862), *Illustrations of the topography and antiquities of the Shires of Aberdeen and Banff* (Aberdeen), Vol. 4, p. 329

67. Storer Clouston, J. (1927), *The Orkney parishes, containing the statistical account of Orkney, 1795-1798* (Kirkwall), p. 62

68. Mather, A. (1970), 'Pre-1745 land use and conservation in a Highland glen: an example from Glen Strathfarrar, North Inverness-shire', *Scottish Geographical Magazine*, *86*, 163-4

69. Gaffney (1960), *The lordship of Strathavon*, pp. 31-2; Miller, R. (1967), 'Land use

by summer shielings', *Scottish Studies*, *II*, 193-221

70. See, for instance, the successive rentals in (1883) *The exchequer rolls of Scotland*, Vol. VI, *1455-1460* (Edinburgh), pp. 223-4; (1888) ibid., Vol. XI, *1497-1501* (Edinburgh), pp. 457-60. (1901) ibid., Vol. XXI, *1580-1588* (Edinburgh), pp. 344-9

71. Thomson (1890), *Register of the Great Seal of Scotland*

72. A general review of the processes involved can be found in Dodgshon, R. A. (1977), 'Changes in Scottish township organization during the medieval and early modern periods', *Geografiska Annaler*, *59B*, 51-67

73. Smith (1895), *The book of Islay*, Appendix III

74. Compare, for example, *The exchequer rolls*, Vol. VI, *1455-1460*, pp. 223-4 with Vol. XXI, *1580-1588*, pp. 344-9

75. Crawford (1966), 'Contributions to a history of domestic settlement in North Uist', 38-9

76. Storer Clouston (1919), *Records of the earldom of Orkney*, p. 37

77. Mackenzie, A., *Inventory of the title deeds of the estate of Easter Moniack belonging to Edward Satchwell Fraser, Esquire of Realick*. Bound Xerox copy in SRO

78. (1906) *Geographical collections relating to Scotland made by W. Macfarlane* (Pubs. SHS), 1st series, *51*, Vol. I, p. 272, affords relevant comment on this aspect in relation to north-east Scotland.

79. Laing, L. (1969), 'Medieval settlement archaeology in Scotland', *Scottish Archaeological Forum*, 69-77; Fairhurst, H. (1969), 'The study of deserted medieval settlements in Scotland (to 1968), I. Rural settlement', pp. 229-35 in Beresford, M. W. and Hurst, J. G. (eds.), *Deserted medieval villages* (London), p. 231

80. Parry, M. L. (1975), 'Secular climatic change and marginal agriculture', *Transactions of the Institute of British Geographers*, *64*, 5-11

81. Fairhurst, H. and Petrie, G. (1964), 'Scottish clachans II: Lix and Rosal', *Scottish Geographical Magazine*, *80*, 152-6

82. Fairhurst (1969), 'The study of deserted medieval settlements in Scotland'

83. See, for example, the Galloway reference in (1874) *Fourth report of the Royal Commission on historial manuscripts*, Part I, Report and Appendix (London), p. 517

84. One frequently finds the phrase, 'the toun and lands of . . .' in land charters or rentals for the Highlands no less than for the Lowlands.

85. Jamieson, R. (ed.) (1876, based on original 1754 edition), *Burt's letters from the north of Scotland* (Edinburgh)

86. See, for example, the (1852) 'Extracts from the court book of the barony of Skene' in *The miscellany of the Spalding Club* (Aberdeen), pp. 218-19

87. Jamieson (1876), *Burt's letters from the north of Scotland*, pp. 28-9

88. The Lour excavation is reported in Dunbar, J. G. and Hay, G. D. (1960-1), 'Excavations at Lour, Stobo, 1959-60' *Proceedings Society Antiquaries of Scotland*, *94*, 196-210

89. Crawford, I. (1974), 'Scot(?), Norman and Gael', *Scottish Archaeological Forum*, *6*, 1

3 THE ORIGINS OF TRADITIONAL FIELD SYSTEMS

R. A. Dodgshon

If we could revisit the landscape of Scotland prior to 1750, the kind depicted so graphically by Thomas Slezer's *Theatrum Scotiae*,[1] we would find an unfamiliar scene. Many of the scattered farmsteads and estate villages which fill the rural landscape today, together with their accompanying network of large, regularly shaped hedged or tree-bound enclosures would be absent. In their place, there existed a different, more naked order. Then, the basic unit of farming, the unit of both operation and co-operation, was the fermtoun or clachan, a frequently huddled, but sometimes planned, cluster of dwellings and outbuildings. Around it was extended a mosaic of small, irregular, unenclosed fields. Their surface would appear scarred, as in so many of Slezer's foregrounds, with gracefully curved but deeply-incised rigs (Plate 1). If we could talk to the farmers who laboured these rigs, we would discover that their property was scattered through-out the toun in the form of intermixed rigs, groups of rigs or parcels, a system of landholding layout known as runrig. If we lingered longer, the more perceptive would soon become aware that within most touns, there was an important areal difference as regards husbandry, with an inner sector of continually cropped arable, and an outer sector that was shifted, fold by fold, from grass to arable and back to grass again in strict rotation: this bilateral organisation of cropping was called infield-outfield. Together, runrig and infield-outfield constituted the basic elements of early Scottish field systems, institutions from whose nature and variations the early Scottish landscape derived much of its character.

To understand them, we must confront a number of problems. First, it is necessary to fix a broad working definition of their nature. Both runrig and infield-outfield possessed a structure, or distinctive form of layout. At the same time, they had a functional or dynamic side to their character. Any working definition must embrace both these aspects. Second, there is the question of their internal and external relationships. Too often past discussion has treated runrig and infield-outfield as inseparable, so much so that the terms have been used as substitutes for each other. Such an approach has contributed nothing but confusion. They could and did exist apart. Nor did they exist in a vacuum, but each had a social, economic and, above all, a tenurial context. Any analytical discussion of their character would be incomplete if it failed to explore their relationship with each other and with their context. Lastly, there is the con-tentious matter of origins, of how and when runrig and infield-outfield first developed.

Defining Scottish Field Systems

Runrig: its Structure and Functional Character

Like subdivided field systems elsewhere, runrig involved a community of land-holders whose individual holdings were fragmented into strips or parcels and intermixed, one with another. Structurally, it can be analysed in terms of its scale, both physical and tenurial, and its form of layout.

Considering the first of these problems, Gray once argued that the hallmark of the Scottish runrig toun was its small size or compactness. What he terms the usual size of unit involved the tilling of less than 100 acres (40 ha).[2] Such a bald statement, though, cannot convey the variety of toun size. With the exception of the north-east, the majority of touns in the eastern Lowlands, from Angus through Fife and the Lothians to the Merse, were probably in excess of 100 ha. For example, a study of eighteenth-century touns in Roxburghshire and Berwick-shire based on a sample of 208 found that 80 per cent exceeded Gray's estimate. In fact, over 50 per cent exceeded 150 ha.[3] In the north-east and in the western Lowlands, toun size was significantly smaller. In these areas, the majority fell within the range 25-100 ha. Larger touns were not absent, but they were not as common as in the Lothians or the Merse.[4] In terms of crude acreage, the largest touns in the south or east of Scotland were those to be found in the Southern Uplands. A 1718 survey of the vast Buccleuch estate shows that the majority of its numerous gerss or pastoral holdings in Selkirkshire, Dumfriesshire and southern Roxburghshire ranged between 250 and 500 ha.[5] However, crude figures need qualifying. The bulk of these acreages comprised upland pasture. Such touns were fortunate if they contained more than 25 ha of arable. A similar qualification can be entered with regard to toun size in the Highlands and Islands. For instance, a 1769 survey of the large Breadalbane estate in Perthshire yields an overall average per toun of 200 ha plus. The bulk of these acreages, though, comprised rough grazings.[6] The same was true of the Assynt estate in the north-west. When surveyed in 1779, its 44 touns averaged nearly 1020 ha each, but less than 50 ha in respect of arable land.[7]

The scale of touns can also be expressed in landholding terms, or in terms of how many tenants they carried. The most obvious source material for this type of information is estate rentals. Unfortunately, there has been little system-atic study of the many sixteenth- and seventeenth-century estate rentals available (see Chapter 5). Our view of tenant numbers per toun, therefore, must still be regarded as patchy. But even from the limited number of rentals examined by the writer, it is clear that touns held by more than one tenant, or multiple tenants, were not overwhelmingly dominant. A study of rentals for south-east Scotland revealed that only 54 per cent of the 263 touns covered by them were held by multiple tenants at some point during the period 1680-1766. However, if the 52 examples of proprietary runrig, or runrig touns that were shared between more than one heritor, are added to the calculation, the proportion increases to almost two-thirds.[8] A comparable analysis of the 1696 *List of pollable persons in Aberdeenshire*, which details whether a person was a tenant or not within each toun, suggests that less than half of all touns had multiple tenants.[9] Work by Lebon on Ayrshire also confirmed that multiple tenancy was significant long before the mid-eighteenth century.[10] Even in the Highlands and Islands, not all touns were held by multiple tenants. Here and there on estates like the Macleod estate on Skye or the Breadalbane estate in Perthshire, single tenant touns were to be found juxtaposed alongside multiple tenant touns.[11] In reply, it might be argued that such a review, based as it is on data for the late seventeenth and eighteenth centuries, may depict runrig at a late stage, a stage when its importance was in decline. After all, a decline in tenant numbers during this period has been documented for areas like the western Lowlands and the Southern Uplands.[12] Rentals available for the fifteenth and sixteenth centuries, though, enable us to answer this question easily. For instance, a Crown rental of 1497 relating to land in Ettrick, Stratherne, Moray, Ayrshire and Galloway shows that even at this point, single and multiple tenancy existed alongside each other.[13]

These same sources suggest that Gray was probably right in assuming that the average multiple tenant toun had 2-6 tenants. Admittedly larger touns can be found. For example, the 1696 *List of Pollable Persons in Aberdeenshire* shows that touns like Cobairdie, Achaber, the Daach of Auchinbor, Pitully, Tullich and Larish had more tenants.[14] So too did many of the proprietary runrig touns in south-east Scotland, with examples like Eyemouth, Coldingham and Eildon having over 20 different heritors.[15] However, generally speaking, there appears to have been a ceiling to the landholding scale of runrig touns. Once they became too complex, many were probably inclined to be split into smaller sub-touns (see Chapter 2). By such means, the landholding scale of touns could be kept to modest levels.

However, by way of a caveat to the foregoing discussion, it should be noted that rentals do not always tell the entire story as regards the landholding structure of touns. In the Lowlands, they omit what appear to have been substantial numbers of cottars. By definition, a cottar was someone who held a small amount of land from a tenant in return for his labour. The owner of a low-lying Perthshire estate put the number of cottars on each of his touns as four and the amount of land they held collectively as 20 per cent of each toun.[16] To judge from the way many reports in the *Old Statistical Account* of the late eighteenth century refer to the recent disappearance of cottars as one of the more significant social changes of the period, they were obviously both widespread and important in the landholding make-up of touns.[17]

In the Highlands and Islands, rentals are a difficult source to use for another reason. The widespread existence of the tacksmen system in the region means that the true number of tenants, let alone cottars, could be concealed. This was a system whereby the entire toun or group of touns was leased to a single tacksman. Often, he was a close relative of the estate owner or clan chief, or a senior member of one of the clan's cadet branches. In turn, the tacksmen then leased out the toun to the working tenants, or sub-tenants, who actually farmed the land.[18] Taking a general view of the problem, some rentals state quite clearly that a toun was leased to a tacksman so that no ambiguity exists. For instance, one drawn up for the Lordship of Strathavon in 1708 declared touns like Easter Blairfindy and Neathor Clashinor as held by tacksmen.[19] In other cases, their existence can be inferred from the way in which groups of touns were recorded in a rental as held by a single tenant. A fine illustration of this is provided by a 1600 rental for the Lordship of Huntly which noted the 40 mark land of Mamoir as set to Allane Camerone McOmildowy. Since it comprised 20 different touns, it can hardly be doubted that McOmildowy functioned as tacksman.[20] Inevitably, where tacksmen existed, rentals afford a very imperfect view of landholding: many of the single tenancies that seemingly existed on estates like the Macleod estate in Skye may, in reality, have been tacksmen controlling a multiple tenant toun.

Yet another problem affecting Highland areas has been outlined by Geddes.[21] Close reading of a 1718 rental for the Seaforth estate lands in Lewis, Kintail and Ross suggested to him that although the rental was arranged in touns, these may not necessarily have been the actual units of farming. This was because within each toun, tenants appear to have been grouped for the payment of rent into pairs or threes. Geddes interpreted this as signifying that such groups farmed separate sections of the toun, so that one was really dealing with a system of touns within touns. Whilst it is not absolutely certain that this was the case, it is a plausible interpretation. If widespread, such an *ad hoc* grouping of tenants within touns would greatly complicate the use of rentals.

Turning to the physical layout of runrig, the intermixture of land belonging to different landholders led to a veritable patchwork of landholding. The complexity of such systems is well conveyed by a toun like Coldingham in Berwickshire, whose 47 different heritors held 1,473 Scots acres in 339 separate strips or parcels.[22] At the other end of Scotland, the runrig toun of Funzie on the Shetland isle of Fetlar had its 189.5 acres of arable shared between its various proprietors in 459 strips or parcels.[23] Such excesses of fragmentation were not exceptional amongst the larger touns. However, it is the style or manner of fragmentation, rather than its extent, that is of most concern to scholars. Unlike comparable systems south of the Border, Scottish subdivided field systems bore a special term of description — runrig. This has led some writers to argue that if it carried a special term of description, then there must be something special about its character. In searching for this mark of distinction, they have looked to its layout and have argued that it involved strips running parallel, or that it comprised the systematic allocation of land between landholders, or that it involved the systematic intermixture of holdings through all the different parts of a toun.

These assumptions can be tested using detailed runrig surveys that became available during the middle decades of the eighteenth century. Even acknowledging that these surveys form only a small sample of the total number of touns that existed, there is little doubt that they make it difficult to accept that the essential meaning of runrig centred on its absolute regularity of appearance on this evidence alone. Two plans, those for West Reston (Berwickshire) and the lands of Claymires and Botarie (Aberdeenshire), have been reproduced in Figures 3.1 and 3.2. In a country possessed of such wide physical contrasts, it would be presumptuous to argue that these plans serve as an illustration for all types of toun. But they do illustrate the difficulties to be faced in matching assumption with fact. The only indisputable conclusion to be drawn from these and similar plans is that arable was arranged into small, irregular units. These units were called *shots* in the Lowlands, but had a varied terminology elsewhere. In Caithness, for instance, they were called *shades*. In parts of the north-east and central Highlands, terms like *croit*, *rhun* and *park* were used. These arable building-blocks of the toun's layout formed a continuous, unbroken area in the more fertile touns. However, in the Highlands and Islands, or wherever land was poorly drained, they might be disjoined and scattered as discontinuous blocks interspersed with pasture. The plan of the lands of Forbes in the parish of Clatt (Aberdeenshire) in Figure 3.3 displays layouts of this type. Such plans, though, yield less support for stock assumptions regarding the landholding layout of runrig touns. If the parallel arrangement of strips, their sequential allocation to landholders or the systematic scattering of strips over a variety of different land types were present, then it was only on a partial basis. Other published plans bear out this discrepancy between assumption and fact.[24]

Of course, it could legitimately be argued that such plans depict runrig on the eve of its abolition. Could it be that we see the system in a decayed form, or after piecemeal exchanges and amalgamations had long since destroyed the symmetry of its original layout? For some scholars, the stability of runrig layouts implied by this question would itself be questionable. The reason being that, for them, the distinctive feature of runrig was the periodic reallocation of strips between landholders.[25] In short, if the orderly layout of landholding was part of its essential nature, then it would have been constantly *re*-created by *re*-division and *re*-allocation of strips. The question of runrig losing its regularity by being frozen, and then undergoing local changes of detail in its layout, therefore, does not arise. This stress on the periodic reallocation of runrig forms part of a myth of archaism which surrounds the interpretation of Scottish field systems. Those who propound this archaism in relation to runrig see it as representing a mid-way point in the evolution of property rights from a purely common property form to severalty, since it doled out strips or land on a *temporary* basis to individuals.[26] The difficulty with this argument is that it lacks substantive support. A few contemporary writers refer to its local practice, such as Pennant's reference to it in the Loch Broom area.[27] Delving amongst estate material has also produced examples. For instance, a 1765 tack for a third of Bellnollo (Perthshire) to a Robert Maxtone refers to his share being 'mark'd out & divided to conform to the Judgement of Birleymen, & as falling to him by lot, to be drawn by him for that purpose'.[28] However, cumulatively,

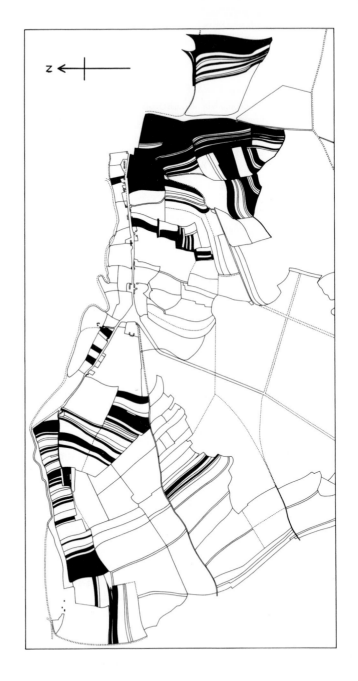

Figure 3.1: Runrig Lands of West Reston (Berwickshire), 1760. The holdings of one landholder have been shaded black.

Figure 3.2: Claymires and Botarie (Aberdeenshire), c. 1760 (after G. Kay, 1962)

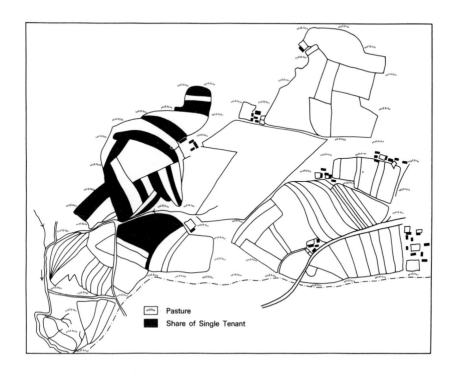

Pasture
Share of Single Tenant

such evidence is not impressive. More serious, there is ample evidence to show that many touns were stable in layout over long periods of time. Proprietary runrig touns form an obvious source of evidence. In fact, examples like Eyemouth (Berwickshire) show rigs being exchanged between landholders to achieve a more convenient layout.[29] In the case of tenant runrig touns, a sure sign of stability is the way many tacks dealt with the problem of allocating shares or holdings by linking it back to the previous occupant.[30] Clearly, this presupposes a continuity of layout for that share or holding. Some writers have tried to rationalise this lack of evidence by seeing 'fixed' runrig as developing out of 'moveable' runrig, the latter being the original state.[31] However, even if this was an acceptable interpretation, it still would follow that some touns had been stable in layout, perhaps for a century or more, by the time they appear in the light of the eighteenth century. There was ample scope, therefore, for localised adjustments in toun layout that might have disrupted any original pattern of regularity.

However, there is another way of reaching back beyond these surveys to the runrig systems of an earlier period. Medieval charters sometimes belie signs of the formalised procedures by which landholders divided their property into runrig. A popular method in eastern Scotland was that known as sun-division.

This involved the identification of a landholder's share in a toun as either the sunny or shadow portion. If the former, he was given the strips which lay to the east or south in any sequence of an allocation; if the latter, he had the strips lying to the west or north. A fine illustration of this practice is to be found in the mid-fifteenth-century 'Depertison betuix Melros [the abbey] and Walter of Haliburton', involving land at Haliburton (Berwickshire). After drawing lots to see who had the sunny and who the shadow half, the land was divided into 'ryndale be four riggs & four till ayther pt.'[32] Another solution to the problem was to assign each person with a rank order in the allocation of strips. Thus a landholder would be described in charters as having the third or fifth rig throughout the toun.[33] Another method adopted was for the toun to be divided out into the required number of shares, and then for the landholders to draw lots for them. The Bellnollo tack that was cited earlier hints at this type of allocation. In a few cases, the exact method used is only partially revealed. For instance, until 1614, 'the Earles and Bishops lands were runrig'd through Orkney and Zetland, the former having two and the latter one.'[34] With each of the foregoing methods, we are clearly dealing with procedures that produced a systematised layout, systematised both as regards the sequence of allocation and in the extent to which a person's holding was spread over the entire toun. The evidence for them is the surest proof available that the intent behind runrig was to produce a regular layout as regards landholding. However, it does not follow automatically that this regularity of layout was the essential meaning of the term runrig, only that this was a characteristic of it.

The disposition of landholding on a runrig basis naturally created logistical problems for farming. Usually, these problems were met by the adoption of a common cropping and grazing routine, one to which the entire toun was subjected. This routine was enforced by rules or acts of good neighbourhood enacted by the local barony or birlaw court. The most critical area was the management of stock. The entire annual cycle of stock movements through the different sectors of the toun — infield, outfield and common pasture — needed to be carefully regulated. Most touns, for instance, maintained a single common herd, to which landholders contributed a fixed number of stock (their stocking *soums*).[35] This made it easier to control such husbandry practices as outfield tathing[36] and to observe the strict dates when stock were herded back and forth across the head dyke,[37] that fundamental line in the toun's spatial organisation which separated infield from outfield and the common grazings.[38] Needless to add, the regulation of ploughing and harvesting were complementary to such stocking controls. Indeed, the one depended on the other.

Infield-Outfield: its Structure and Functional Character

The scale of infield-outfield systems was governed by the broad regional differences in toun sizes discussed earlier. Their disposition within touns also displayed broad differences between regions. In the more fertile and settled parts of the Lowlands, infield and outfield tended to occupy most of the toun and to be more equally balanced as regards acreage. Such touns, in consequence, tended to have only a limited supply of permanent pasture actually within their bounds. For grass, they depended instead on outfield or on nearby commonty which they shared with other touns. In those parts of the Lowlands where drainage was a problem, and throughout the Highlands and Islands, we tend to find much more pasture within touns, so that the spatial organisation of the toun appears based on a tripartite division of land into infield, outfield and permanent pasture. In such touns, infield and outfield could be quite modest in relation to the total acreage of the toun (see Figure 3.3). Of course, in the case of Highland touns, and many around the fringe of the Highlands, there could be a fourth element — shielings. These comprised detached grazings on the more rugged or distant hill ground.

Looking more closely at each of these sectors, infield was commonly disposed around or adjacent to the farmsteads of a toun (see Figure 3.3). This is what one might expect of a field unit that formed an intensively cropped area and which received the bulk of the toun's dung. Although it has been classed as a one-field system, it hardly qualifies as such. Most documented examples appear divided into two or more breaks for the purpose of cropping. The only clear-cut instance of infield being cropped as a single break is the so-called bear-fey land of Galloway.[39] Elsewhere, even the Highlands and Islands could boast two- or three-break systems. Thus, a late eighteenth-century comment on Orkney tells how 'bear succeeded to Oats and Oats to Bear invariably on the same land for centuries'. [40] Similar cropping systems are documented for infields in the Hebrides and in mainland counties like Perthshire.[41] Where a three-break system prevailed, it tended to be either bear, oats and rye, or bear, oats and oats. The latter system was particularly common in the north-east.[42] It formed the basis for J. Wilson's model of infield cropping (see Figure 3.4). Further south, in Fife, the Lothians and the Merse, cropping tended to be heavier, with the insertion of a wheat break instead of oats, and/or longer, through the addition of a pease break. Donaldson's *Husbandry Anatomized* (1697), for example, describes a toun in the south-east whose infield was cropped with barley, oats and pease.[43] However, a roughly contemporary essay by Lord Belhaven described infields in East Lothian as cropped with wheat, barley, pease and oats.[44] Similar cropping systems were to be found in the Merse.[45] These three- and four-break systems were probably long established.[46] However, what does appear recent when seen in mid-eighteenth century tacks is the insertion of a faugh or fallow break into infield cropping schemes: this had the effect of converting the standard three- or four-break systems into four- or five-break ones. Instances of a fallow break being used have been located in the extreme south-east, in Ayrshire and on the Abercairny estate in Perthshire.[47]

Before examining the pattern of outfield cropping, it is worth noting that some touns did not possess an outfield by name. Instead, their infields passed directly into common grazings. The 1718 survey of the Buccleuch estate, for instance, noted touns in the parish of Canoby (Dumfriesshire) as divided simply

Figure 3.3: Lands of Forbes, Clatt Parish (Aberdeenshire), *c*. 1771, Showing the Layout of Infields, Outfields and Pasture

into infield and commonty.[48] On the Assynt estate, meanwhile, the 1779 survey distinguished only between infield and 'sheeling' arable.[49] The vast majority of other early estate surveys, though, do record an outfield developed beyond infield. As in Figure 3.3, it often consisted of 'folds' or 'faulds' scattered over the common grazings of a toun. Only in the more fertile areas did it form a compact cropping zone. Its cropping structure is best explained by reference to Figure 3.4. Each fold formed a cropping break. Figure 3.4 has ten. During

Figure 3.4: Model of Infield-Outfield Cropping (after J. Wilson)

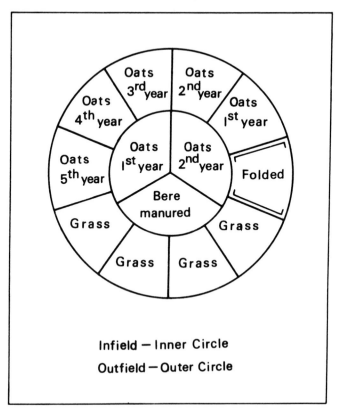

Infield — Inner Circle

Outfield — Outer Circle

any one year, half of these breaks, and therefore only half of the outfield, would be under a crop. Of these five breaks under crop, one would be under its first crop, another its second, another its third, another its fourth, and another its fifth and final crop. Of the remaining five breaks under grass, one would be a tathed break: this meant that during summer, stock would be penned and folded on it at night, thereby manuring it in preparation for its cultivation the following spring. As the newly tathed break came into cultivation, the break which had completed its course of five crops was abandoned back to grass again. Thus, by turns, each break was shifted from grass to arable and back to grass again.

The system portrayed by Figure 3.4 was especially common in the north-east. Elsewhere, variations of detail but not principle can be found. Broadly speaking, outfields in the more fertile parts of the Lowlands were cropped in a more restricted way. Often, only a quarter or a third would be in cultivation for any one year, each break carrying no more than three or four crops.[50] This restricted cropping of outfield has to be seen in context. These touns were usually those in which infield and outfield occupied most of the toun. Under these circumstances, outfield was valued as much for its grass as for its arable supplement.[51] In areas where grass was more abundant, such as in Highland areas, outfield cropping could be more extreme. However, no toun had more than a half of its outfield under crop. Figure 3.4 effectively defines this upper limit.[52] Yet another source of regional variation was the practice in some areas, notably the north-east, of having a part of outfield that was prepared for cultivation not by tathing but by faughing. Faughing was probably a straightforward system of fallow, but turf cuttings may have been added as a manurial supplement.

Just as some touns sought a supplement for their arable by cropping outfield, so also did many seek a supplement for their pasture resources. As already stressed, the extent to which touns had access to extra-toun grazing varied from one part of the country to another. In the south, the hill pastures of the Southern Uplands, the Lammermuirs and the Cheviots had long been parcelled into gerss or pastoral farms. This was a process that had begun with the abbeys back in the twelfth and thirteenth centuries. It was extended with renewed vigour during the fifteenth and sixteenth centuries, again in response to commercial sheep-farming rather than local population looking for new land to colonise as land pressure mounted. This carving up of hill pastures into gerss farms meant that relatively few lowland touns could boast hill pastures: the link between the two had long been broken. In the Merse, for instance, the hill ground which embraced it constituted a separate system of landholding, not a dependent one. Apart from lowland touns like Chirnside, which possessed a large commonty on the flanks of the Lammermuirs, there were few links between upland and lowland. Instead, lowland touns relied more on lowland waste areas like Coldingham, Fogo, Langton and Wilton commonties. Even the use of these appears to have been in decline by the mid-eighteenth century, as farmers opted to have controlled grazing on the farm.[53] In all probability, we would have to go back well into the medieval period to find a time when these lowland touns enjoyed easy access to upland pastures. Certainly, there must once have been a system of summer shielings tied to low-ground touns. Whittington's map of *shiels* in Lammermuir established this;[54] as does the manner in which some low-ground parishes or touns like Chirnside, Duns and Dunbar had outlying areas in Lammermuir attached to them.

In the Highlands, as well as around their fringe, a more extensive system of common grazings and shielings can be found, a system which survived in active use throughout the period under review. Their existence can be vouched for in a number of ways. For example, shielings were so valued that early land conveyances can be found which convey not just a toun, but also its shieling area. Good examples of such charters are available for the Atholl area.[55] There are also contemporary comments on the system, such as that dated *c.* 1722, about the tenants of Over and Nether Glenyla (Angus) and how they go in summer to 'the far distant Glens which border upon Brae Mar and ther live grassing their cattle in little houses which they build upon their coming and throwen down when they come away called sheals'.[56]   Local baron court books also evidence an active use of common grazings and shielings. Typical is the entry in the Forbes baron court to the effect that tenants in the parishes of Kearne, Clatt, Forbes and Achendoe should 'putt ther goods to the hill of Curreyne for pastureing, and every parochen to have ane common hird among them'.[57] Surveys can also yield instances of shielings or common pastures being used. Mention has already been made of references to shielings on the Assynt estate. Further south along the coast, Whittington has mapped shielings and their related touns in Knoydart parish (Inverness-shire).[58] As in southern Scotland, though, the role of Highland shielings and common grazings was not static but subject to revaluation as circumstances changed, with some touns starting to cultivate their shielings and others having them set apart as separate touns by the late seventeenth century.[59] A fuller discussion of the shieling system is presented in Chapter 4.

Tenure, Landholding and Farming

The broad relationship between landholding and cropping, as well as that between what existed on the ground and its tenurial and socio-economic back-ground, represent sadly neglected issues. Perhaps most surprising of all is the past failure to explore runrig's tenurial context. Frequently described as a form of communal tenure, such a classification seems more designed to fit assumptions regarding its layout than the conditions known to surround its tenure.[60] In fact, when rentals or tacks are inspected, they suggest two types of tenure were associated with multiple tenant touns. In one, tenants appear individually as well as jointly responsible for the management and rent of the entire farm and not just a portion of it. In the other, each tenant was assigned, either by their tack or by their rental statement, a separate share of the toun.[61] This distinction enables us to make sense of a conflict which exists in the evidence for early touns. On the one hand, there is the abundant evidence for landholders having their share as so many strips scattered runrig-style through the toun. On the other hand, there is a small but significant body of evidence to suggest that some early touns were farmed in common, only the produce being divided. In past discussions, these two types have been fused into one, with runrig touns being portrayed as those farmed in common. By fixing its tenurial background more clearly, the fallacy of this view becomes evident. Runrig touns certainly involved co-operation over ploughing and harvesting, but the identification of each person's holding, albeit as a scatter of disjoined strips, meant that each had a separately defined share. Logically, such touns were probably underpinned by those tenures in which each tenant was assigned a separate or discrete share. Con-versely, touns farmed in common appear more consistent with tenures making each and every tenant jointly responsible for the entire toun. It is not suggested that these were exclusive categories of tenure and landholding, but their recognition does help clarify runrig's tenurial background.

Looking more closely at this link between tenure and landholding, the manner in which shares were defined also contains much of interest. As with other landholding systems that passed through a feudal stage, a common factor between the different parts of Scotland was the use of land denominational units — ploughgates, oxgates, husbandlands, merklands, pennylands, davachs — to convey touns and holdings. These varied from region to region in a way that imparts considerable character to local and regional conditions. The link between these units and field patterns has been critically reviewed by Barrow and Duncan. Both are agreed that land units of the east and south-east, like the ploughgate of 104 acres, were arranged into large, subdivided field touns. However, they are not so convinced by the runrig character of all early land units north of the Forth. Barrow, for instance, thought that the practice of referring to carucates (Latin for ploughgates) as 'x carucates(s), by name B,C,D, etc. (in the vill of A)' instead of 'x carucate(s) in the vill of A', as in areas south of the Forth, implied that these northern carucates were not part of a runrig system.[62] Similarly, Duncan thought the segmented character of the davach, with its halves and thirds each bearing a separate name, meant that it probably comprised 'small enclosed units of arable'.[63] To agree with these ideas would be to accept that whether a land unit was associated with subdivided fields or not was something implicit in its nature as a land unit. Instead, it is argued here that the association of a land unit with subdivided fields depended on the circumstances of its use. What mattered most for the formation of subdivided fields was the sharing between two or more landholders of a discrete block of arable that functioned as a toun, whether a whole ploughgate or davach or fractions of either. Obviously, where a very large land unit like the davach (it equalled 168ha in the north-east) was broken up into a number of small touns to suit the uncompromising facts of physical geography, the point or period when these touns became shared between landholders may have been delayed compared with the large touns of the south-east. But it does not follow that their propensity to being shared, and therefore to becoming subdivided field systems, was implicit in the nature of the land units used.

Where a toun was shared, landholders usually held so many land units out of the total in the toun. Intermixed and interchangeable with this system of holding designation was one based on explicitly defined shares, such as a half, quarter or third. Examples are commonplace in early rentals or tacks. The most important feature of these share units is that as rights in land, they were open-ended. They did not define a holding down to its last strip, but offered simply the formula for its calculation.[64] Since such shares were interchanged with land denominational units, the latter must perforce have shared the same meaning.

This open-endedness of shares has significance for the debate over runrig's meaning. The reason is simple. If shares were open-ended, then it follows that before landholders could begin farming, they first had to divide their shares into holdings on the ground. The Bellnollo tack illustrates this gap between tenure and landholding admirably. Its appreciation adds a new dimension to the problem, for it implies that a runrig layout constituted a system of shares divided into what some legal sources called *known* property.[65] As an interpretation of runrig's essential meaning, its attractions are fourfold. First, it fits what may be the linguistic meaning not just of runrig, but also its variants like *rundale, red-dail, rendal, run-shade, roinn-ruith* or *rinn-ruithimire*. Second, it may explain why Scottish subdivided fields bore a special term of description compared with systems south of the Border. The answer does not lie in any difference of nature. As the writer has argued elsewhere, English subdivided fields may also be seen as representing shares divided into known property.[66] However, whereas English systems were stable over long periods, Scottish systems were subject to greater change and flux. Even where reallocation was practised only infrequently, it must still have served to remind landholders of the essential condition of their holdings, hence the term runrig. This leads on to the third point, of why reallocation occurred. If it was the open-endedness of tenure and not some deep-rooted cultural trait that created the need to divide land, then logically, the recurrent need to divide land can be linked to the normal changes or breaks of tenure, such as the start of a new lease. Needless to say, in those parts of the Highlands where land was held on a year-to-year basis, this need may have arisen every year. But in the Lowlands, where landholders could have long tacks, then holding layout could have remained stable for generations at a time. Fourth, such an interpretation of runrig affords a basis for explaining the details of its layout as a regular system of subdivided fields. In some charters, we find shares labelled as being 'just and equal'.[67] Work on the division proceedings of proprietary runrig touns in Roxburghshire and Berwickshire has shed light on how this stress on equality was interpreted. Revealingly, it was based on an equality of both extent and value. As one lawyer declared during the division of Auchencraw (1714), how could it be otherwise 'when lands ly runrig'.[68] This double-edged equality is supported by evidence for other parts of Scotland; for instance, a division of land at Buay (Shetland) in 1612 was regulated by the principle of each having 'als mekill in quantitie as qualitie'.[69] The guiding principles behind the laying out of shares are also laid bare by fifteenth-century tacks for the Cupar abbey estate. A 1470 tack for half of Fortar refers to the toun being divided between the tenants 'in all its commodities', whilst another of 1468 for the Grange of Balbrogy talks of the need to balance shares 'until they shall be equal' in terms of quality.[70] When trying to link tenure with landholding, this stress on both quantity and quality must be given a prominent place, for where land was diverse, the only way such an equality could be achieved was by giving each person a share, as at Fortar, of 'all its commodities'.

Like runrig, infield-outfield has suffered from a failure to explore its wider connnections. A hint at what these wider connections might be is provided by work on south-east Scotland. During the study of evidence provided by the division of proprietary runrig touns, a curious anomaly was discovered. Outwardly, these touns referred to their husbandland or merkland assessments as if they embraced both their infield and outfield. However, when it came to the listing of each landholder's actual share of the toun, they were credited with so many husbandlands or merklands of infield plus so many acres of outfield. When the shares of infield were grossed, they equalled the total number reportedly in the toun. The conclusion to be reached was that a toun's assessment only accommodated its infield. Outfield formed the land outside its land-unit framework and consequently was measured solely in acres.[71]

This failure of a toun's land-unit framework to expand with the toun's area was not peculiar to south-east Scotland. There are signs that it was the case in other parts of Scotland, with land units being frozen before the colonising history of the toun had played itself out. One approach is to compare the land-unit assessment of a toun at two widely separated dates. For example, a twelfth-century charter describes Arbuthnot parish (Angus) as comprising 54 ploughgates. This is the same figure quoted by the *Old Statistical Account* as the parish's assessment in the eighteenth century.[72] In case it is argued that this merely proves that parishes like Arbuthnot were fully settled at an early date, one need only compare the total acreage of other touns with their assessment to realise that one was a very loose fit for the other. When such calculations are performed for the Breadalbane or Assynt estates, for instance, it produces not only a wide variation in merkland or davach size, but figures which bear no relation to the estimated size of these units.[73] Only by comparing their infield acreages with their assessments do we obtain a plausible balance. Some early commentators actually acknowledged this inflexible response of assessments to growth. Edmonston, for example, mentioned how 'outsets' in Shetland were never included in the merkland assessment of touns.[74] Compare this with Brand's comment that 'only what is Arable is Accounted for.'[75] More explicit is the eighteenth-century tack for the half of the toun of Coults (Banffshire), which described the tenant's share as '[e]xtending to eight oxgates of land comprehending their intill'.[76]

If accepted, this association between infield and the assessed area of a toun provides a new perspective on its character. In effect, it means that whatever its nature as a farming system, its origin cannot be divorced from the tenurial history of touns, for the institutional rigidity of the one helped shape the form of the other.

The Origin of Scottish Field Systems

Scottish field systems have always played a critical role in the wider debate on field systems. Both runrig and infield-outfield have long been classed as archaic, and as such have provided the anchor in elaborate evolutionary schemes of how field systems developed. Thus, in their recent discussion of the problem,

Baker and Butlin cast infield-outfield in the role of being a primordial field system that was once widespread throughout Britain, but which, in lowland areas, was replaced by the more intensive two- and three-field system from the early medieval period onwards.[77] Writing on Scottish field systems in the same volume, Whittington presented, albeit in provisional terms, an 'attractive hypothesis' on how infield-outfield may have originated in the first place, a hypothesis which links part of it, or outfield, to that most primitive of cropping systems, shifting cultivation. It was that if

> the Scottish agrarian system is seen as a progression from shifting arable farming associated with cattle-keeping to a sedentary form in which cattle remained more important in the wetter west and grain in the drier east, then a stage must have occurred when a more extensive type of arable was changed into a mixture of intensive and extensive. Due most probably to a growing population there would be a stimulus towards the development of an inner ring (infield or intensive zone) and an outer (outfield or less intensive zone) ring: an arrangement forced into existence by the paucity of manure in an area with generally leached acid soils.[78]

Plausibly, he thought the period when this 'stimulus' was applied may have been the twelfth and thirteenth centuries. An important part of Whittington's argument is that once formed, the infield-outfield systems of the more fertile south-east grew by extension of the intensive zone, such systems tending towards 'all-infield systems' and thus being comparable with the more intensive field systems to be found in England.[79] Starting from a completely different premiss are those scholars who see infield-outfield as essentially a one-field system, or infield, which developed into a two- and then a three-field system in lowland Britain, but which in Scotland could only manage a half-hearted extension into outfield. Such radical differences of viewpoint reflect the shortcomings of the evidence available to us. However, much can be done in narrowing down the range of possible interpretations.

The Origin of Runrig

The earliest references to runrig date from the fifteenth century, but these can hardly measure its first appearance in the landscape.[80] A suggestive piece of early evidence published by Barrow is the late-twelfth century reference to a landholder having the fifth rig of the toun of Ballebotlia in Fife.[81] If this was an example of a share being defined by its rank order in a sequence of allocation, then it would extend back the earliest signs of subdivided fields to long before the earliest mention of runrig.

The argument that it was older even than the twelfth century hinges around the assumptions built up concerning periodic reallocation and, in particular, the idea that it extends back to a tribal phase of society when rural communities, bound closely by ties of kinship and mutual obligation, strove constantly to maintain an equality between individuals. In every sense, these early runrig communities were seen as 'little commonwealths', whose organising principle was a socially-based rather than a tenurially-based right of equality. However, as made clear earlier, there is an alternative interpretation of periodic realloca-tion, one which links it to the normal breaks of tenure, such as the start of a new tack, within a shareholding system. The equality of division implicit in such a system makes appeals to any socially-based sense of equality un-necessary. An alternative argument for an early appearance of runrig is provided by Whittington's suggestion that the practical problems posed by the old Scots plough created a need for communal ploughing and land-sharing which expressed itself in runrig.[82] Such an argument, though, is comparable to that advanced by the Orwins for England and must be subject to the same criticisms as the latter.[83]

If the assumptions of runrig's archaism are questionable, what can be assumed? Much seems to depend on whether we regard it as a special type of subdivided field or whether we align its character, and therefore its origin, with those elsewhere. The discussion has already intimated that the second of these alter-natives is the more credible. Once this view is adopted, then the origin of runrig can be sought not in some dimly perceived tribal past, but in the same processes shown to produce subdivided fields elsewhere, namely piecemeal colonisation and partible inheritance.[84] Lack of detailed evidence prevents us from demon-strating beyond doubt how such processes worked to produce subdivided fields in a Scottish context, but there is sufficient to hint at their potential effect. As regards piecemeal colonisation, the manner in which outfields were shared out in proportion to each person's share of infield is exactly the kind of link between new land and old that would, over time, produce a fragmented system of land-holding. The operation of partible inheritance can also be seen at work, but only in select areas.[85]

The Origin of Infield-Outfield

Like runrig, the earliest manuscript reference to either infield or outfield dates from the fifteenth century, when the term 'infeldland' occurs in a tack for the toun of Abirbrothy (Angus).[86] Thereafter, regular references can be found in land charters, but especially from the late sixteenth century onwards. Un-fortunately, most of these early sources refer to the system only in passing. Explicit evidence does not exist before the eighteenth century. We are forced to debate the origin of infield-outfield, therefore, largely in terms of what can be inferred from its character or appearances at a fairly late date in its history.

Two influential ideas in this debate were noted at the outset of this dis-cussion, namely that infield was initially a one-field system and that outfield may have begun its life as a system of shifting cultivation.[87] To accept either would be to attach an early, possibly prehistoric, date to their first appearance. However, neither represents a watertight argument. The first really glosses over the nature of infield in order to instate it as the logical precursor of the two-

and three-field system. As made clear earlier, apart from the Galloway example, there is hardly a recorded instance of an infield that was not divided into two or more breaks for cropping. As the two- and three-field system was no more than a nominal grouping of furlongs into two or three breaks or field units for the purpose of cropping, it is difficult to follow this argument, let alone accept it.

The assertion that outfield was a survival of a primitive system of shifting cultivation is equally questionable. As Whittington clearly states, when taken to its logical conclusion it presupposes that outfield preceded infield since it formed the more basic system.[88] However, as yet, no one has grappled with the serious obstacles to such an interpretation. The most serious is that it rewrites the history of touns and their cultivated land in a way that is inconsistent with accepted models of their evolution. Can we realistically believe that the entire history of colonisation from the initial foundation of these outfield systems down to the eighteenth century was accommodated merely by the formation of an intensive infield within them? Was the outward growth by assarting from an original nucleus not a feature of Scottish touns? More important, given such an interpretation, how do we make sense of land assessments which define only the inner heart of touns, or their infield? On a different tack, the stress on outfield's shifting system of cropping as a truly primitive feature has been found plausible only because, like the view of infield as a one-field system, it glosses over the detail of its on-the-ground organisation. Simply switching grass to arable and back to grass again in strict rotation did not make it a primitive system. After all, Kerridge sees this sort of convertible husbandry as one of the key innovations in his sixteenth- and seventeenth-century 'Agricultural Revolu- tion' in England, an innovation which he derives from the grass-field husbandry (i.e. outfield) of northern England.[89] In short, to classify outfield as primitive requires a more searching analysis of its character than has hitherto been accorded it. We cannot rely on the infamously disparaging comments of the late- eighteenth-century Improvers to value the system for us, as some discussions have done. Of course, to cast doubt on its antiquity is not to say that a system of shifting cultivation was not once practised in prehistoric Scotland. Work by palaeobotanists like Turner demonstrates that it probably was[90] (see Chapter 1). But it is another question altogether to show that these early systems had an unbroken lineage down to the outfield systems of late medieval Scotland.

In fact, an alternative model of infield-outfield development can be con- structed which uses the tenurial distinction between infield and outfield that was outlined earlier. Seeing infield as assessed land and outfield as non-assessed land establishes a sequence of development, the former appearing before the latter. Being the initial nucleus of the toun, and the area defined by its assess- ment, it was only to be expected that infield should acquire an intensive character as regards cropping. How outfield acquired its character in this scheme of development poses more difficult problems. One explanation put forward focuses on the movement of stock and the use made of their manure. Virtually all detailed descriptions of outfield make it clear that it was tathed before being cropped and that tathing took place during the summer prior to its cultivation. Perhaps because of the generalised view taken of outfield cropping, past discussion has overlooked the vital fact that once in cultivation, each outfield break was automatically removed from further tathing. If the manure provided by stock during summer was not to be wasted, landholders were forced to move their stock to a new tath break. It was this straightforward logistical fact that explains why each cultivated break of outfield appears one crop removed from the next (see Figure 3.4) and why, in addition to the cropped area, there was always a new break being tathed ready for cropping the following spring. Needless to say, set in motion, this simple attempt to exploit manurial resources to the full produced a pattern of convertible husbandry.

Attempts to see infield as a one-field system or outfield as a system of shifting cultivation have a built-in chronology for when they first developed. To admit either would mean a prehistoric or, at the latest, an early historic dating for this first stage of infield-outfield development. Of course, the question of when complete infield-outfield systems took shape is a separate issue. Mention has already been made of Whittington's proposal that complete infield-outfield systems may have emerged for the first time over the twelfth and thirteenth centuries, when extensively cropped outfields were supplemented by intensively cropped infields. An even later date for their integration has been built around the argument that infield constituted assessed land and outfield non-assessed land. Such an argument implies that infield was the land colonised up to the point when new land ceased to be incorporated into land units. This is unlikely to have been earlier than the twelfth or thirteenth centuries and may have been later in some areas. However, it does not follow that this formed the period over which outfield first developed. As Chapter 2 showed, whilst population was growing over the twelfth and thirteenth centuries, the pressure on land may not have been as acute as in southern Britain. It would be quite reasonable to assume that the capacity of touns as fixed by their assessments was sufficient for the needs of the day, without recourse to an outfield cropping supplement. The final freezing of assessments, therefore, may only signify a *terminus post quem* for outfield development. Taking a more positive view, to see outfield as non-assessed land is to accord it a very distinct tenurial status that could not easily be ignored by early charters or rentals. For this reason, the sudden build-up of references to outsets and then outfield over the fifteenth and sixteenth centuries may herald their pioneer appearance on the ground.[91]

The study of how field systems developed cannot be regarded as a progressive debate, with a single interpretation being accepted and then slowly refined by ongoing work. Instead, successive scholars have tended to constantly recharge the debate with new ideas and interpretations. The resultant diversity of viewpoint is especially apparent with regard to Scottish field systems. As the foregoing essay has tried to show, there are still quite sharp differences of viewpoint on both their nature and development. However, it is almost certain that the basic problems confronting us are matters more of history than prehistory. Once this is acknowledged, then it enhances the relevance and value of searching early documentary sources. This chapter has demonstrated some of the results and value of this type of research. Although it may be too early to reach any definitive conclusions, these will surely only be reached by such an approach.

Notes

1. Slezer, J. (1693), *Theatrum Scotiae* (Edinburgh), especially plates nos. 21, 32, 34 and 35

2. Gray, H. L. (1915), *English field systems* (Cambridge, Mass.), p. 70

3. Dodgshon, R. A. (1975a), 'Towards an understanding and definition of runrig: the evidence for Roxburghshire and Berwickshire', *Transactions of the Institute of British Geographers* (hereafter *Trans. Inst. Br. Geogr.*), 64, 15-33

4. Apart from eighteenth-century pre-improvement surveys, such as Scottish Record Office (hereafter SRO), RHP 14088 (Riccarton and Cessnock) and RHP 5199 (Leslie estate, Aberdeenshire), an indirect measure of toun size in these areas is afforded by early assessment lists. See, for example, Reid, R. C. (ed.) (1960), *Wigtownshire charters* (Publications of the Scottish History Society, hereafter Pubs. SHS), 3rd series, 51, 2-14

5. SRO, RHP 9629, survey of Liddesdale, 1718, and Roxburgh MSS., Floors castle, Computation of the lands adjacent to the Waters of Bowmount and Kail 1769

6. McArthur, M. M. (ed.) (1936), *Survey of Lochtayside 1769* (Pubs. SHS), 3rd series, 27, 1-207

7. Adam, R. J. (ed.) (1960), *John Home's survey of Assynt* (Publ. SHS), 3rd series, 52, 50-1

8. Dodgshon (1975a), 'Towards an understanding and definition of runrig'

9. Stuart, J. (ed.) (1844), *List of pollable persons within the shire of Aberdeen 1696* (Aberdeen, 2 vols.)

10. Lebon, J. H. G. (1946), 'The process of enclosure in the western lowlands', *Scottish Geographical Magazine* (hereafter SGM), 62, 105

11. Macleod, R. C. (ed.) (1938), *The book of Dunvegan* (Third Spalding Club), pp. 148-53; MacArthur (1936), *Survey of Lochtayside 1769*, pp. 1-207

12. Dodgshon, R. A. (1972), 'The removal of runrig in Roxburghshire and Berwickshire 1680-1766', *Scottish Studies, 16*, 126-7

13. Burnett, G. (ed.) (1888), *The exchequer rolls of Scotland*, vol. XI, *A.D. 1497-1501* (Edinburgh), pp. 387-460. Further comment on the balance between individual and multiple tenure, together with reasons as to why individual tenure 'without cottar help was out of the question', can be found in Whittington, G. (1973), 'Field systems of Scotland', pp. 512-79 in Baker, A. R. H. and Butlin, R. A. (eds.), *Studies of field systems in the British Isles* (Cambridge), pp. 544-5

14. Stuart, (1844), *List of pollable persons,* Vol. I, pp. 155-71, 392-412 and 424-9

15. Dodgshon (1975a), 'Towards an understanding and definition of runrig', 21

16. Wight, A (1778), *Present state of husbandry in Scotland* (Edinburgh), Vol. 3, p. 356

17. See, for example, (1794) *Old statistical account*, Vol. II, pp. 140, 159, 224, 357; (1793) *Old statistical account*, Vol. IX, pp. 199 and 442. See also Whittington (1973), 'Field systems of Scotland', pp. 544-5

18. A discussion of tacksmen occurs in Cregeen, E. (1968), 'The changing role of the house of Argyll in the Scottish Highlands', pp. 153-92 in Lewis, I. M. (ed.), *History and social anthropology* (London)

19. Gaffney, V. (ed.) (1960), *The Lordship of Strathavon* (Third Spalding Club), p. 194

20. (1859) *The miscellany of the Spalding club* (Spalding Club), 4, 310-19

21. Geddes, A. (1948-9), 'Conjoint-tenants and tacksmen in the isle of Lewis 1715-26', *Economic History Review*, 2nd series, I, 54-60

22. SRO, Home-Robertson MSS., Billie 2068

23. Thomson, W. P. L. (1970), 'Funzie, Fetlar: a Shetland runrig township in the

nineteenth century', *SGM*, *86*, 178

24. See, for instance, Geddes, A. (1938), 'The changing landscape of the Lothians, 1600-1800, as revealed by old estate plans', *SGM*, *54*, 132-3; Third, B. M. W. (1957), 'The significance of Scottish estate plans and associated documents', *Scottish Studies*, *1*, 52

25. See Grant, I. F. (1930), *The social and economic development of Scotland before 1603* (Edinburgh), p. 105; Geddes (1938), 'The changing landscape of the Lothians', 131; Uhlig, H. (1961), 'Old hamlets with infield-outfield systems in western and central Europe', *Geografiska Annaler*, *43*, 308-9

26. In particular, see D'Olivier Farran, C. (1953), 'Runrig and the open field system', *Juridical Review*, *65*, 134-49

27. Pennant, T. (1774), *Tour in Scotland and voyage to the Hebrides 1772* (Chester), Vol. II, p. 201. Good summaries of further data for the Highlands and Islands can be found in Handley, J. E. (1953), *Scottish farming in the eighteenth century* (London), pp. 48-9; Gray, M. (1957), *The Highland economy 1750-1850* (Edinburgh), pp. 19-20

28. SRO GD24/1/32, Abercairny MSS., Article of Agreement, Bellnollo, 1765-73

29. Historical Manuscripts Commission (1894), *First report on Marchmont Muniments*, Appendix III, p. 197. See also p. 219

30. Typical are the 1765 tack for half of Drummy Easter 'to Patr. & John Taylor as presently possessed by Robert Murray there' (SRO GD24/1/32) and the 1473 tack for 'a third part of Mortoun, viz., that part which William Foyd held, is let for five years to George Chapman'. In Rogers, C. (ed.) (1880), *Rental book of the Cistercian abbey of Cupar Angus* (London), Vol. I, p. 170

31. See, for example, Handley (1953), *Scottish farming in the eighteenth century*, pp. 48-9

32. (1837) *Liber Sancte Marie de Melros* (Bannatyne Club), Vol. 2, pp. 518-19. A fuller discussion can be found in Dodgshon, R. A. (1975b), 'Scandinavian "solskifte" and the sunwise division of land in eastern Scotland', *Scottish Studies*, *19*, 1-14

33. An example is cited in Barrow, G. W. S. (ed.) (1971), *The acts of William I King of Scots 1165-1214* (Edinburgh), pp. 432-3

34. Mitchell, A. (ed.) (1908), *Geographical collections relating to Scotland made by Walter Macfarlane* (Pubs. SHS), *53*, Vol. III, 1

35. See, for example, Gunn, C. B. (ed.) (1905), *Records of the baron court of Stitchill 1665-1807* (Pubs. SHS), *50*, 146; Historical Manuscripts Commission (1872), *Third report* (London), p. 406

36. Examples can be found in Wills, V. (ed.) (1973), *Reports on the annexed estates 1755-1769* (Edinburgh), p. 27; Thomson, J. M. (ed.) (1919), 'The Forbes baron court book 1659-1678' in *Miscellany of the Scottish History Society* (Pubs. SHS), 2nd series, *19*, 299.

37. Typical is the example in (1855) *Black book of Taymouth* (Bannatyne Club), p. 364

38. For discussion of head-dyke, see Robertson, I. M. (1949), 'The head-dyke – a fundamental line in Scottish geography', *SGM*, *65*, 6-19

39. Mitchell (1907), *Geographical collections* (Pubs. SHS), *52*, Vol. II, 103-4

40. Cited in Marwick, H. (1970), *The place-names of Birsay* (Aberdeen), p. 115

41. Macdonald, J. (1811), *General view of the agriculture of the Hebrides or western isles of Scotland* (Edinburgh), p. 22; (1793) *Old statistical account*, Vol. IX, Caputh, Perthshire, p. 494

42. Wilson, J. (1902), 'Farming in Aberdeenshire: ancient and modern', *Transactions of the Highland and Agricultural Society*, 5th series, *14*, 72; (1793) *Old statistical account*, Vol. VIII, Muthill, Perthshire, p. 513

43. Donaldson, J. (1697), *Husbandry anatomized* (Edinburgh)

44. Hamilton, J., 2nd Lord Belhaven (1699), *The countrey-man's rudiments or advice to the farmers of East Lothian, how to labour and improve their ground* (Edinburgh), p.16

45. Dodgshon, R. A. (1975c), 'Farming in Roxburghshire and Berwickshire on the eve of improvement', *Scottish Historical Review*, *54*, 141-2

46. Donaldson, G. (ed.) (1949), *Accounts of the collectors of thirds of benefices 1501-1542* (Pubs. SHS), 3rd series, *42*, especially 29 *et seq*.

47. Dodgshon (1975c), 'Farming in Roxburghshire and Berwickshire', 142; Maxwell, R.

(1743), *Select transactions of the honourable society of improvers in the knowledge of agriculture in Scotland* (Edinburgh), p. 213; SRO, GD24/1/32, Abercairny MSS., tacks 1739-77

48. SRO, RHP 9629, Survey of Liddesdale, 1718

49. Adam (1960), *John Home's survey of Assynt,* 1-49

50. Details of outfield cropping systems in the extreme south-east are provided by Dodgshon (1975c), 'Farming in Roxburghshire and Berwickshire', 144-5. A comparable system is described by Buchan-Hepburn, G. (1794), *General view of the agriculture of the county of East Lothian* (Edinburgh), p. 49; Hamilton, (1699), p. 16

51. See Dodgshon (1975c), 'Farming in Roxburghshire and Berwickshire', 147-50

52. See, for example, the description of outfield at Kilmartin (Argyllshire) in (1793) *Old statistical account*, Vol. VIII, Kilmartin, p. 98. The example published by Wilson (1902), 'Farming in Aberdeenshire', 72, also affords an instance of an outfield cropped for 5 years then rested 5 (see Figure 3.4).

53. Dodgshon (1975c), 'Farming in Roxburghshire and Berwickshire', 149-50

54. Whittington (1973), 'Field systems of Scotland', p. 570

55. Typical is a clare constat of 1681 which refers to touns in Atholl together with their shielings of Ruichragin and Ruichragvrichie. SRO, *Calendar of charters and other original documents of E. J. Ferguson Esq of Balemund 1328-1811*, p. 94

56. Mitchell (1907), *Geographical Collections,* 36

57. Thomson (1970), 'Funzie, Fetlar', 318

58. Whittington (1973), 'Field systems of Scotland', p. 568

59. Gaffney (1960), *The Lordship of Strathavon*, pp. 31-2; Miller, R. (1967), 'Land use by summer shielings', *Scottish Studies, II*, 193-221

60. The most explicit statement of this view is D'Olivier Farran (1953), 'Runrig and the open field system', 134-9

61. A fuller discussion of this distinction can be found in Dodgshon (1975a), 'Towards an understanding and definition of runrig', 16-17; Dodgshon, R. A. (1975d), 'Runrig and the communal origins of property in land', *Juridical Review, 50*, 192-6

62. Barrow, G. W. S. (1972), *The kingdom of the Scots* (London), p. 266

63. Duncan, A. A. A. (1975), *Scotland: the making of the kingdom* (Edinburgh), p. 319

64. The most obvious illustration of this point are those multiple tenant or multiple heritor touns in which each tenant or landowner was given an identical half or third. See Dodgshon (1975d), 'Runrig and the communal origins of property', 196-8

65. Dodgshon (1975a), 'Towards an understanding and definition of runrig', 114

66. Dodgshon, R. A. (1975e), 'The landholding foundations of the open field system', *Past and Present, 67*, 3-29

67. Dodgshon (1975a), 'Towards an understanding and definition of runrig', 28-9; Burnett, J. G. (ed.) (1951), *Powis Papers 1507-1594* (Third Spalding Club), pp. 148-9; Hamilton, H. (ed.) (1945), *Monymusk papers 1713-1755* (Pubs. SHS), 3rd series, *39*, 21; Johnston, A. W. (ed.) (1921-33), *Old lore miscellany of Orkney, Shetland and Sutherland*, Vol. 9, p. 125

68. Berwickshire sheriff court, Duns, register of decreets, vol. 1713-16, Feb. 1715

69. Barclay, R. S. (ed.) (1962), *The court book of Orkney and Shetland 1612-1613* (Kirkwall), p. 18

70. Rogers (1880), *Rental book of the Cistercian abbey*, vol. I, pp. 143 and 157

71. Dodgshon, R. A. (1973), 'The nature and development of infield-outfield in Scotland', *Trans. Inst. Br. Geogr.*, *59*, 1-8

72. Information derived from Skene, W. F. (1876), *Celtic Scotland* (Edinburgh), Vol. III, p. 259

73. For the former, see Dodgshon (1973), 'Nature and development of infield-outfield', 11. For the latter, see Adam (1960), *John Home's survey of Assynt*, 50-1

74. Edmonston, E. (1809), *A view of the ancient and present state of the Zetland islands* (Edinburgh), Vol. I, pp. 147-8

75. Brand, J. (1883, reprinted from the 1701 edition), ed. by Brown, W., *A brief description of Orkney, Zetland, Pightland-Firth and Caithness* (Edinburgh), p. 225

76. Mitchie, J. G, (ed.) (1901) *The records of Invercauld* (Spalding Club), p. 472

77. Baker, A. R. H. and Butlin, R. A. (1973), 'Conclusion: problems and perspectives',

pp. 619-56 in Baker and Butlin, *Studies of field systems*, pp. 655-6

78. Whittington (1973), 'Field systems of Scotland', 573

79. Ibid., 576-7

80. The earliest published reference is usually taken to be that in (1842) *Registrum de Dunfermlyn* (Bannatyne Club), 285

81. Barrow, G. W. S. (ed.) (1960), *The acts of Malcolm IV King of Scots 1153-1165* (Edinburgh), p. 227

82. Whittington (1973), 'Field systems of Scotland', 545

83. Dodgshon (1975e), 'Landholding foundations', 3-9, provides a critique of the Orwins' ideas on subdivided fields. For their original argument, see Orwin, C. S. and Orwin C. S. (1938), *The open fields* (Oxford) Ch. IV

84. See discussion in Baker and Butlin (1973), *Studies of field systems*, pp. 635-53; Dodgshon (1975e), 'Landholding foundations', 3-29

85. See, for instance, Peterkin, P. (1820), *Rentals of the ancient earldom and bishopric of Orkney* (Edinburgh), p. 20

86. Rogers (1880), *Rental book of the Cistercian abbey*, vol. II, p. 170

87. Apart from Whittington (1973), 'Field systems of Scotland', 573, see also Grant (1930), *Social and Economic Development of Scotland,* 108; Symon, J. A. (1959), *Scottish farming: past and present* (Edinburgh), p. 22; and Orwin and Orwin (1938), *The open fields*, p. 38

88. Whittington (1973), 'Field systems of Scotland', 573. See also Uhlig (1961), 'Old hamlets', 305

89. Kerridge, E. (1967), *The agricultural revolution* (London)

90. Turner, J. (1975), 'The evidence for land use by prehistoric farming communities: the use of three-dimensional pollen diagrams', pp. 86-95 in Evans, J. E., Limbrey, S. and Cleere, H. (eds.), *The effect of man on the landscape: the Highland zone* (Council for British Archaeology Research), Report no. 11

91. Dodgshon (1973), 'Nature and development of infield-outfield', 15-16

4 THE TRADITIONAL PASTORAL ECONOMY

A. Fenton

In the past, writers on Scottish farming have laid more emphasis on the arable than on the grazing. Yet the economic balance of farming communities depended on the integration of these two sides, and there is no doubt that the ending of runrig in the Highlands was as much brought about by changes in the grazing as by changes in the organisation of the arable. Though a number of studies take grazing into account, their geographical coverage is patchy, and a full picture for the whole country remains to be worked out. In this chapter two areas are considered, one where the use of shielings was a mark of the traditional pastoral economy, and one covering Orkney and Shetland, where it was not. Though further subdivision of the shieling areas could be made,[1] this is not undertaken here in any detail, in order to retain a broad perspective.

The Background and the Approach

The characteristic settlement unit of the areas under review was the multiple-tenancy farm, of which an example is preserved as an open-air museum at Auchindrain, near Inveraray in Argyll. These farms constituted the wintertown, or main village, and they were usually complemented by the shieling huts in the hills. Within and around the wintertowns the land was held in a form of runrig with intermingled strips and patches of grass and arable, the arable being on machair ground where plough cultivation was the norm, or on peaty or stony ground where spade or caschrom cultivation prevailed, in association with lazy beds. Cereal crops consisted of oats, bere, and sometimes rye; but from the third quarter of the eighteenth century, potatoes increasingly came to replace cereals. This fact alone meant that stock had to depend more on grass than in the past, when more straw was available for fodder. In general, the Highland farming system worked, as in Lowland Scotland, on the infield-outfield system, though much modified to suit a different environment. In fact, some farms had no infield, and others had no outfield. The use of fertilisers such as seaweed and composts of animal manure, turf and peat, and peat-ash, allowed continuous cropping of a horticultural intensity on some of the arable areas.

The wintertown could vary in size, up to about a dozen farms or sometimes fifteen to twenty, as in Strathnaver in Sutherland.[2] The infield and outfield areas jointly were separated from the moorland grazing by a head-dyke, a wall of stone or turf or both. Beyond the head-dyke, at distances varying according to terrain, lay the shieling area or *airidh*.

In approaching the subject of the pastoral economy, it is necessary to use a variety of sources — topographical literature, travellers' accounts, family papers and estate plans, place-names and dialect terminology. What follows is an attempt to use such sources to throw light on the organisation of grazings, with special reference to shieling systems and their ultimate decline, and to areas where no shieling system appears to have existed.

Pastoral Farming on the Mainland and Western Isles

The pastoral nature of the Highlands and Western Isles, and their virtues as a natural breeding ground for cattle, is frequently mentioned by early writers, such as John of Fordun (1380), John Major (1521), Hector Boece (1527) and others. The Highlanders or 'Wild Scots' had a wealth of sheep, cattle and horses, and the islands of Argyll were more profitable 'in store of bestial, than ony cornis'.[3] In the sixteenth and seventeenth centuries detailed descriptions of the Western Isles show that, for the most part, the islands had an intermixture of small-scale arable and stock farming, with a few places such as Ascrib, Lingay and Iuvard being specified as used for 'scheling'.[4] In this respect, the northern and western edges of Scotland matched the Hebrides.[5]

If travellers and observers were aware of these pastoral emphases, the lairds were even more conscious of them, for the grazings had value which could be extracted in the form of rent through their factors or tacksmen. In this there is a contrast with the grazings of Orkney and Shetland, which were untaxed under the form of udal tenure that existed there, though whether it was udal or feudal, the actual functioning of the interrelationships between the tounlands with their infield and outfield arable, patches of meadow grass and other grazing, their surrounding dykes, and the hill- or moor-grazings beyond was essentially the same. In Scotland generally, the grazings were feudal appurtenances, subject to confirmation in charters, as shown for example in Banffshire land transactions of 1562,[6] and on the lands of Glenfyne (Argyll), in a charter to the Lamonts, dated 1701.[7]

The degree of complexity in the use of shielings and grazings can be judged in several ways. The nature of their produce was reflected in the content of rents paid in kind. The lands and shielings on the borders of Kintail in Ross-shire, for example, paid £40 Scots in money, and for the rest had to deliver to the laird annually a 'sufficient white plaid', three stones of butter, twelve cheeses, a fat kid, a fat calf, and one mutton or good sheep, according to a lease of 1642.[8] The grazing of Shalvanach in Inverness-shire paid nearly 40 merks, one wether, one kid, one stone of butter, and two stones of cheese, and Alexander Chisolm paid to his mother for the lands of Muckuroch 200 merks Scots with two stones of butter, four stones of cheese, two wethers and one kid, whilst his foster son, 'a child of seven year old, possesses the graseings of Corrie, Glascory and Milardie by cowes complimented him by Archibald Chisolm', the rent being 200 merks for the first two and 100 merks for Milardy.[9] Examples of such rents are numerous, and they are not confined to the produce of cattle, but to that of sheep and goats as well in many instances. In general the name given to payment for pasturage was *grass-mail*. This could be exacted from all the tenants on an estate, as at Stichill in Roxburghshire in 1663, when the tenants were required to pay their grass-mail duty,[10] or it could apply to payment for grazing a particular number of animals. In Perthshire in the 1790s, for example, the grass-mail of a sheep was valued at two or three shillings,[11] and in Galloway in 1742, the grass-mail of two stots (young bulls or oxen) amounted to £2.[12]

Conversely, grazing could form part of a worker's wages. Shepherds in Selkirkshire, who ranked high in the Border farm-worker hierarchy, got eight soums of grass for wages in the late eighteenth century, or the equivalent in value of this amount. This entitled them to 10 cows or 80 sheep in payment for their services.[13]

In parts of the country, and surviving especially in the north-east into the eighteenth century, there were *grassmen*, tenants with no land but only a right of pasture, and to this extent different from cottars. A grassman lived in a *grasshouse* which could have a byre (cow-shed) attached.[14] The method of occupying the pasture could vary. Either the grassman, as part of his fee, was allowed to keep a stirk (steer) along with his master's herd, or else, less commonly, he had in addition to his house and kail-yard the right of having a cow fed, not with the farmer's cows but with his herd of young cattle.[15] Either way the use of grass was a form of payment for this class. In Kincardineshire in 1618, tenants of the barony of Urie had the right to pasture stock on the Mounth according to established use, and fines were exacted if any stock strayed on to the home grass of their neighbours.[16] Weak animals that could not travel had to be herded, and a cow needed to give milk to a sick person had to remain. Otherwise the ruling was, as in Glenorchy (Perthshire) in 1621-3, that all the cows, cattle, horses and sheep had to be put outside the head-dykes from about 1 May to 8 June, and in this area there was a further move to the more distant shielings where they remained till about 15 July.[17] Here, as in several other areas, the movement of animals was a two-stage operation, intended to make maximum use of the available feed.

Organisation of Grazings

Grazings constituted a major and profitable resource, to be 'farmed' with as much care as the arable. The two-stage movement to the shielings was part of this care, but there were other complementary aspects nearer home, for grazings did not only lie beyond the head-dykes. In the central Highlands there was a small grazing plot near the house, the 'door land', reminiscent of the Shetland *tounmal*, for baiting horses at mealtime and tethering cows.[18] A grazing strip between two arable patches or in a corner of a ploughed field was known in

Lowland Scots as a *lizour* (Old Scots *lesow*, to pasture, *c.* 1420; Old English *læswian*, to graze). The terms *loan* and *loanin*, both known from the fifteenth century, in Old Scots, and frequently surviving in place-names, applied to a strip of grass of varying width that ran through the arable areas of a settlement, linking the houses with the common grazing ground, and serving the combined functions of a grazing area for tethered beasts, a driving road, a milking place in reasonable weather, and a common green where social activities went on. This was an essential and multifunctional part of any joint-farming community.

Such grazing units lay within the head-dykes of the settlement, and served especially for the animals that were required for everyday use, in particular the milk-cows, and at certain times, the horses or work-oxen. The general stock of cattle grazed, in part, on sections of the outfield pasture, to which they were confined by earthen dykes, as a means of fertilising these sections for cropping with oats, but otherwise the animals ran on the common grazings outside the dykes. In order to conserve the resources, the number of beasts a tenant could have on the common pasture was, or should have been, related to the number of winter stock the holding could carry. That is to say, the basic control was the amount of winter fodder that could be produced from the arable patches in the form of straw, and from the meadow patches in the form of hay. The common pasture was usually calculated in *soums*, the term being applied to the number of livestock a certain grazing area could maintain, generally assessed at one cow or a proportional number of sheep varying from three to ten according to district, or else to the unit of pasturage that could support a certain fixed number of livestock.

What the soum meant, in concrete terms, varied from area to area and from time to time. In 1323, for example, a grant of six acres of arable was made in the tenement of Auchcairnie (Kincardine), bounded by a cart road, a new ditch, a burn, and the moor of Cambon. With it went the right of common pasturage in the King's Thanage of Kincardine for 2 horses, 10 oxen, 12 cows and 100 sheep with their followers up to one year old, with freedom to dig peats and turf. The loaning in Auchcairnie was 12 ells broad in 1633-4.[19] In Dunbartonshire, in 1673, every mailing in Gartclosh was to hold two soums of kye (cows) and every two mailings one horse. Evidently there was a great deal of trouble with 'over-soumes', caused by strangers without rights grazing their cattle. In 1678, the West side mailings in Kirkintilloch were assessed at four soums for kye with a last year's calf, i.e. a year-old stirk, and the East side mailings at three soums of kye with a last year's calf. It was ordained that oversoums should be got rid of, and a roll of cows made. No grass was to be set for cow grazing at less than 24 shillings Scots.[20]

In 1700, attempts were being made at Stichill, in Roxburghshire, to make a balance between sheep and cattle. Though the runrig possessors of the Mains were allowed to put on a certain stent (allowance) of sheep, it was thought that this could be spoiling the ground, and especially the cow pastures. According to the new regulations, therefore, no tenant was to put more sheep on his possession than what amounted to 'the halfe of his Sowmes conform to the Stent', and the number of sheep was to be agreed for each soum by the several possessors.

Where anyone possessed only one soum in the Mains, that was to be a cow or an ox, but not a sheep. He could not introduce his own sheep, nor those of another. With the consent of the majority, different pastures were to be kept for the sheep and cows and oxen in the summer. The herd was to feed his own cows apart from the rest of the cattle. Any attempt at overstenting led to forfeit, half of the animals going to the informer, and the other half for the use of the poor.[21] On information available for Midlothian for the mid-seventeenth century, it appears that a year-old horse, assessed at two soums, required as much grass as 6 year-old cows or oxen, 20 sheep, 40 lambs or 168 goats.[22]

The system of souming was as much part of farming in Lowland Scotland in pre-enclosure days as it was in the Highlands, then and later. It is, however, unsafe to try to judge the Lowland Scottish situation by that of the later Highland evidence, for souming was not fixed once everywhere and for all time. It could change to suit changing needs, and there was much local variation, though the balance between numbers of stock on the summer grazing and the numbers kept tethered or herded at home, and the numbers overwintered, was always in theory maintained. Parallels between the eighteenth century and earlier Lowland Scottish practice and the later Highland practice are, however, often astonishingly close.

In the late nineteenth century, grazing rights in the Outer Hebrides varied according to terrain and place, a soum being reckoned as a cow with her progeny, which could be a calf, a calf and a stirk, a calf and a stirk and a two-year old quey, or a calf, stirk, quey and a three-year old heifer. It could vary, therefore, from one to four animals. The usual system of equivalents, the *colpachadh*, was 1 horse = 8 foals, 4 one-year-old fillies, 2 two-year-old fillies, 1 three-year-old filly and 1 one-year-old filly, or 2 cows. Cows were, therefore, rated higher than in seventeenth-century Midlothian. One cow was equated with 8 calves, 4 stirks, 2 two-year-old queys, 1 three-year-old quey and 1 one-year-old stirk, 8 sheep, 12 hoggs, 6 lambs, or 16 geese. A sheep and a two-year-old hogg were equivalent, as were 2 sheep and 3 one-year-old hoggs.[23]

Because of the close link with the environment, it is difficult to make a general statement about souming equivalents. A further complication was the use of small islands for grazing, the townships of the adjacent land each having certain rights, or the capacity of the island itself being fixed. Figures have been noted for the island of Great Bernera, off Lewis, for example.[24]

Various ways of souming or stenting the common grazings were employed. Crofters in a township might have had equal shares, the general common might have been shared by several townships, or the grazings could be in two parts, split between machair and hill. The souming could be worked out on the basis of each £1 of rent (which was sometimes a fraction of a pound) or on the acreage of the croft. If rents varied, the souming per croft varied, though a complicating factor could come from an enlargement to the common grazing, and in such enlargements shares tended to be equal. At Blairmore and Culdrain, East Sutherland, for example, the crofts had soumings of 1 to 36 sheep on the old common pasture, but equal soumings of 3 sheep each on a 263-acre enlargement. Further variation came from attempts to control the selective grazing of sheep. They were excluded from many common grazings in mainland Argyll and in Lochaber, or could be grazed for limited periods only, as at Ruaig in Tiree, where cows could be replaced by sheep, in the ratio of 1:4, only from 1 May to 15 November. The grazing of horses was also limited in some areas such as Airds, Muckairn (Argyll), where they were allowed only 3 months of the year on the common grazings.

Souming equivalents also showed variety according to the quality of the grazings. A cow, for example, was equal to 4 to 6 sheep in the Western Isles, up to 8 in Harris, 5 in Melness (Sutherland), in Achancarran (Assynt), at Gravir in Lewis, and in Tiree, 6 at Milltown, Applecross (Ross-shire) and only 3 in Shetland. The general effect of equivalents, in latter days, has been to favour sheep at the expense of cattle. On occasion, stock additions could sometimes be made to the stated soumings. At Ireland and Bigton in Shetland, extra milk-cows could be grazed, but not geese. At Blairmore and Culdrain in Rogart, East Sutherland, two cattle beasts could be grazed morning and evening above the souming. At Trislaig, Lochaber, a crofter who wanted to keep a horse could graze it on the common as well as his cattle. In summer and autumn, extra hoggs could be kept to replace ewes to be cast later in the year. Four extra were allowed in East Harris and at Airdens, Criech (Sutherland) and at Maywick, Biston, Ireland, Channerwick and Levenwick in Shetland, one extra hogg for every five sheep.[25] The system of souming, therefore, was never an inflexible one, but could be sensitively adapted to suit changing times and conditions, provided the estate or the grazings committee made sure the individuals obeyed the regulations, and agreed among themselves.[26]

Shieling Systems

A joint-farming community, especially one in a highland area, cannot be understood if attention is focused only on the farm-village (the fermtoun of earlier Lowland Scotland) within the dyke that enclosed its arable. The dyke itself was not a barrier, but a means of correlating the arable and pastoral elements in the economy. It could itself be moved if the settlement expanded.[27] It was opened in the autumn after the crops were off the ground, and the village lands then became part of the common grazings, as long as the runrig form of land use survived. It was sealed in spring, and the stock kept outside, away from the growing crops. In this way it acted as a kind of control valve, regulating both crops and grazings until the enclosure of individual crofting units, usually with stob and wire fences, began to do away with the need for it. The fully functional community in the Highlands also required its remoter grazings, the shieling areas, to complete it, and it is no accident that the joint-farming village is often referred to as the 'wintertown', with the implication that the summer quarters were the shieling huts (Plate 2). This dual character of the traditional pattern of settlement in highland areas is perhaps the most remarkable demonstration of the value attached to the grazings and of the part played in the economy by cattle, and to a lesser extent sheep and goats, and their products.

The annual seasonal migration of people and stock to the hill grazings is an ancient custom in many parts of the world, traceable in Scotland through place-names ending in, for example, -shiel, -ary (Gaelic airidh), and -setr, to at least the twelfth century. It survived in Lewis until the twentieth century, and in the higher-lying parts of Scotland generally, including the Borders, until the eighteenth century.[28] The precise way in which the shielings related to the townships remains to be clarified, but in Sutherland, for example, 'every town-land, davoch (ten-penny land), and even each farm, had their district shealings',[29] and the same was true in Perthshire. The primary relationship was with the farm rather than with the individual.

In the Highlands, the introduction of commercial breeds of sheep, especially the Blackface and the Cheviot, and the conversion of countless former townships into sheep-farms (and, later, sometimes deer-forests) in the late eighteenth and early nineteenth centuries was what effectively ended the use of the shieling areas by the people of the wintertowns. It has been argued that before this time the hill grazing was not fully utilised because it was in part too rough for cattle, and because the number of cattle that could be overwintered was limited by the amount of winter fodder available, but on the other hand too intensive grazing by sheep can lead to a deterioration of the vegetation, and sheep cannot trample down bracken in the same way as cattle.[30] This, however, is an over-generalisation. In earlier times the shieling areas were not exclusively grazed by cattle (though the emphasis lay here), but by sheep and goats as well.[31]

As in Scandinavia, the grass was utilised in more than one stage. About Whitsun, the sheep and cattle were put on to the grazing ground behind the arable, known as the gearraidh, cùl-cinn, sliabh or beinn, when the first grass had appeared. This 'clearing' of the townland was evidently a matter of much importance, for several Gaelic names are applied to it: reiteach a bhaile, glanadh a bhaile, fuadach, cartadh, cu(r)sgaradh, u(r)sgaradh. In some areas, such as at North Tolsta in Lewis, such spring grazing areas had a special 'spring dwelling', tigh earraich, bigger than the huts in the hills, and with a room that could be used for cattle on stormy nights. Such intermediate dwellings were in use till about 1936.[32] In the central Highlands, where shielings could sometimes be very distant, there were also intermediate grazing areas. When the hills were turned into sheep-farms, the summer migration still continued for a time to the grazings in the nearer glens and corries, but in a modified form, with cows and servants only.[33] On Lochtayside, several farms each had their remoter shielings as well as a 'sheel' immediately above their farms (see Figure 4.1).[34] They were near enough for the milk to be carried home each day, and their function was little more than that of shelter huts.[35]

In the Hebrides, the move to the shielings proper took place in June, after the fields had been tilled. Sheep, younger and older cattle and horses all went together, the men and horses carrying materials to repair and re-roof the shieling huts, the women carrying bedding, meal, cooking and dairy equipment. The men left once the women and young folk had been settled in. Most of the available evidence suggests that the shielings were places for the women and children, whilst the men saw to jobs at the wintertown and worked at fishing. However, it is possible that going to the shieling was at one time more of a family affair. In a discussion of the disarming of the Highlanders after the Jacobite attempt of 1719, for example, it was stated that any who refused to give up their arms were to have their houses burned and their stock removed,

> which last may be putt in execution in the Winter, butt in this season [July] they are on the mountains with their Cattle, and will be able easily to avoid any Parties of the Troops that might be sent to take them or their Cattle.[36]

Figure 4.1: Farm Boundaries and Shielings, North Lochtayside, 1772

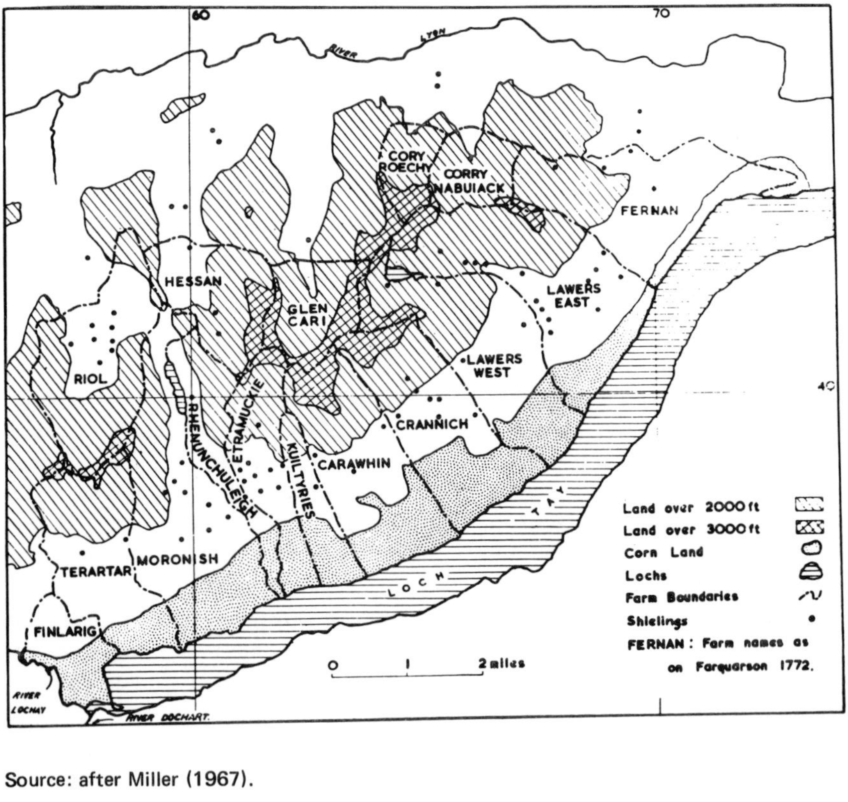

Source: after Miller (1967).

It sounds from this as if the men were at the shielings too. Similarly, an observer in the late eighteenth century saw in Glen Garry at the head of the valley of Atholl entire families with their flocks gathering in the evening around groups of huts.[37] In Ulva, Argyll, where the shieling system lasted till about 1800, it also appears that the men went to the shielings, returning from time to time to the wintertown in the course of the summer, to farm and to fish.[38]

In the central Highlands the system was more complex, and fairly intensive use was made of the hill grazing areas by spreading the grazing over a longer period of time. There were two phases of movement to the shielings. The first was the 'small flitting', when boys or young herdsmen were sent with the young horses, dry mares and animals not required about the farm or township, and the chance was taken to repair the huts, make heather beds, and see to a stock of fuel. The milk-cows and women went later, at the 'big flitting'.[39] Sometimes the huts were also used as bothies (shelter huts) in winter by herdsmen who remained to look after yeld or young cattle or horses left to range freely there after the milk-cows had returned, as in Glenlyon in 1727, and in Caithness and Sutherland in the late eighteenth to early nineteenth centuries.[40]

At the same time, in certain areas, efforts were made to conserve hill grazings. In Sutherland about the beginning of April a grass-keeper or *poindler* was hired to look after the grass of the shielings, and drive off or pound trespassing cattle, so that there would be plenty of feed for the stock that came in mid-June. The Badenoch people also had poindlers in 1767.[41] The herdsmen who went with the animals at the time of the small flitting served a similar purpose, as did the herding system in Strathavon, Banffshire. Here, the landowners sent up their herdsmen a week or two in advance of the stock to keep other people's cattle off their grass, as well as the numerous horses that roamed around, each capable of eating two or three times the amount of pasture needed for a cow.[42] Young and yeld cattle and horses did not have to leave the shieling areas when the milking stock was there, but were herded on the moor edges and rougher grazings.[43] In late-eighteenth-century Argyll, every farm hired a man to guard pasture from trespassing stock, known as a *grass-keeper* or *chaser*.[44] In Renfrewshire in 1762, 'muir-masters' were appointed to ensure that no 'outentown beasts' were pasturing on the common grazing.[45] In the sixteenth century, the overseer of a moor was the 'mure grieff'.[46] By means of such appointments, a considerable degree of control could be exercised over the grazings, at both individual family and at estate level.

Modification of the Shieling System

Extended use of the hills and moors meant that the summer shieling areas could double up as hill grazings in the modern sense, especially in mainland Scotland, but though these two aspects coexisted for some time, the one was eventually superseded by the other. In the case of the more distant Perthshire shielings, for example, the introduction of commercial sheep-farming from the end of the eighteenth century led to their being disjoined from the farms to which they had belonged, and to their being let as separate possessions, even though their former link with the land to which they belonged had been so strong that when the lands changed hands the shielings often remained with them. Two or three such old shieling areas could make a large sheep-farm, where a good shepherd's house could be built. Such farms sometimes got the name Newton, to mark the new creation.[47]

Such erosion of the old shielings reflected the commercial emphases on sheep-farming in the late eighteenth and nineteenth centuries. An older form of erosion, however, was the spread of settlement which, by converting former shielings into areas of permanent occupation, enforced the taking over of ever remoter areas for grazing purposes. The creep of permanent settlement up the valleys has been documented for Corgarff and Avonside in north-east Scotland. Cattle at the shielings were brought together at night in a particular place, with or without an enclosure, and such well-manured sites were the first to be cropped, as an extension of the outfield manuring or tathing technique. Once cultivation started, the Corgarff people caused some trouble by occupying the remoter Faevait shielings. One of the first improvement places on Avonside was Torbain, set out from the grazing lands of Achnahyle by birleymen in 1768. Patches of cultivation appeared soon thereafter at a number of other places. This creep of improvement up the glens, in several eighteenth-century spurts, was encouraged by the Duke of Gordon and his factor, since it gave an opportunity for increased rents after a first year of cultivation free or at a low figure, and it speeded the dissolution of the shieling system even without the intervention of sheep- or deer-farming. The same was happening with the Duke's Lochaber shielings in 1769, and in Strathavon, as tacks were renewed, an opportunity was sometimes taken to separate shielings from the farms. Robert Farquharson, for example, had to renounce his right to the shielings of Lettermore and Blairnamarrow when he got the tack of Achriachan and Findron in 1721. In some cases shielings continued as part of the holding, it being stipulated in the lease whether part of the ground should be cultivated or not. Generally speaking, the divorcing of shieling grounds from holdings was completed in Strathavon between 1784 and 1791.[48]

A comparable situation existed in Assynt in Sutherland, where 246 shielings were divided in the 1760s between 42 joint-tenancy farms. The shielings here were marked by the cropping that went on around those nearest the farms, and sometimes also the remoter ones. The Inver shielings, surveyed in the 1760s, were even said to be better adapted for tillage than the farm infields, and gave better yields. In effect, the Assynt shielings were being used to quite a considerable degree as an extension of the outfield.[49] In such cases, it is inaccurate to regard the shielings as a departure from the infield-outfield model[50] partly because shieling areas could sometimes be used in the same way as the outfield, and partly because the infield and outfield do not in themselves constitute a model, but are part of a system. In the same context, even in the Highlands and Islands not every runrig village possessed or made use of a shieling if there was sufficient local pasture or an extensive outfield for milk cattle, though in such cases the young beasts, sheep and goats would still use the common pastures in summer.[51] In Argyll, Inverness, Perth and Ross, shielings tended to be higher lying, averaging, for example, 220m O.D. in Morvern,[52] and cropping did not come into the question.

Long-distance Movements of Cattle

In areas where sheep farms replaced shielings, change was of a revolutionary nature, since it had a fundamental effect on the settlement pattern, especially around the northern and western coasts, leading to the clearance of people from many long-inhabited districts and the creation of new farm-village settlements in much less favourable places, usually close to the sea. However, where the grazing of cattle for commercial purposes, for the droving trade, was concerned, change was less drastic, more evolutionary, and showed that the grazing areas were capable of natural development. The dual use of hill grass for intensive shieling, grazing by milk-cows and extensive stock-grazing is one aspect of this, with the subsequent complete change-over to hill grazing. This duality characterised the eastern and central Highlands, and may antedate the eighteenth century. It dates from the seventeenth century in Skye, where, as a result of the demand for cattle by dealers from the Lowlands, who had to get them in time for Lowland markets, the date of the return from the shieling was brought forward from the beginning of harvest to mid-August. Already in 1580 a cattle fair had been established in Portree. Dealers buying cattle there swam them across to the mainland and then drove them on foot to fairs such as those at Falkirk and Stenhousemuir in mid-September. To support this trade, the grazing of herds of black cattle on the moors and hills of Skye was probably going on in the sixteenth century alongside the summer grazing of individual families, the produce of whose stock was undoubtedly also counted amongst the *marts* (Gaelic *mart*, a cow for killing) for winter slaughter that Skye was even then exporting to the Lowlands. This source of ready money for paying the rent led to over-grazing. When Samuel Johnson was there in 1775, he noted that the cattle were not as small as was commonly believed, and that the price they fetched was £2 or £3 a head. Over-grazing is suggested by his comment that they went from the islands very lean, and were not offered to the butcher till they had been fattened for some time in English pastures.[53] They were, it has been said, 'Highland bones to be covered with Scottish and English beef', even though the Skye breed was reckoned to be amongst the best.[54] In 1798-1800, Lord Macdonald was complaining about the number of squatters and others who grazed cattle on his Skye estates in summer, without making payment. John Blackadder, who surveyed the estate at that period, summed up the economic ideal: that each farm should grow enough to support the possessors without their having to go to the market for grain, and that the grazing or yearly cost of the cattle should pay the rent. In this way, the importance of the grazing was recognised by both laird and tenant. The Skye pattern paralleled that of Strathavon.[55] In the mid-nineteenth century there were still many disputes over the hill grazing in Portree, which had to be shared between small tenants, cattle dealers and others,[56] but by this time the practice of transhumance had become rare in Skye generally, and had not been particularly common since 1811, following evictions for sheep-grazing and the effective end of runrig.[57]

There was a cattle trade between the Highlands and the Lowlands in the sixteenth and seventeenth centuries, and even before the Union of 1707 travellers might observe 'a prodigious number of Scotch Cattle, coming from the Mountains to be sold' in the neighbourhood of Carlisle.[58] Although, from the viewpoint of early-nineteenth-century economics, the 'pastoral life is unfriendly both to industry and population', nevertheless cattle which could be transported on the hoof were Scotland's chief export between the Union of the Crowns in 1603 and the Union of the Parliaments in 1707. Scotland was described as, at that period, 'little else than a mere grazing field to England'. Cattle remained amongst Scotland's chief exports till the 1750s, after which it began to fall lower in the lists.[59]

Droving transformed Galloway from a backward area into one of the main commercial grazing centres for producing cattle, with people like Sir David Dunbar of Baldoon taking a lead in the 1680s, not only in selecting cattle for quality, but also in setting up grazing enclosures,[60] which in Scotland antedate enclosures for arable purposes. The cattle-droving trade from the Highlands into Lowland Scotland and beyond also became more organised in the later seventeenth century, though it seems to have been a necessary part of the trade that cattle should be cheap. At the time of the Union of 1707, the average price of cows was about 20 to 27 shillings sterling. In 1736 in Colonsay they were around 25 shillings a head. But prices gradually rose. In 1763, a Yorkshire drover was paying 2 guineas a head at the Falkirk tryst for cattle from Skye. By the 1770s they were fetching £1 10s to £2 10s, and £4 by the 1790s. By this period the greater part of the 100,000 animals driven annually to England came from the north. To these prices has to be added the cost of droving. In the early nineteenth century it cost 7s 6d a head to take a drove from Caithness to Carlisle, and the further journey to Norfolk for sale and fattening for slaughter could have cost a further £1. The demand in England was constant due largely to the growth of London and the needs of the army and navy for meat, until the market collapsed around 1815. Some concept of the overall value of this trade can be got from the fact that in 1747 an estimated annual loss of stock to cattle thieves, amounting to about £37,000 sterling, was not enough to disrupt droving or prevent banks from providing credit.[61]

The resulting economic incentives were so strong that their reflection was felt strongly in the grazing grounds, not only through increases in the stock of native cattle, but also through the taking of Lowland cattle to the shieling grounds of the eastern Grampians for summer feeding. This led at first to overstocking and a consequent pushing of the shieling grounds further up the glens, for example on the Mar estates. Edinburgh and Glasgow, as rapidly expanding centres, also exercised a considerable influence on most parts of Scotland by providing market and consumption centres.[62]

Thus the commercial incentives of the seventeenth and eighteenth centuries were fundamental in bringing change to the shielings of the central and eastern Highlands, as well as to islands like Skye, though for a long time the high-lying Highland pastures were not fully utilised through the controlled herding of cattle, in contrast to the careful herding of sheep on sheep farms by store-masters who normally came from the south. Even the servants, it was said, were not properly dressed for cattle-herding. They had only a tartan jacket, kilt and brogues, whereas the shepherds from the south of Scotland had clothes of warm coarse cloth, warm stockings of a double thread, strong thick shoes, and a large thick plaid.[63]

The picture of shieling life as conveyed by late-eighteenth- and nineteenth-century sources is not necessarily that of an old tradition. The long survival of the use of domestic shielings in Lewis is partly due to a rough, boggy terrain that made the island difficult to exploit for sheep-farming, allied to a greater density of small crofting units, few of them viable in themselves. The tradition here, as it survived, possibly lies closer to the kind of land use by summer shielings that prevailed in earlier days, but even so it would be rash to project backwards recent conditions in Lewis and generalise them for other parts of Scotland. On the one hand, the displacement of the native sheep by commercial breeds swept shielings away. Even here, however, change was not always immed-iate and absolute. In Glenlyon, Perthshire, the introduction of the Blackface did not lead to an immediate break in summer shieling-going. Tenants were encour-aged to adapt the shielings, and to use them as bases for overwintering two-year-old wedders, giving the grounds a different kind of grazing emphasis, more akin to their use as grazing areas for black cattle for the droving trade. At the same time, some landlords taught their tenants to set up club-stocks of hardy Blackface sheep that needed little or no winter shelter and in such cases there was little immediate visible impairment to the shieling system. By about 1800, club-stocks of Blackface were the rule in this area, and the grounds were used throughout the winter. For the time being the cattle herds remained undiminished in size.[64]

On the other hand, the trade in black cattle led to a more intensive use of the shieling by cattle over much of the Highland area, and eventually turned the shielings into hill grazings. It also gave rise to the concept of Scottish shielings as places primarily for cows and their followers, whereas up to the seventeenth century, and much later in several places, a mixture of stock went to the shielings, including native sheep and goats. For a time this domestic mixture was able to survive alongside the more commercial grazing interests and to interlock with it to some extent. But either way, the shielings declined and largely disappeared in the first half of the nineteenth century or even earlier, in company with the runrig system of farming itself, mainly because the arable and pastoral aspects of the economy intermeshed so closely that if one element was cut off the other could survive only if the nearer grazings around the township could be developed in some way, as by re-seeding in modern times.

It is remarkable that at the time when the shielings were in full use, little attention was paid in the Highlands to the making of hay for winter fodder. Only patches of bog- and meadow-hay were cut in the vicinity of the houses, the animals having been excluded from them when they were in the hills from May till July. Hay for the winter tended to be cut after the grain harvest, not before it, and since it coincided with potato work and the seasonal rain, it was treated very much as an afterthought.[65] The lack of hay was a deficiency of which lairds were well aware. Already by 1729, the Duchess of Gordon was teaching the right way of making hay, and several gentlemen in the northern shires were said to have begun sowing French grasses which were ready for grazing in April, as against May for natural grass.[66] In the 1780s, Robert Gray, at Skibo, in Sutherland, got 200 stones of hay an acre from sown grass-seed, and used hay rotationally, with three years of hay, one of pasture, and then three years of oat-crop. In Ross-shire, 'hay, not known here formerly, is now the ordinary food of horses and cows.' All the same, grass-seeds were still a novelty in that county, though at Bindhill the tenant had erected stone-walled enclosures within which grass-seed could be sown, and at Tarlogie, red clover and rye-grass were being used for hay, and white clover, ribwort and trefoil for pasture grass, with some cowslip seed as well because the cows liked it.[67] But such occurrences were patchy and confined to the big estates that could afford to enclose. Under unfenced runrig conditions, there was little profit in artificial grasses, and the crofters' ultimate solution was to change over to an economy with a main emphasis on sheep, once the keeping of commercial breeds had percolated down the social scale.

Pastoral Farming in the Northern Isles

In Orkney and Shetland, though there is little or no evidence for a shieling system, grazing was nevertheless of great importance, both in itself and as a guide to the development of the settlement pattern. In earlier days settlement expansion was accomplished by the gradual absorption of grazings, as indicated by place-name elements like -quoy (Old Norse kví, a fold, animal enclosure) and -setter or -ster, the former more common in Orkney, the latter in Shetland. -Setter represents two Norse words, setr, a dwelling-place, homestead, and sætr, a hill area for grazing stock, which cannot be phonologically distinguished from each other, and so the geographical position of such farm-names has to be taken into account. It cannot be assumed that a -setter name indicates former transhumance. However, the Gaelic airidh, Early Irish airge, a shieling, may be preserved in Orkney in the farm-names Arie in Sanday, Airy in Stronsay and Birsay, and Arian at Stromness,[68] and perhaps Errival in Papa Westray and Airafea in Sanday and Stronsay.[69]

In Shetland, the hill-grazing area is now known as the *scattald*, but formerly an older name, derived from Old Norse *hagi*, was applied to it. It survives in place-names taking the form 'the Hoga', 'the Hogen of . . .', or compounded as in Lambhoga, Hogaland, Hogali, Hogapund,[70] as well as in a number of noun compounds. These are *haglet* (Old Norse *hagi* + Norwegian dialectal *leite*, place, spot), an enclosed piece of hill pasture, or a piece of ground habitually grazed by a flock of sheep or herd of cattle; *hagmark,* ʮagmet, *hagstane*, a mark or boundary stone indicating the dividing line between two hill pastures, kept in memory till the mid-eighteenth century by the custom of riding the boundaries, *riding the hagri*;[71] *hogaland* (Old Norse *haglendi*), used in Unst for pasture for cattle;[72] *hogaleave*, leave given, in return for payment, to graze stock, cast peats, or cut coarse grass and heather for thatch on another man's pasture, and so to some extent equivalent to grass-mail.[73] The term *hagi* itself could mean unenclosed pasture ground, enclosed pasture and the part of the hill pasture nearest the settlement,[74] as well as common pasture shared between a number of settlements. It could itself be divided into areas, as indicated by names like *doon-hogin* and *ophogin* in Foula, and *hemhoga* in Yell.[75]

All these terms point to the *hagi* as the grazing area. The more recent term, *scattald* (Old Norse *skat*, tax + possibly Old Scots *hald*, holding), is more complicated. The scattald was a fixed unit, referring to a complete unit of settlement with the whole of the lands available to it, as is made clear by a sixteenth-century source that speaks of clearing, burning and reclaiming new corn lands on 'ony part or partis of the inscattell callit infeild or outscattell callit outfeild', and of making 'habitationis saittis and quoyis thairupon'.[76] Here the term is tied firmly to the arable areas, which evidently consisted of patches amongst considerable stretches of moor and rough grazing. If 'scattald' had applied from the beginning to the grazing area, it could not have been a taxation unit, for tax seems always to have been levied on the cultivable land, even in areas where the pastoral emphases were strongest. Quoylands were untaxed because they evolved in former grazing areas. The scattald, therefore, should be seen as originally referring to the whole multiple-farm settlement unit, at a period when the associated hill grazings still bore the name of *hagi*. The date at which 'scattald' became restricted in sense to the grazing areas is not certain, but it seems to have occurred during the eighteenth century,[77] indicating the relatively greater emphasis put on grazing in Shetland, from which the bulk of the evidence for the hagi-scattald interchange comes, as opposed to Orkney.

In the township areas, within the hill-dykes, there were a number of grazing possibilities. In Shetland the *tounmal* (Old Norse *tun-vollr*, a strip of the infield) was a piece of grazing on rough land near or around a tenant's house, for grazing tethered stock,[78] sometimes lying in a continuous strip with the tounmals of other tenants, as in parts of Fetlar.[79] The equivalent piece of land in Orkney, however, was for arable, not grazing, and paid tax, whilst the Shetland tounmals did not do so.[80] *Outbreks*, pieces of land taken in from the moor or grazing areas, were a common means in Orkney of expanding the arable elements of the settlement. Once broken in, they became taxable,[81] though they gradually eroded the amount of close-at-hand grazing.

The meadows that lay within the dykes were subject to formal organisation. During a reorganisation at Inner Stromness in Orkney, for example, in 1624, a large meadow was divided into two for the two urisland or ounceland units that made up the 'town' to use year about. A plank (approximately 40 fathoms square) of grass at Graves in Holm appears to have been individually apportioned to the tenants in Easter Graves.[82] The equation of patches of grazing with rigs is suggested by rig-names like *dyeld* (Old Norse *deild*, portion), *flet* (Old Norse *flöt*, plain) and *flaa* (Old Norse *flá*, strip of meadow land), all of which originally referred to patches of grass, as does the element *-ing*, meadow, in the names of cultivated rigs. There was either a spread of arable at the expense of grass, or an interchange of grass and arable strips from time to time.

Rigs or the bigger units known as *sheeds* were generally divided from each other by strips or patches of grass which could sometimes be taken in for cultivation. In Orkney, an *inbreck* was a piece of pasture land newly broken up for cultivation. A *merkister* (cf. Faroese *merkisgarður*) was an unfenced strip of grass kept for the grazing of tethered animals in the 'town'.[83] The Shetland equivalent was the *merkigord* (Old Norse *merkigarðr*, a dividing dyke). A narrow, grass-grown piece of land between two cultivated patches, or an angular piece of land or a green spot amongst heather was a *ger*, *gyr(o)* or *garrick* (Old Norse *geira*, triangular strip).[84]

The township of Funzie in Fetlar, Shetland, may be used to show the way in which grass and arable mingled within the townsland area (see Figure 4.2). In 1829 there were 459 separate pieces, of which 439 lay runrig, not in individual possession, and all unenclosed. A survey showed that 24 patches of meadow averaging 0.3ha were each held by groups of three tenants; 2 patches averaging 1.25ha by groups of seven; 1 patch of 0.5ha by groups of two; 92 patches of grass averaging 0.3ha by individuals; 9 patches averaging 0.29ha by groups of three; and 1 patch of 3.84ha by a group of nine. Two patches of corn-land were held in one case in lieu of meadow shares. Thus 131 of the 459 separate pieces, or nearly 40 per cent, were meadow or an equivalent for it.[85]

The sharing of grass could be done by joint use, or by rotation of townsland units. Where a tenant group shared a meadow in Fetlar, the individuals cut and cured the hay jointly and afterwards divided it equally. The same happened at Uyeasound in Unst, but here a woman from a neighbouring settlement was asked to do the dividing. At Tresta in Fetlar, four small pieces of meadow rotated annually amongst four crofters until 1965. The meadow at Sandness in the West Mainland of Shetland is still held in shares, though the hay has not been cut on it for several years.[86] There were 20 to 30 patches of grazing at

Figure 4.2: Township of Funzie, Fetlar (Shetland), 1829

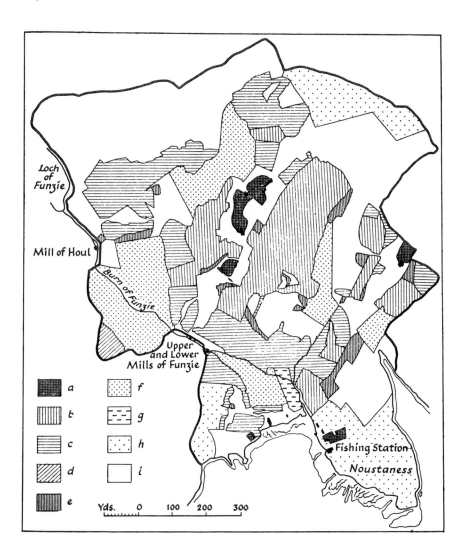

The mixture of arable and grass in the township of Funzie, Fetlar (Shetland), 1829

a. Yards of crofts
b. Infield
c. Outfield
d. Shared outfield
e. Outbreaks

f. Meadow
g. Corn land in lieu of meadow
h. Shared grass
i. Grass held by individuals
Common grazing lay beyond the dyke

Source: after Thomson (1970).

Noss in the South Mainland, for which lots were cast each May. The boundaries were marked out afresh each year by digging lines of holes.[87] On the slope of the Noup of Norby the grazing was held by ten tenants holding three strips each, changed annually till at least 1964. The grass was unfenced and the animals grazed on the tether.[88] The annual reallocation of meadow-grass can be traced back in Orkney to the seventeenth century, under the name of *meadow skift*.[89]

The place of the individual tenant in the system can be seen in Fetlar. William Henderson, tenant of Thoft in Funzie, shared a yard with another tenant and had half of the tounmal, about 0.03ha. As one of nine tenants, he had an arable infield rig in each of the nine blocks of rigs, totalling 1.15ha. His 23 outfield rigs were each much smaller, and totalled 1.06ha. He had a seventh share in each of the large meadows of Smirkeylda and Backadyeald, and co-operated with his neighbours in Thoft and Gardie in making hay on eight sections of the Heart of the Mires. He had nine patches of grass, a third share in three patches of grass, and shared Noustaness with all the other tenants. His total holding within the dykes amounted to 8.08ha (above average for the period and place), so that his grazing, exclusive of access to the scattald, amounted to 5.87ha, or 72.55 per cent of the whole.[90]

Conclusion

The traditional pastoral economy is a matter of some complexity, with a good deal of regional variation not only in relation to geography, but also to underlying administrative systems. The lack of direct taxation of grazing grounds in the Northern Isles, for example, may be seen as a reflection of the formal udal basis of the law. The eastern and central Highlands, and the areas that lay adjacent to the Lowlands, including parts of the Inner Hebrides, had their own kind of development, and in the Outer Hebrides, especially Lewis, the long survival of the shieling system is due to a set of highly localised factors.

In terms of the crofter in a township or the individual tenant in a multiple-tenancy farm, the way the links between arable and grazing areas functioned were of prime economic importance and there was much variation in relation to time and to place. The breaking of these links due to clearances for sheep farms, or to the absorption of shieling areas into hill grazings, or to the fragmentation of holdings and the establishment of numerous small crofts or outsets on the Shetland scattalds, or to the widespread mid-nineteenth-century reclamation of moor and hill areas in Orkney, were part and parcel of the breakdown of the old runrig system of communal farming, of which the grazing organisation was an integral part. This breakdown has left problems that legislation has yet to solve.

Notes

1. Fenton, A. (1976), *Scottish country life* (Edinburgh), pp. 124-36

2. Fairhurst, H. (1967), 'The rural settlement pattern of Scotland, with special reference to the west and north' in Steel, R. W. and Lawton, R. (eds.), *Liverpool essays in Geography* (London) p. 197, Fig. 1, and p. 198

3. Brown, P. H. (1893), *Scotland before 1700* (Edinburgh), pp. 10-11, 46, 60, 72

4. Munro, R. W. (1961), *Monro's Western Isles of Scotland and genealogies of the clans 1549* (Edinburgh and London); Martin, M. (1884), *A description of the Western Isles of Scotland c. 1695* (Glasgow)

5. Caird, J. B. (1964), 'The making of the Scottish rural landscape', *Scottish Geographical Magazine* (hereafter *SGM*), *80*, 74-5

6. Fraser, W. (1883), *The chiefs of Grant* (Edinburgh), Vol. III, pp. 419-21

7. Lamont, N. (1914), *An inventory of Lamont papers, 1231-1897* (Scottish Record Society), p. 317

8. Mackey, W. (1887-8), 'Life in the Highlands in the olden time', *Transactions of the Inverness Scientific Society and Field Club*, *II*, 220

9. MacPhail, J. R. N. (ed.) (1916), *Highland papers II* (Publications of the Scottish History Society) (hereafter Pubs. SHS), *12*, 303-5

10. Gunn, C. B. (ed.) (1905), *Records of the baron court of Stitchill 1655-1807* (Pubs. SHS), *50*, 28

11. Robertson, J. (1799), *General view of the agriculture of the county of Perth* (Perth), p. 322

12. Paton, H. (ed.) (1933), *Session book of Penninghame* (private circulation), Vol. II, p. 377

13. Douglas, R. (1798), *General view of the agriculture of Selkirk* (Edinburgh), p. 315

14. Hamilton, H. (ed.) (1945), *Selections from the Monymusk papers (1713-1755)* (Pubs. SHS), third series, *39*, 9

15. Pratt, J. B. (1870), *Buchan* (Aberdeen), p. 23

16. Barron, D. G. (ed.) (1892), *The court book of the Barony of Urie in Kincardineshire* (Pubs. SHS), *12*, 26

17. Innes, C. (1855), *The black book of Taymouth* (Bannatyne Club), pp. 355, 364

18. Marshall, W. (1794), *General view of the agriculture of the central Highlands of Scotland* (London), p. 30

19. Cramond, W. (1894), *Animals of Fordoun* (Montrose), pp. 16, 45

20. Pryde, G. S. (ed.) (1963), *The court book of the Burgh of Kirkintilloch* (Pubs. SHS) *53*, *52*, 13-14

21. Gunn, C. B. (1905), *Records of the baron court of Stitchill*, p. 146

22. Fenton, A. (1963), 'Skene of Hallyard's Manuscript of Husbandrie', *Agricultural history review* (hereafter *Agric. Hist. Rev.*), *11*, 68-9

23. Carmichael, A. (1884), 'Grazing and agrestic customs of the Outer Hebrides' in *Report of Her Majesty's Commissioners of Inquiry into the condition of the crofters and cottars in the Highlands and Islands of Scotland* (Edinburgh), pp. 468-9

24. MacGregor, A. A. (1935), *The haunted isles* (London) pp. 250-1; Carmichael (1884), 'Grazing and agrestic customs', pp. 158-9; Whitaker, I. (1959), 'Some traditional techniques in modern Scottish farming', *Scottish Studies*, *3*, 173-4

25. Argyll, Duke of (1883), *Crofts and farms in the Hebrides* (Edinburgh), p. 8; Darling, F. F. (1955), *West Highland survey* (Oxford), pp. 206-7; Owen, T. M. (1959), 'The role of the township in a Hebridean crofting community', *Gwerin*, *2*, 153-4: Coull, J. R. (1963), 'Melness', *Scottish Studies*, *7*, 186; Coull, J. R. (1968), 'Crofters, common grazings in Scotland', *Agric. Hist. Rev.*, *16*, 146-50; Caird, J. B. (n.d.), *Park – a geographical study of a Lewis crofting district* (Glasgow and Nottingham), p. 5

26. Moisley, H. A. (1960), 'Some Hebridean field systems', *Gwerin*, *3*, 25-6

27. Robertson, I. M. L. (1949), 'The head-dyke: a fundamental line in Scottish geography', *SGM*, *65*, 6-20; Gailey, A. (1963), 'Agrarian improvement and the development of enclosure in the south-west Highlands of Scotland', *The Scottish Historical Review*, *42*, 105-25

28. Fenton, (1976), *Scottish country life*, pp. 124-6

29. Henderson, J. (1812), *General view of the agriculture of Sutherland* (London), p. 80

30. Coull (1968), 'Melness', 152-3

31. Cf. Forbes, R. (1886), *Journals of the Episcopal visitations of the Rt. Rev. Robert Forbes* (London), pp. 143-4

32. MacDonald, D. (1950), 'The historical geography of North Tolsta' (typescript, National Museum of Antiquities of Scotland), 91192; Geddes, A. (1955), *The Isle of Lewis and Harris* (Edinburgh), p. 83

33. Marshall (1794), *General view*, p. 46; Stewart, A. (1928), *A Highland parish* (Glasgow), p. 193

34. McArthur, M. M. (ed.) (1936), *Survey of Lochtayside,1769* (Pubs. SHS), third series, *27*, 127

35. Cf. MacKellar, M. (1887-8), 'The shieling: its traditions and songs', *Transactions of the Gaelic Society of Inverness*, *14*, 136

36. Dickson, W. K. (1895), *The Jacobite attempt of 1719* (Pubs. SHS), *19*, 278

37. Marshall (1794), *General view*, p. 46

38. (1845) *New statistical account*, vol. 7, Ulva, Argyllshire, p. 346

39. Campbell, D. (1895-9), 'Highland shielings in the olden time', *Transactions of the Inverness Scientific Society and Field Club*, *5*, 68

40. Menzies, D. P. (1894), *The 'red and white' book of Menzies* (Glasgow), p. 371; Henderson, J. (1812), *General view of the agriculture of Caithness* (London), p. 146; Henderson, J. (1812), *General view of the agriculture of Sutherland* (London), p. 80

41. Henderson (1812), *Sutherland*, p. 80; Gordon Castle MSS.; *Scottish national dictionary* s.v. *Poind*; Robertson, J. (1808), *General view of the agriculture of Inverness* (London), p. 197

42. Gaffney, V. (1960), *The Lordship of Strathavon: Tomintoul under the Gordons* (Third Spalding Club), pp. 25-6, 81

43. Henderson, J. (1812), *Caithness*, p. 146

44. (1795) *Old statistical account*, Vol. XIV, Kilfinichen and Kilvicuen, Argyllshire, p. 197 (note)

45. (1762) *Session papers, Syme v. Pollok*, 10 Dec.

46. (1881) *Register of the Privy Council of Scotland 1590* (Edinburgh), Vol. 4, p. 499

47. Robertson, J. (1799), *Perth*, pp. 68-9, 337, 339-40; Stewart (1928), *A Highland parish*, pp. 191, 193

48. Gaffney (1960), *The Lordship of Strathavon*, pp. 20-1, 28-32

49. Adam, R. J. (ed.) (1960), *John Home's survey of Assynt* (Pubs. SHS), third series, *52*, 3, 4, 6, 12, 14, 23, 28, 31, 43-5, 48; Miller, R. (1967) 'Land use by summer shielings', *Scottish Studies*, *11*, 198-200

50. Whittington, G. (1973), 'Field systems of Scotland' in Baker, A. and Butlin, R. (eds.), *Studies of field systems in the British Isles* (Cambridge), p. 567

51. MacSween, M. D. (1959), 'Transhumance in North Skye', *SGM*, *75*, 81

52. Gaskell, P. (1968), *Morvern transformed* (Cambridge), p. 14

53. Johnson, S. (1775), *A journey to the Western Islands of Scotland* (London), p. 185

54. MacCulloch, J. (1824), *The Highlands and Western Isles of Scotland* (London), Vol. III, pp. 89-103

55. Fenton (1976), *Scottish country life*, pp. 132-3

56. (1845) *New statistical account*, Vol. 15, Portree, Skye, Inverness-shire, p. 227

57. MacSween, M. and Gailey, A. (1961), 'Some Shielings in North Skye', *Scottish Studies*, *5*, 83

58. Taylor, J. (1903), *Journey to Edenborough in Scotland* (Edinburgh), p. 157

59. Walker, J. (1812), *An economical history of the Hebrides and Highlands of Scotland* (London and Edinburgh), Vol. I, pp. 307-9; see also Haldane, A. R. B. (1952), *The drove roads of Scotland* (London and Edinburgh); and Bonser, K. J. (1970), *The drovers. Who they were and how they went: an epic of the English countryside* (London and Basingstoke)

60. Symson, A. (1823), *A large description of Galloway 1684* (Edinburgh), p. 41

61. Ferguson, W. (1968), *Scotland 1689 to the present* (Edinburgh and London), p. 168; Lenman, B. (1977) *An economic history of modern Scotland* (London), pp. 88-9

62. Cf. Whyte, I. D. (1974), 'Agrarian change in Lowland Scotland in the seventeenth century' (unpublished PhD thesis, University of Edinburgh), pp. 170-9, 182-4

63. Walker (1812), *Economical history*, Vol. I, pp. 314-16

64. Campbell (1895-9), 'Highland shielings', 87

65. Fenton (1976), *Scottish country life*, p. 136

66. MacKintosh, W. (1729), *An essay on ways and means of inclosing, fallowing, planting etc. Scotland, and that in sixteen years at farthest* (Edinburgh), XLIV, XLVI, p. 169

67. Wight, A. (1778-94), *Present state of husbandry in Scotland*, Survey IX (Edinburgh), pp. 5, 253, 275, 281, 291

68. Marwick, H. (1922-3), 'Antiquarian notes on Sanday', *Proceedings of the Orkney Antiquarian Society*, *I*, 23

69. Marwick, H. (1924-5), 'Antiquarian notes on Papa Westray', *Proceedings of the Orkney Antiquarian Society*, *3*, 36-7

70. Jakobsen, J. (1901), *Shetlandsøernes Stednavne* (Copenhagen), pp. 64, 101-2

71. Neven, G. (1933), 'The Scattald Marches of Yell, Shetland, 1667', *Old-Lore Miscellany of Orkney Shetland Caithness and Sutherland*, *9*, 140-1; O' Dell A. C. (1939), *The historical geography of Shetland* (Lerwick), p. 240, Hibbert, S. (1822), *A description of the Shetland Islands* (Edinburgh), p. 458; (1845) *New statistical account*, vol. 15, Tingwall, Whiteness and Weisdale, p. 64; Jakobsen, J. (1897), *The dialect and place-names of Shetland* (Lerwick), p. 109; Saxby, J. M. E. (1908), 'Shetland phrase and idiom II', *Orkney and Shetland Miscellany, Old-Lore Series, 1,* 269-70

72. Jakobsen, J. (1928), *An etymological dictionary of the Norn language in Shetland* (London and Copenhagen)

73. Johnston, A. W. (1910-12), 'Scattald Marches of Unst in 1771', *Old-Lore Miscellany of Orkney Shetland Caithness and Sutherland, 3,* 162-3; *4,* 193; *5,* 125; Edmonston, A. (1809), *A view of the ancient and present state of the Zetland Islands* (Edinburgh), vol. I, p. 149

74. Hibbert (1822), *Description of the Shetlands*, p. 458; Angus, J. S. (1914), *A Glossary of the Shetland dialect*, s.v. (Paisley); O'Dell (1939), p. 242

75. Jakobsen (1928), *Etymological dictionary*, s.v.

76. (1575-6) *Register of the Privy Seal* (Edinburgh), 7, 75/1

77. O'Dell, A. C. (1939), 242-43

78. Hibbert (1822), *Description of the Shetlands*, p. 427

79. Thomson, W. P. (1970), 'Funzie, Fetlar: a Shetland run-rig township in the nineteenth century', *SGM*, *86*, 176-7

80. Clouston, J. S. (1932), *A history of Orkney* (Kirkwall), pp. 346-60; Marwick, H., (1929) *The Orkney Norn* (Oxford), pp. 192, 231, Marwick, H. (1923-34), 'Impressions of Shetland', *Proceedings of the Orkney Antiquarian Society*, *12*, 17

81. Peterkin, A. (1820), *Rentals of the ancient earldom and bishoprick of Orkney* (Edinburgh), Vol. II, pp. 2, 41, 131; Clouston, J. S. (1914), *Records of the earldom of Orkney 1299-1614* (Pubs. SHS), second series, 7, 84, 322, 373-4; Mooney, J. (ed.) (1952), *Charters and other records of the city and Royal Burgh of Kirkwall* (Third Spalding Club), pp. 8, 23

82. Clouston, J. S. (1920), 'The Orkney Townships', *Scottish Historical Review*, *17*, 26-7

83. Cf. Marwick (1929), *The Orkney Norn*, 113-14

84. Jakobsen (1928), *Etymological dictionary*, s.v.; Firth, J. (1920), *Reminiscences of an Orkney parish* (Stromness), p. 149; Marwick (1929), *The Orkney Norn*, s.v.

85. Thomson (1970), 'Funzie, Fetlar', 181

86. Ibid., 180-1

87. Venables, U. (1956), *Life in Shetland* (Edinburgh and London), p. 22

88. Coull, J. R. (1964), 'Walls: a Shetland crofting parish', *SGM*, *80*, 141

89. Clouston, J. S. (1925), 'An Orkney "Perambulation"', *Scottish Historical Review, 22,* 196: Marwick (1929), *The Orkney Norn*, 83

90. Thomson (1970), 'Funzie, Fetlar', 181-3

ACCELERATED CHANGE

5 THE EMERGENCE OF THE NEW ESTATE STRUCTURE

I. Whyte

Throughout seventeenth-century Scotland the estate was the basic unit of land organisation and, personified in the proprietor, of decision-making. The extent of land under other forms of management — the burghs or small owner-occupiers — was limited.[1] Scottish rural society lacked a substantial middle class and was dominated, economically and politically, by a few large landowners. Although small owner-occupiers, the 'bonnet lairds', did exist,[2] they were neither numerous nor prosperous enough to play a dynamic role comparable to the English yeomen.[3] Rural society was polarized into landowners on one hand, and the bulk of rural society belonging to the tenant class and below on the other. It has been claimed that the interests of proprietor and tenant in Scotland at this time were irrevocably opposed;[4] the evidence of court books shows that in the short term this was often so. However, both groups were bound together by their common dependence upon the same resource, the land. The economic success or failure of one group had repercussions on the other and the estate community was interdependent in many ways.

An important yet neglected aspect of Scottish historical geography is the study of the processes by which the feudal, subsistence-oriented rural society of the sixteenth century developed during the next two hundred years into a highly capitalistic one. The Scottish rural landscape was essentially modified by two forces: technical changes (for example enclosure, new crops and rotations) and organisational changes. While the former made the most immediate and spectacular contribution to the transformation of the landscape (see Chapters 7, 8 and 9), they could not have been successfully implemented without the latter, which maximised their efficiency. While developments in agricultural practices undoubtedly occurred in the seventeenth and early eighteenth centuries,[5] organisational changes at this period probably made a greater contribution to the long-term evolution of the rural landscape. The social and economic developments which were involved occurred largely within the framework of the estate, taking the form of alterations in the relationship between landlord and tenant and modifications in the character of tenant farming. The study of estate organisation and management is thus central to a consideration of the changes in rural society which laid the foundations for the better-documented and more visually dramatic changes of the later eighteenth and nineteenth centuries.

Historical geographers have concentrated their attention on the period after about 1760 when the pace of agrarian change was most rapid and for which there are abundant, easily-handled sources. Yet the writings of the Improvers and the wealth of late-eighteenth-century descriptive literature are often misleading, inaccurate or deliberately biased regarding earlier periods and these distortions have influenced previous work.[6] As a result, the period between the Reformation in 1560 and the Union of 1707 has been dismissed as one of rural stagnation or even as a decline from a supposed golden age of medieval monastic agriculture, the nadir being represented by the famines of the later 1690s.[7] However, on looking back from a time of rapid change preceding periods inevitably appear stagnant and dynamic elements are diminished.[8]

Recent research[9] has suggested that the traditional model of the Scottish rural landscape as being the product of revolution rather than evolution has been partly conditioned by these later sources.[10] There is a need to assess the agrarian economy of pre-eighteenth-century Scotland in terms of contemporary, not retrospective, sources. Of these, private estate papers are perhaps the most important, though not the only, category.[11] The supposed paucity of early material in Scottish archives partly reflects a lack of rigorous searching. A vast bulk of material awaits examination. The present study is merely an introductory survey based on papers relating to estates throughout Lowland Scotland from the Solway to the Moray Firth, and the southern and eastern fringes of the Highlands, which are available in the Scottish Record Office and National Library of Scotland.

Organisational Changes within the Estate

Estate Structure and Management

Due to the predominance of large estates in Scotland, the ways in which they were managed had a great impact on rural society and on the landscape. Estate management was influenced by the character of rural society, the layout of the estate, its resources and the needs of its proprietor. The landowner's role depended upon the size of his estate and his own status and ambitions. Small proprietors with limited incomes tended to live permanently on their lands, overseeing most of the business and expenditure. Landowners with occupations outside their estates — in trade, the law or politics — left much of their administration to a hierarchy of paid officials (see Figure 5.1). This also applied where estates were large or fragmented.

The factor acted for the proprietor in all estate business. He collected rents, disposed of produce, took day-to-day decisions regarding expenditure and convened the baron court on behalf of his master.[12] On sizeable estates the factor was in charge of large sums of money and had considerable responsibility.[13] The chamberlain was concerned with keeping accounts, collecting rents and giving receipts to the tenants,[14] while the baillie presided over the baron

Figure 5.1: The Estate Hierarchy

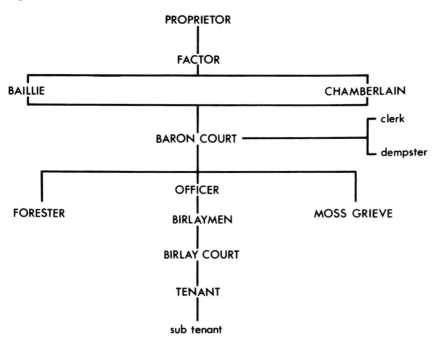

court under the aegis of the proprietor or factor.[15]

The baron court was, until the abolition of heritable jurisdictions in 1747,[16] a key element in estate administration. Its jurisdiction was over the barony, which might extend further than the estate to include small feuars.[17] The power of such courts had declined from the Middle Ages.[18] By the seventeenth century their remit was confined to the trial of minor cases of assault, misdemeanors such as debt, and infringements of good co-operative agricultural practice, or 'good neighbourhood'.[19] The court protected the proprietor's interests, allowing him to enforce his rights and claim his dues without going to higher authorities. A landlord might use it to recover rent arrears,[20] or to take action against damage to his property.[21]

The court could be used more positively to compel tenants to undertake and safeguard improvements of benefit to everyone on the estate such as the planting of trees and the sowing of legumes.[22] It was also an allegedly impartial source of justice in disputes between the tenants themselves, particularly breaches of good neighbourhood, such as the damaging of crops by stray animals.[23] Baron courts have been viewed as instruments of oppression,[24] and could doubtless have functioned as such. However, surviving court books show that they were rarely concerned with imposing additional burdens. Smout considered that they provided a forum where tenants could assemble and interpret custom;[25] this must certainly have been so with disputes concerning good neighbourhood. However, the structure and function of the court did not necessarily prevent innovation in agriculture. Some were instrumental in encouraging tenants to adopt improvements. More commonly they protected innovations instituted by the proprietor, such as planting and enclosure. Hamilton was probably more fair in his assessment of the baron court when he considered that one of its functions was 'the general improvement of agriculture'.[26]

It is probably wrong to assign a stagnant or progressive role to the baron court as an institution. The extent to which it legislated for agrarian change by trying to enforce the improving statutes of the Scottish Parliament,[27] or by protecting improvements undertaken independently by the proprietor, reflected in great measure the personality of the individual landowner. Families with progressive ideas, such as the Clerks of Penicuik or the Barclays of Urie,[28] could use it to compel their less enlightened tenantry to undertake improvements which they would otherwise have been unwilling to carry out. More indirectly, it could have been used to add force to improvement clauses in tenants' leases. On the other hand, proprietors who were content with the *status quo* might have imparted a backward air to the business of their courts. In wider terms the court's significance is clear: it lay at the heart of estate administration, providing an institution which was, when properly used, fairly impartial and before which each individual, including the proprietor, was equal at law if not always in practice.[29]

The officer was the executive of the factor and chamberlain[30] (Figure 5.1), travelling from farm to farm, receiving abuse from refractory tenants and sometimes even liable to assault.[31] On some estates specialist officers were given charge of timber and peat resources to ensure that they were efficiently utilised.[32] The officer was aided by birlayment, part-time voluntary helpers appointed from the tenantry. This system was similar to the 'lawrightmen' of the Northern Isles and had parallels in northern England.[33] Birlaymen were tenants in whom the proprietor or his officers placed particular trust and who could be relied upon to give impartial verdicts under oath in disputes between tenants or with the proprietor. They were normally unpaid and were reappointed annually. Their duties were to maintain good neighbourhood and provide assessments in valuations or disputes. To this end they sometimes had their own birlay court, under the jurisdiction of the baron court, in which such cases could be dealt with immediately and informally.[34]

An important aspect of estate administration was that most positions in the hierarchy could be, and often were, held by tenants. Factors of large estates were sometimes members of cadet branches of the family, even small proprietors in their own right.[35] However, in many cases they were tenants with their own holdings on the estate. This applied even more frequently to the baillie and chamberlain, while the officer and birlaymen were invariably tenants who were sometimes only appointed with the prior consent of their fellows.[36]

Thus, in its general form though not necessarily in particular instances, estate administration involved much of the community, though inevitably the interests of the landowners predominated. It could be argued that factor, baillie and chamberlain, because of the salaries which they received, would have been 'laird's men'. However, they were usually tenants too, facing the same pressures as their fellows and consequently likely to have been sympathetic to their problems within a framework which was essentially paternalistic.

The structure of estate management was flexible and did not prevent agricultural improvement. It could accommodate the needs of proprietors bent on developing their estates as well as landowners who were content to let their lands continue at a semi-subsistence level. The same structure continued into the eighteenth century and served the Improvers in their turn. Estate management was neither backward nor stagnant in itself. However, the impetus for change had to come from the landowners, the only people with potential resources, power and breadth of vision to institute improvements. The way in which the administrative hierarchy was used reflected the outlook and attitudes of individual landowners.

Changing farm structure

During the seventeenth century a number of important organisational changes began to occur within the framework of the estate community. One of the most significant was the gradual modification of farm structures. Three types of farm existed in Scotland at this time: those with multiple holdings, comprising joint-tenant farms where two or more tenants held a single lease and combined to pay the rent, and multiple-tenant farms where tenants leased individual holdings, usually specific fractions of a farm, and paid rents separately. Single-tenant farms which were leased by only one husbandman also existed. Smout has suggested that joint-tenant farms were the most primitive type and single-tenant farms the most advanced, implying an evolutionary sequence.[37]

Joint-tenant farms inevitably involved communal working. They can only be distinguished from multiple-tenant farms where the conditions of tenancy are specified: this normally occurs only in leases. These suggest that such farms were widespread but not numerous. Out of over 2,900 leases from estates throughout Lowland Scotland which were studied, only 275 involved joint tenancy. In 116 of these the tenants were related — specifically father and son, or brothers — or had common surnames implying kinship. Farms of this type may have been essentially the same as single-tenant farms in the way in which the working of the land was organised. The difference in tenure may have been due merely to individual family circumstances: for example, where a father who relied on the labour of one or more sons arranged a joint lease to encourage them to stay at home. This type of joint-tenant structure was not especially backward — it was merely an organisational variant of a relatively advanced type of unit, the single-tenant farm. However, where there was no family relationship between joint tenants a more ancient structure does seem to be implied. Such farms do not appear to have been common in Lowland Scotland by the seventeenth century.

On multiple-tenant farms tenants were involved in co-operative agriculture due to a lack of the capital and equipment needed to operate independently. The need to divide the shares of this type of farm by quality as well as quantity with strict regard to fairness led to the fragmentation of tenant runrig where each tenant's share was intermixed with those of his fellows in a series of parcels, sometimes with a degree of regularity, the shares of land usually being fixed but possibly sometimes liable to periodic reallocation (see Chapter 3).[38] This in turn reinforced the need for communal working.

On single-tenant farms the husbandman had to be self-sufficient in equipment and manpower. Instead of the bulk of the work being done by the tenants themselves, as on multiple-holding farms, it was undertaken mainly be sub-tenants and hired servants. The tenant was as much an overseer as a direct participant. Such a unit was potentially more efficient, as the tenant was not hampered by the constraints of communal working. In terms of organisation, it was a modern farm.

It has been suggested that multiple-holding farms were dominant, indeed universal, in pre-improvement Scotland.[39] However, single-tenant farms were common throughout Lowland Scotland and numerous in many districts. The poll lists of 1696 allow the farm structure of Aberdeenshire at this date to be mapped (Figure 5.2). Unfortunately, poll tax records are fragmentary or lacking in detail for other parts of Lowland Scotland. Elsewhere the proportion of single-tenant to multiple-holding farms can be determined from rentals listing the number of tenants per farm. Because of the complete coverage for Aberdeenshire it is useful to begin with this county and work outwards. While it cannot be considered a microcosm of seventeenth-century Scotland, it was nevertheless a large and varied county topographically and economically. When the percentage of single-tenant farms per parish (excluding smallholdings) is calculated, marked variations are apparent (Figure 5.2). There is a broad correlation between areas where single-tenant farms dominated and arable lowlands: the Garioch, the district around Aberdeen, the valleys of the Ythan and Deveron. Few upland or semi-upland parishes had high percentages of single-tenant farms. The areas with the most developed farm structures were thus mainly lowland and arable.

When the poll lists are examined in detail, a further upland-lowland contrast emerges. Multiple-holding farms in Highland parishes like Glenmuick had many tenants – up to 12 – with few or no cotters and servants.[40] By contrast, many Lowland multiple-holding farms had only two or three tenants with several subtenants and servants. The labour force and holding size on this type of farm was comparable to that on adjacent single-tenant ones. The implication is that on these lowland multiple-holding farms the tenants maintained sufficiently large work-forces to be independent. They were in a different class from the impoverished husbandmen of Glen Muick; in such cases the communal element may have meant little more than the tenants living together in the same ferm-toun.

Figure 5.2: Percentage of Single-tenant Farms per Parish, Aberdeenshire, 1696

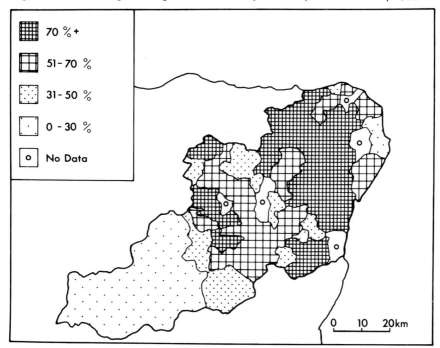

Figure 5.3 shows single-tenant farms as a percentage of all farms on estates for which detailed rentals are available for the period 1660-1707. Single-tenant farms were common on many estates. If estates north of the Tay are classified by their rent structure[41] into predominantly arable, mixed or pastoral, an analysis of variance test shows that the differences between the samples are significantly greater than those within them, arable estates having higher percentages of single-tenant farms. Thus the pattern of farm structure which has been demonstrated for Aberdeenshire occurred more widely. In the Southern Uplands the farm structures of pastoral areas were more developed than on the fringes of the Highlands. In the latter area there were again differences between upland and lowland multiple-holding farms. Highland farms often had many tenants — on the Strathbran estates six, seven or eight were frequent while one even had twenty.[42] On Lowland farms two or three tenants were usual and over four uncommon in most areas. That this situation was dynamic and not static can be seen by comparing rentals and the Aberdeenshire poll lists. A gradual reduction of tenants was widespread (Table 5.1). This process was identified by Dodgshon in south-east Scotland in the early eighteenth century and was considered by him to have been the most painless way of moving from a multiple to a single-holding structure, allowing consolidation from tenant runrig in the process.[43] It thus appears that such changes were

Figure 5.3: Percentage of Single-tenant Farms on Various Estates, 1660-1707

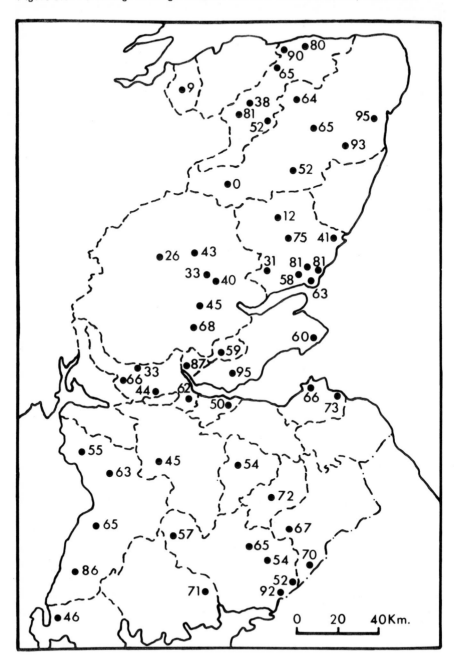

occurring quite widely in Lowland Scotland. A rural society dominated by wealthier capitalist farmers was starting to emerge with a greater proportion of subtenants, servants and labourers, whose stake in the land was becoming tenuous or had vanished entirely. The creation of a commercially-oriented structure of this kind was a prerequisite for other improvements.

Table 5.1: Changes in Tenant Numbers

Estate	County	Dates	Consolidation	
			Consolidation to single-tenant farms (per cent)	Consolidation within multiple-tenant framework (per cent)
Aboyne	Aberdeen	1600-96	0	0
Fiddes		1552-1696	50	0
Forbes		1552-1696	35	29
Huntly		1600-96	38	16
Skene		1639-96	43	0
Brechin	Angus	1634-94	38	37
Carmyllie		1622-92	30	10
Kellie		1678-1707	13	5
Panmure		1622-92	11	16
Strathbran	Perth	1655-91	0	0
Grandtully		1625-99	0	3
Penicuik	Midlothian	1646-84	0	25
Cassillis (Kyle)	Ayr	1639-82	11	6
Cassillis (Carrick)		1639-99	17	0
Castle Kennedy	Wigtown	1622-65	8	5

Changing Tenurial Structure

At the same time, related changes were taking place in the tenurial position of many farmers. Insecurity of tenure has been blamed for the lack of improvement in pre-eighteenth-century Scottish agriculture by denying tenants a long-term stake in the land which they farmed and discouraging the investment of capital and labour in it.[44] The granting of written leases for substantial periods has been seen as an important innovation in Scottish agriculture.[45] It has been assumed that before the eighteenth century husbandmen were normally tenants-at-will, holding their lands by verbal agreements and liable to summary eviction.[46] Where written leases or 'tacks' were granted, it has been claimed that they were invariably short; systems of annual leasing or of three- to five-year tenures have been suggested.[47] The introduction of long written leases has been regarded as an innovation of eighteenth-century improvers.[48]

An examination of over 2,900 leases dating from the late sixteenth century

to the first decade of the eighteenth suggests that their introduction in significant numbers first occurred in the early seventeenth century, if not before
(Figure 5.4). Written leases pre-dating the late sixteenth century are rare. Many

Figure 5.4: Numbers of Written Leases Surviving per Decade

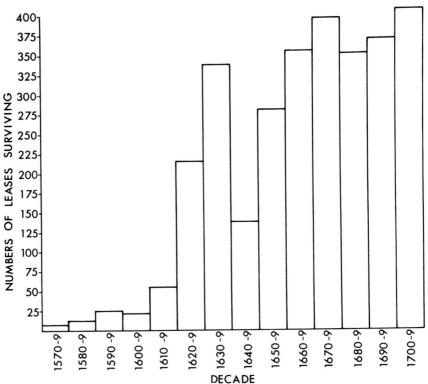

more exist for the 1620s and 1630s, a period which other evidence suggests
was one of modest prosperity.[49] After a slump during the troubled 1640s and
1650s there is a sharp rise in the number of surviving leases which date from the
period between 1660 and the end of the century, again a time of relative peace
and prosperity.[50] It is probable that the leases which have survived are only a
fraction of those which once existed. This can be shown from isolated rentals
indicating which tenants possessed written leases. In most cases few or none of
the corresponding tacks have survived. Leases, although formal legal documents,
did not have the survival value of charters or sasines confirming land ownership
as opposed to tenancy.

While Figure 5.4 may be partly weighted by the tendency for more material
to survive from the later part of the century, it is likely that there was a significant increase in the proportion of tenants with written leases on many estates
during the seventeenth century. Rentals giving details of tenure are rare, but

Table 5.2: Percentages of Tenants with Written and Verbal Leases on Certain Estates

Estate	County	Date	Percentage Written Tacks	Percentage Verbal Tacks	Percentage Not Known	Total No. of Tenants
Cassillis	Wigtown	1622	23	70	7	72
Crawford	Lanark	1638	80	20	0	58
Cassillis	Wigtown	1655	51	38	11	55
Breadalbane (L. Tay)	Perth	1674	39	61	0	119
Penicuik	Midlothian	1680	80	20	0	35
Hailes	E. Lothian	1682	55	45	0	30
Strathbran	Perth	1701	33	67	0	89
Balquholly	Aberdeen	1705	70	17	13	25
Fyvie	Aberdeen	1705	62	36	2	43

they show the importance of written against verbal agreements on particular estates. Table 5.2[51] demonstrates that on six of the nine estates with a reasonably large number of tenants, over 50 per cent had written leases. On four estates the majority was substantial. The two Cassillis rentals indicate that the proportion of tenants with written leases increased between the 1620s and the 1650s. The same trend occurred at Penicuik and Fyvie later in the century. At Penicuik 71 per cent of the holdings set by verbal agreements in 1680 were held with written tacks in 1700 and at Fyvie 62 per cent of the tenants with verbal agreements in 1705 were recorded as being obliged to accept written leases in the near future.[52]

The Breadalbane and Strathbran rentals are exceptions to this pattern. On these estates in Highland Perthshire, where multiple-holding farms with large numbers of tenants predominated, written leases were less common. This suggests that there was a link between progressive attitudes towards farm structure and tenancy. Table 5.2 also suggests that on some estates at least, the decision to grant either a written or a verbal lease was a matter for individual negotiation between a proprietor or his officers and specific tenants, rather than a blanket decision applied to the whole estate.

While the granting of increasing numbers of written leases may have been widespread in Lowland Scotland, it was not universal. Practice on the Buccleuch estates, covering much of the central Borders, was different. There tenants held their land from year to year, the holdings being reallocated at annual 'land settings'.[53] But this did not mean that the Buccleuch tenants went in constant fear of eviction. The attitudes of the proprietors, possibly inherited from the tight-knit loyalties of Border warfare, were paternalistic. Holdings could, and did, pass from father to son for generations.

When the lengths of surviving leases are examined, tacks of over ten years' duration comprise 36 per cent of the total, the percentage per decade tending to rise from the early part of the century onwards. On some estates 19-year leases, the length which later became standard in many parts of Scotland, and which represented a fair compromise between the interests of landlord and tenant, were first introduced in substantial numbers during the 1620s and 1630s. However, this early policy was not successful everywhere.[54]

The trend towards granting written, and especially long, leases reflected changes in the relationship between proprietor and tenant, as did holding enlargement and the reduction of tenant numbers. It was related to the more commercial attitudes which began to appear in Lowland Scotland during the seventeenth century.[55] Tenants were increasingly selected more for their competence than with regard to tradition. This was especially important in arable areas where increased grain production depended upon the co-operation of the tenantry. In pastoral areas much commercial activity, particularly the droving trade, was directly controlled by the landowners and there was less need to encourage the tenantry.[56] In arable areas the desire to increase their rents transferred some of the bargaining power regarding conditions of tenure to the tenants. In some cases factors went to considerable lengths to secure able tenants and some of these successfully held out for lower rents or longer leases.[57] On the Craigends estate in Renfrewshire the proprietor recorded his efforts to induce particular tenants to take holdings by offering them 19-year leases.[58] If they accepted long tacks they received some remission of rent for the first two or three years. The position of proprietor and tenant had changed markedly from the early part of the century when many tenants had paid large grassums, lump sums which were often equal to three times the annual rent of the holding, to secure a 19-year lease.[59]

Marketing and the Commutation of Rents

While farms, tenures and the basic structure of rural society were being slowly modified along more commercial lines, the tenant farmer was also becoming more involved in marketing. The traditional economy has been characterised by payments in kind as principal rents, by small payments in produce (kain rents) for the proprietor's household, and by labour services. By the end of the seventeenth century principal rents in the pastoral areas of Lowland Scotland had been almost entirely converted to money. Only along the Highland edge did the payment of principal rents in live animals and their produce continue.[60] In arable areas a start had also been made on commuting 'fermes', or grain rents, to money. The earliest known instances of this were on estates around Edinburgh from the 1640s.[61] The capital provided a guaranteed market for produce as well as acting as an important outlet for exports. By the time of the Union in 1707 partial commutation of grain rents had spread to other areas, including the western Lowlands and north-east Scotland.[62] There was also widespread conversion to money of kain rents and labour services. Commutation forced tenants to become more closely involved in a money economy. It was linked to an increase in the number of periodic market centres, especially between 1660 and

1708 when over 300 new non-burghal centres were authorised.[63] Urban growth and an increasing, if irregular, export trade in agricultural produce was encouraging internal marketing to break free from the constraints of the burghal system. This induced proprietors to begin transferring the responsibility for marketing estate produce to their tenants, though this process was still far from complete by the early eighteenth century.

Bulk Trade

While tenants were becoming more commercially minded, the trade in bulk produce, handled by the proprietors, was also growing. For east coast estates from Berwickshire to Orkney there is evidence of an expansion in the grain trade, especially after 1660. Part of this trade met the demands of Scotland's growing urban population: Edinburgh and Glasgow were particularly large consumers. There was also a developing export market. In the later seventeenth century, large quantities of grain were sent to Scandinavia and the Low Countries while England also imported considerable amounts of Scottish grain after a poor harvest.[64] In the pastoral sector the counterpart was the droving trade in live animals to England. This existed in the first half of the century but expanded substantially once competition from Ireland was removed in 1667. The rearing of sheep and especially cattle for the English market was sufficiently lucrative for several proprietors in Galloway to build large complexes of enclosures in which animals were cross-bred and fattened. The increasing profits from the grain and livestock trades may well have helped to finance the widespread conversion and rebuilding of country houses and the laying out of landscaped parks which occurred in the last forty years of the seventeenth century.

Rural Landscape Changes

Enclosure and the Country House

Social and economic development in Scotland had been hindered by three centuries of war with England and by internal political instability. With the exception of the Civil War period in the 1640s and 1650s, the seventeenth century brought more settled conditions and a spread of law and order. After the Union of the Crowns in 1603 the Borders were pacified, and although raiding continued along the margins of the Highlands, landowners throughout Lowland Scotland turned to litigation rather than force to settle their disputes. In the rural landscape this was marked by a modification of the bleak, functional lines of the fortified house and castle to produce the more decorative 'Scottish Baronial' style. After the Restoration in 1660 this trend continued with the conversion of many castles by the addition of new non-defensive wings, as at Traquair House, and the building of new country mansions on a classical model, such as Kinross House and Hopetoun House[65] (see Chapter 10).

Following English and Continental fashion, the new and converted country houses were surrounded by 'policies' or enclosed planting and parkland. This small-scale ornamental enclosure began to take on a more commercial role on many estates by the end of the century. In some cases the mains, or home farm, was also enclosed and farmed commercially by the proprietor. This encouraged experiments with new agricultural practices: convertible husbandry and selective breeding were tried on some estates.[66] In a countryside almost devoid of timber, landowners soon realised the value of large-scale block planting as a long-term investment. Around Yester House in East Lothian there were several thousand acres of young trees by the end of the century.[67] Elsewhere the scale of block planting was smaller but several other landowners could probably have claimed, like the Earl of Strathmore, that the trees which he had planted would, when mature, be equal in value to a year's rental of the estate.[68]

Enclosure perhaps reached its greatest extent in Galloway, where the growth of the droving trade stimulated the construction of large parks. Sir David Dunbar's cattle park at Baldoon, near Wigtown, was estimated to have been four and a half kilometres long and over two and a half wide, but other examples of similar scale are known.[69] While enclosures of this type often involved the expropriation of several former farms, as at Castle Kennedy in Wigtownshire,[70] their management was kept strictly in the hands of the proprietors.

The amount of enclosure which had been achieved by the end of the seventeenth century was small in terms of the landscape as a whole, especially when compared with England. It consisted of islands of improvement in a sea of open-field, infield-outfield cultivation, and unenclosed rough pasture. Where estates were small but wealthy, as in the Lothians, these islands were quite thickly scattered. However, a start had yet to be made on enclosing the tenants' lands. The Military Survey of 1747-55 (Plate 6) shows that during the first half of the eighteenth century progress in this direction was slow. Nevertheless, the enclosed policies and mains formed a nucleus from which more widespread enclosure could be commenced. They also provided experience in new agricultural techniques which were later developed and extended by the first of the eighteenth-century 'Improvers' when sufficient capital was available and the economic situation was more favourable. The work of the 'Improvers' and the spread of enclosure in the eighteenth century are discussed by Adams (Chapter 7) and Caird (Chapter 9).

Rural Housing

Rising living standards for at least some of the tenantry were reflected in improved housing in the later seventeenth century. Early in the century evidence suggests that housing conditions were universally poor throughout Scotland. The typical tenant's house was cruck-framed and built of impermanent materials by the occupier himself, landlords supplying only the main timbers.[71] Poor housing standards were doubtless aggravated by the prevalence of short leases which discouraged the investment of labour and capital in improvements. The typical farmstead was a long house, a plan favoured by the use of crucks.[72]

There were, however, differences in the size and quality of houses depending upon the status of their occupiers. Larger tenants possessed houses with enough living space to be divided into two or three rooms, though single-room dwellings with central hearths were probably more common (Plate 3).

The progressively enlarged holdings which were being created in arable areas were accompanied by improved building construction. The long house began to be replaced by the courtyard farmstead where the outbuildings were grouped into one or two wings adjoining the dwelling house rather than in a single continuous range (Plate 4). The factor's house at Belhelvie, north of Aberdeen, with its two storeys, glazed windows and selection of specialised outbuildings perhaps typifies the dwellings of the new capitalist tenant farmers.[73] An important innovation was the spread of lime mortar, allowing crucks to be dispensed with and fully load-bearing walls to be constructed. At Lasswade, near Edinburgh, tenants were occupying two- and even three-storey farmhouses built with stone and lime by the end of the century.[74] The concept of permanency in rural housing was changing from a dwelling which would stand for the duration of a short lease to one which would last for two generations or more. The construction of such houses may have been encouraged by the spread of longer leases, and certainly indicates a willingness by both tenants and proprietors to invest more capital and labour in agriculture. They also reflected growing social differentiation, since labourer's cottages do not appear to have improved significantly.

Conclusion

The foregoing survey has necessarily been wide-ranging. It has emphasised the changing position of the tenant within the estate community in seventeenth-century Lowland Scotland. Social and economic change occurred largely within the framework of the estate, taking the form of alterations in the relationship between landlord and tenant, and modifications in the character of tenant farming. The study of estate structure and management is thus central to a consideration of the organisational changes in rural society which prepared the way for the transformation of the Scottish rural landscape in the eighteenth and nineteenth centuries.

In adopting a more commercial orientation, rural society in the more progressive areas of Lowland Scotland, particularly the east coast, was becoming polarized into a smaller class of prosperous tenants and a larger group whose direct dependence on the land was diminishing. As these changes occurred, co-operative husbandry declined and the selection of suitable tenants became determined more and more by their ability than by traditional paternalistic considerations. The creation of a modern farm structure thus commenced well before the 'classic' period of agricultural improvement.

Landscape changes also occurred. Their scale was greatest in a few limited areas such as the Lowlands around the Forth and Tay estuaries, under the influence of urban markets and in some cases of urban capital, and in the south-west, with the stimulus of the droving trade. This helps to explain why these were the first areas to develop fully commercialised farming systems in the eighteenth century.[75] The extent to which the rural landscape was modified in these areas prior to 1707 has probably been underestimated. Elsewhere landscape changes were more limited yet still important. Processes of holding amalgamation and consolidation modified the character of the traditional fermtoun and the relationships between its occupants. Improvements in tenure, commutation and developments in marketing fostered more commercial attitudes. These were directly expressed in the landscape by improved housing conditions and new farmstead layouts, and probably indirectly by more dynamic attitudes to agricultural production leading to improved farming practices. The experiments of landowners with new systems of husbandry within enclosed mains and policies began to provide a basis of experience which would in time transform the entire landscape.

Overall, the evidence suggests that the character of Scottish rural society and the rural landscape did not remain static during the seventeenth and early eighteenth centuries. Development was sometimes faltering, but in the long term it accelerated slowly. Change was interrupted by the Civil Wars, the famines of the 1690s and the Jacobite rebellions of the early eighteenth century, but progress was never halted for long. The experiments of early-eighteenth-century improvers such as Cockburn of Ormiston and Grant of Monymusk can thus be seen more meaningfully as a direct continuation of seventeenth-century trends rather than as isolated, aberrant phemonena.

It must be emphasised that these changes were slow. They were not evident to contemporary writers and have thus escaped detection till recently. However, they appear to have been the result of conscious decision-making by landowners. This was probably a response to improving economic circumstances and even to new fashions. Proprietors were becoming involved in large-scale trade in agri-cultural produce. The old feudal society was passing. A more dynamic and business-like approach to estate management was appearing. Such forces had repercussions on the rural landscape and society as a whole.

It has only been possible to outline some of the changes which occurred and to suggest broad regional differences. These were based partly on economic contrasts between arable and pastoral farming. They were also due to a time lag between the more progressive areas around the larger burghs and more remote interior districts. The major burghs, especially Edinburgh, may have acted as centres from which new attitudes were diffused into the countryside. Of equal significance was their role as markets for agricultural produce and outlets for the export trade.

The evidence which has been discussed suggests that too much emphasis has been placed on the crop failures of the 1690s. These now appear as an isolated combination of uniquely severe weather conditions rather than the culmination of a long-continued agricultural decline. They undoubtedly checked progress, but further research spanning the late seventeenth and early eighteenth centuries will probably reveal a pattern of continued slow, unobtrusive development with only a temporary reverse.

There is a need for more research on agrarian change at this period before the chronology of development, its underlying causes and its spatial variations become clear. There is no shortage of sources on which to work. For estates where runs of accounts and rentals have survived with supporting documents such as leases and other estate papers, detailed case studies would be particularly valuable. Accounts, factors' reports and correspondence, classes of documents which are most abundant for larger estates, may clarify the changing nature of proprietor/tenant relationships. Estate papers are also the main source for landscape changes such as enclosure and improved building construction. It would be valuable if the earlier phases of some of the changes which have been described could be pinpointed more accurately. The relative paucity of sources for the early part of the seventeenth century may have led to an underestimation of its importance.

Enough evidence is now available to indicate the need for a reassessment of the chronology and nature of agrarian change in Scotland from the sixteenth to the nineteenth centuries. Rural society and the agrarian landscape were by no means unchanging and the developments which occurred at this time formed the foundations in which the more spectacular and better-recorded achievements of the traditional 'Agricultural Revolution' were laid.

Notes

1. Grant, I. F. (1930), *The social and economic development of Scotland before 1603* (Edinburgh), pp. 267-9

2. Sanderson, M. H. B. (1973), 'The feuars of kirklands', *Scottish Historical Review* (hereafter *Scot. Hist. Rev.*), *52*, 117-48; Grant (1930), *Social and economic development of Scotland*, pp. 265-86

3. Batho, G. (1967), 'Noblemen, gentlemen and yeomen' pp. 276-305 in Thirsk, J. (ed.), *The agrarian history of England and Wales* (Cambridge), Vol. IV

4. Ferguson, W. (1968), *Scotland, 1689 to the present* (Edinburgh), p. 73; Fullarton, F. (1793), *General view of the agriculture of Ayr* (Edinburgh), p. 69

5. Developments such as liming, new rotations and the expansion of the arable area are discussed in detail in Smout, T. C. and Fenton, A. (1965), 'Scottish agriculture before the Improvers – an exploration', *Agricultural History Review, 13,* 73-93 and Whyte, I. D. (1979), *Agriculture and society in seventeenth-century Scotland* (Edinburgh)

6. Whyte, I. D. (1976), 'Scottish historical geography: survey and prospect', *Occasional research papers No. 8* (Department of Geography, University of Edinburgh), pp. 27-8; Devine, T. M. and Lythe, S. G. E. (1971), 'The economy of Scotland under James VI', *Scot. Hist. Rev., 50,* 99

7. Smout, T. C. (1969), *A history of the Scottish people 1560-1830* (Edinburgh), pp. 224-6; Symon, J. A. (1959), *Scottish farming, past and present* (Edinburgh), pp. 51-63, 89-102

8. Carter, I. (1971), 'Economic models and the recent history of the Highlands', *Scottish Studies, 15,* 101

9. Whittington, G. (1975), 'Was there a Scottish agricultural revolution?', *Area*, 7, 204-6; Smout and Fenton (1965), 'Scottish agriculture'; Whyte, I. D. (1974), 'Agrarian change in Lowland Scotland in the seventeenth century' (unpublished PhD thesis, University of Edinburgh)

10. The 'revolution' view was summed up in Caird, J. B. (1964), 'The making of the Scottish rural landscape', *Scottish Geographical Magazine* (hereafter *SGM*), *80*, 72-80

11. This source is discussed in Whyte (1974), 'Agrarian change', pp. 22-33

12. The duties of factors were set out in their commissions. See, for example, Scottish Record Office (hereafter SRO) GD 16/27/53; GD 6/1470; GD 26/5/299

13. SRO, GD 224/943/4, account book, 1653

14. SRO, GD 248/39, accounts, 1622-32; GD 16/30/67, accounts, 1630

15. SRO, GD 6/1023, 1026, contract, 1641; court records, 1643

16. Barron, D. G. (ed.) (1892), *The court book of the barony of Urie 1604-1747* (Publications of the Scottish History Society) (hereafter Pubs. SHS), *12*, vii

17. Dickinson, W. C. (ed.) (1937), *The court book of the barony of Carnwath* (Pubs. SHS), *29*, xxiii-xxxvii

18. McIntyre, P. (1958), 'The franchise courts', p. 377 in *An introduction to Scottish legal history* (Publications of the Stair Society)

19. Barron, (1892), *Court book*, vi

20. Extracts from the court book of the barony of Skene 1613-33, *Spalding Club Miscellany* (1892), *5*, 210

21. SRO, GD 1/300, court book, 1666; Barron (1892), *Court book*, 92; Gunn, C. B. (1905), *Records of the baron court of Stichil* (Pubs. SHS), *50*, 50

22. SRO, GD 26/2/1, court book, 1596; Gunn (1905), *Records*, 50

23. SRO, GD 16/36/18, court book, 1648

24. Handley, J. E. (1953), *Scottish farming in the eighteenth century* (Edinburgh), p. 89

25. Smout (1969), *A history of the Scottish people*, p. 115

26. Hamilton, H. (1963), *An economic history of Scotland in the eighteenth century* (Oxford), p. 49

27. The improving legislation of the Scottish Parliament is discussed in detail in Whyte (1974), 'Agrarian change', pp. 70-111

28. Barron (1892), *Court book*, xxix-xxxix; SRO, GD 18/695

29. McIntyre (1958), 'The franchise courts', 375

30. SRO, GD 26/2/1, court book, 1596; GD 45/18/150, tack, 1617

31. Dunlop, J. (ed.) (1957), *Court minutes of Balgair* (Publications of the Scottish Record Society), *87*, 6-7

32. Whyte (1974), 'Agrarian change', pp. 63-7

33. National Library of Scotland, MSS. 31.2.8; Bouch, C. M. L. and Jones, G. P. (1961), *A short economic and social history of the Lake Counties 1500-1800* (Manchester), pp. 150-4

34. SRO, GD 18/695, court book, 1664; Barron (1892), *Court book*, 24; Gunn (1905), *Records*, 9

35. SRO, GD 237/88/5, accounts, 1668

36. Whyte (1974), 'Agrarian change', pp. 67-9

37. Smout (1969), *A history of the Scottish people*, p. 113

38. Dodgshon, R. A. (1975), 'Towards an understanding and definition of runrig – the evidence for Roxburghshire and Berwickshire', *Transactions of the Institute of British Geographers, 64*, 15-34; idem, 'Scandinavian solskifte and the sunwise division of land in eastern Scotland', *Scottish Studies, 19*, 1-14

39. Third, B. M. W. (1953), 'The changing rural geography of the Scottish lowlands 1700-1820' (unpublished PhD thesis, University of Edinburgh), 3, 5

40. (1840) *List of pollable persons within the shire of Aberdeen 1696* (Publications of the Spalding Club), *I*, 171-9

41. Smout (1969), *A history of the Scottish people*, pp. 129-30

42. SRO, GD 121/224, rental, 1691

43. Dodgshon, R. A. (1972), 'The removal of runrig in Roxburghshire and Berwickshire 1680-1766', *Scottish Studies, 16*, 122-6

44. Handley (1953), *Scottish farming*, p. 120

45. Kay, G. (1962), 'The landscape of improvement', *SGM*, *78*, 100-11

46. Ferguson (1968), *Scotland*, p. 73; Smout (1969), *A history of the Scottish people*, p. 137

47. Grant (1930), *Scotland before 1603*; Handley (1953), *Scottish farming*, p. 85

48. Symon (1959), *Scottish farming, past and present*; Smout (1969), *A history of the Scottish people*, p. 274

49. Lythe, S. G. E. (1960), *The economy of Scotland in its European setting 1550-1625* (Edinburgh), pp. 24-75; Devine and Lythe (1971), 'The economy of Scotland', 50

50. Smout and Fenton (1965), 'Scottish agriculture', 75-7

51. SRO GD 25/9/47, bundle 7; GD 237/201; GD 112/9/25; GD 18/708; GD 16/1607; GD 24/673; GD 248/216; GD 28/2273, rentals

52. SRO, GD 18/708, rental, 1654; GD 28/2273, rental, 1705

53. SRO, GD 224/935/3, report, 1693

54. Sinclair, Sir John (1814), *General report on the agricultural state and political circumstances of Scotland* (Edinburgh), Vol. I, p. 191

55. Whyte (1974), 'Agrarian change', pp. 368-70

56. Ibid, pp. 269-72

57. SRO, GD 45/20/12, 14-17, accounts, 1669, 1671-4

58. Dodds, J. (ed.) (1886), *Diary and general expenditure book of William Cunningham of Craigends* (Pubs. SHS), *2*, 13

59. SRO, GD 25/9/73 – the series of tacks for the 1630s.

60. SRO, GD 112/10, box 1, bundle 1 and 2, tacks, 1600-1700; GD 121/121, tacks 1640-50

61. SRO, GD 18/704, 712, 714, rentals, 1646, 1663, 1667

62. Whyte (1974), 'Agrarian change', p. 368

63. Smout and Fenton (1965), 'Scottish agriculture', 79

64. Smout, T. C. (1963), *Scottish trade on the eve of the Union* (Edinburgh), p. 210; Woodward, D. (1977), 'Anglo-Scottish trade and English commercial policy during the 1660s', *Scot. Hist. Rev.*, *56*, 157, 165

65. Smout (1969), *A history of the Scottish people*, pp. 108-10; see also Ch. 10

66. Convertible husbandry, e.g. SRO, GD 26/548, 552, GD 45/18/496/2, GD 24/602. Selective breeding, e.g. SRO, GD 45/18/535, GD 112/9/15

67. Cox, E. H. M. (1935), *A history of gardening in Scotland* (London), pp. 48-9

68. Miller, A. H. (ed.) (1890), *The Glamis book of record* (Pubs. SHS), *10*, 32

69. Mitchell, A. (ed.) (1908), *Macfarlane's Geographical collections*, (Pubs. SHS), *52*, II, 78

70. SRO, GD 25/9/63, accounts, 1640s-50s

71. Whyte, I. D. (1975), 'Rural housing in Lowland Scotland in the seventeenth century – the evidence of estate papers', *Scottish Studies*, *19*, 55-68

72. Ibid, 57-64

73. SRO, GD 45/20/214

74. SRO, GD 18/722, rental, 1694

75. Gray, M. (1973), 'Scottish emigration – the social impact of agrarian change in the rural lowlands 1775-1875', *Perspectives in American History*, *7*, 119-22

6 THE PATTERN OF LANDHOLDING IN EIGHTEENTH-CENTURY SCOTLAND

L. Timperley

Power and landownership have been synonymous in Scotland from time immemorial and in this the eighteenth century was no exception. Although the century saw considerable changes in all sectors of Scottish life, the landowning class continued to dominate the constitution, the economy, and society as a whole. From the ownership of land the landowning class derived both wealth and the basic right to govern the country. There was no truly free land market as 'ownership was artificially protected, politically recognised, and valued as the basis of social distinction.'[1] The higher ranks of the landowning class were thus endowed with a permanence and stability which helped give eighteenth-century Scotland an appearance of calm which contrasted with the turbulence of the seventeenth century and the social tensions of the nineteenth.

The political system in eighteenth-century Scotland was blatantly undemocratic and had the effect of concentrating political power into the hands of a small number of wealthy families. The right to vote was restricted to that section of the landowning class who held land or superiorities directly of the Crown valued at 40 shillings old extent, or £400 Scots valued rent. In 1788, no county electorate exceeded 200 and the majority were less than half this figure. Even these totals were inflationary as of the 2,655 voters registered, 1,318 were fictitious, that is they were created by local magnates to ensure their hold over parliamentary elections.[2] Landowners did not consider the acquisition of votes by purchase or favour as corrupt, and both county and burgh elections were often controlled by a single large landowner. Overlying this system of local influence was the web of patronage controlled by the 'manager' who ensured that the Scottish representation at Westminster accorded with the policy of the party in power.[3] To the prospective voter he could offer places on the civil list of Scotland, pensions, posts in the customs, excise and post office, as well as procure commissions in the army and, occasionally, office in the British government, thus further cementing the powerful position of the landowning elite. Eligible candidates for parliamentary elections were themselves few in number, restricted not only by the legal requirement that each candidate should have his name on the Register of Voters for the county in question, but by the limited number of constituencies,[4] the expense of travelling to, and living in, London, as well as the political system itself. Election to the House of Lords was solely the preserve of the Scottish peers (about 150 in all) who elected sixteen of their own number to sit in Westminster. The Crown controlled this 'election' and the 'King's List' nominating certain peers was invariably accepted.

Local government was 'a system of unplanned survivals and wayward digressions'[5] under which the landowning class again had total power. Before 1747, the peers had their heritable stewartries, sheriffdoms and regalities, and after the Militia Act of 1797, they could become Lords Lieutenant. The other wealthy landowners could become Commissioners of Supply or Justices of the Peace. As heritors, landowners had an active say in the administration of poor relief and education within the parish, as well as being all-powerful on their own estates (see Chapter 5). Local government posts were unpaid, and without the acceptance of these duties as a responsibility of their class by the landowners, the country could not have been administered as it was.

The economic life of eighteenth-century Scotland was also under the control of the landowning class, although their power lessened in the last decades of the century as industrialisation and urbanisation increased (see Chapter 13). Agriculture, with its associated secondary and service industries, provided the majority of Scotsmen with their means of livelihood throughout the century, although methods and organisation altered dramatically. The Scottish landowner had the reputation of being the most absolute in Britain and had more recent ties with the old feudal system than his English counterpart, but once the profitability of the new methods had been proved, the majority of landowners accepted the need for change and efficiency. In the industrial sector the land-owning classes also made a significant contribution. Interest was directly proportional to the relationship of any industry to the landowner's estate and thus an industry using raw materials, power or surplus labour found on an estate was considered worthy of encouragement. Investment in larger concerns was not common, and as entrepreneurs in industry and commerce landowners were not always successful, but as providers of long-term investment in roads, harbours, canals and planned villages, they had no equals. There is no doubt that without the approval, if not always the active help, of the landed classes, the processes of change in Scotland would have been severely curtailed.[6]

As a consequence of political and economic power the landowning class formed a social elite moulded by their superior education and culture. Changes in manners and mode of life within the century were as dramatic as the changes seen in agricultural methods and had their base in increasing incomes coupled with contact with English society. The landed class, although the most highly educated in Scotland, made little direct contribution to eighteenth-century cultural achievements. They served, however, as patrons of the arts, and Scottish intellectuals in general 'were so emotionally dependent on the approval and support of the landed classes that it is scarcely conceivable that the cultural golden age could have taken place if the gentry and nobility had been unwilling to become its patrons'.[7]

The landowning class of eighteenth-century Scotland was therefore an elite which ruled absolutely. The opportunity for oppression was enormous, but on the whole the landowners ruled sensibly and fairly. They were not as inward-looking and defensive in attitude as many other ruling elites in Europe. Inter-marriage with families of merchants, lawyers, burgesses and industrialists, as well as the purchase of estates by men who had made their fortunes in other spheres, meant that class distinctions were not strong. There was a desire to maintain the social position of the landowning class, but the revitalising effect of new blood and money was not ignored.

Despite the obvious importance of this class, little detailed information is available on the basic structure or organisational framework of the eighteenth-century Scottish landowning class. The aim of this chapter is to reconstruct the pattern of landholding. It is hoped that from this reconstruction light will be shed on other aspects of eighteenth-century life, such as the timing and character of agrarian improvements, the distribution of policies and the location of planned villages. Such a picture of the Scottish landholding pattern must be the result of an amalgamation of many and various sources, carefully and painstakingly pieced together, as detailed sources, comparable to those used in English studies, are not available.[8] To achieve this for the whole of Scotland at ten- or twenty-year intervals would be an impossible task and therefore one year must be chosen as the optimum for study.

The choice was not difficult, for in a work primarily concerned with the agrarian sector of the economy, 1770 stands out as being of great significance. Many historians have argued that it was about this date that the take-off into self-sustained growth occurred in the agrarian sector.[9] If the industrial sector of the economy is taken into consideration, 1780 would probably be a more appropriate date, but the landowners' interests lay in rural society and few were to expand their horizons beyond using limited parts of the new technology to enhance the local economy. The choice of 1770 is further vindicated by the availability of a wide range of contemporary documents and books relating to the land after this date, reflecting the activity and interest evoked by the changes occurring. A picture of landholding about this date would reflect the traditional society of the early eighteenth century, while at the same time holding the elements vital to the substantive economic changes which took place in Scottish agriculture in the latter decades of the century.

Sources of Evidence

The most valuable sources available for the reconstruction of the pattern of landownership are valuation rolls which can be used to give a basic framework to the study. These rolls were compiled for each county in order that every proprietor might pay a just share of any land tax demanded by Parliament.[10] In each roll teinds, feu duties and the income from mills and fishings, as well as the profits from land, were assessed;[11] but each is unique, for it was not until 1802 that a set format was laid down for the county clerks to follow. As a result, valuation rolls vary in the quality of information they give, to which is added the problem that the dates of compilation of the three or four which exist for each county show little correlation.[12] Few exist for the eighteenth century, for although it had been the practice to revise the rolls annually until 1667, thereafter it was decreed that the assessment in force in 1660 (that is the actual rental of 1656) was to be used for taxation purposes. Clerks of supply no longer found it necessary to rewrite the roll unless changes in ownership made the old one unworkable or unless they were requested to do so by a superior. In this situation it is obvious that the sums noted against each farm or estate became more and more obsolete as the century wore on, but the relative position of one owner to another was roughly maintained.

Having obtained rolls as near 1770 as possible and having processed them to take into account boundary changes and the individual character of each roll, the gaps in information were filled as far as possible by using estate plans, lists of freeholders, valuation rolls of individual estates and landowners, the minutes of the meetings of the commissioners of supply, lists of heritors signing documents pertaining to parish affairs, the *Old statistical account* and other secondary sources. All this information was set down, by county and parish if possible, in a *Directory of landownership*.[13] This *Directory* does not, however, give a complete picture of landownership in 1770 on two counts. First, the ownership of 6.5 per cent of the valued rent is unknown, and second, the dates of the valuation rolls used for nine counties are outside the optimum decade of 1765-75. However, by dividing counties first by the date of the relevant valuation roll, and second by the quality of information, assessment can be made of how numbers changed over time and what effect the gaps in information would have on the ownership pattern of a county.[14]

The Landowning Classes

Historians generally accept that the system of landownership in Scotland gave rise to three broad categories of owners who enjoyed heritable tenure — the nobles, the lairds and the bonnet lairds.[15] The nobles were the closest to the King in the feudal pyramid and were distinguished by their aristocratic rank and by the fact that most of them acknowledged the King as their immediate feudal lord. The lairds were far more numerous, much less exclusive and more diverse in origins. Although there was a wide range of income and consequently of social prestige and political power within this class, in general they can be defined as having an unearned income from rents, mortgages, government office or a profession which enabled them to live a more comfortable life than that of the bonnet lairds. As there was no check on subinfeudation in Scotland, land could be granted by any vassal to be held of him, and so the freeholder as found in England never emerged in Scotland. The bonnet laird, roughly equivalent to the owner-occupier of England, was mainly limited to areas where Church or Crown had feued land in small parcels. The dividing lines between these three categories were determined by social status and political function. The lairds were able to mix socially with the nobility and the bonnet lairds, but they were shut out from the exclusive privileges of the former and had a way of life different from that of the latter. To some degree the members of each group were conscious of belonging to a distinct class which held a particular position in the social hierarchy and exercised the political functions peculiar to itself, but when economic and financial criteria are considered, a more meaningful and fundamental division into landlord and owner-occupier can be discerned.[16]

The problem now arises of correlating the information given by the valuation rolls with a classification based on real incomes. While it may have been the case that the basic division into landlord and owner-occupier is one of function because the available sources are limited, financial criteria have to be used, which in turn allows the further subdivision of the former group. As no previous work has been attempted on landed incomes in Scotland on a national scale and contemporary data as used in English studies do not exist,[17] a less direct approach is necessary. Valued rent is the real rent of 1656 which had become frozen to give a nominal value for various units of agrarian income. By assessing the trends in the rise and fall of rents within Scotland in the eighteenth century and by then applying these to the base of 1656, a rough guide can be obtained as to the agrarian income of landowners. Total income cannot be assessed because income from government office, funds, mortgages or a profession is not included, but it is unlikely that the hierarchy shown by the valuation rolls would be radically altered by this additional income, as it was the wealthier landlords who had more cash to invest and the political power to gain government sinecures. It is also true that no account of spasmodic improvements on a local or regional basis can be allowed for, as an average has to be taken for the country. By using all available national evidence,[18] it would appear that between c. 1660 and c. 1740 the national average of real rent doubled; between c. 1660 and c. 1770 it increased threefold; between c. 1660 and c. 1793 it increased 7.6 times; and between c. 1660 and 1811 it increased a massive 15 times. The rate of increase diminished in the last few years of the Napoleonic Wars, so that by 1815 the figure was probably about 15.5 or 15.6 times that of c. 1660.

Having worked out a rule by which real rental can be assessed, the problem now becomes one of relating income to specific socio-economic groups of landowners. By noting the comments made by contemporary writers such as Adam, Fullarton and Sinclair and modern writers such as Graham, Slaven and Smout on the relationship of income to status, the rough subdivision outlined in Figure 6.1 can be obtained. It should be noted at this point that Figure 6.1 refers to individuals only, but corporate bodies and institutions also owned land in eighteenth-century Scotland. For the purpose of this work the term 'institution' has been widened to include mortifications, kirk assessments and Crown property. Similarly, 'corporate bodies' include not only entries relating to town and trade associations, but also companies such as the York Buildings Company and groups of creditors.

The Pattern of Landholding *c*. 1770

Only 2 per cent of individual landowners held land in more than one county
and of these the majority owned land only in two counties, most having two
separately operated estates rather than one estate divided by an accident of
boundary.[19]

Figure 6.1: The Subdivisions of the Landowning Class

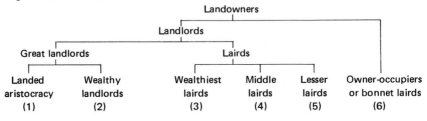

Numbers relate to valued rent possessed by each, in £ Scots:
1. above £4,000 Scots
2. £2,000-£4,000
3. £1,000-£2,000
4. £500 -£1,000
5. £100-£500
6. below £100

The pattern of landholding which emerges shows clearly that, unlike her
neighbour England, Scotland's landholdings show a specific pattern.[20] The great
landlords had a much smaller share of the total wealth in the western half of the
central belt than in the eastern and a much higher share in the Borders than in
the Highlands, with the exception of Sutherland. The Highlands emerge as a
distinct area affected by distance from centres of population, rugged topography
and poor soils and climate, as do the traditional Border counties of Roxburgh,
Selkirk and Dumfries, which had for many centuries been the buffer zone against
English attacks. In the intervening area there is a distinct east/west split in the
pattern of landholding which has more to do with historical than geographical
factors (see Figure 6.2).

The west and central region in 1770 had the lowest percentage of its counties'
valued rentals controlled by the great landlords, being less than 35 per cent in
every case. Conversely, the percentage controlled by the lairds, averaging 63 per
cent, is high, and in the majority of counties it is the lesser lairds who control
the highest portion of the county (Table 6.1). In keeping with this pattern, the
average of 17 per cent controlled by the bonnet lairds is the highest in the
country (the national average being 5.5 per cent), as is that of the 16-24 owners
found on average in the parishes of this area.

It is in this region that the remnants of the sixteenth- and seventeenth-century
feuing of Church and Crown lands can most clearly be seen in the pattern of
landholding.[21] Much was feued in small lots, and despite the intervening years

Figure 6.2: The Pattern of Landholding, 1770

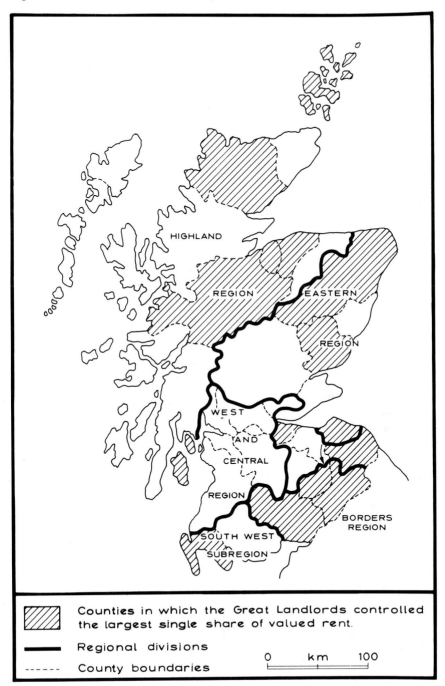

HIGHLAND

REGION

EASTERN

REGION

WEST

AND

CENTRAL

REGION

BORDERS
REGION

SOUTH WEST
SUBREGION

Counties in which the Great Landlords controlled
the largest single share of valued rent.

Regional divisions

County boundaries

0   km   100

Table 6.1: The Pattern of Landholding in the West and Central Region, 1770

County	Percentage of Valued Rent Controlled			
	Great Landlords	Lairds	Bonnet Lairds	Institutions and Corporate Bodies
Ayr	34.1	54.9	10.2	0.8
Lanark	27.8	54.0	13.5	4.7
Renfrew	26.8	62.7	8.2	2.3
Dunbarton	19.5	60.5	15.7	4.3
Stirling	9.4	68.4	13.7	8.5
Clackmannan	22.1	64.6	13.3	0
Kinross	0	77.5	20.3	2.4

and a general trend away from small landholdings, bonnet lairds or portioners were still prevalent in areas of the west, especially north Ayrshire, Lanarkshire and Dunbartonshire, with holdings often less than 50 or even 20 acres.[22] The lesser lairds also prospered in these counties, perhaps as a result of feuing or the amalgamation of existing feus, for in most they controlled the largest share of the valued rent. Further east in Stirling and Kinross, the great landlords had even less control and the lesser lairds correspondingly more.

The sub-region of the south-west, comprising Wigtownshire and Kirkcudbrightshire, is transitional between the characteristics of the west and central region and the Borders (Table 6.2). Thus the percentage of the valued rental of these counties owned by the great landlords is higher than in the west and central region but less than in the Borders. Conversely, the percentage controlled by the bonnet lairds is less than in the former but more than in the latter. Further evidence of the hybrid nature of these counties is seen in the fact that, although there is a definite peak in the percentage owned by the lesser lairds, the highest percentage is controlled by the landed aristocracy, as in the Borders.

Table 6.2: The Pattern of Landholding in the South-West Subregion, 1770

County	Percentage of Valued Rent Controlled			
	Great Landlords	Lairds	Bonnet Lairds	Institutions and Corporate Bodies
Wigtown	49.4	45.3	3.8	1.5
Kirkcudbright	39.1	54.9	3.6	1.4

In the Borders region the largest share of each county's wealth was in the hands of a few individuals, for although the percentage controlled by the great landlords was over 65 per cent, the share held by the wealthy landlords was only on a par with counties in the central lowlands (Table 6.3). Extensive areas of marginal land in proximity to the English Border had made it expeditious to set up large estates in the past. The number of lairds was correspondingly small, and, on the whole, percentages decrease with valued rent for each of the three classes of laird, but bonnet lairds have a more haphazard representation. East Lothian is included in this region, as it has a pattern of landholding similar to the main Borders region, although differences become apparent when changes over time are discussed.

Table 6.3: The Pattern of Landholding in the Borders Region, 1770

County	Percentage of Valued Rent Controlled			
	Great Landlords	Lairds	Bonnet Lairds	Institutions and Corporate Bodies
Dumfries	65.7	27.6	6.7	0
Selkirk	65.1	33.6	0	1.3
Roxburgh	73.6	22.0	5.4	1.0
East Lothian	69.7	26.7	1.4	2.2

The core of the Eastern region is formed by the counties of Midlothian, Peebles, Fife, Kincardine and Perth, although the last is so large and so situated that it of necessity includes part of the Highlands. There are also two pairs of counties, namely Aberdeen and Angus, and Berwick and West Lothian which, while not distinctive enough to warrant subgrouping, do show the influence of adjacent regions. In the majority of counties the percentages controlled by the great landlords are slightly less than those controlled by the lairds, the averages being 41.5 per cent for the former and 50.2 for the latter (Table 6.4). In the case of the four other counties the situation is reversed, with the great landlords on average owning 50.8 per cent and the lairds 45.3. It is interesting to note that the percentages controlled by the wealthy landlords range only from 16.7 per cent to 22 per cent, so that variations in the proportion owned by the great landlords are due mostly to variations within the landed aristocracy which range from 20.2 per cent to 34.1 per cent. As with the Borders, the percentages controlled by the bonnet lairds vary from county to county, the average being 3 per cent.

The pattern of landholding in the Highland region is not entirely uniform, the counties of Caithness, Ross and Cromarty and Argyll showing slightly different characteristics from the main group of counties. Moray, Nairn, Inverness, Bute, Sutherland and Orkney all show a pattern of landholding where the great landlords predominated over all others in the proportion they controlled (Table 6.5). Although the figures for Banff and Bute do not entirely fit in with this pattern, this is due more to a fault in the source material than to any marked deviation in the pattern of landholding.[23] In Inverness-shire the figures are distorted slightly by the fact that six estates valued at a total of £11,334 Scots were, in 1770, in the hands of the Annexed Estates Commission and are therefore grouped with Institutions rather than under individual owners who temporarily lost control between 1745 and the 1780s.[24] In these counties the

Table 6.4: The Pattern of Landholding in the Eastern Region, 1770

County	Percentage of Valued Rent Controlled			
	Great Landlords	Lairds	Bonnet Lairds	Institutions and Corporate Bodies
Midlothian	40.8	53.9	3.7	1.6
Peebles	41.0	50.7	2.8	5.5
Fife	44.4	48.7	3.7	3.2
Perth	41.4	47.7	5.1	5.8
Kincardine	39.7	50.0	0.5	9.8
Aberdeen	50.0	44.2	1.3	4.5
Angus	49.7	46.2	3.0	1.1
Berwick	50.5	48.5	3.5	0.5
West Lothian	53.2	42.4	4.4	0

percentages controlled by the landed aristocracy are much higher than that of the wealthy landlords, with the exception of Nairn and Bute. In these small counties a landowner with an estate valued at over £4,000 Scots would have controlled over quarter of the total.

Table 6.5: The Pattern of Landholding in the Highland Region, 1770

County	Percentage of Valued Rent Controlled			
	Great Landlords	Lairds	Bonnet Lairds	Institutions and Corporate Bodies
Moray	57.6	39.0	1.2	2.2
Banff	26.2	64.8	6.0	3.0
Nairn	55.8	42.3	1.2	0.7
Inverness	40.8	39.9	3.8	15.5
Sutherland	67.7	31.6	0.7	0
Orkney	54.1	38.7	7.1	0.1
Bute	52.8	38.1	9.1	0
Argyll	46.0	51.2	1.9	0.9
Caithness	44.4	47.3	1.6	6.7
Ross and Cromarty	40.0	50.1	0.9	9.0

In the remaining counties of Caithness, Ross and Cromarty and Argyll, the great landlords controlled only 40-46 per cent of the total, whereas the lairds controlled 47-51 per cent. It has been noted that the eighteenth-century social structure of Caithness and Ross and Cromarty showed them to be enclaves of the Lowlands[25] and this is also reflected in the pattern of landholding existing in 1770, which had more in common with that of Midlothian than with that of their Highland neighbours. At the other end of the scale, another characteristic feature of these Highland counties is the small percentage controlled by bonnet lairds, except in Orkney where unique circumstances prevailed.

Although not included in the national system owing to the nature of the source material, Shetland cannot be entirely omitted.[26] It is clear that the pattern of landholding was similar to that of neighbouring Orkney, the system of udal tenure serving to accentuate the share held by the smaller owner-occupiers or udallers.[27] Hence of the total merklands recorded in the rental, 78 per cent were listed under udal lands.

In addition to the 33 counties, there are also data concerning the cities of Edinburgh and Glasgow (Table 6.6). Comparisons are difficult as the twentieth-century boundaries give Edinburgh a much larger landward portion of eighteenth-century Midlothian than Glasgow acquired from Lanark and Renfrew. This is reflected in the relative valuations of the cities, for Edinburgh had a total of £77,000 Scots, whereas Glasgow had only a quarter of this. Potential variations are masked, but were unlikely to be large as the landholding pattern outside the two royal burghs was subject to similar pressures in 1770.

Table 6.6: The Pattern of Landholding in the Cities of Edinburgh and Glasgow, 1770

| City | Percentage of Valued Rent Controlled[a] | | | | | | | |
	1	2	3	4	5	6	Corporate Bodies	Institutions
Edinburgh	0	15.2	24.9	18.3	22.1	6.9	1.5	11.1
Glasgow	0	0	5.8	7.4	35.2	21.3	7.3	23.0

a. The numbers one to six heading the columns refer to the subdivisions of the landowning class listed in Figure 6.1.

Individuals, although owning the vast majority of the landed wealth in 1770, were not the only element in the pattern of landholding as corporate bodies and institutions also owned estates. Corporate bodies accounted for a very small proportion of the valued rent of the counties of the Highlands and Borders, but were more numerous in the two intervening regions. Much of the wealth thus controlled in the eastern region was in the hands of the York Buildings Company[28] and the majority of the remainder in the hands of towns or burghs. In the west and central region the picture was more diverse with towns, companies and trade associations all being represented, as in the lands covered by the cities of Glasgow and Edinburgh.

On paper, institutions appear to be more evenly spread over the country, but this is only partially true, as in the Highland region 6 out of 13 entries related to the Crown and a further 4 to the Forfeited Estates commissioners. In the Borders region the entries related to hospitals, colleges and other charitable organisations. The eastern region had by far the greatest number and variety of institutions, whereas the west and central region, although large, had surprisingly few. In the cities of Edinburgh and Glasgow the number of institutions tends to reflect the differences between east and west, as the former had eight entries and the latter only two.

Change in the Eighteenth Century

Was there any significant change in this pattern from the beginning of the century up to 1770? The dearth of contemporary evidence for the early years of the century reflects the general apathy and lack of stimulus to inquiry that were characteristic of the time. Valuation rolls are the only records to give any statistical data, although even these are few in number and of varying quality.[29] It is clear that in the Highland region there was a fall in the average number of owners per parish in all counties where statistics are available. Thus in Morayshire, the average per parish fell from 8.3 (1667) to 6 (1773); in Ross and Cromarty, from 7.8 (1743) to 6.1 (1756) and to 5 (1794); in Argyllshire, from 14.4 (1684) to 11.5 (1751); and in Caithness, from approximately 10 (1702) to 7.1 (1751) and again to 6.3 (1790s). In the Borders, evidence is more scanty, although from the figures relating to Roxburgh, where the average number of owners per parish fell from 12.1 (1678) to 10.1 (1771), it would appear that here too estates were diminishing in number. Statistics for the west and central region came from the counties of Lanark, Renfrew, Ayrshire and Stirling. From the evidence it appears that these counties did not experience a fall in numbers as large as those of other regions. Thus in Ayrshire, the average number of owners per parish fell from 21 (1705/8) to 19.2 (c. 1770) and in Renfrew, from 16.6 (1654) to 14.1 (1735). In the eastern region, statistics exist for the majority of counties and in all cases the average number of owners per parish diminishes in the early part of the century. Thus in Berwick, the average number per parish fell from 16.5 (1680) to 12.8 (1772), in Aberdeen from 8.9 (1674) to 5.5 (1771), in Kincardine, from 8 (1657) to 6.3 (1771) and in Midlothian, from 16.1 (1680) to 12 (1771).

In the opening decades of the century the percentage of the total agrarian wealth owned by the large landowners increased in every county to the detriment of the lesser and bonnet lairds, the amount varying with the pattern of landholding within the county. The depressed economy saw little demand for land except from the wealthier established owners, and in areas such as the west and central region, where aristocratic influence was small, change was less marked. There is ample evidence that the forces favouring aggregation were considerably weakened in the thirty years up to 1770, and indeed in some cases the process was reversed despite increasing activity in the land market. As the economy prospered, prices rose and the economic forces working against the small landowners lessened, allowing many to hold on to their land. In addition, the established landowners faced increasing competition for estates as merchants, planters and lawyers with profits from other fields competed for estates. Thus in Morayshire, although the average number of owners per parish fell from 8.3 to 5.5 between 1667 and 1747, it fell only another 0.5 between

1747 and 1773. Similarly in the eastern region: in Peebles, the average number of owners per parish increased from 6.6 to 7.4 between c. 1736 and 1761, and in Aberdeen, it increased marginally from 6.5 (1741) to 6.7 (1754). In Kincardine, there was only a marginal fall between 1744 and 1771, from 6.5 to 6.3.

Evidence for the last part of the century is more abundant, although often still of a random nature. The statistics presented in Table 6.7 form the basis of the following discussion supplemented by evidence from valuation rolls, the *Old Statistical Account* and other secondary sources. It is worthy of note that the figures quoted in the final column are not always complete, as Sinclair himself notes that his evidence relating to the lowest group of valued rent is weak in places.

In the west and central region, although aristocratic control was small and competition from newcomers high, consolidation of holdings still took place in many counties, the number of large estates increasing in Lanark, Ayr, Stirling and Clackmannan, remaining stable in Kinross and Renfrew, and decreasing only in Dunbarton. The accompanying fall in numbers in the other classifications seen in Ayr, Stirling and Clackmannan is reversed in Lanark, denoting fragmentation of holdings, as one would expect in a county so involved in urbanisation and industrialisation. This is reflected by the fact that the average number of owners per parish rose from 23.3 (1770) to c. 34 (1790s).[30]

In the Border region, although there was a high level of aristocratic control, aggregation was severely limited, as there was a very active land market. Competition for residential estates in areas both beautiful and not too distant from the centres of population meant that newcomers were actively purchasing estates in this area. Hence in Roxburgh, where in 1770 over 62 per cent of the agrarian wealth was controlled by 15 members of the landed aristocracy, the turnover of the other 200 or so holdings was high.[31] Under such conditions there was a slight upward trend in numbers of owners, as seen in Selkirkshire, where numbers rose from 41 (1770) to 43 (1786) and again to 44 (1814); in Dumfries, where they rose from 413 plus four groups of heritors (1770) to 445 (1814) and in Roxburgh, where numbers increased from 220 plus 19 groups to 349, also between 1770 and 1814.

The general trend in the counties of the eastern region was again towards the larger estates, resulting in a decline in the number of owners between 1770 and 1814 in most counties, with the exceptions of Midlothian, Angus and Kincardine. In Midlothian, there was clearly a move towards the middle and smaller estates, to be expected near the capital city, whereas in the other two counties changes were marginal. East Lothian, although having a pattern of landholding akin to the Borders, shows changes akin to those found in Fife or Perth where the great landlords increased at the expense of the other two classes.

When the figures for 1770 and 1814 seen in Table 6.7 are compared for the counties of the Highland region, it becomes clear that in every case the great landlords were consolidating their position at the expense of the lesser landowners. Thus in the Highlands, where aristocratic control was actually less than

Table 6.7: Number of Landowners: the County Totals of 1770 and 1814 Compared (in £ Scots)[a]

County	above £2,000 Sc		£500-£2,000 Sc		Below £500 Sc	
	1770	1814	1770	1814	1770 (+ group)	1814
Aberdeen	26	28	85	88	144 (+ 1)	114
Angus	20	16	56	59	158 (+ 3)	191
Argyll	10	17	52	43	138 (+ 2)	131
Ayr	14	20	65	51	680 (+ 3)	200
Banff	4	9	25	17	148 (+ 3)	14
Berwick	21	22	67	59	109 (+ 12)	152
Bute	2	2	3	2	39	6
Caithness	5	5	13	11	32	14
Clackmannan	2	4	11	6	24 (+ 4)	22
Dumfries	4	10	31	30	378 (+ 4)	405
Dunbarton	3	1	13	19	162	136
East Lothian	22	23	37	29	138	133
Fife	34	45	108	102	497 (+ 10)	491
Inverness	6	12	17	18	107	57
Kincardine	7	11	32	29	35	46
Kinross	0	0	6	7	154	161
Kirkcudbright	9	7	37	40	238	354
Lanark[b]	7	9	46	50	779 (+ 6)	1096
Midlothian[c]	17	10	67	92	418 (+ 1)	569
Moray	8	7	19	18	45	23
Nairn	3	3	5	3	8	9
Orkney	3	4	13	11	304	195
Peebles	5	6	19	21	65	54
Perth	31	39	100	95	662 (+ 1)	621
Renfrew	6	6	25	22	173 (+ 5)	300
Ross & Crom.[d]	8	13	31	27	69	55
Roxburgh	29	33	48	55	143 (+ 19)	261
Selkirk	9	9	20	20	12	15
Stirling	3	9	40	29	522 (+ 3)	109
Sutherland	3	2	4	3	19	8
West Lothian	8	8	20	22	139 (+ 2)	122
Wigtown	7	6	17	16	105	83
Zetland	0	0	0	0	0	0

a. This information comes from the *Directory* and Sir John Sinclair's *General Report*, p. 122.

b. Figures for 1770 and 1814 include Glasgow. Proprietors owning in both are allowed for.

c. Figures for 1770 and 1814 include Edinburgh. Proprietors owning in both are allowed for.

d. Figures for 1814 are those of Ross and Cromarty added together and no allowance can be made for proprietors owning in both counties.

in the Borders, aggregation was more marked because of a lack of competition from newcomers.

Overall, therefore, in the decades after 1770, just as in those previously, the eighteenth century saw a movement towards larger estates. In certain areas, especially near urban centres, it was reversed, giving a less marked trend overall, but it was evident nevertheless. The most vital factors in this later period were the influx of newcomers and a very active land market, rather than large shifts of control from one class of landowner to another.

There is little evidence relating to any changes which might have occurred in the number or size of estates controlled by institutions or corporate bodies. Of the two most important institutions in 1770, the Crown saw no change in its property within the century and the Forfeited Estates Commission had only a transient effect on the pattern of landholding. The same can be said of the York Buildings Company, which was the largest corporate body in 1770, but which had little lasting effect. It is unlikely that the property controlled by other members of these categories changed much within the century. The price of land was so high that the majority of institutions and corporate bodies had little chance of acquiring additional property and on the other hand, once acquired, property was rarely sold unless it could be feued to good advantage.[32]

Conclusion

If the basic continuity and slowness of change in the pattern of landholding is considered, along with the growing importance of non-economic motives for the possession and acquisition of land, one is almost justified in regarding this pattern of landholding as a social system within which economic change operated. The great landlords controlled just over 50 per cent of the total agrarian wealth of Scotland in 1770, although county figures range from 0 to 73.6 per cent. Change was slow over the century but always the larger estates retained their position, or grew, for the sale of land by this class was rare. The lairds nationally controlled 41.6 per cent of the total in 1770, and change within the century meant a decline in the power of the lower orders of this class early in the century, although this was almost halted in the second half, especially in the 1790s. Unlike the great landlords, however, the lairds saw a change in their membership under the influence of a very active land market. The bonnet lairds were the most numerous class, though controlling only 5 per cent of the land in 1770. This class saw a continuous diminution in its numbers in the eighteenth century, the tide only being stemmed temporarily late in the century when rising prices coupled with increased opportunities for additional employment helped the small owner to make an adequate living.

The pattern of landholding which has emerged can throw new light on many subjects associated with the eighteenth-century landowner. The connection between the pattern of landholding and the timing and character of agrarian improvement is not a simple one, but it is clear that the size of an estate had an indirect effect. In the early stages it was the wealthy enthusiast who undertook new methods on a small scale, but as the obvious advantages of the new husbandry became apparent, then the hard core of lairds began implementing the new methods. In general, these men were landlords who relied on their estates for their income. Their crucial role in the Improving Movement is discussed by Adams in Chapter 7. The pattern of landholding can also bring a fresh viewpoint to the study of the changing landscape in eighteenth-century Scotland. The distribution of policies will reflect the pattern of landholding, as they were most numerous in areas where the lairds predominated and sparse in areas where one landowner or a multiplicity of feuars existed (see Chapter 10). Again, the small landowner had neither the land nor the money to plant more than a few trees as a windbreak, whereas the wealthier landowner had the resources to plan for the future and consequently reafforest large areas if he chose. Similarly, the location of planned villages depended on a variety of factors, but there is no doubt that it took a wealthy man to undertake such a scheme and he required an estate large enough to support such a village community (see Chapter 12).

In addition to research building on that already completed for the eighteenth century, there is also a need for more data on a national level. There has been no other study made of the landholding pattern in Scotland except Millman's work on the 1970s,[33] and although sources are few as one enters the seventeenth century, there is no such dearth in the nineteenth. There is also room for work at a local level, for although studies in depth have been attempted, these need to be correlated and wide gaps exist. Scope also exists for work on other fronts associated with landholding, such as the activity and character of the land market, the incomes of landowners, and the condition of the smaller landowners, especially in the early decades of the eighteenth century.

Notes

1. Saunders, L. J. (1950), *Scottish democracy 1815-1840, the social and intellectual background* (Edinburgh), p. 15

2. Adam, Sir C. E. (1887), *A view of the political state of Scotland in the last century* (Edinburgh)

3. Mackie, J. D. (1966), *A history of Scotland* (London), p. 279

4. There were 30 county and 15 burghal constituencies in Scotland after 1707

5. Pryde, G. S. (1960), *Central and local government in Scotland since 1707* (London), p. 8

6. Lythe, S. G. E. and Butt, J. (1975), *An economic history of Scotland 1100-1939* (Glasgow), p. 109

7. Smout, T. C. (1969), *A history of the Scottish people, 1560-1830* (London), p. 506

8. Mathias, P. (1957), 'The social structure in the 18th century; a calculation by Joseph Massie', *Economic History Review* (2nd series), *10*, 30-45; Thompson, F. M. L., 'The social distribution of landed property in England since the 16th century', *Economic History Review*, *19*, 505-17; Mingay, G. E., 'Enclosure and the small farmer in the age of the industrial revolution', *Economic History Society, Studies in Economic History* (London), 40-2

9. Handley, J. E. (1963), *The agricultural revolution in Scotland* (Glasgow), p. 1; Adams, I. H. (1975), 'Economic process and the Scottish land surveyor', *Imago Mundi, 27*, 13-18; Third, B. M. W. (1953), 'The changing rural geography of the Scottish lowlands, 1700-1820' (unpublished PhD thesis, University of Edinburgh), II, Ch. 6

10. This tax was at first an extraordinary way of raising money invoked only in emergencies, but it became more and more common, until by the eighteenth century it was an annual occurrence.

11. Mackie, J. D. (ed.) (1946), *Register of brieves, 1286-1386: Thomas Thomson's memorial on old extent* (Stair Society Publication)

12. There were, however, two Exchequer Orders in 1771 and 1802 demanding that copies of the valuation rolls were to be sent to the Office of the Presenter of Signatures. The response was far from complete, but there is a definite clustering of rolls in the years after these orders.

13. Timperley, L. R. (1976), *A directory of landownership in Scotland c. 1770* (Scottish Record Society), new series, *5*

14. See Timperley, L. R. (1977), 'Landownership in Scotland in the 18th century' (unpublished PhD thesis, University of Edinburgh), pp. 106-27. The percentages quoted hereafter come from these amended statistics at county and national levels

15. Smout (1969), *A history of the Scottish people*, p. 137

16. Mingay, G. E. (1963), *English landed society in the 18th century* (London), p. 8. Although the nomenclature used in this work is similar to that used by Mingay, comparisons cannot be made, as the levels of income used for each subclass are much lower in Scotland than in England

17. Gregory King, Joseph Massie and Patrick Colquhoun produced statistics for 1688, 1760 and 1803 respectively; see Mathias (1957), 'Social structure in the 18th century'

18. Sinclair, Sir John (1791-9), *The statistical account of Scotland . . .* (OSA) (Edinburgh), Vol. 20 (appendix), p. 87; *idem*, Vol. 21 (Edinburgh), pp. 471-2; *Scots Magazine* (1748), 228; Sinclair, Sir John (1814), *General report of the agricultural state and political circumstances of Scotland* (Edinburgh), Vol. I, p. 123; Wilson, R. (1815), *An enquiry into the causes of the high prices of corn and labour* (Edinburgh), pp. 47-9, quoted in Smout (1969), *A history of the Scottish people*, p. 310; Smout, T. C. and Fenton, A. (1965), 'Scottish agriculture before the Improvers – an exploration', *Agricultural History Review, 13*, 73-93; Smout (1969), *A history of the Scottish people*, p. 291; Handley, J. E. (1953), *Scottish farming in the 18th century* (London), pp. 269-70

19. No discernible pattern emerges when the numbers of owners owning in more than one county are considered on a regional basis.

20. Thompson, F. M. L. (1963), *English landed society in the 19th century* (London), p. 32

21. See Symon, J. A. (1959), *Scottish farming past and present* (Edinburgh), Chs. 3-5; Athol Murray in McNeill, P. and Nicholson, R. (1975), *An historical atlas of Scotland c. 400-c. 1600* (St Andrews); Sanderson, M. H. B. (1973), 'The feuars of kirklands', *Scottish Historical Review, 52*, 117-48; and McNeill and Nicholson (1975), *Historical atlas of Scotland*

22. Slaven, A. (1975), *The development of the west of Scotland 1750-1960* (London), p. 61

23. See Timperley (1977), *Landownership in Scotland*, pp. 114-15

24. See the inventory of records held in the Scottish Record Office (SRO) under the E700-788 series for a list of those who forfeited estates.

25. Donaldson, J. E. (1938), *Caithness in the 18th century* (Edinburgh), p. 39; and Cruickshank, J. B. (1961), 'The Black Isle, Ross-shire: a land use study', *Scottish Geographical Magazine* (hereafter SGM), *77*, 3-14

26. No valuation roll exists for this county but a rental of 1772 gives much information. See Timperley (1976), *Directory of landownership*

27. Udal tenure, found in the islands of Orkney and Shetland in the eighteenth century, was of Norse origin. Each udaller paid a tribute called 'scat' to the Crown as immediate superior, but had no charter or sasine in return, undisturbed possession being considered proof enough. Under Norse law, land was divided equally among the children of a deceased person and so by the eighteenth century a multiplicity of udallers existed

28. The York Buildings Company, originally chartered in 1691, was bought in 1719 by Mr Billingsley and his associates, who floated a joint-stock fund to purchase forfeited estates. At first the company appeared successful but over-expenditure soon led to financial difficulties. Company officials could not deal with the problems arising on estates where

agriculture was primitive and the people fiercely loyal to their previous landlords. After much litigation and the sale of the estates one by one, the company was dissolved in 1829

29. All the statistics quoted in this section regarding average numbers of owners per parish come from the respective valuation rolls listed by county and date in the E106 series in the SRO. Exceptions are those entries dated 1790s which come from the respective parishes in the *Old statistical account* and those of 1814 which come from Sinclair (1814), *Statistical account of Scotland*, p. 122

30. This figure is based on entries in the *Old statistical account* and is a very rough approximation

31. Sommerville, T. (1861), *My own life and times, 1741-1814* (Edinburgh), pp. 359-60

32. A good example is the land dealings of Hutcheson's Hospital, Glasgow: see Kellet, J. R. (1961), 'Property speculators and the building of Glasgow', *Scottish Journal of Political Economy, 8*, 213-17

33. Millman, R. (1969), 'The marches of the Highland estates', *SGM, 85*, 3, 172-81; (1970) 'The landed properties of Northern Scotland', *SGM, 86*, 186-203; *idem* (1972), 'The landed estates of Southern Scotland', *SGM, 88*, 126-33

7 THE AGENTS OF AGRICULTURAL CHANGE

I. H. Adams

Although the dynamics of economic and geographic change in eighteenth-century Scotland have attracted considerable interest, a recent debate as to the existence of an Agricultural Revolution typifies the rudimentary level of understanding so far attained.[1] Yet sufficient research has been completed to appreciate what happened, even if the interrelationships of the various strands remain less well understood. To understand why it happened demands further research, and not primarily in the field of geography, for the radical changes that occurred were determined by people, and not by geography.

Scotland's take-off on the path of sustained economic change had to await a transformation of will by a small group of people, the landowners, who had it in their power to control the pace of change in society. The desire for change manifested itself in the later years of the seventeenth century, but the agricultural depression of the 1690s, followed by years of glut at the beginning of the eighteenth century, did little to nurture economic conditions favouring the long-term reorganisation of agriculture. The political uncertainties of the time were resolved neither by the Act of Union, nor by the 1715 Rebellion, and they remained unresolved during the first significant economic developments in the late 1720s. The foundation of the Society of Improvers in 1723 and the establishment of the Board of Manufacturers in 1727 gave sufficient impetus to encourage several landowners to embark on the improvement of their estates. A low plateau of development ensued but the caution shown by the large majority of landowners was subsequently justified, for the Rebellion of 1745 bore witness to the fact that underlying political uncertainties had lingered in stronger measure than many had thought. Thereafter, in apparent unison, Scottish landowners went about improving their estates with a verve that reached fever pitch.

This chapter is about the role of people as agents of geographical change. People in this case are individuals, for when one examines agrarian changes which amount to the complete subversion of an established system and the establishment of a new authority, individuals must count. The revolutionaries in this case are a band of people called 'Improvers', who were generally landowners, but occasionally included tenants.[2] The fact that the improvers had authority over their lands prior to the changes made them no less revolutionary, for they were a very small and closely linked group.

Although blood relationship and marriage did not themselves imply the certain diffusion of agrarian change, they did establish a pattern of peer relationships across the country which reduced the friction of geographical distance on the interchange of ideas. In particular, a great interest, and almost interference, was manifested by relatives when it came to the improvement of each others' estates. As an example of this cross-fertilisation we can examine the activities of the 8th Earl of Kinnoull and his cousin the 6th Earl of Findlater (Figure 7.1). When the Earl of Kinnoull was absent abroad, Findlater looked after his estates and acted as his commissioner. Both earls took a strong interest in Findlater's nephew, James Grant of Grant, and his improving activities. When Findlater died in 1770, Kinnoull became the commissioner for the young 7th earl, who spent most of his life abroad. Similarly, Findlater's brother-in-law, the 2nd Earl of Hopetoun, was the curator-in-law for his cousin's insane son, the 3rd Marquis of Annandale. Thus the influence of blood relationships on agricultural improvement extended from the shores of the Solway Firth to the shores of the Moray Firth.

Figure 7.1: Network of Blood and Marriage Relationships for Sir James Grant of Grant

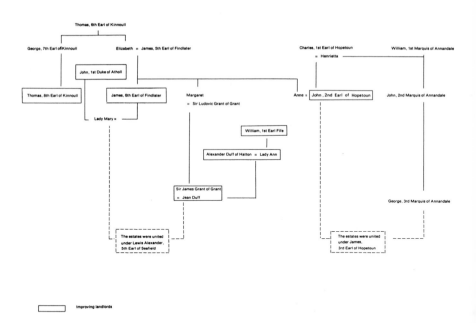

Network of blood and marriage relationships among improving landlords from whom Sir James Grant of Grant received advice.

Landowners had little competition for the political or economic power they possessed at this time, and few other groups came anywhere near their level of prestige. Closest were the judges of the Court of Session, and occasionally the merchant barons of the tobacco trade. The towns rarely threw up men of any real stature, Provost George Drummond of Edinburgh being a prominent exception. For the most part the burghs were rather sad places, whose leaders wallowed in their own corruption. The landowners filled the political positions themselves, or with their nominees, and their patronage was essential to enable professional men to gain a living. Thus when the great changes occurred in the period 1748 to 1770, they exercised authority with mutual support, evidence of which has been preserved in letters, memoranda and reports in the family muniments of the aristocrats of Scotland. From these documents one can construct the networks of communication in the business of agrarian change (Figure 7.2). It is clear that here was a tightly knit group of men determined to institute great changes in the fabric and society of Scotland. They began to make those changes on their own, and on the Annexed Estates, for there they could exercise the authority to make an Agricultural Revolution.

The Annexed Estates

The Annexed Estates comprised the 13 largest of the estates originally forfeited to the Crown by the attainder for treason of owners implicated in the 1745 Rebellion. Ardsheal, Arnprior, Barrisdale, Callart, Cluny, Cromarty, Kinlochmoidart, Lochgarry, Locheil, Lovat, Monaltry, Perth and Struan were singled out for special attention as part of the government's scheme to eliminate the threat of Jacobitism by removing some of the basic causes of discontent and disaffection in the Highlands. The Annexing Act of 1752 (26 Geo. II c.41) provided that the rents and profits arising from them were to be used solely for the

> purpose of civilising the inhabitants upon the said estates, and other parts of the Highlands and Islands of Scotland, the promoting amongst them the Protestant religion, good government, industry and manufactures, and the principles of duty and loyalty to his Majesty, his heirs and successors.

The commissioners appointed under the Act fulfilled its terms and carried out large-scale improvements in agriculture and forestry, encouraged the fishing industry, promoted linen and other manufactures, erected schools and churches and improved communications, until their efforts were brought to an end by the Disannexing Act of 1784 (24 Geo. III c.57).

The commissioners' schemes depended largely on accurate information about the extent and resources of the estates under their charge, which extended from the remote sea lochs of Wester Ross to the fertile lands of Strathearn, the estate of Perth alone spreading over fifty miles from the lower course of the Tay to the flanks of Ben More. The Annexing Act had expressly empowered them to have the lands surveyed and plans made 'setting forth the extent and different

Figure 7.2: Network of Improvers

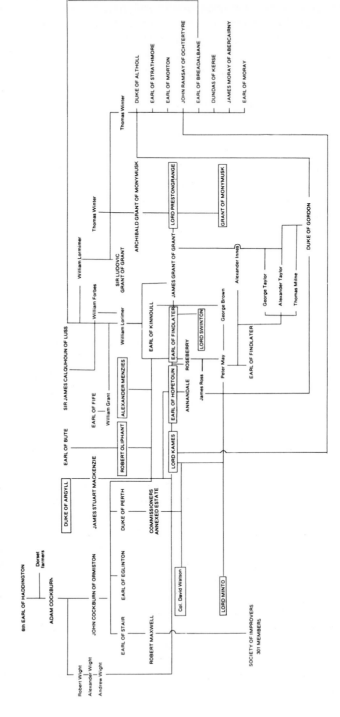

Each line represents documented flows of information. Every Scottish county is represented in the diagram.

qualities of the grounds, the several advantages and disadvantages arising from their situation and what improvements may be made upon the same'. Though there was a long delay in appointing the commissioners under the Act, once appointed they wasted no time before applying themselves to this very question. One of the commissioners, Lieutenant-Colonel David Watson, to whom William Roy had been responsible in his Military Survey from 1747 to 1755, laid before their first meeting, on 23 June 1755, a paper entitled 'Instructions to the surveyors to be employed in surveying the Forfeited Estates', which was amended and approved at the next meeting on 30 June.[3] This proved to be one of the most important documents in the history of agricultural improvements in Scotland, for the commissioners included twenty of Scotland's leading landed proprietors, and its terms were to be echoed repeatedly in the instructions given by individual landowners to their own surveyors over the next few years.[4] Time and again the pioneering activities of the commissioners, be it mineral surveys, land-use surveys, drainage schemes or planned villages, stimulated others to emulate them.

Agricultural Revolution

All too often the Agricultural Revolution has been measured in terms of the introduction of new crops, lime, rotation or enclosures, but in essence it was a revolution in the management of the countryside of which these innovations were only a part. New economic goals were the key element, towards which 'rational principles' were adopted that can be described as the application of Newtonian science to agriculture.[5] The scientific aspect, however, stressed geometry and numeracy, and the numeracy especially valued was money. Thus the customary elements such as rents in kind, services and thirlage were replaced by this most accountable of commodities. Once commutation was begun, the whole of the land could be re-evaluated and brought into full production: in simple terms the rent yield per unit was increased. Reorganisation implied the creation of ideal management units (the individual farm), the demand for scientific agricultural practices (the lease), and a diminution of people on the land (the prohibition of subletting).

The Agricultural Revolution demanded the action of different agents — the pioneers, the generators, the adopters, the implementors and the managers — to give it the momentum for universal adoption. The pioneers were a group who introduced the novel ideas in the face of general hostility and often their singular lack of success, at times leading to bankruptcy, confirmed the sceptics' convictions. The generators were a group, usually of considerable power in society, who recognised the benefits of improvement and were able not only to reorganise their own lands, but also to create the necessary infrastructure, for example the construction of turnpike roads by Commissioners of Supply. When success had the imprimatur of respectability, it was then emulated by the adopters who did not wish to be seen lagging behind their peer group or superiors. In order to execute change, these three categories required the services of implementors and in Scotland, implementors were mainly land surveyors and principal estate officials who had a firm grasp of the new methods. Finally, there were the managers, mostly commissioners and factors, who nurtured the new system to its full potential.

Improvement in Practice

Geographical analysis of innovation diffusion and adoption has portrayed the individual decision-taker as a neutral character. The main element has been space through which information is assumed to flow exogenously towards the potential innovator. On the other hand, economic historians have stressed the role of certain individuals – Coke of Norfolk,[6] Henry Home, Lord Kames,[7] Grant of Monymusk,[8] Sir John Sinclair of Ulbster,[9] Jethro Tull,[10] Arthur Young[11] – at the expense of the vast majority of self-effacing improvers. Neither of these positions allows adequate explanation of the speed and comprehensiveness of change in Scotland during the second half of the eighteenth century.

The complexity of the decision-making process leading to improvement and the interaction of landowner, implementors and managers can best be illustrated in the context of a specific example.

The Landowner

The estates of the Grant of Grant family lay in Strathspey and extended up into the Cairngorms. The lands had been in the family's hands for centuries and were run in the time-honoured fashion of the clan in which the chief's status was largely linked to the extent of land possessed and the number of people he commanded. The turning-point for the Grant estates came in 1763 when Sir Ludovick Grant made over the management of his lands to his son James. In the following ten years James Grant initiated 'agricultural and social improvement, in settlement schemes for disbanded soldiers, and from 1765 in founding his new town of Granton'.[12] James Grant was held in considerable esteem by contemporaries for his role as an agricultural improver, but a detailed examination of the records indicates he had a considerable capacity for allowing others to make his reputation for him. It is possible to reconstruct something of the network of communication around Grant which fostered the diffusion of 'improving' ideas (Figure 7.3). It seems that he was so showered with advice from relatives and well-wishers that at times it reached nagging proportions. His cousin, Lord Deskford, was one of his most assiduous and not altogether appreciated advisers. In February 1761, he wrote to James Grant:

Plate 1: Haddington (East Lothian), 1693
The small town of Haddington lay in the centre of a 'hearth area' for agricultural improvement in Scotland; but even here the parks around the houses and mains of the progressive landowners, and the town crofts were the only enclosed features in the landscape of the 1690s. The town fields are still cultivated in open-ridged strips. There are few trees except in the gardens and orchards of the town. The bare hills of the Lammermuirs form the backdrop. (Source: J. Slezer, *Theatrum Scotiae*, London, 1693.)

Plate 2: Sheiling Bothies on Jura (1790)
The temporary huts of turf and stone built around a timber frame on the mountain pastures of Highland communities attracted much attention from English visitors in the eighteenth century. These visitors often failed to appreciate their temporary nature, and the dwellings and their inhabitants were frequently condemned for their primitive construction and slothful disposition. (Source: T. Pennant, *A Tour in Scotland I*, London, 1790.)

Plate 3: Thatched One-storey Cottages near Scone (Perthshire), 1693
Rural housing standards of the tenantry began to improve in the late seventeenth century.
Until that time one-storey cottages were frequently cruck-framed consisting of a single room
with a central hearth, and constructed from impermanent materials. Long houses divided
into two or three rooms were found in some areas. Such cottages fronted directly onto the
unpaved street and sometimes had no back yard. (Source: J. Slezer, *Theatrum Scotiae*,
London, 1693.)

Plate 4: Enclosed Farmstead near St Andrews (Fife), 1693
On progressive estates, larger tenants were provided with improved farmsteads. Long houses
were replaced by courtyard farms with barns and byres grouped around an enclosed rick-
yard. The farmhouse was sometimes of two storeys and became a more permanent dwelling
of stone and lime. An enclosed vegetable garden and orchard were frequently located beside
the farmstead. (Source: J. Slezer, *Theatrum Scotiae*, London, 1693.)

Plate 5: J. & C. Blaeu's Map of Lothian and Linlithgow (1654)
Blaeu's *Atlas Novus* provides the first comprehensive cartographic coverage of Scotland. The finely-engraved maps allow a number of elements in the rural landscape to be discerned, particularly settlements, roads and parks. Some of Blaeu's maps, including this one of Lothian and Linlithgow, are based directly upon the manuscript surveys of Timothy Pont made in the 1590s. The large number of enclosed parks in the vicinity of Edinburgh, and the Esk and Tyne valleys, are a notable feature of the developing countryside. (Source: J. & C. Blaeu *Atlas Novus*, Amsterdam, 1654.)

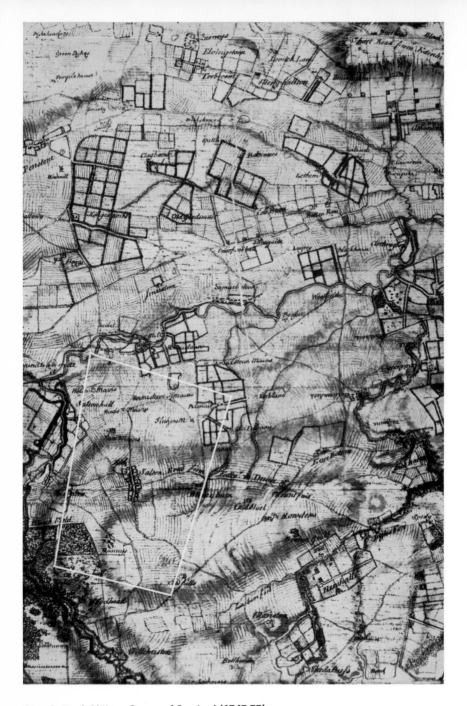

Plate 6: Roy's Military Survey of Scotland (1747-55)
The Military Survey of Scotland provides an incomparable record of the Scottish rural landscape towards the end of the first phase of 'Improvement'. The houses and mains of many landowners had been rebuilt and enclosed in the first half of the eighteenth century and feature on the Survey as islands of rectangular fields bordered by shelter belts. Beyond the mains farms, however, lay extensive areas of unimproved and unenclosed land which were to be the focus for the phase of accelerated agricultural change in the late eighteenth century. A comparison of the outline area with Plate 7 illustrates this second phase of change. (Source: British Museum, Maps C9b.)

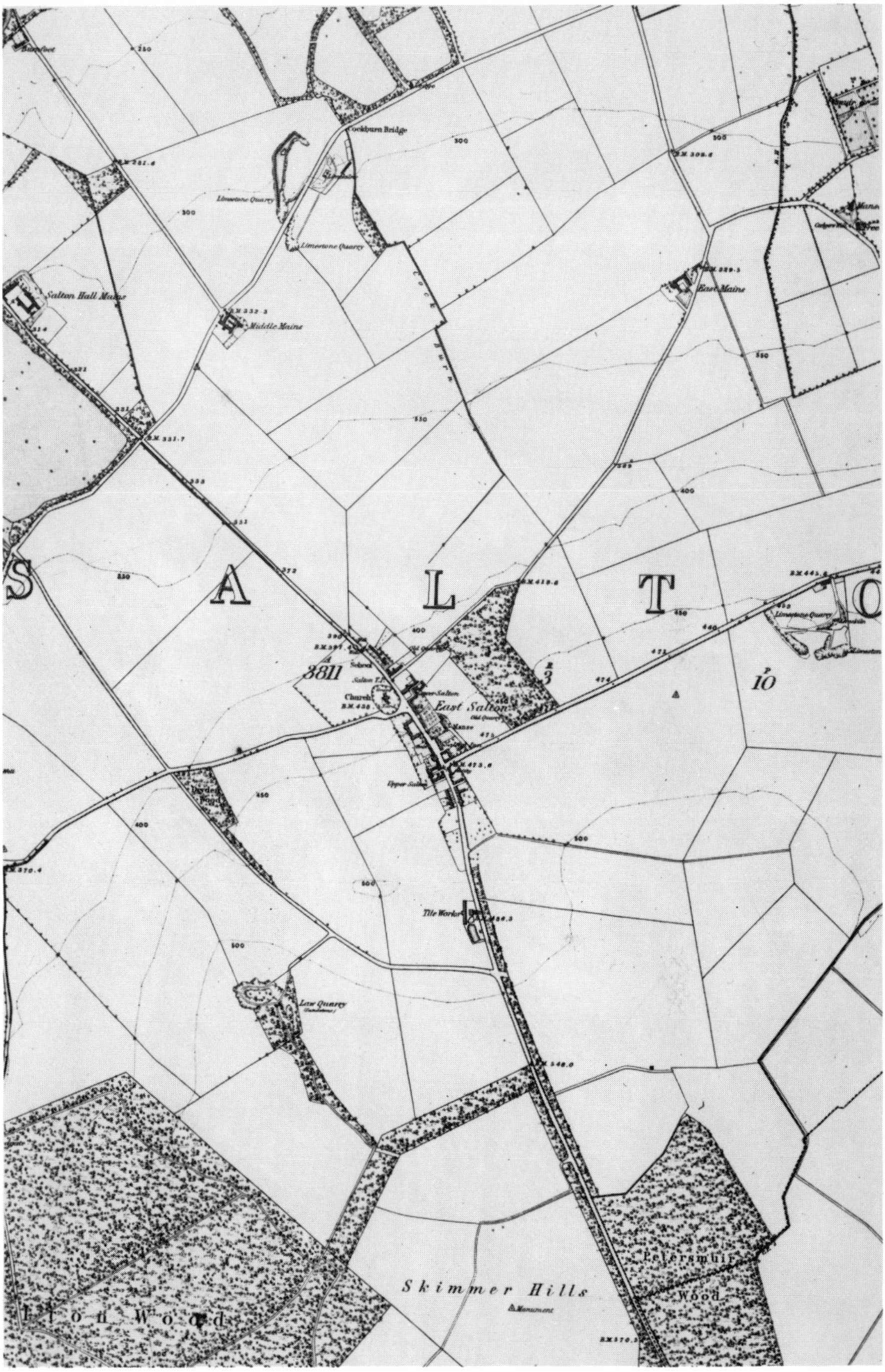

Plate 7: The First Edition Ordnance Survey 6 Inch to 1 Mile Plan (1855)
The culmination of the process of enclosure and its impact on the Scottish rural landscape
is recorded on the Ordnance Survey's first edition 6 inch plans. A comparison with Plate 6
illustrates the scale of landscape change: the road network has been reorganised, fields
enclosed with hedges and walls, new courtyard farmsteads erected, quarries opened for
building stone and for lime and shelter belts and fox coverts planted. (Source: sheet XIV
first edn O.S 1:10,560, East Lothian.)

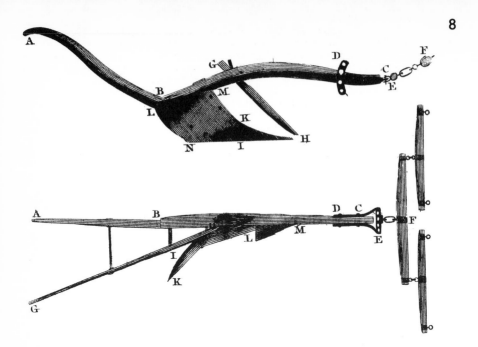

Plate 8: Small's Swing Plough

Small's swing plough was first introduced on farms in east Berwickshire in *c.* 1763 and by about 1780 was commonly in use throughout south-east Scotland. The new plough was lighter than older, wooden ploughs and it needed fewer draught animals and less manpower to operate. However, it was more easily damaged by stones in the furrows and its advantages were quickly lost in tilling crooked and uneven ridges. The levelling of ridges thus quickly followed its adoption. (Source: Sir John Sinclair, *An account of the systems of Husbandry of Scotland II appendix 5*, Edinburgh, 1813.)

Plate 9: Cultivation Ridges, near Greenlaw, Berwickshire

High-backed and curved ridges were a characteristic feature of arable land before the levelling and straightening of ridges that was encouraged by the adoption of farm machinery in the late eighteenth and early nineteenth century. Where relict cultivation ridges survive on the landscape they thus provide an indication of the date of cultivation. In southern Scotland, ridging of the land tended to disappear in the mid-nineteenth century with the introduction of tile drainage. (Source: M.L. Parry.)

Plate 10: Cultivation Ridges in the Eastern Lammermuir Hills

The different types of ridges indicate the approximate date of reversion of the farm land to moor. Key: 1, 1m = curved, high-backed ridges dating from before *c.* 1800; 2a, 2b and 3 = straight ridges of varying width dating from after *c.* 1800; e = post-improvement enclosure; f = post-improvement farmstead standing on pre-improvement settlement site; d = recent plough for afforestation; s = open sheep drains; u = uncultivated moorland (Laughton, Berwickshire, 1970). (Source: Ordnance Survey, reproduced by permission of the Controller, HMSO, Crown Copyright Reserved.)

10

11

12

Plate 11: Auchterarder Estate (Perthshire), 1948
Auchterarder House and its policies with the home farm on their western edge. The field
shapes are partly adapted to the topography and are thus not as regular as in many landscapes derived from the improvement period. The frequent shelter belts, tree-lined field
boundaries and well-built courtyard farms are clearly shown. Within the informally-planted
policies, the large, square kitchen garden, distant from the house and hidden by trees, is
especially prominent. (Source: Ordnance Survey, reproduced by permission of the
Controller, HMSO, Crown Copyright Reserved.)

Plate 12: Auchterarder Estate (Perthshire), 1973
Landscape change in the post-1945 period has been on a scale which, in some areas, rivals
that of the late eighteenth century. At Auchterarder field boundaries have been ploughed
out, shelter belts and hedgerow trees removed and substantial new barns and machinery
sheds built. Change has been greatest in the policies where parkland and plantations have come
under the plough. (Source: Ordnance Survey, reproduced by permission of the Controller,
HMSO, Crown Copyright Reserved.)

Plate 13: The Crofting Landscape of North Uist (1966)
Machair strips of hay, oats and potatoes are scattered around uncultivable sand dunes and
outcrops of Lewisian gneiss. In the foreground cultivation has reverted to semi-natural
vegetation and the area is made over to a bird sanctuary. (Source: John Dewar Studios,
Edinburgh.)

Plan
OF
Enclosures with Clumps of Planting,
& Ponds for Cattle

Plate 14: Plan for Enclosing and Planting Fields (1813)
Few model field layouts were published in the books and periodicals of the Improvement
Era but the general principles were well known and widely adopted. Fields were large and
rectangular where topography and estate bounds allowed. Their corners were frequently
planted with copses and their edges lined with a shelter-belt. Additional detail illustrated
here are the locations of gates (B) and a single pond (A) designed to serve four adjacent
fields. (Source: Sir John Sinclair, *An account of the systems of Husbandry of Scotland I*,
Edinburgh, 1813, p. 43.)

Plate 15: Hatton House (Midlothian), 1719
The country houses of the aristocracy were rebuilt or enlarged in the seventeenth century
with both Classical and Baronial architectural motifs in evidence. The gardens surrounding
such houses were enclosed with brick or stone walls which often had pavillions or summer
houses at the corners. Fountains, ponds, statuary and sundials formed part of the design
while the garden plots were laid out with great formality. Evergreens, such as holly and yew,
were clipped while fruit trees were grown espaliered on the walls. Plantations of Scots pine
or sycamore sheltered the houses. (Source: J. Slezer, *Theatrum Scotiae*, London, 1719 edn.)

Plate 16: Inveraray Castle (Argyllshire)
Robert Morris's designs for the Duke of Argyll's Inveraray Castle, executed between 1745
and 1761, were an early and influential exercise in castellated Gothick style. The Scottish
landscape, especially the Highland margins and Southern Uplands, provided an ideal setting
for mansions conforming to the ideals of the picturesque. Such designs led ultimately to the
nineteenth-century revival of Scots Baronial. Inveraray is set in an irregularly landscaped
park of the eighteenth century, though a nineteenth-century formal garden has been added
beside the house. The view across Loch Fyne and the remodelled burgh of Inveraray are an
integral part of the landscape setting. (Source: John Dewar Studios.)

15

16

Plate 17: Inveraray Village (Argyllshire)
Inveraray is perhaps the most attractive of the planned villages in Scotland since it was designed to be part of the carefully-contrived landscape created for the Dukes of Argyll. The two- and three-storey cottages are more pretentious than in most planned villages but their lack of front gardens, large back yards and solid construction are more typical. The provision of public buildings (church, school and factor's house) rectangular market place, broad street and coherent layout is also characteristic. (Source: John Dewar Studios.)

Plate 18: Fife Street, Dufftown (Banffshire) 1880
Dufftown was laid out for the fourth Earl of Fife in 1817. It is therefore one of the 'second generation' of planned settlements. Its plan is a crooked-armed cross with a central square in which stands the Baronial tower. The mixture of one- and two-storey cottages fronting directly onto the street is characteristic, while by 1880 the burgh was paved and lighted. Newly-planted trees are perhaps an attempt to alleviate the harshness of the scene. Dufftown's economy was centred upon a distillery and agricultural service functions, the mainstay of many of the villages established on the Highland margins. (Source: Aberdeen University Library (G.W. Wilson Collection) C. 3421.)

Plate 19: Helmsdale (Sutherland)
Helmsdale was developed in the period between 1817 and 1830 as part of the comprehensive reorganisation of the Marchioness of Sutherland's estates. The 'clearance' of small tenants and cottars from the uplands to make way for sheep and deer is one of the most published and less honourable aspects of the Improvement, but there were constructive corollaries such as the new fishing ports exemplified by Helmsdale. (Source: John Dewar Studios.)

Plate 20: Plan of Helmsdale, 1820
Helmsdale River provided a fine natural harbour for the newly-established herring fishing fleet while the improved road and new bridge linked the site to Inverness and to Dunrobin, centre of the Sutherland estate. The town was laid out on an extensive grid plan between town and quayside. Already, by 1820, no less than nine firms had established fish warehouses on the quayside and the first street of the settlement had been built. (Source: J. Loch, *An account of the improvements on the estates of the Marquess of Stafford*, London, 1820, p. 126.)

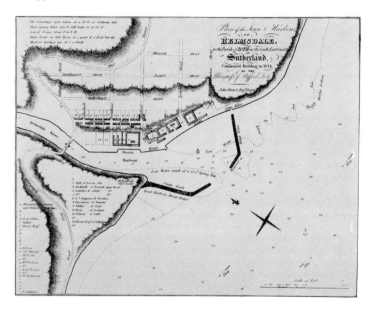

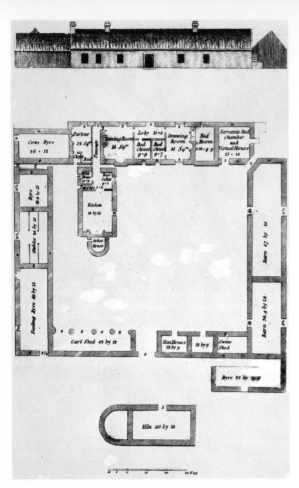

Plate 21: Model-farm Plan (Banffshire), 1812
Model-farm plans are found in great profusion in the books and new farming journals
generated by the Improving Movement. Some of the layouts were of buildings that had
actually been erected, others were more idealised. Almost all such plans consist of a large
yard with the farmhouse forming one side, and barns, byres and stables the other sides. In
the Lowlands farmhouses were normally two storey but in the upland margins, such as in
Banffshire, the traditional longhouse form was retained, though built in stone and lime-
rendered. (Source: D. Souter, *General view of the agriculture of the county of Banff*,
Edinburgh, 1812, p. 90.)

Plate 22: Relict Alder Coppice, Philorth (Aberdeenshire)
This grove of alders at Philorth shows the form of relict coppice. There is much evidence
of 'bogs' or woods of alder in northern Scotland being informally coppiced for local use
from the sixteenth century onward, but there is little evidence of formal coppice management. The principal commercial demand for alder was for gunpower charcoal and arose in
the nineteenth century when management was already on the wane. (Source: J.M. Lindsay.)

Plate 23: Stanley Cotton Mills, River Tay (Perthshire)
Stanley mills were established in 1785, by a partnership which included a landowner
(George Dempster of Dunnichern) and an inventor-manufacturer (Sir Richard Arkwright).
The mills are, from left to right, Brick Mill (started *c.* 1786), Mid Mill (*c.* 1850) and East
Mill (*c.* 1800). Although their situation was marginal to the cotton-manufacturing region of
Scotland, they occupied a fine water-power site. By 1834 East and Brick Mills had 200
horsepower at their disposal, some of which was used to drive power-looms. A substantial
village developed beside the mills. (Source: J. Shaw.)

I consider Money laid out by a Gentleman to promote Industry upon his Estate as being really laid out at more than common interest . . . besides thinking of Improving the Country you should this summer begin to think of the disposition of your Grounds and Plantations.[13]

Deskford further recommended Grant to talk to the Duke of Argyll about trees 'for in that matter he must be allowed to have merit'.

Figure 7.3: Distribution of the Principal Participants in the Improving of Sir James Grant's Speyside Estates

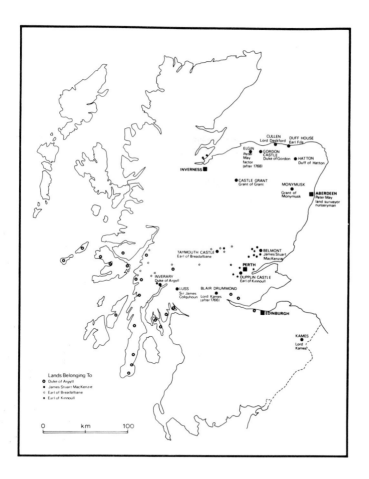

Note the wide influence of some landowners and the regional concentration in the north-east, Perthshire and the north central Lowlands.

Archibald, 3rd Duke of Argyll, was indeed one of the most prolific of the early improvers. From the time he succeeded his brother in 1743, till his death in April, 1761, Inveraray became the focus of improvements of unprecedented scale: the new town of Inveraray was begun, a new castle was built, policies were laid out, and surrounding lands were transformed into new farms and woodlands (Plates 16 and 17). Next Deskford suggested that Grant should

> make the acquaintance with Miller at the Physick Garden at Chelsea, and you should see Mr. Gray's Nursery at Fulham and Gordon's at Milend. And, if you have not done it already, it would be right before you came down to make a Tour for two or three days through some of the best disposed Gardens in the neighbourhood of London.[14]

Again, two months later, Deskford was further encouraging Grant to become an improver even though he had had no reply from his earlier letter:

> I intend to be at Castle Grant this year when you form your plan for laying out your ground within sight of the house. If you fix upon your time for that purpose, it would be right to have a surveyor there, to put your resolve upon paper; and if I know the time soon, I can appoint Peter May, the best surveyor in Scotland to be there.[15]

The Implementors

James Grant of Grant was able to command the loyal service of implementors of outstanding calibre, including his old tutor William Lorimer and land surveyors such as Peter May and his appretices.[16]   The key man in the improvement of the Grant of Grant estates was William Lorimer (1717-65). He was the son of William Lorimer of Dyttach, who rose to become chamberlain to the Earl of Findlater. Lorimer junior was a bursar at Marischal College, Aberdeen, and on 12 November 1737 he was appointed by the Earl of Findlater to be school-master at Deskford. A year later he was promoted to Fordyce school.[17] He remained in this post until 1747, when he became tutor to James Grant.[18] In the late 1750s, Lorimer spent a short period in Albany, New York, but then returned to the service of his former pupil, without a formal position, but on a retainer of £100 per annum. Thus, by 1760, the various men who were to initiate change were gathered in Castle Grant. James Grant, the son of the landlord, filled the role of the adopter; his tutor, William Lorimer, provided the intellectual power, while Lord Deskford was the generator providing advice in many forms, especially recommending implementors such as Peter May, the land surveyor.

To understand the motivation of the people involved, it is necessary to look into their minds and to see what questions they were asking. Did they seek abroad for ideas and assistance? Did they relate agrarian change to wider matters such as the economic, political and social consequences of their actions?

Fortunately, a document survives which throws considerable light upon such questions. It was drawn up by William Lorimer for his own use at the outset of his work on the Grant of Grant estate and details the tasks which Lorimer planned ahead:

> To get a surveyor of ground from the South of Scotland who understands not only measuring and laying out of ground, but also farming and country improvements.
>
> To inform myself of all the methods of improvement both in agriculture and manufactures practised in the South of Scotland and in the Low Countries.
>
> To inform myself of the different sorts of tenures of landlords and tenants both in the Lowlands and Highlands. How the linen manufacturers are carried on: lint-fields and bleaching . . . .
>
> To get books of all kinds on the policy and agriculture of Scotland.
>
> To enquire about the proper method of recovering lands over-run by sand.
>
> To know how the elections are going on, both now, and at last elections the different connections and interests.
>
> To know the Gentlemen of the County of Moray, their families, connections and estates.
>
> Do. of Inverness.
>
> To get all the knowledge about planting in Argyllshire and Banff.
>
> The situation of the Forfeited Estates, particularly those annexed to the Crown.
>
> To introduce burning of limestone both in Urquhart and Strathspey.
>
> To converse with the most sensible farmers in Strathspey about the best way of improving ground.
>
> To enquire the nature of tenures between masters and tenants in England.
>
> What is the manner of settling manufactures?
>
> The best way of cultivating and improving the woods, what parts are to be cut and sold, and to what place they are to be carried.
>
> The whole scheme of Government now in England, and the nature of Feudal tenures . . .
>
> The way of breeding cattle, sheep and horses.
>
> The different ways of inclosing ground and improving soil.
>
> The different measures of corn, and liquids and Scotch money.
>
> The way of collecting the rents in this country.
>
> The connection of the great families in Scotland.
>
> The price of building here and in England.
>
> The price of day-labour here and in England.
>
> Servants' wages.
>
> What are the number of people in Grant Estate, and people in the neighbourhood.
>
> Account of the Sinking Fund, the stocks, South Sea year, etc.
>
> The different companies that carried on trade.
>
> The best way for preserving grain in granaries.

[To which was added in James Grant's hand]

> The whole progress in making malt liquor.
> What is necessary to qualify a man to stand for a county, what for a
>   burrough.[19]

Early in 1763, we find Lorimer writing out the drafts of letters which bear Grant's signature asking the factors of the various parts of the estate to

> as soon as possible make out and send me a clear and distinct abstract of the
> rental, by which you collect, distinguished into different columns, such as,
> the name of the tenant, and his farm or possession, his meal and money-rent,
> customs, and services, and the time of the expiration of tack.[20]

The purpose of this inventory is quite clear for he goes on to declare, 'you are to acquaint the tenants that I am extremely desirous they should all begin to improve, at least some parts of their grounds with lime.' Later in the instructions he repeats this stress on lime: 'Let me know what progress liming has made in your collection, and what methods you would propose to make it universal, for I am determined to introduce it in every part of my estate, both Highland and Lowland.'

A good example of the care that Lorimer exercised in his inquiries can be seen in the questionnaire sent to James Stuart Mackenzie of Rosehaugh, brother of the 3rd Earl of Bute. Mackenzie owned estates in Angus, Perth and Ross and Cromarty, and bore a considerable responsibility for his brother's estate on the island of Bute (Figure 7.3). Furthermore, he was in constant touch with Lord Deskford, from whom he borrowed Peter May, the land surveyor, to survey his own estates; May later became Bute's factor at Mount Stuart near Rothesay.[21] Both the pattern of land ownership and the system of communication between landowners thus served to accelerate the spread of improving ideas (see Chapter 9).

Lorimer sent out similar questionnaires to Sir James Colquhoun, of Luss in Dumbartonshire, and William 'Burnside' Grant, chamberlain and forester to Earl Fife. The advice contained in the replies was presented by Lorimer in a paper dated 1 October 1763, entitled, 'Remarks upon the management of Farms and Woods collected amongst friends in Scotland'.[22]

To reinforce this advice Lorimer wrote a further 179-page report — 'Things requiring Mr. Grant's attention when he goes to Strathspey'[23] — pressing his employer to make decisions. Indeed, we can trace through Lorimer's words the complexity of the improvement process:

> Lord Deskford advises you to take Peter May or some such surveyor & with
> him go over your whole Estate next summer — from thence get a general
> idea of it & next year cause him begin a real & written Survey of the whole.[24]

This sentence was quoted verbatim in a letter by William Forbes which repeats earlier advice given by Archibald Grant of Monymusk, which was itself taken from a paper read by Colonel David Watson to the commissioners of the Annexed Estates in 1755.

In September 1763 Lorimer wrote a report on the 'Present State of Urquhart' in which he observed,

> When the tenants received new leases in 1760 they generally paid a grassum equal to one year's rent, which was rather unequal, as it must be supposed that among so many farms there must be some vastly better than others. This shews the Propriety, nay Necessity, of a survey but it is done in time as the tacks don't expire till Whitsunday, 1770.[25]

The timing of the expiration of leases was critical, for it was necessary for all farms to go out of lease at once. This was attained by putting farmers on an annual lease as their old leases, usually of seven or nine years, fell in. Thus, at the point of enclosure all these leases appeared to be of the onerous one-year variety, leading many authors to assume that this had been a permanent and debilitating feature of the old agrarian system. Besides the necessity of having all the land free for a comprehensive replanning of the estate there was also a longer-term objective — to make sure that all farmers were put on to the new long leases simultaneously, so that if complete reform was ever again contemplated by the landlord, he would avoid the long delay experienced by the early improvers. Thus the annual lease in this circumstance was an example not of rapacious, but of far-sighted, landlordism.[26] The enthusiasm for the wide-scale expiry of leases at the same time diminishes in the periods of agricultural depression, since landowners found that it could be difficult finding tenants when many farms became vacant simultaneously.

Lorimer's contribution to the improvement of the Grant estates was cut short by his early death in January 1765, while on his way to Italy seeking relief from ill-health.[27] Yet he played an outstanding role in the initial stages of agricultural improvement and much that has been attributed to the master was in fact the brain-child of the servant. James Grant of Grant was perfectly aware of his debt to an old friend for in January 1769 he wrote, 'And had he lived I should have remitted whatever his exigencies might have required during his stay in Italy, as I never could have done too much for that excellent man to whom I lay under the greatest obligations.'[28] Progress of change on the estate never faltered and the transformation of mansion house, policies, farm lands and the laying out of the new town of Grantown-on-Spey progressed steadily through the 1770s.

Estate Officials

In the 1750s and 1760s the great landlords found it difficult to find the right kind of men to implement the new ideas in agriculture and estate management. With their English upbringing men like James Stuart Mackenzie could be forgiven for their jaundiced view of the Scottish scene, illustrated in his correspondence with the Earl of Findlater (Lord Deskford):

> I observe there is hardly such a thing as what they call in England a land steward, regularly bred to that service; what is called a factor here seems to be only a sort of agent and receiver, which is a mightly small part indeed of an English land steward's business, who does not employ three days in the year receiving rents, but his great and material business is attending to the proper laying out of farms, and instructing the tenants in the cultivation of their lands . . . But what I have heard, there are not half a dozen such land stewards in all Scotland.[29]

Mackenzie was well aware that Lord Deskford had the best of these in Peter May, who was training a cadre of surveyors which would yield several important cartographers as well as distinguished estate managers.

James Stuart Mackenzie's remarks were unfair, however, for he failed to recognise that the existing structure of estate management in Scotland was fundamentally different from that in England. On a typical large Scottish estate in the mid-eighteenth century the rents were collected by a local factor giving part-time attendance only to his duties. On a number of estates, for instance those of the Duke of Buccleuch, such officials were known not as factors but as 'chamberlains'.[30] Remittances might be made by those factors directly to the owner, who would audit their accounts, but more commonly they were passed to his Edinburgh-based *doer* or law-agent. In some estates the factor with responsibility for the area surrounding the principal mansion house, such as Cullen House or Gordon Castle, also acted as the general receiver, taking remittances from the other factors and acting as *primus inter pares*. When a proprietor was abroad or was a minor, overall supervision was often exercised by commissioners appointed from among the relations, friends and advisers of the owner, though sometimes commissioners were appointed for more limited purposes, such as the set (lease) of a part of the estates. In some instances the auditing by the owner or his *doer* passed to the general receiver or commissioner, as with the Earl of Bute, but the century from 1750 onwards saw the general adoption of independent audit by accountants.[31]

The growth of this profession is characteristic of the changes taking place in the Scottish economy at this time. The first *Edinburgh Directory*, published in 1773, contains the names of seven accountants and in Glasgow in 1783 there were six. A century later, there were nearly two hundred in the two cities.[32] The early estate accountants owed much to the professional training of Alexander Farquharson, Clerk of Accounts to the great Buccleuch estates in the minority of Henry, 3rd Duke of Buccleuch, for his pupils ultimately became responsible for audit on almost all the great estates. Lower down the scale were the clerk, ground officer, farm grieve, forester and gardener, as well as the household staff. Duties could be combined and designations of various posts were by no means consistent, but there existed a structure which was to evolve into a modern system of estate management that ultimately outshone many an English great estate.

Land Surveyors

One of the most important agents of change on an estate was the land surveyor. The ability to measure land, to use scientific instruments, to calculate results accurately, to draw maps, and to judge the quality and potential worth of land, fixing rents so as not to bankrupt tenants, required skills of the highest order. Numerate men of this calibre with agricultural experience were not abundant and for many years from the 1720s to 1760s land surveyors were drawn from a variety of professions, including schoolmasters, nurserymen, architects and farmers.

Figure 7.4: The Growth of the Scottish Land Surveying Profession

The professional contribution of land surveyors in Scottish economic development measured by man years, 1700 – 1850

The profession had only a brief life in Scotland. In the first quarter of the eighteenth century there was not even enough work to keep one land surveyor fully employed (Figure 7.4). From the mid-1720s, however, there was sufficient growth in demand to keep about ten surveyors in constant work until 1748 when the opportunities expanded almost exponentially until 1770, when there were seventy land surveyors fully employed. For example, George Brown left his master Peter May in 1769 to set up on his own, but when James Ross, factor to the Duke of Gordon, tried to recruit him on a salaried basis, Brown confidentially rejected the offer:

> My present inclination is more disposed to prosecute my business in the way I am than to engage by the year. I was recommended by Mr. May to Brodie, and Brodie recommended me to some of the neighbouring Gentlemen, so that I have found plenty of business even in my first outset.[33]

The vitality of these early land surveyors is amply illustrated by the life of Peter May (Figure 7.5). From 1755, May had been employed by the Forfeited Estates commissioners to survey the annexed estates of Lovat and other lands as well as continuing his private commissions and running a profitable nursery garden in Aberdeen. Early in 1765, Alexander Innes, commissary of Aberdeen, tried to engage May for Grant of Grant but found the surveyor fully engaged for the whole season.[34] At this time frustration drove James Grant of Grant to consider other surveyors — John Home was one and another, recommended by Sir Archibald Grant of Monymusk, was James Robertson from Northumberland. Lord Findlater continually pressed Peter May to survey the Grant estates, but in September 1766 May had to point out to Findlater,

> I am much obliged to your Lordship for recommending me to Mr. Grant, there is nobody I would serve with more pleasure or greater attention, but I am afraid it will be late to begin him after I have done at New and your town of Rothes settled.[35]

It was not until 1767 that a cryptic entry appears in the diary of James Grant, the clerk at Castle Grant, 'Mr May came to Castle Grant and his men too.'[36]

After 1770, demand slackened off and land surveyors such as Peter May and George Brown became factors to the Earls of Findlater. Other men of the north-east school of surveyors such as Alexander and George Taylor and Thomas Milne had to leave Scotland in search of work. The two brothers went to Ireland and built a considerable reputation for their cartographic skills.[37] Thomas Milne left Scotland in 1785 to begin a residence of 21 years in England, where he surveyed several counties before making his most ambitious work, *Milne's Plan of the Cities of London and Westminster*.[38] Depressed conditions continued until the early 1790s and only returned to the position of 1770 in 1810. There was considerable opportunity for employment during the years of boom up to 1815, but thereafter the profession declined in spite of increasing industrialisation until the coming of the Ordnance Survey in the 1850s rendered their services generally unnecessary.

In little over a century Scottish land surveyors produced over 50,000 plans. The importance of this output extended far beyond the cartography itself, for they were in the business of planning a new landscape. In what was an open and largely incoherent farming scene, half moorland with few trees, they created

Figure 7.5: The North-East School of Land Surveyors

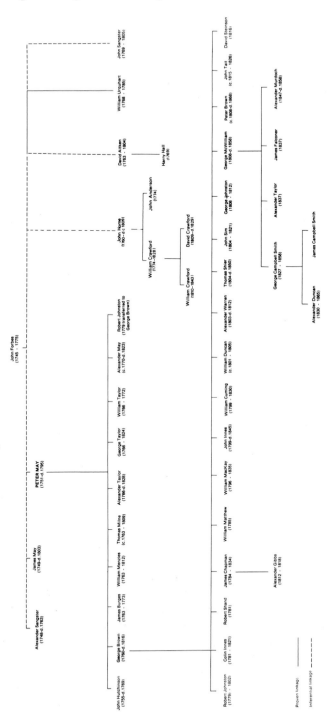

The Northeast School of land surveyors: the passage of professional skills through proven master/
trainee relationships for 120 years of Scottish land surveying.
The diagram illustrates the passage of professional skills from Peter May to the coming of the Ordnance
Survey in the 1850s.
N.B. the dates represent the span of professional careers unless otherwise stated.

an ordered, geometrical, fenced and wooded landscape (Plates 6 and 7). Moreover, the land surveyor needed to establish the potential of the land to yield higher rent and to identify the means of achieving this — by enclosure, by liming, by the construction of new farmhouses, and by a host of other improvements (see Chapter 9).

The Agricultural Revolution in Scotland was thus a unified attempt to increase profit from the landlord's main asset — land. As Peter May recorded in a letter to the factor to the Duke of Gordon, 'I am still wandering thro' the fields, which turns out a disagreeable business in this bad weather. I find the rents of Deskford will double in many places, and I believe will rise two thirds on the whole.'[39] Moreover, the relationship between land surveyors and landowners meant that the improving activities of surveyors spread rapidly across the country. This is indicated by a letter from Peter May to James Grant of Grant:

On my way north I was recommended to my Lord Kinnoull by my Lord Findlater. I stayed some days at Dupplin [Castle] and was made happy in the good company of a great man. His Lordship was remarkably entertaining and we travelling sometimes through church and state and now and then made an excursion even the length of Strathspey [i.e. about Grant's estates], which he promises to visit next summer and I have undertaken to be his travelling governor. He is extremely anxious about you and your country affairs and was much pleased at the accounts I gave him of it . . . My next stage was Belmont Castle, the country seat of Lord Privy Seal, where I made a pretty long sederunt. His Lordship and Mr. Menzies applied to my Lord Findlater that I should survey his estates in Perth and Angus . . . He has a very fine estate but not at all well managed . . . I dined with Lord Kames at Aberdeen, who is very anxious about Strathspey. We had a long conversation about it and he has suggested some useful things. He recommends to push on industry slowly rather than rapidly; success is more certain and the expense much less.[40]

Agricultural Societies

In the diffusion of new ideas the importance of agricultural societies is not easy to establish, although their existence and their membership can readily be identified. In particular, the question arises as to whether they were a primary or secondary diffusing force. It is reasonable to argue that the societies themselves represent a secondary diffusion, because they were set up only when interest had been aroused. The earliest association of this nature, 'The Honourable the Society of Improvers in the Knowledge of Agriculture in Scotland', was founded at a meeting held at Edinburgh on 8 June 1723.[41] Its secretary was Robert Maxwell of Arkland in Dumfriesshire and he was probably the author of the *Treatise concerning the Manner of Fallowing* which the Society published in 1724. Maxwell seems to have remained the driving force and in 1743 he published the *Select Transactions of the Honourable the Society of Improvers in the Knowledge of Agriculture in Scotland*. At this time the Society had 301 members, of whom the great landowners were well represented: the Dukes of Atholl, Hamilton and Perth, the Marquises of Lothian and Tweedale, and the Earls of Balcarres, Breadalbane, Dunmore, Findlater, Glasgow, Haddington, Hay, Hopetoun, Kinnoull, Kintore, Lauderdale, Morton, Seaforth, Stair, Strathmore, Traquair, Wemyss and Wigton. Another group consisting of 86 members, some 29 per cent of the membership, were Edinburgh lawyers. They have been dismissed as an irrelevant force in the diffusion process, but it has only been recognised recently that these men, in their role of *doers*, commissioners and factors for estates all over Scotland, were in a unique position to disseminate both knowledge and action.[42] The aim of the Society was clearly to stimulate the diffusion process: 'to correspond with the most intelligent in all the different customs in the nation, concerning their different ways of managing their grounds, that what may be amiss may be corrected and what is profitable imitated'. Here was an explicit attempt to overcome geographical barriers to diffusion by the power of the pen.[43]

The Society of Improvers began a long tradition of farming societies and agricultural shows which remains a significant force to the present day. Of the lesser societies founded under its influence, the Ormiston Agricultural Society, established in 1736 by John Cockburn of Ormiston, was one of the most influential. Its rather special attribute was the estate of Ormiston, which acted as a demonstration unit for young tenant farmers who were sent for training from as far as the Moray Firth lowlands. Yet one must be cautious about attributing too much influence to pioneers such as John Cockburn and Robert Maxwell, for they went bankrupt in 1748 and 1750 respectively — and that was one lesson that would *not* have gone unnoticed.

Most of the longer-lived societies date from the 1780s, by which time the main force of structural change had been initiated in the large estates. Their role was probably more important in diffusing information about piecemeal improvements which could be incorporated into the reformed structure. An illustration of this kind of activity can be seen in the work of the *Farmers Society* at Glasgow around 1790. Here the seed merchants had been supplying farmers with rye grass seed which lasted only one year, so the society purchased seed for themselves 'from the best foreign markets',[44] and this was distributed to various parishes 15 to 20 miles around the city. In time, such societies, as that at Glasgow, became social clubs, but that alone did not diminish their role in the diffusion of the new order: rather it put it on a more informal basis.

Agricultural Publications

'Behold another volume on husbandry: exclaims a peevish man on seeing the title-page: how long shall we be pestered with such trite stuff?' Such was the opening sentence in the preface of Lord Kames's *Gentleman Farmer*. And the reply was, 'as long, sweet Sir, as you are willing to pay for it: hold out your purse, and wares will never be wanting.' It is probable, however, that the publications themselves had little influence in promoting agrarian change. They were designed to grace shelves, to honour past actions in need of posthumous justification, and to be successful the author had to over-state the case for improvement. What better way to do it than by completely disparaging past systems? Lord Kames condemned most books on the subject as booksellers' productions, or in today's terms, coffee-table publications, whose authors 'deliver their precepts from a study lined with books without even pretending to experience'.

Figure 7.6: The Availability of Agricultural Books in Eighteenth-Century Scotland

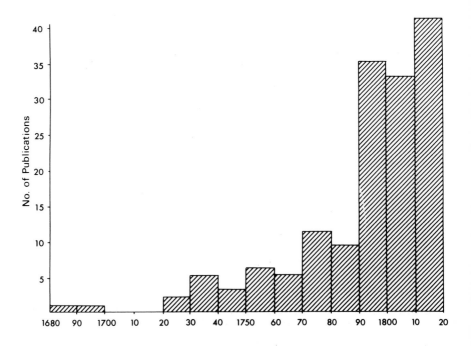

The most active period of publishing was well after the main phase of improvement.

Experience was the most sought-after quality, for the varied geographical conditions in Scotland rarely coincided with the generalisation of the printed page. Prolific writers such as Arthur Young and Sir John Sinclair were institutionalising a movement which was well past its initial dynamic phase. If the evidence shown in Figure 7.4 is accepted, then the dynamic phase in

Scotland lasted from about 1748 to 1770; thereafter most of the literature simply supported an established position. The list of agrarian literature published in Scotland, or of English origin and known to have been read in Scotland, reveals an interesting trend (Figure 7.6). From small beginnings with the publication of the *Scots Gard'ner*[45] in 1683, which coincided with the late seventeenth-century desire for modernisation of the Scottish economy, there was little development in the first two dead decades of the eighteenth century, before the revival of interest in agrarian improvement of the 1730s. A further slack period was followed after 1770 by a flourishing agricultural publishing trade, especially during the prosperous years of the French Wars.

Although the part played by agrarian literature was a minor one, there were some instances in which books were purchased with the object of advancing agriculture. The commissioners of the annexed estates ordered one copy of 'Young's writings and Dickson's Treatise' to be given to the factors on the annexed estates at Barrisdale, Coigach and Monaltry, and two copies to each of the factors on the larger estates of Perth, Lovat and Cromarty 'for the benefit of the tenants on these estates'.[46] They were somewhat optimistic, for most of the tenants spoke only Gaelic. An entry to William Lorimer's 'Memorandum' for him 'to get books of all kinds on the policy and agriculture of Scotland' shows that one literate man at least made the effort, but in his case he found the advice wanting. Of Jethro Tull's work he noted, 'Tull's husbandry too expensive. A rational husbandry may be carried on for less.'[47]

Conclusion

The evidence appears overwhelming that Scotland experienced an Agricultural Revolution, masterminded by a small, highly motivated group of people with the aim of enjoying the highest standard of living possible. The rising aspirations of the landlords reverberated right through, or rather down, the social scale. Everybody in society suddenly faced economic and geographic change, save only the St Kildans. As to the dating of this event, one can say it started in the immediate aftermath of the 1745 Rebellion which laid to rest any future for the Jacobite cause and left no alternative than to follow the Hanoverian English mode of living. The landlords made their lands into efficient income machines, the successful farmers enjoyed a substantial living, and the rest began the long trek either to the town or to the New World. In the initial phase which was over by 1770, the commissioners of the annexed estates were by far the most important stimulant to change. From 1754 the Commission formed a powerhouse of ideas and example which stimulated change throughout the country. These were the years of overpowering intellectual vitality in Scotland that we know as the Scottish Enlightenment. While the relative agricultural backwardness had been a reflection of the cultural isolation, the Agricultural Revolution was a facet of the intellectual whirlwind that swept across the land. Man had come to believe that the new science made all things possible.

Notes

1. Whittington, G. (1975), 'Was there a Scottish Agricultural Revolution?' *Area*, *7*, 204-6; and correspondence relating thereto by D. Mills and M. Parry (1976), *Area*, *8*, 237-9; and I. H. Adams and I. D. Whyte (1978) *Area*, *10*, 198-205

2. Historians have used this term to head chapters or substantial sections addressed to agrarian change: Symon, J. A. (1959), *Scottish farming* (Edinburgh); Hamilton, H. (1963), *Economic history of eighteenth-century Scotland* (Oxford); Smout, T. C. (1969), *A history of the Scottish people 1560-1830* (London)

3. Scottish Record Office (hereafter SRO), Forfeited Estates papers E 721/1, pp. 12, 14

4. Reprinted in full in Adams, I. H. (1974), *Descriptive list of plans in the Scottish Record Office*, *3*, IX (Edinburgh); influence can be seen in the Duke of Gordon's instructions to Alexander Taylor in 1770, in *idem* (1970), *Descriptive List of Plans in the Scottish Record Office*, *2*, IX (Edinburgh); in the Earl of Hopetoun's instructions to John and James Tait in 1758, in *idem* (1971), *The Mapping of a Scottish Estate*, 22-3 (Edinburgh); and in James Grant of Grant's instructions to Peter May in 1767, in *idem* (1979), *Peter May, land surveyor, 1752-1795* (Publications of the Scottish History Society) (hereafter Pubs. SHS), 4th series, *15*

5. For example, Lord Kames in his preface to *The gentleman farmer* (p. xi) remarked, 'though they would require the elucidation of a Newton, or a Boyle'.

6. Parker, R. A. C. (1975), *Coke of Norfolk. A financial and agricultural study 1707-1842* (Oxford)

7. Lehmann, W. C. (1971), *Henry Home, Lord Kames, and the Scottish Enlightenment* (The Hague); Ross, I. S. (1972), *Lord Kames and the Scotland of his day* (Oxford)

8. Hamilton, H. (1945), *Selections from the Monymusk papers, 1713-1755* (Pubs. SHS), 3rd series, *39*

9. Mitchison, R. (1962), *Agricultural Sir John: the life of Sir John Sinclair of Ulbster 1754-1835* (London)

10. Wicker, E. R. (1957), 'A note on Jethro Tull: innovator or crank', *Agricultural History, 31*, 47-8; Fussell, G. (1973), *Jethro Tull: his influence on mechanised agriculture* (Reading)

11. Gazley, J. G. (1973), *The life of Arthur Young 1741-1820* (Philadelphia)

12. *History of Parliament. The Commons 1754-1790*, *II*, members A-J. This is a typical example of the public reputation of an Improver.

13. SRO (Seafield muniments), GD 248/672/4, Correspondence of James Grant, 1760-9

14. Ibid.; for details of these nurseries see Harvey, J. H., 'Mid-Georgian nurseries of the London region', *Transactions of the London and Middlesex Archaeological Society*, *26*, 293-308

15. SRO (Seafield muniments), GD 248/672/4, correspondence of James Grant, 1760-9

16. Adams (1979), *Descriptive list of plans*

17. SRO, CH 2/91/2, pp. 44-6, Deskford Kirk session minutes; CH 2/158/6, pp. 268-9, Presbytery of Fordyce minutes, 1727-47 (I thank Dr I. D. Grant for these references)

18. SRO, CH 2/158/7, p. 12, Presbytery of Fordyce minutes, 1747-69. There is an elegy to Lorimer by John Grant, brother of James Grant of Grant, in the *Scots Magazine*, *27* (1765), 323; see also Dixon, G. A. (1975), 'William Lorimer on forestry in the Central Highlands in the early 1760s', *Scottish Forestry*, *29*, 191-210

19. SRO (Seafield muniments), GD 248/40/3, volume of notes

20. SRO (Seafield muniments), GD 248/38/1, notes on the management of farms and woods

21. Adams (1979), *Descriptive list of plans*

22. SRO (Seafield muniments), GD 248/38/1, notes on the management of farms and woods

23. Ibid.

24. SRO (Seafield muniments), GD 248/250, Grant of Grant correspondence, 1762-8

25. SRO (Seafield muniments), GD 248/38/1, notes on the management of farms and woods

26. Other examples of this type of annual lease have been found on the estates of the Duke of Gordon, Marquis of Annandale and the Earl of Findlater, all eminent improvers.

27. *Records of Marischal College,* I, p. 439n

28. SRO (Seafield muniments), GD 248/2082, p. 293, letter book Grant estates, 1764-9

29. SRO (Seafield muniments), GD 248/3408/6

30. Adams, I. H. (1971), 'Division of the commonty of Hassendean 1761-1763', *The Stair Society*, Miscellany I, 181

31. Grant, I. D. (1979), 'Landlords and land management in north-eastern Scotland 1750-1850' (unpublished PhD thesis, University of Edinburgh)

32. Institute of Chartered Accountants of Scotland (1954), *A history of the chartered accountants of Scotland from the earliest time to 1954* (Edinburgh), p. 173

33. SRO (Gordon Castle papers), GD 44/49/22, surveying estates, 1769

34. Alexander Innes (1727-88), an advocate in Aberdeen, was an agent for James Grant of Grant and active in the formation of the new town of Grantown and settlement of marches with the Duke of Gordon. In 1771 he purchased the estate of Cowie in Kincardineshire.

35. SRO (Seafield muniments), GD 248/346/5, letter 1766

36. SRO (Seafield muniments), GD 248/1542, fo. 27v letter book of Sir James Grant of Grant, 1787-92; for a copy of Peter May's proposals for surveying the Grant estates see Adams (1979), *Descriptive list of plans*

37. Adams, I. H. (1975), 'George Taylor, a surveyor o'pairts', *Imago Mundi* (2nd series), *27*, 55-64

38. Bull, G. B. G. (1956), 'Thomas Milne's land utilization map of the London area in 1800', *The Geographical Journal*, *122*, pp. 25-30

39. SRO, Gordon Castle papers, GD 44/49/22, surveying estates, 1769

40. SRO (Seafield muniments), GD 248/250, Grant of Grant correspondence, 1762-8

41. Ramsay, A. (1879), *History of the Highland and Agricultural Society*, (Edinburgh), pp. 19-27

42. Grant (1979), *Descriptive list of plans*, pp. 211-17

43. Campbell, R. H. (1964), *State of the annual progress of the linen manufacture 1727-54* (Edinburgh)

44. Sinclair, Sir J. (1791-9), *Old statistical account*, Vol. 18, Strathblane parish, Stirlingshire (Edinburgh), p. 567

45. Reid, J. (1683), *The Scots Gard'ner . . . published for the climate of Scotland* (Edinburgh)

46. SRO (Exchequer Records), E.721/11, p. 38, Minutes of Board Meeting, Annexed Estates Commissioners, 29 January 1770. The books referred to are presumably Young, A. (1767), *The farmer's letters to the people of England, containing the sentiments of a practical husbandman . . .* (London); and Dickson, A. (1762-70), *Treatise on Agriculture* (2 vols.)

47. SRO (Seafield muniments), GD 248/37/4, volume of notes by William Lorimer

8 CHANGES IN THE EXTENT OF IMPROVED FARMLAND

M. L. Parry

Agricultural change in Scotland during the eighteenth century, like that in many developing economies, occurred in two ways — in the structural base of farming (the organisation of estates and farms) and in the farming system (the mix of farming technology, knowledge, labour and capital). The modification of the Scottish rural landscape was the product of these underlying changes; and it is for this reason that the study of landscape change during the Improving Movement is important, because it not only increases our comprehension of the landscape of the present but also represents an effective record of socio-economic change in the past.

Two fundamental types of landscape change can be identified. First, there was a substantial upgrading of the agricultural infrastructure, that is of the *quality* of the agricultural landscape. Such changes included improvements in enclosure to accommodate new ideas in crop rotation and stock control, improvements in access to make full use of new machinery, and improvements in the design of farm buildings. Landscape changes of this kind are discussed by Caird in Chapter 9.

Second, there was a substantial extension of the area of improved farmland in all parts of Scotland, that is in the *quantity* of farmland. A variety of commercial and technological factors combined to push the frontier of reclaimed land deeper into the lowland mosses and higher up the valley sides. At the same time, for reasons considered later, there was an acceleration in the rate of abandonment of high and remote farms. Indeed, the national pattern of improved farmland and unimproved moorland was sufficiently modified over the period 1750-1820 to represent a major alteration in the face of the Scottish countryside. This essay asks where, when and why such changes occurred. It first considers the general literature on changes in the extent of Scottish cultivation and compares the Scottish trends with those elsewhere in northern Europe. There then follows an account of the unpublished evidence for changes in cultivation at a national scale, and discussion of a method for mapping, dating and explaining such changes at the regional and local level.

Definitions

Throughout northern Europe the slopes of hill areas are traversed by a boundary

177

between unreclaimed moorland and improved farmland. In Scotland the boundary is often a distinct one between natural vegetation and sown crops; but sometimes it may comprise a more gradual transition from degraded pasture invaded by sedge and bracken to closely grazed rough grassland. Because of this there is a need for precise definition of terms.

In England and Wales the distinction between moorland and farmland has frequently been identified by reference to the upper limit of small, permanent enclosures.[1] The field boundaries were often recorded on large-scale maps of the eighteenth and nineteenth centuries and were thus a convenient indicator of the agricultural frontier. In Scotland, however, enclosure came late to the farming scene and cultivated plots which shifted within the outfield area were not bounded by internal enclosures. The only boundary feature of the outfield was the head-dyke, a pre-enclosure drystone or turf wall which separated the semi-wild stock on hill pasture from the arable and meadow land below. The head-dyke, however, was an immovable feature which did not reflect shifts of cultivation limits that occurred below it; and in the late eighteenth and early nineteenth centuries it was frequently breached to allow the reclamation of land above. It should also be noted that, contrary to earlier opinion,[2] the head-dyke was not a universal feature: much of the Southern Uplands show little signs of it.

A study of the head-dyke, such as that by Robertson,[3] is therefore not as rewarding as it might seem; more relevant is examination of the upper limit of land that was reclaimed by ploughing and was sown with cereal crops and, from the 1770s onwards, root-crops and improved grasses. It can be located on aerial photographs by reference to relict cultivation ridges that survive under a mantle of heather or rough grass. This limit of cultivation by the plough, which (with the exception of the caschrom) was the only means of extensive reclamation in upland Scotland prior to the use of surface seeding and controlled grazing in the later nineteenth century, corresponds with the 'moorland edge' marked on all Ordnance Survey maps from the first edition of 1843-78 onwards.[4] It marks the effective frontier of improved farmland.

The Literature

The lack of an integrated approach to landscape study has been responsible for the scant progress made, until quite recently, in reconstructing Scottish landscape history. In particular, we still know little about the history of Scotland's upland margins save that which has come to light indirectly from local studies of settlement evolution. The most detailed studies hitherto completed have been in western Argyll and Inverness. Here the evidence is that, following some widespread desertion of settlements and retreat of agriculture during the plagues of the seventeenth century,[5] there occurred a peak of cultivation around the mid- and late eighteenth century in northern Skye, Ardnamurchan and Kintyre.[6]

Elsewhere in Argyll and, to the north, in Sutherland, the widespread desertion of crofts and abandonment of pockets of cultivation occurred as a result of enforced 'clearance' for sheep-farming over the period 1800 to 1840. In Morvern (Argyll), for example, every single property changed hands between 1813 and 1844. However, the land sales and evictions peaked at different times in different parts of the region. In eastern Lochaber, on the estate of Glengarry, there was some early clearance in the 1780s, and at Lochiel the main movement took place in 1803;[7] yet further west it was delayed until the 1820s and 1830s in Knoydart, 1838 in Ardnamurchan,[8] and 1819-25 on the Argyll estates.[9] The massive and well reported clearances in Sutherland occurred mainly over 1807-21. Most of this clearance occurred in areas where cultivation had never been extensive and where it is misleading to refer to changes to a continuous limit of cultivation. For this reason, and because the Highland clearances have been quite fully discussed elsewhere,[10] they will not be considered in this chapter.

In the Southern Uplands there is some evidence both of retreat from the very high levels of settlement mapped by Timothy Pont in the 1590s, and of a few new farms being established on former moorland in the eighteenth century.[11] Elsewhere the record is scant. The general assumption has been that a stagnating economy in the late Middle Ages saw some retreat of cultivation limits,[12] but until recently this had not been tested, nor had the belief that the net cultivated area in Scotland expanded during the Improvement era.[13] There is little evidence from which to draw a general pattern: the mid-eighteenth-century peak of reclamation in the west contrasts with a probable peak around the time of Timothy Pont in the south-west. We cannot, at this stage, extrapolate either trend to other regions, but it is instructive to place them in the context of trends that are more fully documented elsewhere in Britain and in northern Europe if only because, while acknowledging the great contrasts in society and economy that occurred within the wider region, some similarities of the interaction between the commercial stimulus for reclamation and the physical restraint of the upland environment may help us to comprehend the processes and trends that prevailed in the past.

In England sufficient evidence has now emerged for Exmoor and Dartmoor, for the Black Mountains, the Pennines and North Yorkshire Moors, and for the Mendip Hills to enable a pattern to be identified.[14] This suggests that, in these uplands, rapid advance in the tenth and eleventh centuries slowed in the late medieval period — with widespread retreat occurring in less favoured areas — and was resumed in a piecemeal and erratic fashion from about 1550 to 1780. Thereafter it accelerated rapidly with parliamentary enclosure and an inflated wartime economy in the late eighteenth and nineteenth centuries.

In Wales more scant evidence points to some retreat of cultivation limits in the late Middle Ages, with subsequent expansion during the Napoleonic Wars.[15] In Ireland the early trend is not clear, but there appears to have been a substantial degree of reclamation during the Napoleonic Wars — though whether this was primary reclamation of virgin moor or secondary reclamation of long-abandoned farmland is not clear.[16]

In Norway, to which Scotland before the Union may have borne a close similarity, there was a substantial retreat of high-lying settlement and farmland between about 1350 and 1500. It seems to have occurred throughout the country, the rates of farm desertion for some regions reaching 65 per cent, but never falling below 40 per cent.[17] This raises the possibility that Scotland witnessed retreat on a similar scale before the Improvement era and that subsequent reclamation in the eighteenth and nineteenth centuries occurred largely on long-abandoned farmland, a possibility that bears strongly upon the discussion in this chapter.

The Context of the Problem

Prelude

In order to examine the pattern of change over 1750-1820 it is important to understand the trends which led up to eighteenth-century movements of the cultivation limit. These may best be illustrated by examination of south-east Scotland — East Lothian and Berwickshire — because it is for this area that the analysis of subsequent change is most complete.

In this region the earliest unbroken limits of cultivation had been established in the mid-twelfth century by the grange farms of the Border abbeys. A study of place-names in the grant charters and in the abbey rentals has shown that the highest surviving farms in the Lammermuir Hills date from this period. Some of these were substantial, for example the grange at Spertildon (now Gammelshiel, Berwickshire), which stood at 300 m O.D., contained in 1300 two carucates (c. 108 ha) of tillage, 1,400 sheep and 16 cottages for shepherds and their families.[18]

How much of this land was later abandoned to moor is not known, but large areas of abandoned cultivation ridges occur adjacent to steadings which are known to have flourished in about 1300, and at least a dozen steadings mentioned in early monastic charters do not appear on detailed maps of the sixteenth and seventeenth centuries. Some may have been deserted because they were unviable, others were certainly abandoned as a consequence of the English invasions in the fifteenth century. In the upper Merse of Berwickshire the Exchequer Rolls indicate that in 1497 and 1499 the lands were so wasted that either they were not laboured or the crops were destroyed.[19]

Most reversion seems to have occurred, however, in the late seventeenth and early eighteenth centuries. Fourteen farmsteads located by Timothy Pont in his survey of 1583-96, and whose sites have been located on aerial photographs or in the field, were abandoned before 1750[20] but after 1627 (since they are mentioned in documents of that year[21]). Moreover, a further 37 settlements mentioned in charters or rentals of the late fifteenth or sixteenth centuries likewise disappear from the documentary or map record before 1750 and seem mostly to have been abandoned some time after about 1650, particularly after 1690.[22] Some abandonment was due to the amalgamation of farms — on the Roxburghe, Dunglass and Biel estates at least seven farms were absorbed by their neighbours.[23] On the marginal land at higher levels, however, there is evidence that farmsteads and farmland were being abandoned for their lack of economic viability. In the parish of Langton the Reports of 1627 recommended a reduction in rent for three farms and a moratorium on the rent of a further three[24]; and it is probably not a coincidence that of these six farms three were abandoned before 1750.[25] Smout and Fenton have referred to this trend as one of 'clearances for sheep farming on the classic pattern', though there is, as yet, little evidence to confirm this.[26]

The Limit of Cultivation c. 1750

Although the limit of cultivation in south-east Scotland saw some downhill retreat in the century between 1650 and 1750, it still stood at a remarkable elevation in the mid-eighteenth century. Its location at about this time can be reconstructed for almost the entire country from the Military Survey drawn up under the direction of General William Roy between 1747 and 1755.

In terms of landscape detail the Military Survey is the single most valuable record of eighteenth-century Scotland. Drawn at a scale of about 1:36,000, the coloured manuscript sheets record the location of farmsteads, cultivated land and roads with some locational inaccuracy but with remarkable comprehensiveness of detail[27] (Plate 6). In south-east Scotland a comparison of the Survey with other county maps and estate documents revealed only 35 farmsteads omitted in error, these amounting to less than 5 per cent of the total then in existence.[28] In addition, there was close correspondence between the location of aerially mapped abandoned farmland and the cultivation symbols of the Military Survey. Thus the cultivation limits marked on the Military Survey apparently reflect with a reasonable accuracy the cultivation limits of the mid-eighteenth century.

The location of these cultivation limits is illustrated in Figure 8.1, which has been plotted from the 1:144,000 reduction of the Military Survey. This reveals the surprising height and remoteness of the farmed area, which extended far up the glens that penetrate the Highlands from the south-east, such as Glen Esk, Glen Clova, Glen Shee and Glen Garry, and far into the Cairngorms from the Don, the Cabrach and along Speyside. In the Southern Uplands it is clear that the limits of cultivation extended to the very ends of Nithsdale and Annandale, and far up the many headwater valleys of the Tweed; and in the valleys that breach the Lammermuir plateau cultivation was mapped at elevations frequently exceeding 350 m O.D. and is confirmed by evidence of relict cultivation ridges on aerial photographs.

In contrast to the high-level cultivation in the glens, Figure 8.1 also emphasises the large tracts of uncultivated low or moderately elevated land which had

Figure 8.1: The Distribution of Improved Farmland in Scotland, c. 1750 and c. 1860

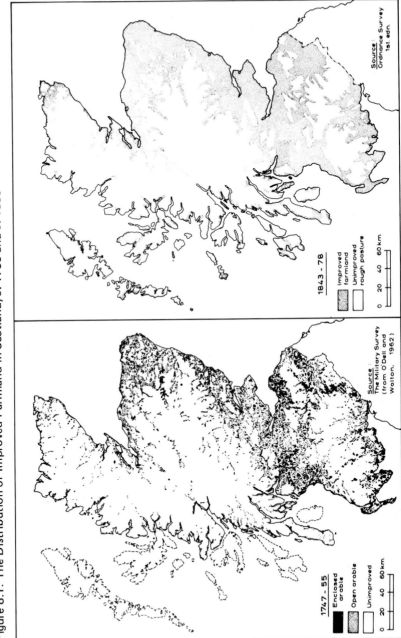

For explanation, see text. (Data for c, 1750 after O'Dell and Walton)

evidently been 'leap-frogged' during the early upward advance. Much of the Upper Merse (*c*. 190 m O.D.) in Berwickshire and Roxburghshire remained unimproved moor, as did much of the coastal region of Kirkcudbrightshire and the Machers of Wigton. The foothills of the Sidlaw Hills in Angus lay un-reclaimed, and substantial areas of upland plateau in Aberdeenshire and Banffshire had been ignored in favour of the higher but more sheltered straths and glens. The Black Isle and Tain peninsula had apparently been reclaimed only at their fringes.

The scale and pattern of change which occurred in the next hundred years can be assessed by comparing the limits of the cultivated area marked on the Military Survey with the location of the moorland edge on first-edition Ordnance Survey maps, which are available at six-inch or one-inch scales from 1843 in the south and from 1878 in the north (Plate 7). The scale of change between 1750 and 1860 is surprising (Figure 8.1). On the one hand there occurred a substantial retreat from the high land in strath, glen and valley; on the other, there seems to have been widespread reclamation of the lowland mosses and lower plateau uplands — a consolidation into the farmed area of islands of moor that had been avoided in earlier times.

By 1860, there were few blocks of moor interrupting the blanket of lowland arable, and the limits of cultivation were by now more clearly represented by a contour line along the Scottish hillside. Many of those areas reclaimed between 1750 and 1860 were moderately elevated and characterised by poorly drained podsols: for example, the improved land of the Upper Merse now extended to the very foot of the Lammermuirs and Cheviots. In Ayrshire the outliers of foothill at Maybole were reclaimed; and in north-east Aberdeenshire the hills above New Pitsligo and Old Meldrum were taken in.

While there was advance on the lowland, there was retreat at high level. Almost every strath and glen where cultivation had once extended beyond 300 m O.D. saw the permanent abandonment to moor of its most remote farmland, often land which had been initially reclaimed far back in the Middle Ages. The details of this retreat are not apparent at the small scale illustrated in Figure 8.1, and their full discussion must await analysis at the large scale in the latter part of this chapter. But the broad comparison that has been made between the pattern for 1750 and 1860 has indicated that the overall trend was one of consolidation and rationalisation — the reclamation of islands of moor at lower levels, and the retreat from elevated farms in the sheltered glens. The net change was probably one of massive gain to the farmed area: the national area of crops and grass recorded in the Board of Trade June Returns for 1866 was 1.7 million ha (or 21 per cent of the land area),[29] while a rough measure of the cultivated area recorded by Roy amounts to less than 1.2 million ha (15 per cent).

It is possible to establish the details of these national trends by reference to reclamation and reversion at the regional level. The subsequent sections of this paper therefore attend to the detailed mapping and dating, first, of the advance and consolidation of improved farmland and, second, of the rationalisation of the moorland edge by retreat.

Advance and Consolidation

Sources

There is no nationwide source of evidence on reclamation in Scotland until the collection of acreage data was initiated by the Board of Trade in 1866. What might appear to be an earlier and partially comprehensive source has drawbacks: reports by parish ministers in the *Old Statistical Account* (1791-9) (hereafter *OSA*) included comment on the expansion or contraction of cultivation since 1760, but these reports cannot be regarded with much confidence, being based at worst on hearsay and at best on a partial view of the local farming scene. Morgan's study of all 21 volumes of the *Account* revealed 105 parishes (out of a total of 893) which reported some expansion, but there seems to be no regional pattern in their distribution.[30] Only seven parishes acknowledged contraction of the cultivated area — all in the west, and especially in southern Argyllshire (Lochgoilhead, Kilmorich, Strachur and Stralachlan) — and the most frequent explanation given was the letting of farms to immigrant sheep farmers.[31] Since it is known from other sources that substantial contraction did occur in many parishes, but it is not mentioned in the *Account*, the source is certainly not comprehensive.

It is possible, however, to map and date areas of reclamation at the local level from a time-series of large-scale county maps carefully selected for their original-ity and comprehensiveness.[32] If care is taken to discount the effect of increasing comprehensiveness in the map series, then the appearance of 'new' farmsteads in mid-series is an indication of the establishment of new farms and points to the location of associated reclamation of moor. For the Lammermuir Hills levels of accuracy in the map series may be regarded as sufficiently high by 1770 to indicate that additions to the maps represent new farmsteads. The sites of these farmsteads were located on aerial photographs or on the ground, and their layout and structure were examined in order to confirm their date of establishment. The use of aerial photographs and estate plans also enables identification of the probable extent of reclamation related to the new settle-ment.

The advantage of county maps and aerial photographs as data sources for this type of survey is that they are spatially comprehensive, that is they yield evidence throughout the area of study in contrast to estate plans and rentals which may provide evidence over a restricted area for which the documents are extant. The comprehensive mapping of reclamation provides a framework upon which the second stage of the survey — its dating — can be implemented. Many intakes can be approximately dated by reference to the morphology of cultivation ridges where these were abandoned soon after reclamation —

abandonment which quite frequently occurred during the 'heady' days of the Improvement era. The morphology of these ridges — straight, low and with a high ridge:furrow ratio — has been demonstrated to be dependable evidence of post-Improvement cultivation, and the aerial survey of all areas of relict ridges can safely distinguish between those which were abandoned before and those abandoned after the Improvement era (Plates 9 and 10).[33] The broad base of this approximate dating provides a surface upon which to extrapolate from specific dating of a limited number of sites that is enabled by the study of surviving estate documents. This complementary use of spatially comprehensive and spatially restricted sources can be employed to reconstruct the chronology of reclamation at the local level.

The Chronology in South-east Scotland

At the time of the Military Survey the limit of cultivation in south-east Scotland followed a very different line from that 75 years later (Figures 8.2 and 8.3). In the 1750s it lay at very high levels at the headwaters of the Monynut and Whitteadder which breach the Lammermuir from the south-east. Here cultivation extended up to 360 m O.D. and was associated with farms like Friardykes and Mayshiel which had a history reaching back to the monastic period. Similarly,

Figure 8.2: The Limit of Cultivation in South-East Scotland *c*.1750, and Farm Abandonment 1750-1825

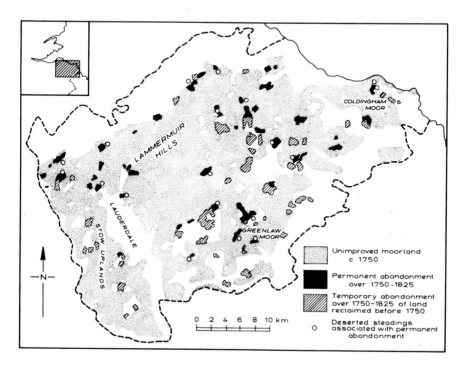

on the upper reaches of Lauderdale there is evidence on the Military Survey, confirmed by relict cultivation ridges and settlement sites on aerial photographs, of cultivation up to 400 m O.D. In general it is fair to say that at no time since the mid-eighteenth century have the furthest limits of improved farmland been at so high a level.

In contrast there lay, at much lower levels, extensive upland moor (for example, over much of the Stow Uplands at 230 to 350 m O.D.) and unreclaimed lowland mosses (for example, those lying at c.125 m O.D. at Westruther and Greenlaw). The cultivation limit thus ranged from 400 m O.D. at Tollis Hill above a headwater valley of the Leader to below 150 m O.D. on the lowland mosses of the Upper Merse.

Table 8.1: Reclamation and Reversion in South-East Scotland, 1750-1825

| | Reclamation | | | Reversion | |
	No. of steadings established	Associated primary reclamation (ha)	Additional temporary reclamation (ha)	No. of steadings abandoned	Associated permanent reversion (ha)	Additional temporary reversion (ha)
1750-70	29*	1,150	1,000*	21	80	2,500*
1770-1800	31	1,140	2,000*	70	150	500*
1800-25	49	2,940	1,500*	54	240	1,500*

*estimates

Sources: county maps, aerial photographs, 1st edn Ordnance Survey, field survey.

In 1750 the moorland area of the Stow Uplands and Lammermuir Hills probably exceeded 61,700 ha, but by 1825 it had been reduced to 56,490 ha. The location, timing and process of this trend is of especial interest: the distribution of new farms (80 in all) which appear between 1770 and 1825 reveals a distinct bias toward the Stow Uplands, lowland mosses and eastern uplands (Table 8.1, Figure 8.3). About 4,080 ha of primary reclamation in previously unreclaimed moorland were associated with 18 of these new farms, and an additional 3,500 ha were taken in once again from long-abandoned farmland. The distribution of primary reclamation which is illustrated in Figure 8.3 can only partly be confirmed by the extant documentary record, but is believed to be accurate.

Most of this reclamation seems to have taken place after 1780. With the recovery of prices, first in the 1750s but particularly from 1762, the unreclaimed moorlands were regarded rather differently than twenty years before. In 1776 a renowned 'Improver' declared: 'I present to the view of my reader an immense moor between Greenlaw in Berwickshire, and Fala in Mid-Lothian, as a desirable subject for an improving farmer, now that there is access to lime by a turnpike-road.'[34] Yet there is surprisingly little evidence that this offer was accepted.

Figure 8.3: The Limit of Cultivation in South-East Scotland *c.*1750, and Reclamation 1750-1825

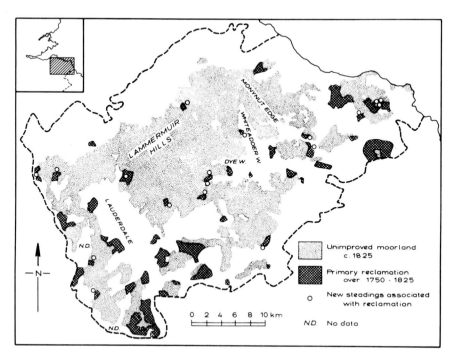

Moreover, Andrew Wight's reports (1778) for the commissioners of the annexed estates make no mention of reclamation in south-east Scotland.[35] This was apparently largely delayed until the 1780s and 1790s when it is frequently recorded in the *OSA*.[36] In the parish of Melrose, which comprises the southern part of the Stow Uplands, the output of grain was reckoned to have doubled between 1760 and 1790 owing to the extension of arable land; and on the estate of Marchmont substantial intakes of arable occurred on three farms at the edge of lowland mosses soon after the price of oats reached its first peak just before 1800.[37]

At the higher levels reclamation was characterised by a few isolated schemes which were, as often as not, spectacular failures. One of the earlier schemes was that of Riddel Lodge above Lauderdale, the entire farm being laid out in the 1760s with 140 ha of newly improved land. One half of this farmland had been abandoned back to moor by 1808 and the remainder had reverted by 1820.[38]

In general, the reclamation of the high moors was delayed until the 1790s, and was then mainly put to turnips or clover for sheep: and a second leap in grain prices after 1803, together with improving access in the hills which allowed the transport of lime, encouraged intake even of the remote haughs.[39] This advance seems to have continued up to about 1816 after which the crash in cereal prices and runs of poor seasons conspired to induce rapid abandonment. One remarkable exception was the cultivation of 35 ha in 1818 on Tullis Hill in upper Lauderdale which, at 360 m O.D., must have represented an unrealistic investment even in times of high prices and fine summers.[40]

The Chronology Elsewhere

Walton's comparison of the Military Survey with Thomson's *Atlas* of 1828 for the north-east of Scotland reveals a similar trend to that in the south-east.[41] Over the period 1750-1825 new farms were 'planted' on the peat-covered interfluves of Buchan or on the unreclaimed fluvio-glacial sands of the lowland valleys. The empty spaces on Roy's map in the lowland north-east were quickly filled up. On the Banffshire plateau there was widespread intake, particularly on the Hill of Aultmore which was 'studded far and wide with the cottages of the poor'.[42]

Reclamation programmes which received wide publicity in the *Statistical account* and the Board of Agriculture Reports were generally the more spectacular. For example, reclamation of Kincardine moss between Aberdeen and Stonehaven was directed by the estate owners themselves and involved the investment of substantial sums.[43] Elsewhere, however, reclamation was piecemeal, and was undertaken by cottagers who were given, rent-free, a plot of moor on the condition that they brought it into cultivation. Many of these people had been dispossessed of their livelihoods on older farmland either by the break-up of farming townships or by the amalgamation of single-tenant farms. For example, in the parish of Kilmuir (Easter Ross) the *OSA* reported that '300 acres of muir have been brought into cultivation in the last 25 years by heritors allowing "mealers" to build huts on the muir.' They had been given an advance of twenty shillings to build a house, a small 'acknowledgement' in hens and eggs and a promise of seven years free of rent.[44]

In the south-west Highlands the limited cartographic evidence points to limits of cultivation being near their maximum extent in the second and third quarters of the eighteenth century. Gailey believes that Wilson's map (1786-7) of the Tayvallich peninsula in North Knapdale (Argyllshire) captures the effective maximum and that Bald's map (1809) does likewise for Ardnamurchan.[45]

Retreat and Rationalisation

It is also possible to reconstruct the path of retreating cultivation by a study of aerial photographs (Plates 9 and 10).[46] The quantity and distribution of permanent abandonment, mapped in this way, can be confirmed by reference to the location of deserted farmsteads detected from the sequence of county maps and checked in the field, while further confirmation is available from surviving estate plans. The abandonment can then be dated approximately by reference to the morphology of relict cultivation ridges. In south-east Scotland, 98 per cent of all abandonment could, by this means, be ascribed a date of abandonment either before or after the time of Improvement.[47] This dating can be supplemented by reference to the time of disappearance of farmsteads from the county map sequence, and can in a few instances be pin-pointed for specific years from a time series of estate plans and rentals.

The spatially comprehensive but general dating from aerial photographs and county maps, supplemented by specific but spatially limited dating from documents, enables the chronology of retreat by the cultivation limit to be discerned at two levels – the synoptic trend at the regional level, and the specific trend at the local level.

The Chronology in South-east Scotland: Regional Trends

At least 145 farmsteads were abandoned in the Lammermuir Hills between about 1750 and 1825 and permanent reversion associated with this retreat of settlement probably exceeded 480 ha. Most reversion was the product of farm amalgamation rather than of the abandonment *en bloc* of marginal farms, but a substantial part (24 steadings) occurred at high level in the upper valleys of the Whiteadder, Bothwell and Monynut waters (Figure 8.2). Most abandonment over 1750-1800 was of old-established settlement, with the occasional reversion of recent intakes, but over 1800-25 the trend was towards the permanent reversion of new farmland. In these years about one-sixth of the reversion was of land probably reclaimed after 1650, while the remainder was of land first reclaimed in the Middle Ages.

Temporary abandonment was more commonly the product of farm amalgamation and generally occurred at lower levels. It seems to have been most prevalent in the 1760s and 1770s and in the 1820s. Indeed, a great wave of both permanent and temporary reversion occurred after the initial fall of cereal prices had been compounded by further falls in 1814 and 1815.[48] Reclamation, which had continued in optimistic fashion even over 1813-16, now ceased and much new land was abandoned back to moor.[49] The pace of retreat accelerated in the 1820s and 1830s and new farms, such as those at Riddel Lodge (Lauder parish), were abandoned in their entirety.

By the mid-1830s the combined effect of low prices, high rents and poor seasons (in 1816 and 1817) had eaten into the wartime profits of the previous twenty years. A submission by one local estate owner to the Select Committee on the State of Agriculture (1836) noted of his neighbours: 'from being generally in comfortable circumstances (in 1816) the great majority of them were soon reduced to little better than a state of bankruptcy, with the high money rents that they had contracted.'[50]

In summary, it is clear that, while the pace of high-level abandonment which had characterised the preceding century slowed considerably, there was still a marked retreat over the period 1750-70, though it is probable that this was balanced by reclamation at lower levels. Over 1770-1800 sectoral advance at lower levels became more marked and more than balanced high-level retreat, and by the turn of the century the limits of cultivation stood at their highest levels since the fourteenth century. Over 1800-25 sectoral advance accelerated, but was increasingly balanced by the reversion of high arable land, and after 1825 overall limits of cultivation saw substantial retreat due to increased reversion and reduced intake. In all, 5,230 ha of arable were taken in from the moor over 1750-1825 and 4,500 ha of formerly improved land were abandoned (Table 8.1). These represent 10.0 per cent and 8.6 per cent, respectively, of the entire area above 250 m O.D. in the Lammermuir Hills.

The Chronology in South-East Scotland: Local Trends

For those areas in which a time-series of farm rentals or estate plans survive, it is frequently possible to reconstruct the detailed chronology of more local trends by reference to the convergence of evidence from both the spatially restricted and spatially comprehensive sources. One example of such a reconstruction will suffice, though it should be noted that this is one of many which could be constructed for various parts of Scotland.

The sample chronology is based upon evidence from a study of ridge morphology, county map sequence and documentary record on part of the Marchmont estate in Berwickshire. It illustrates that there occurred here a complex history of continually contracting arable from the mid-eighteenth to the mid-nineteenth century (Figure 8.4). All that remains today of five sizeable arable farms in the seventeenth century are small islands of pasture around two much- diminished steadings. Bedshiel, which in the eighteenth century was a village large enough to support a schoolmaster,[51] now barely supports one farming family. This contraction of improved farmland is a trend that has, of course, been typical of much of marginal Scotland.

Table 8.2 and Figure 8.4 illustrate the details of the local trend. The two main phases of retreat seem to have occurred, first, at some date before 1800 (probably in the late seventeenth and early eighteenth centuries) and, second, over 1800-1825.

The Chronology Elsewhere

A detailed chronology of retreat, of the kind now available for south-east Scotland, is not yet available for other regions of Scotland. All we may do is speculate on the basis of partial surveys and point to the directions in which further and more detailed study would be most rewarding.

There are almost no published conclusions concerning abandonment elsewhere in Scotland, in the century or so leading up to the 1750s. Specific exceptions to this rule are commentaries upon the reversion of farmland in Kintyre and upland Banffshire resulting from famine and plague in the 1650s and 1690s.[52]

For the period 1750-1825, however, there is more information. In the north-east, Walton's comparison of the Military Survey and Thomson's *Atlas* indicates a substantial withdrawal from the very highest limits (over 400 m O.D.) in the

Figure 8.4: The Chronology of Contracting Farmland, 1760-1850, at Bedshiel, Greenlaw Parish (Berwickshire)

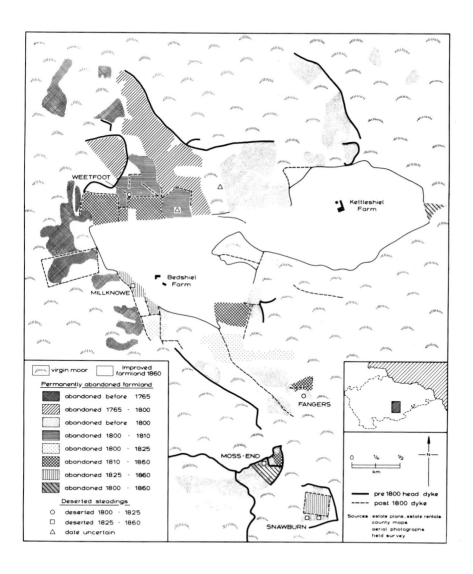

headwater valleys of the Dee above Inverey (Aberdeenshire) and above Duthil in Nairn.[53] Contraction from the high-level frontier of earlier advance seems also to have occurred in the west — in Ardnamurchan and Southend on Kintyre, for example, the distribution of abandonment occurs precisely in those remote

Table 8.2: Permanent Reversion at Bedshiel, Greenlaw (Berwickshire)

Date of reversion	area of reversion (ha)	source of evidence
pre-1765 unspecified	49.5	aerial photographs, MSS.
pre-1800	157.0	ridge morphology
1765-1800	52.5	MSS.; county maps
1800-10	31.0	SRO GD 158/20; county maps
1800-25	41.0	SRO GD 158/20; county maps
1825-60	12.5	county maps
1800-60	41.0	ridge morphology
Total	371.0	

MS. sources: Plan of Marchmont (1765), Marchmont House, Berws.
Plan of Bedshield Acres (1791), Marchmont House, Berws.

haughs that also characterised abandonment in the south-east (Figure 8.2). It has not yet been possible to date this retreat with any accuracy, though it probably occurred before 1800.

Gailey's analysis of the height frequency of settlements marked on the Military Survey (but which now lie in ruins or have disappeared completely) reveals that the desertion of farmsteads and reversion of high-lying farmland went hand in hand.[54] There was a widespread retreat both of the upper limits of cultivation and the upper limits of settlement.

Widespread desertion of settlement has also been found in Glen Lednock (c.200 m O.D., Perthshire). Here at least 52 settlements, some comprising more than 20 separate structures, have been identified on the ground. They were probably inhabited in 1783 because they were mapped by James Stobie at about that date.[55] The timing of their desertion has not yet been ascertained, but probably occurred in the early nineteenth century. Similar widespread retreat of both agriculture and settlement occurred in upper Glen Esk, Angus, at about 250 m O.D. Here, at Berryhill behind Keeny Burn, an exodus of the last tenants in about 1812 has left an entire valley of relict cultivation ridges and ruined steadings.[56]

The Forces for Change

A basic premiss behind this survey has been that understanding the spatial pattern of particular landscapes should enable an increased comprehension of the processes underlying landscape form; and since these processes may be common to different areas they, in turn, provide the basis for the more general comprehension of landscapes elsewhere. It is therefore instructive to evaluate the forces behind changes in the cultivated area in those parts of Scotland for which we have a full chronology, because a knowledge of these will increase our comprehension of changes in the cultivated area that occurred in other, less well documented, regions of Scotland. These forces can be classified as commercial, technological and institutional. Those of a social and political nature, which less directly touched upon change in agriculture, will not be considered here.

The Commercial Stimulus for Change

There were four fundamental commercial stimuli for changes in the extent of improved farmland at work in seventeenth- and eighteenth-century Scotland, changes which lie at the root of the Improving Movement as a whole. The first of these was the move from a quasi-subsistence towards a commercial farming economy. Evidence of this may be found in the move to farm rents payable in cash rather than in kind. On the estates of Innerwich, Cockburnspath and Belton, which included land on the Lammermuir Hills, a major phase of rent commutation occurred over 1710-70. By 1740 one-third of the rentals were paid in cash and by 1770 most upland farms were paying a full money rent.[57] On lower farms this trend occurred a good deal earlier (see Chapter 5).

A second commercial stimulus was the rising price paid for agricultural commodities. Over 1700-50 cereal prices in Scotland had remained remarkably stable.[58] The slow growth of demand was accommodated by increases in productivity and the lack of a rise in prices was apparently reflected in low rents and continuing retreat by the limit of cultivation; but in the late 1770s the prices of oats and wool exhibited pronounced falls.[59] Bankruptcy among tenant farmers became commonplace and several estates adopted policies for the elimination of small farms at the moorland edge.[60] After the outbreak of war in 1793 prices rose steeply and, following a brief recession in 1802-3, resumed the climb to a peak in 1809-15 when the price of oats was double the average for 1770-90, while the price of sheep had increased by 300 per cent and that of wool by 250 per cent. The greater increases for stock prices probably explain the quantity of new land put down to turnips and grass for fodder rather than to cereals which would otherwise have given the quicker return to capital; and the reliance on roots and grasses was clearly an important factor in delaying the reversion of upland arable until the fall in stock prices after 1819. Yet, as the value of meat and wool had risen more sharply in the early years of the war, so they fell more steeply than cereals after 1820 and encouraged swift reversion, first to long ley and, later, to rough pasture.

A third commercial stimulus for reclamation was the rising value of farmland, a trend illustrated by the growth of farm rents. Over the thirty years prior to 1794 the rent for poor arable land in East Lothian had quadrupled, reflecting the changing balance between rising market prices and more stable costs of production.[61] Over the following fourteen years the rent for similar land seems to have almost doubled, and in the following decade increased by a further 10 per cent.[62] During the war years 1793-1815 the total rental of the estate of Marchmont rose by 93 per cent, an indication of the increased demand for land by prospective tenants;[63] and on those estates which offered vacant farms to the highest bidder rents rose even more steeply.

A fourth factor affecting the timing and pace of reclamation was the availability of capital, for the costs of moorland reclamation were substantial. Towards the end of the boom years, sufficient capital had been accumulated by tenant farmers from the profits of the previous decade, but before 1800 reclamation projects were largely financed by landowners.[64] The new incentive to estate activity in reclamation came from underlying changes in the institutional structure of farming.

Changes in Institutional Structure

After about 1750, merchants, lawyers and manufacturers increasingly bought into landownership for prestige and security of investment. The extent of transfer was considerable, for example two-thirds of Roxburghshire changed hands between 1750 and 1815.[65] The move brought both more capital into agriculture and, with the division of estates for sale, a reduction in their average size. In the Lammermuir Hills and Stow Uplands the number of separate estates rose from 107 in 1771-2 to about 120 in 1791-8, 134 in 1884 and 140 by 1870.[66] The increasing incidence of owner-occupancy led to greater attention to estate management and to both more intensive and more market-oriented farming.

Parallel to this, there occurred an increase in size of farms from amalgamation which frequently resulted in the abandonment of remote arable that was once cultivated from the subordinate steading. In the Lammermuir Hills as a whole, the number of farms decreased from about 1,000 in the seventeenth century to about 840 by 1800, 720 by 1850 and 580 by 1900. Between 1770 and 1850, the period of most amalgamation, the average size of farms increased by 21 per cent.[67]

Changes in Farming Technology

The stimulus of increased profitability promoted a widespread adoption of new farming techniques by the new generation of farmers and proprietors. Many of these techniques are discussed elsewhere in a more general context (see Chapter 9), but some relate particularly to changes in the extent of the farmed area.

More hardy strains of oats were widely adopted by Southern Upland farmers in the 1790s and these, in addition to turnips and rye-grass which were adopted over 1770-90, opened up wide areas of the moorland fringe as potential arable.[68] These, and the introduction of improved rotations, probably doubled the productivity of upland farmed under the old outfield system.[69] Improved breeds of sheep, particularly the Cheviot, were widely adopted in place of the Blackface on more sheltered ground and much of the new intake was probably put over to the provision of fodder for these.[70]

A major deterrent to the intake of new land was the cost of enclosure to keep stock out of the turnips and oats. This may explain the tardiness with which reclamation responded to rising prices in the 1780s. It was not until the late 1790s that the prices of both grain and livestock fully overcame objections to the intake and cropping of open land; and even then the reclamation which followed seems to have been envisaged only as a short-term investment because few of the intakes were enclosed. Indeed, none of the land later abandoned in upland south-east Scotland exhibits signs of enclosure. Consequently, when profits shrank after 1815, the new lands were soon abandoned. Thus the scarcity of pre-existing enclosure in the uplands not only retarded the advance of cultivation but ensured that much of it was only temporary.

A whole range of new implements was increasingly adopted in the late eighteenth and early nineteenth centuries and the swing-plough, in particular, had a major impact on the productivity of marginal arable land in Scotland (Plate 8). It was introduced into lowland parishes in the south-east in the 1770s and 1780s and into upland parishes in the 1790s, and enabled the construction of straight, low cultivation ridges which reduced the proportion of land wasted in the furrow from an average of one-third to one-fifth of the total area under the plough.[71] As a result of these changes productivity per unit area of cultivation would have increased by 13 per cent, which would have led, in circumstances of stable demand, to a matching reduction in the area under cultivation.

Increases in productivity also derived, of course, from a variety of other innovations. Cultivation was now perennial throughout the farm rather than on the infield alone, thus the area under tillage, which had traditionally been (at most) only two-thirds of the farm at any one time (the infield and one-half of the outfield) was now increased by 50 per cent. In addition, the seed: yield ratio of oats, which in the Middle Ages probably averaged 1 : 3, had increased to over 1 : 5. By 1820, after contraction on to the best land, it may have been 1 : 7.[72]

The sum effect on the productivity of arable land in Scotland must have been substantial: an increase of 13 per cent from the levelling of cultivation ridges, about 15 per cent from the move to perennial cultivation and probably another 40 per cent from increases in the return to seed. The suggestion is that, on average, the productivity of arable land in southern Scotland almost doubled between 1760 and 1820 — and it is interesting to note that this calculation is confirmed by the estimates of contemporary observers.[73] Such substantial increases in productivity probably account for the widespread contraction of tillage both before and after the 'boom' period. Only over 1790-1815 did the intensification of production fail to keep pace with demand and the farmed area undergo a marked expansion.

Conclusions

The extent of improved farmland is logically related to the size of the food market and output per unit area. Thus the explanation for nation-wide trends of advance and retreat by the limit of cultivation over 1750-1820 is found in the balance between, on the one hand, the growth in demand from a growing population and a booming wartime economy and, on the other hand, the increased supply from improving agricultural productivity. The overall result was a rationalisation of the boundary between improved farmland and unimproved moorland — a retreat from the high unproductive sites in the staths and glens that were first reclaimed in the Middle Ages and an advance on to the open moors of moderate elevation. The progress of these changes varied greatly as the diffusion of commercial, institutional and economic stimuli worked its way outwards from the hearth areas in the south-east and south-west. Thus the retreat of cultivation and desertion of high-lying settlements which occurred in south-east Scotland in the late eighteenth century was not apparent in Sutherland until twenty or thirty years later. Indeed, it is possible that the extent of desertions of farmsteads over 1770-1800 in the Lammermuirs represents an early phase of settlement 'clearance' that was not altogether unrelated to those of the nineteenth-century Highlands.

The net gain in output by Scottish agriculture was substantial — an increase in the farmed area by 40 per cent over 1750-1825 in concert with 100 per cent increases in productivity. The change to the Scottish landscape was also both extensive and lasting. At least 200,000 ha of low-lying moorland were reclaimed for the first time and remain improved today; and, in contrast, the sites of deserted farmsteads and heather-covered cultivation ridges comprise a relict landscape that is very much a characteristic feature of the valleys in the Southern Uplands and of the Highland glens.

The picture is, of course, far from complete. In particular, little is at present known of those changes in settlement and agriculture that occurred in the Highlands before about 1780. The method of mapping and dating the path of reclamation and reversion, and in particular the use of aerial photographs as a data source, should be useful here. The task ahead must be to develop a more detailed national picture by testing in other areas the ideas that have been developed in this chapter.

Notes

1. Eyre, S. R. (1961), 'The upward limit of enclosure on the East Moor of Derbyshire', *Trans. Inst. Br. Geog.*, *23*, 61-74

2. Robertson, I. M. L. (1949), 'The head-dyke: a fundamental line in Scottish geography', *Scottish Geographical Magazine* (hereafter *SGM*), *65*, 6-19

3. Ibid.

4. Parry, M. L. (1976), 'Abandoned farmland in upland Britain: a reconnaissance

survey in southern Scotland', *Geographical Journal, 142* 101-10

5. After the passage of both plague and destruction brought by Leslie's army in the 1640s, 29 out of 55 holdings in the parishes of Kilcolmhill and Kilbaan in Kintyre were recorded as wholly waste, and 13 as partially waste. See McKerral, A. (1948), *Kintyre in the seventeenth century* (Edinburgh), p. 78

6. MacSween, M. D. (1959), 'Transhumance in north Skye', *SGM, 75*, 75-88; Gailey, R. A. (1960), 'Settlement and population in Kintyre, 1750-1800', *SGM, 76*, 99-107; Gailey, R. A. (1963), 'Agrarian improvement and the development of enclosure in the south-west Highlands of Scotland', *Scottish History Review* (hereafter *SHR*), *42*, 105-25

7. Turnock, D. (1970), *Patterns of Highland development* (London), pp. 25-6

8. Ibid., pp. 27, 29

9. Gaskell, P. (1968), *Morvern transformed* (Cambridge), p. 25

10. Adam, R. J. (1972), *Papers on Sutherland estate management, 1802-16* (Publications of the Scottish History Society), 4th series, *8* and *9*

11. Lebon, J. H. G. (1937), 'Ayrshire' in Stamp, L. D. (ed.), *The land of Britain, the report of the Land Utilization Survey* (London), Part 1, pp. 1-83; Lebon, J. H. G. (1952), 'Old maps and rural change in Ayrshire', *SGM, 68*, 104-9

12. Geddes, A. (1951), 'Changes in rural life and landscape: 1500-1955', pp. 126-34 in Geddes, A. (ed.), *Scientific survey of south-east Scotland* (Edinburgh)

13. Ibid.; Third, B. M. W. (1957), 'The significance of Scottish estate plans and associated documents', *Scottish Studies, 1*, 39-64

14. See Orwin, C. W. (1929), *The reclamation of Exmoor* (Oxford); Hoskins, W. G. and Finberg, H. P. R. (1952), *Devonshire studies* (London); M'Caw, L. S. (1936), 'The black mountains' (unpublished PhD thesis, University of Manchester); Eyre (1961), 'limit of enclsoure'; Roberts, B. K., Turner, J. and Ward, P. F. (1973), 'Recent forest history and land use in Weardale, northern England', pp. 207-21 in Birks, H. J. B. and West, R. G., *Quaternary plant ecology* (London); Chapman, J. (1961), 'Changing agriculture and the moorland edge in the North York Moors' (unpublished MA thesis, University of London); Baker, A. R. H. (1966), 'Evidence in the "Nonarum Inquisitiones" of contracting waste lands in England during early fourteenth century', *Economic History Review* (hereafter *EHR*), *19*, 518-32; Williams, M. (1971), 'The enclosure and reclamation of the Mendip Hills, 1770-1870', *Agricultural History Review* (hereafter *AHR*), *19*, 65-81

15. Jones, G. R. J. (1965), 'Agriculture in north-west Wales during the late Middle Ages', pp. 47-53 in Taylor, J. A. (ed.), *Climatic change with special reference to Wales and its agriculture* (University College of Wales, Aberystwyth), Memo. No. 8; and see Thomas, D. (1963), *Agriculture in Wales during the Napoleonic Wars* (Cardiff)

16. Connell, K. H. (1950), 'The colonization of waste land in Ireland, 1780-1845', *EHR* (2nd series), *3*, 44-71

17. Sandnes, J. (1971), *Ødetid og Gjenreisning* (Oslo), pp. 130-95; Salvesen, H. (1976), 'The agrarian crisis in Norway in the late Middle Ages', pp. 58-60 in Dyer, C. C. (ed.), *Medieval Village Research Group Report*, no. 23

18. Bannatyne Club (1846), *Liber Sancte Marie de Calchou, 1113-1567* (Edinburgh), pp. 82, 465

19. *Letters and Papers*, Henry VIII, xx, ii: 20, quoted in Royal Commission for Ancient and Historical Monuments (Scotland), *Inventory of the monuments and constructions in the county of Berwickshire*, p. xxiv

20. Parry, M. L. (1976), 'The abandonment of upland settlement in southern Scotland', *SGM, 92*, 50-60

21. MacGrigor, A. (1835), *Reports on the state of certain parishes in Scotland (1627)* (Maitland Club, Edinburgh)

22. Parry, M. L. (1973), 'Changes in the upper limit of cultivation in south-east Scotland, 1600-1900' (unpublished PhD thesis, University of Edinburgh), pp. 200-27

23. Ibid., p. 229

24. MacGrigor (1835), *Reports*, pp. 16-19

25. Parry (1976), 'Abandoned farmland'

26. Smout, T. C. and Fenton, A. (1965), 'Scottish agriculture before the Improvers, an exploration', *AHR, 13*, 73-93

27. For details see Skelton, R. A. (1967), 'The Military Survey of Scotland, 1747-55', *SGM*, *83*, 5-16

28. Parry, M. L. (1975), County maps as historical sources', *Scottish Studies*, *19*, 15-26

29. Ministry of Agriculture, Fisheries and Food (1968), *A century of agricultural statistics* (London), p. 6

30. Morgan, V. (1969), 'The First Statistical Account as a basis for studying the agrarian geography of late eighteenth century Scotland' (unpublished PhD thesis, University of Cambridge), p. 20

31. Ibid., p. 22

32. Parry (1975), 'County maps'

33. Parry, M. L. (1976), 'A typology of cultivation ridges in southern Scotland', *Tools and Tillage*, *3*, 3-19

34. Kames, Lord (1776), *The gentleman farmer* (Edinburgh), p. 67

35. Wight, A. (1778), *The present state of husbandry in Scotland* (Edinburgh)

36. Sinclair, Sir J. (1791-9), *Statistical account of Scotland*, Vol. XIII, pp. 391, 223; Vol. XII, p. 44; Vol. VI, pp. 135, 157, 438-9; Vol. XXI, p. 485, Vol. IX, p. 78 (Edinburgh)

37. Ibid., Vol. IX, p. 78; *Report relative to the lordship and estate of Marchmont, 1819*, Scottish Record Office (hereafter SRO), GD 158/20: 49, 59, 69

38. Plan of Riddel Lodge, 1808, SRO, RHP 1215/1; Plan of part of the farm of Tullis Hill (1820), SRO, RHP 1258

39. For reclamation in the 1790s see Hepburn, G. B. (1794), *General view of the agriculture and rural economy of the county of East Lothian* (Edinburgh) p. 96; Lowe, A. (1794), *General view of the agriculture of the county of Berwick* (London), p. 104. For reclamation after 1803 see Kerr, R. (1809), *General view of the agriculture of the county of Berwick* (London), p. 343

40. SRO, RHP 1258

41. Walton, K. (1963), 'Regional settlement', pp. 87-99 in O'Dell, A. C. and Mackintosh, J. (eds.), *The north-east of Scotland* (Aberdeen)

42. Sinclair (1791-9), *Statistical account*, Vol. IX, p. 216, quoted by Walton (1963), 'Regional settlement'

43. Sinclair (1791-9), *Statistical account*, Vol. VI, p. 477

44. Ibid., Vol. V, p. 183

45. Gailey (1963) 'Agrarian improvement'

46. For further details see Parry, M. L. (1976), 'Abandoned farmland in upland Britain', *Geographical Journal*, *142*, 101-10

47. Parry (1976), 'A typology of cultivation ridges in southern Scotland'

48. Mitchison, R. (1965), 'The movements of Scottish corn prices in the seventeenth and eighteenth centuries', *EHR* (second series), *18*, 278-91

49. SRO, GD 158/20: 57, 59, 61

50. *Third report of the select committee appointed to enquire into the state of agriculture* (1836), Minutes of Evidence, Q: 9932

51. Gibson, R. (1905), *An old Berwickshire town* (Edinburgh), pp. 4, 32, 120-2, 235

52. Walton (1963), 'Regional settlement'

53. Ibid.

54. Gailey (1960), 'Settlement and population'; Gailey (1962), 'The evolution of Highland rural settlement with particular reference to Argyleshire' *Scottish Studies*, *6*, 155-77

55. Bain, E. C. (1972), *A short guide to deserted settlements in Glen Lednock* (Strathearn Archaeological Society, Auchterarder)

56. Personal communication, April 1978, M. F. Michie, Glenesk Museum

57. SRO, GD 6/1703, 1709, 1712, 1717/1, 1727, 1762, 1742, 1755, Rentals of the Barony of Innerwick and Thornton; SRO, GD 206/2/7/171/1-5, Rentals of Cockburnspath; SRO GD 73/1/11, Rental of the Baronie Belton

58. For details see Mitchison (1965), 'Movements of Scottish corn prices'

59. Parry (1973), 'Changes in the upper limit of cultivation', p. 370

60. For example the Marchmont Estate, see note 36; for the Dunglass estate see Reading University Library, EAS 1/2/25, 27 and 1A/1/15-48, Accounts of the Dunglass estate; for the Biel estate see SRO, GD 6/1769/1, 9, 15

61. Hepburn, G. B. (1794), *General view of the agriculture and rural economy of the county of East Lothian* (Edinburgh), p. 128

62. Kerr, R. (1809), *General view of the agriculture of the county of Berwick* (London), Appx. p. 56; SRO, GD 158/20: 10-11

63. SRO, GD 158/20: 11

64. Smout, T. C. (1964), 'Scottish landowners and economic growth 1650-1850' *Scottish Journal of Political Economy*, *11*, 218-34

65. Smout, T. C. (1969), *A history of the Scottish people, 1560-1830* (London), p. 283

66. Parry (1973), 'Changes in the upper limit of cultivation', p. 359

67. Ibid., p. 362

68. Kerr (1809), *Berwick*, pp. 244-5; Lowe, A. (1794), *General view of the agriculture of the county of Berwick* (London), p. 96; *Farmer's Magazine* (1803), 'Account of the district of Lammermuir, drawn up in 1794' *4*, 507-11; Robertson, G. (1829), *Rural recollections* (Irvine), p. 333

69. *Farmer's Magazine* (1811), 'Comparative view of East Lothian husbandry in 1778 and 1810', *11*, 51-68, 204-23, 343-53, 515-23

70. Fairbairn, J. (1823), *A treatise upon breeding, rearing and feeding Cheviot and Black-faced sheep* (Edinburgh); Sinclair (1791-9), *Statistical account*, Vol. XIII, p. 386

71. Parry (1976), 'A typology of cultivation ridges in southern Scotland'

72. Lowe (1794), *Berwick*, p. 96; Kerr (1809), *Berwick*, p. 244, *Farmer's Magazine* (1811); Robertson (1829), 'Comparative view of East Lothian husbandry', 383

73. Robertson (1829), *Rural Recollections*, p. 383

THE RESHAPED COUNTRYSIDE

9 THE RESHAPED AGRICULTURAL LANDSCAPE

J. B. Caird

The landscape of rural Scotland generally presents a strikingly planned, geo-metrical appearance of ordered fields, mostly rectangular or square in shape, with farmsteads deliberately placed at a site convenient for planned, commercial operations, and the basic layout enclosed by farm and field boundaries of stone dyke, hedge, or post and wire fence interspersed with shelter belts and plantations and linked by farm roads. While the overall shape of some of the farms can be linked to the earlier landscape, most of the present landscape stems basically from the period of agricultural improvements broadly from 1700 to 1850. Estate plans and documents and correspondence make it clear that changes were under way on a limited scale on a few estates early in the eighteenth century; an examination of Roy's Map shows that landscape change was under way in the Lowlands of Scotland by the middle of the eighteenth century (Plate 6) and by the last decade, almost all the writers of the *Statistical Account*[1] mentioned activity which was changing the face of their parishes; by the time of the *New Statistical Account*[2] the reshaping of the landscape was near completion, as the following excerpt from the parish of Airlie in Angus makes clear: 'almost all the fields are enclosed, either with hedges or dry stone dykes. The former, with the interspersed woodlands, give to a great part of the parish a warm, clothed appearance'.[3] By about 1850, the old ordering of the landscape and its concomitant settlement patterns had largely disappeared over much of Scotland and on some estates change was accomplished in a short period, while in others change proceeded over a longer period. There was both evolution and revolution in the reshaping of the agricultural landscape.

The agents of change were the proprietors of the estates who took the deci-sion to remodel their estates. Some of them, for example Cockburn of Ormistoun[4] and the Duke of Argyll,[5] closely superintended the detailed plan-ning, while others commissioned land surveyors to draft the new structure of their properties.

The Process of Change

The Role of the Land Surveyors

The crucial role played by land surveyors in the Improving Movement has been stressed by Adams in Chapter 7, but it is important to note also that the geometrical lines of the landscape of rural Scotland can be largely attributed to their work alone. The earliest members of this professional group, established around 1730, were schoolmasters (often mathematicians) and were first employed in divisions of commonties, measuring areas and laying out boundaries between the proprietors, hence the geometrical lines. From dividing commonties, where legal decisions became permanent landscape features, they progressed to surveying and planning the new estate landscapes of the improving period. Some of the larger estates employed English surveyors such as Thomas Winter, a Norfolk surveyor employed by Sir Archibald Grant of Monymusk. Not only did the land surveyors draw up plans of the estates but they also indicated the quality of the land, particularly the soils, and their suitability for various types of land use. From their measurements and drawings, boundaries of estates, farms and fields, bounded by dykes, hedges and ditches, emerged as landscape features.[6]

If the land surveyors, the country planners of their time, have left an indelible mark on the agricultural landscape, their plans[7] provide evidence for the date and character of landscape change. William Cockburn, a surveyor employed by the Forfeited Estates commissioners to survey the estate of Perth, drew up the survey on which Figure 9.1(a) is based.[8] From Bald's plan of Ardnamurchan and Sunart it has been noted that in 1807 only one farm, Ardnastang, had been lotted.[9] Two plans of Newton (Midlothian),[10] by different surveyors in 1754 and 1756, indicate the speed of the transformation on the estate from hamlet cluster and rigs to rectangular fields, shelter belts and a new house and formal garden, underlining the point that on some estates at least, agricultural improvement was accomplished at a revolutionary pace. Reid's plan of North Uist,[11] 'drawn up in 1799 when Lord MacDonald was intent on improving this estate', provided the basis for the lotting of the farms into crofts and the rectangular croft boundaries were superimposed on the plan, probably in 1813 when the crofts were created.[12] Adams has remarked of those professionals of the improving period that 'Before him he saw an open, fragmented scene, half moorland, but he visualised an ordered, geometrical, fenced landscape.'[13] The land surveyors, beyond doubt, established the lines and much of the detail of the present agricultural landscape.

Enclosure

The hallmark of the reshaped landscape was enclosure, but here it must be stressed that there were some early enclosures or 'Parks' around the lairds' houses long before the improvers began to reshape the landscape. In the parish of Kirkoswald in Ayrshire

> there were several enclosures, and some very fine old trees, about Cullean Castle. But the fences were mostly of stone. Of these enclosures, the most remarkable was that called the Cow park of Cullean, containing about 50 acres (20 ha), which had been in pasture for two hundred years, yet there is not, to this day, to be seen in it the smallest spot of fog. There was also

the park of Turnberry, containing about 460 acres (186 ha), which was enclosed with stone about the beginning of the century, and has been in pasture ever since.[14]

These parks stem from an Act of James IV in 1503 which ordained landowners to have parks and to plant at least one acre (0.4 ha) of wood in areas where there was no significant forest[15] (see Chapter 10). Among the first areas to be enclosed by the improvers were the commonties, grazing and peat-cutting areas possessed in common by several proprietors. Adams has recorded over 200,000 ha of known former commonties.[16] These areas were apportioned among the several proprietors. Hassendean commonty, lying at 183-274 m O.D. in the Southern Uplands, was divided between 1761 and 1763 and the surveyor's boundaries became estate boundaries, while along the central line from which the division was made, the St Boswell Fair Road was laid down.[17] By 1766, the divided common was integrated into the general pattern of improvement of the estate and a 101-ha has been created with a farmhouse now called Hassendean Common. In this case, full integration took place, but some of the higher areas remain as grazings attached to individual farms. Some of the early enclosures of commons did not proceed without opposition, as in Galloway, where the proprietors made grazing parks to facilitate the store cattle trade with England and some of the early dykes were pulled down.[18] In north-east Scotland common grazings persist in the parishes of Cabrach, Corgarff, Glass and Glenlivet,[19] and in the Highlands and Islands they are still the rule in crofting areas and remain unenclosed from adjacent commons. Only since the 1950s have parts of these crofters' common grazings been apportioned to individual townships and to individual shareholders as extensions to their crofts.

Enclosure within Individual Estates

As early as 1661,[20] an Act of Parliament gave protection to landlords making enclosures and enjoined every proprietor of lands of an annual value of £1,000 (Scots) to enclose four acres (2 ha) annually for ten years. Even before the Act, an early reference to enclosure occurs on a Lothian estate in the 1650s: '30 or 40 akers (12 to 16 ha) in proper division and inclosure for accommodating the family in necessaries and corns' and 'a sheep park of 10 acres (4 ha) inclosed with a stone wall'.[21] In Kirkliston parish, West Lothian, the only enclosed land in the late seventeenth century was the laird's gardens, the tenants' kailyards and the churchyard.[22] After 1700, some enclosures had begun on estates such as Whitekirk and Tynningham, in 1707, Ormiston, in 1718,[23] and Monymusk, after 1734, although afforestation had begun in 1719.[24] General enclosure of estates in the Lowlands started in earnest in the period 1765-75 and on upland estates a quarter of a century later. Before enclosure was fully implemented, consolidation of the intermixed strips of tenant runrig had taken place on some estates, as Third has demonstrated at Newton near Dalkeith, where the eastern part of the farm had only one tenant in 1754 while the western part still had three tenants.[25] Geddes suggested that where only a few tenants had their lands consolidated, enclosure took place on these lands and the rest of the farm remained in runrig.[26] Such partial consolidation did not involve movement of the tenants from the fermtoun. Whittington also makes the case that there had been gradual expansion of the cultivated area with new settlements and some consolidation over a long period before the improving movement had properly begun,[27] and Dodgshon has shown that in Roxburgh and Berwickshire, multiple tenancy on farms was gradually reduced to single tenancies[28] (see Chapter 5): thereafter full enclosure could begin. If these examples are of a slower *evolution*, Storrie's work in Ardnamurchan and Islay demonstrates that both *evolution* and *revolution* took place.[29]

The new enclosures on individual estates were organised to suit the new agricultural structure and methods of single-tenant, commercial farming. The size of the farm depended on the ideas of individual proprietors or their advisers but it would appear that many of the older farm boundaries were broadly retained, as Figure 9.1 demonstrates. The first enclosures took place around the mansions of the proprietors and on the Mains or home farms and were often very regular in layout: this is evident from Roy's Map (Plate 6). In the Barony of Auchterarder, part of the annexed estate of Perth, Cockburn's plan of 1755 (Figure 9.1(a)) shows the division of the barony into farms. Wight's account of 1778 comments on each of the farms.[30] Powhillock 'was bounded by a stone wall upon the west and north and by a public road on the south' but had no internal enclosures. The western side of Kirkhill was enclosed: East Kirktown was 'mostly enclosed with stone dykes, except a small part with ditch and hedge'. The marsh between Clartiemire and the neighbouring estate, 'a crooked run of water', had been straightened by 1778. The remaining farmland, apart from the Boreland Parks, a soldiers' settlement after 1763, and according to Wight 'in wretched condition', had been enclosed and subdivided in large fields of moorland with stone walls. Wight recommended that enclosure of these farms be carried out, but this advice does not appear to have been followed during the period of annexure. Enclosure took place in the early nineteenth century[31] with some rearrangement and straightening of boundaries and the addition of the farm at Kirkton Park in the western half of the barony; in the eastern half, the laird had built a mansion, laid out policies and created a home farm which absorbed Kirkhill and West Forden. Since 1950, East Fordoun (formerly Middle Fordoun) has been added to the home farm unit. Powhillock was added to East Kirkton while Clartiemire has also disappeared to become part of Newbigging, which was truncated to enlarge East Fordoun. Internal enclosure abolishing the distinction between infield and outfield was undertaken throughout the barony and plantations and shelter belts were added, both ornamenting and diversifying the fieldscape (Plates 11 and 12). The sites of the farmhouses and steadings are in several cases close to the original fermtouns. In this example, one of the farms, Nether Fordoun, remained intact, but the boundaries of the others were altered; three farms disappeared and one was

Figure 9.1: The Barony of Auchterarder (Perthshire), 1775 and 1970

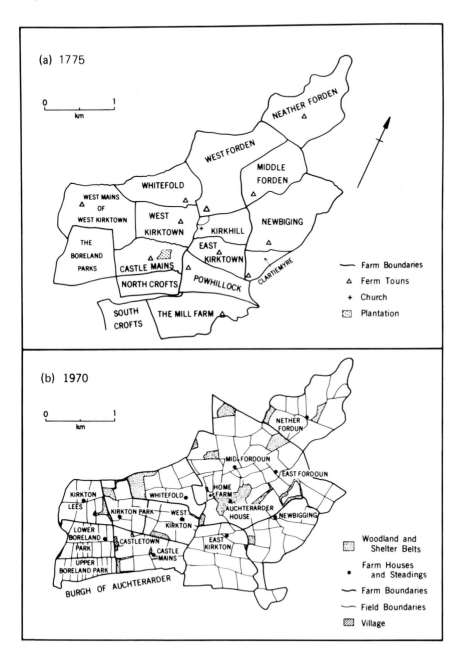

added. How general this particular form of reorganisation was is not clear, but in lowland areas reorganisation was generally thorough.

In upland areas, reorganisation lagged behind the richer lowlands. In the higher land of north Ayrshire and adjoining Renfrewshire, Lebon has demonstrated the different forms of enclosure which he terms 'evolved' as opposed to replanned, with infield being enclosed in small fields and the outfield in larger units giving a spider's web pattern to the new farms. By leaving the buildings of the fermtoun intact less investment was required to enclose these farms. It was probably uneconomical to replan such small estates as comprehensively as their lowland counterparts.[32]

On even poorer land at higher elevations in highland areas, reorganisation led to the abandonment of small tenant farming and its replacement by extensive sheep farms. There was little enclosure of the limited arable land and sheep fanks were sometimes constructed from the ruins of former dwellings. Examples can be cited from Kintyre, where 70 per cent of the former hamlet clusters above 120 m lie abandoned,[33] and from Upper Strathdon (Aberdeenshire)[34] and Glenfernate (Perthshire).[35] Many of these higher farms were at or near the upper limits of cultivation and the hard winter of 1782 may have been the cause of the abandonment, although in Upper Banffshire numerous smallholdings were removed and replaced by large consolidated farms. Displaced persons were accommodated in the new planned villages such as Tomintoul.[36] Parry has quantified this withdrawal in the Lammermuir and Stow Uplands, showing that it began to occur as early as the second half of the seventeenth century with 12 abandonments. There were a further 21 from 1750 to 1800, which he reckons may have been due to the beginnings of amalgamation of farms, 54 between 1800 and 1825, and 70 between 1825 and 1860, most of them at the upper limits of cultivation.[37]

In the south-eastern Highlands the reshaped landscape developed later than in the Lowlands and Southern Uplands. At Lix, in the upper Tay basin, Fairhurst has traced the evolution of the three farms of the Barony of Lix using a combination of studies of estate plans and documents and archaeological techniques. Reorganisation at Lix took place from c. 1780 to 1853 and it is clear that the hamlet clusters, the remains of which are still visible, were built c. 1780. Both Western and Middle Lix were let to two tenants: Wester Lix was consolidated under one tenant in 1816 and Middle Lix in 1845 with the present farmhouse built close to the hamlet cluster. Easter Lix, on the other hand, had eight tenants in 1796, but eleven in 1810, and eight, plus seven cottagers, in 1828: persons displaced from other reorganisations were added to this farm which was finally abandoned in 1853 and added to the neighbouring farm of Acharn.[38] Robertson has established from the enumerator's books of the Census that fermtouns were still numerous in south-west Argyll in 1841 and that craftsmen formed a substantial proportion of their population. By 1891, 60 per cent of these multiple tenancy farms had become single tenancies and a further 24 per cent had been abandoned.[39] This suggests that in the southern Highlands multiple tenancies continued into the middle of the nineteenth century and hamlet clusters survived. But gradually, by tenant reduction, the single farm replaced them and this parallels Dodgshon's findings. At Auchindrain, near Inveraray, the last of the multiple tenants retired in 1963 and the hamlet cluster has been developed as a museum of farming life. Enclosure thus came about on farms in three ways, by tenant reduction, by division of farms and, very probably at the termination of leases, with multiple tenancy being replaced by single tenancy on the replanned estates.

Smallholdings

In the Lowlands, the single farmstead set within a planned field system was the norm while in upland and highland areas, grazings attached to the farm in a single consolidated unit were the usual pattern which emerged in the Southern Uplands and the south-east Highlands. However, in the pre-improvement period, there were other groups of people apart from the tenants and subtenants who also shared in the land of the farms — cottars, crofters, mailers and pendiclers, some of whom were also tradesmen.[40] If the small tenants and cottages at Easter Lix disappeared, provision was made for smallholdings at Balquidder where the number of tenants was reduced from 32 to 12 and 8 of the 12 were given small self-contained crofts on the former farms of Wester and Mid Achtow (Figure 9.2). Another croft was allocated to a craftsman, the blacksmith. A remnant of the older system remains in as much as crofts 10, 11, 12 and 13 were jointly allocated pieces of the haughland. The former common pasture was detached from these crofts and added to the farm of Auchtubhmore.

Other smallholdings were created by dividing existing farms. The Boreland Parks at Auchterarder (Figure 9.1) are one example of the soldiers' settlements which were developed on certain of these Annexed Estates in 1763. Soldiers discharged after the Seven Years' War were given plots of up to 1.2 ha; at Strelitz, also on the Perth estate, 63 rectangular plots were laid out.[41] Three acres (1.2 ha) were insufficient to support a family, and by the early nineteenth century the plots at Strelitz had been integrated with neighbouring farms, but the geometrical field pattern is still evident on the landscape.

With the displacement of large numbers of tenants and other occupants of farms and the laird's desires to develop the land resources of the estates, moor and moss land were available for development. The moss of Kincardine was settled by crofters attracted to it in 1767 by leases of 38 years for three hectares of peat moss with no rent paid in the first seven years. By 1774, 13 tenants had cleared 42 ha of moss and as more crofts were let, the peat was gradually removed and the underlying clays brought into cultivation. As the leases ran out or were sold, the holdings were gradually amalgamated in the nineteenth century.[42]

In the north-east of Scotland, reclamation of moss land was also encouraged by the estates on the fringes of the newly enclosed farms and displaced persons were permitted to squat on former grazing lands. By dint of great effort in paring off the peat, trenching the land, removing stones and building dykes, these

Figure 9.2: Balquidder (Perthshire), 1750 and 1862

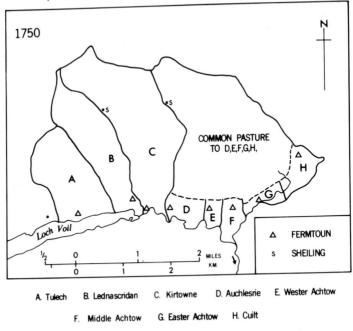

A. Tulech   B. Lednascridan   C. Kirtowne   D. Auchlesrie   E. Wester Achtow

F. Middle Achtow   G. Easter Achtow   H. Cuilt

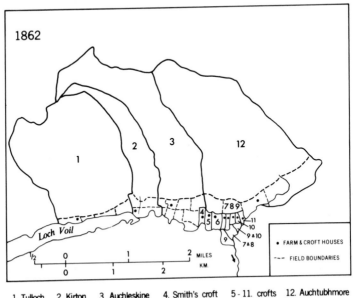

1. Tulloch   2. Kirton   3. Auchleskine   4. Smith's croft   5 - 11. crofts   12. Auchtubhmore

Sources: 1750 map of Barony of Balquhidder by Will Cockburn. Forfeited Papers, Register House, Edinburgh.
Ordnance Survey, Six Inch, Perthshire, Sheet C1V, 1866.

settlers created smallholdings with single-storey thatched houses. On the Seafield estate, on the Davoch of Grange, they were encouraged by a bounty of five pounds per acre reclaimed. Some who were given short leases were evicted at the end of the lease, their hard-won land being added to neighbouring farms.[43]

At Castle Fraser, smallholdings were let to married labourers 'whose dwellings stood in the way of improvement upon the newly arranged farms' and 'who would hire themselves to farmers at busy seasons'.[44] In 1827 a proprietor settled crofters on a shallow soil on 'flat, half worn out moss' between Stonehaven and Aberdeen. He gave them improving leases for 27 years, stipulating that one acre (0.4 ha) be improved in the first year, half the croft within nine years and that cottages of stone and lime of not less than nine by four metres be erected: the proprietor provided windows and a grant of five pounds. In his report he congratulates himself on raising a considerable rental by this reclamation of land formerly used for pasture and peat banks.[45] Most of these smallholdings in the north-east were developed on poor, bleak land on the interfluves of the lowlands and such reclamation was still in progress as late as the 1850s. The inhabitants of these smallholdings found employment as day labourers on farms or work in quarries or as peat-cutters.[46] Some assessment of their numerical importance in the reshaped landscape can be made from the fact that out of 11,422 holdings in Aberdeenshire in 1867, no fewer than 5,525 paid rents of between £4 and £20.[47] The work of extending the cultivated areas is reckoned to have absorbed the growing rural population of the north-east up till the 1880s.[48]

In Banffshire, the lower lands were consolidated and the Braes of Glenlivet laid out in crofts.[49] The landscape of Easter Ross was reshaped in a similar fashion with the valley floor in Strathpeffer being rearranged in commercial farms and the upper slopes and valley benches settled with crofts as at Heights of Auchterneed. Proprietors in this area also placed mealers and cottagers on areas which could be improved. For example, in the central area of the Black Isle, such as the crofts at Balvaird, the land was laid out mainly in rectangular holdings. These reclaimed areas were further expanded in the 1840s with the settlement round Loch Ussie of persons cleared from Strathconon and the imprint of these holdings remains even after amalgamation.[50] Associated with village developments, smallholdings were also made available to villagers[51] (see Chapter 11).

Thus, in the reshaping of the agricultural landscape, a considerable number of smallholdings were created in the north and east, largely from the reclamation of moor and moss land. Many of these holdings proved to be ephemeral, although in the north-east many did survive.

Smallholdings in the North and West — the Crofting Landscape

North and west of the Great Glen and particularly on the islands apart from the Orkney mainland, the reshaped landscape took on a different form. In the southern and eastern Highlands sheep farms had been formed and this pattern was repeated in inland Sutherland and parts of Easter Ross. The hamlet clusters of the straths were emptied from 1806-20 in Sutherland and the farms amalgamated and let to sheep farmers.[52] After this reorganisation, apart from farmhouses, shepherd's cottages and small areas enclosed for the provision of winter keep, the straths had a very reduced form of settlement. The population was removed to the coasts and holdings were carved out at Bettyhill and Helmsdale (Plates 19 and 20) or round the west coast peninsulas, for example in Assynt.[53] In Lochaber, the small tenants were removed from the upper glens and given holdings lower down or at the mouth of the glens, as at Bohuntine or Inverroy, or settled on the stony raised beaches, as at North Ballachulish and elsewhere along Loch Linnhe, thus freeing the inland areas for sheep-farming.[54] These crofts were almost always long, rectangular strips of land extending from the moor to the coast or from the lower valley slopes to the river and were grouped in townships with the settlement laid out in a linear form. The first crofting townships appear to have been established at Drimnin in Morven on the Argyll estates when two small farms were divided among 19 small tenants.[55] In 1803, holdings of from 1.6 to 4 ha were created in Tiree,[56] part-time holdings with the tenants seasonally employed in kelp-making. In Mull in the same year, the creation of crofts had displaced cottars and the Duke instructed his factor that part of a farm be 'cut down into small lots . . .for such as are most destitute'.[57]

This pattern of dividing farms into crofts was followed over much of the west coast and particularly in Skye, the Outer Hebrides and Shetland. The arable land was lotted but was not enclosed, although the surveyor employed in laying out the North Uists crofts specifically envisaged that the holdings would be enclosed.[58] The pastures became common grazings shared by the tenants. Without enclosure of the individual crofts, few improvements were made. Figure 9.3 demonstrates the expansion of the cultivated area which accompanied the reshaping of the Iochdar district of South Uist in 1818. Before the creation of the crofts there were four farms, Ardivachir, Kilaulay, Linique and Balgarva. In the lotting process a further six townships were added, the clusters disappeared and were replaced by houses built on the new crofts as illustrated at Ardivachir. In Benbecula between 1805 and 1829, as a result of the lotting, the cultivated area was expanded by 54 per cent.[59]

Not all the farms were lotted in this fashion. Tacksmen working the land with subtenants remained until the 1840s in South Uist when a further reorganisation took place and large grazing farms were created on the former tacksmen's farms. In other crofting areas, farms were created from former crofting townships and were surrounded by solidly built stone dykes, with internal field divisions and slated farmhouses and steadings on the Lowland model. As a result of these clearances, those who did not emigrate or migrate to the Lowlands were given subdivided crofts in the remaining townships or allocated crofts on former common pastures. With growing pressure of population, the inner areas of township common pastures were reclaimed to extend the arable land.[60] The

Figure 9.3: Iochdar, Island of South Uist, Before and After Lotting

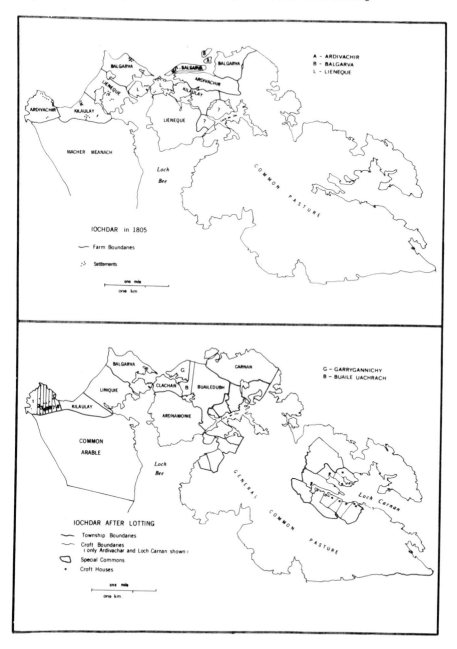

crofting landscape was further reshaped in the late nineteenth century and in the twentieth century by a programme of land settlement which was enacted throughout the Highlands and Islands and which restored most of the farms and grazings lost during the clearances to crofting tenure.[61] Since 1955, enclosure of the crofts has taken place. Some general common grazings shared by several townships have been subdivided and enclosed, and pasture improvement schemes have been carried out by surface seeding on apportionments either on an individual or a township basis, while common arable land has been apportioned to individual tenants.[62]

If consolidation and lotting was general in the crofting districts, a few townships were never lotted and remain in fixed runrig, for example Gloup in the Shetland island of Yell, and Drumbuie in Wester Ross. Caithness, Orkney and southern Argyll conform more to the Lowland pattern of reshaped landscapes but contain some crofting areas. The reshaping of the agricultural landscape in the north-west fringe and the islands apart from the Orkney mainland gave birth to a predominantly crofting landscape (Plate 13).

The New Elements of the Reshaped Landscape

The broad lines of the reshaped landscape have been discussed and the new elements will now be described. Enclosure brought with it regular fields: the character of the fences varied according to taste, micro-climate and materials available; the former hamlet clusters were replaced by new farmhouses and steadings and a road system evolved.

Fields

The layout of the fields was dependent on the size of the farm, type of soils, and on the type of farming envisaged. The field patterns laid out by the improvers were generally rectangular rather than square, but some of the less regular boundaries took account of the topography and streams. Rectangular fields facilitated ploughing and could be conveniently divided with temporary fences for folding animals on turnips. The size of fields was dependent on soil type: fields on light, dry soils were larger so as 'to accelerate ploughing, harrowing and reaping',[63] and smaller on clay soils. The number of fields on the farm was related to the rotation to be adopted; on a six-course rotation, six fields or multiples of six were laid out and fields of roughly equal size facilitated the rotation. Large fields were generally preferred to small fields as hedges and trees reduced the agricultural area, but round the steadings smaller parks were laid out to facilitate movements of stock. Field sizes vary throughout Scotland: in Renfrewshire, fields of 2 to 5 ha probably reflected the emphasis on dairying.[64] Cockburn of Ormiston set a limit of 4 ha on his fields: in

Roxburgh and Berwickshire, the fields were of 6 to 12 ha on the clay soils and 12 to 20 ha and even 28 ha on the lighter soils, reflecting the large farm sizes.[65] At Lindertis in Angus, on a farm of 240 ha, the fields varied between 6 and 10 ha according to the nature of the soil.[66] There are few diagrams of field layouts in the literature, with only one in Sinclair's *Account of the Systems of husbandry*[67] (Plate 14), and one in Loudon's *Encyclopaedia of Agriculture*,[68] neither are examples from actual layouts; this was the land surveyor's province. Where estates were completely replanned, or where smallholdings were laid out on reclaimed land and in crofting areas, field or smallholding layouts tended to be more regular. Where the process of improvements was more evolutionary, as in upland Ayrshire, less regular field layouts characterise the evolved landscape.

Fences

The actual form of field enclosure used was either stone dykes, hedges or ditch, and this depended on local availability of materials and on the whim of the proprietor or the land surveyor. In areas where stone was plentiful it was used, particularly in areas of stony boulder clay where the boulders removed from the fields were made into dykes. Tenants at Monymusk were required by the terms of their leases to build dry stone dykes surmounted by three rows of turf and were at liberty to take the stones from the fields but further stone would be provided if necessary.[69] On areas where there was much surplus stone, consumption dykes were built such as the dyke at Kingswells, 8 km west of Aberdeen; the West Dyke is 457m long by 8m wide and the East Dyke 305m long by 2m wide,[70] but such enormous dykes are rare. On the upland areas of Kilbarchan parish in Renfrewshire, simpler dykes were built and the lands were 'mostly enclosed with rickle stone dykes, gathered from the land'.[71] In Denino parish, Fife, the dykes were more substantial: 'dry stone dykes, topped with a layer of stones placed upon their edges, and the whole cast with lime'.[72] In Caithness, flagstones were set upright to form field boundaries. Such stone walls replaced turf or feal dykes which had been used before the period of the improvements.

Hedges added variety to the landscape. In Hamilton parish, 'the fields are generally surrounded with earthen mounds dug out of a trench, in the face of which, a row of whitethorn has been planted.'[73] Sometimes ditches were dug on both sides of the line of fences and a thorn hedge planted on top. Hawthorn was the commonest plant used, although blackthorn, beech and elder, with an occasional plant of honeysuckle, were used in some areas and trees, spaced at intervals, were incorporated. To give more stability, combinations of dykes and hedges were sometimes built as in North Berwick parish: 'hedges with a small stone dyke, 0.6 to 0.75m in height, behind them'.[74] Within the policies on some estates, a sunk fence or ha-ha was built, an earth bank faced with masonry on one side with a thorn hedge planted on top if shelter was more important than the view.[75] In other cases, particularly in flat, carse areas, simple open drains were used to divide the fields, but usually a hedge was planted on top of the mound formed by the excavated materials. The writings of the improvers contain detailed instructions for constructing dykes, hedges and ditches, and once the lines of the fields were laid out by the land surveyors, laird or tenant created the enclosure from material locally available, or in the case of hedging material, from cuttings of hawthorn or nurserymen's plants. Wire fences with metal or wooden posts were added to the forms of enclosure about 1820.[76]

Shelter Belts

If farm and field boundaries had a practical role, shelter belts were not only functional but were also designed with aesthetic considerations in mind: the enclosures at Forgandenny (Perthshire) 'were surrounded with a single, double or triple row of trees, which at once shelter and beautify the country'.[77] Shelter belts were recommended to be from 15 to 18m wide.[78] On the better soils of the farms, ash, beech, elm and sycamore were used: on poorer soils, alder, birch, rowan and willow were planted,[79] but a wide variety of species, including conifers, was used. Along roads and avenues leading to mansion houses, lines of trees were often planted and to increase the appearance of the rural surroundings, Loudon, who styled himself 'landscape gardener and improver', proposed that 'on ground consisting of rising knolls, banks and vallies, the former should generally be planted to increase the effect'.[80] The role of shelter belts has always been to provide shelter rather than timber: tree-planting on farms, especially in exposed areas, has always had this particular role.[81] On poorer land and on steep uneven slopes unsuited to agriculture, plantations rather than shelter belts were laid down.

Farm Buildings

While most of the eighteenth-century writers were unanimous in stating the need for improved farm buildings, Lord Belhaven was writing as early as 1699 on the proper methods of laying out farm houses and farm buildings.[82] The older buildings in the hamlet clusters consisited of groups of *maisons elementaires* with people and cattle under the same roof in thatched buildings of turf, un-mortared stone or clay in certain limited areas. Thus the new farm buildings were a great advance and were also integral to the new methods of farming. By the end of the eighteenth century, 'in all the improved districts of Scotland . . .not only the houses, but even the offices were now slated, and many of the latter are distinguished for excellent arrangements, by which labour is greatly facilitated.'[83] If small, two-storey, symmetrically designed houses were being built for small estate proprietors and as manses in the late seventeenth century, this had become the basic prototype for the new farmhouses of the eighteenth century which were built of stone and lime with slated or pantiled roofs. Brick was rarely used unless there was a local brickworks. The plan of the farm steadings sometimes incorporated the house on one side of a courtyard or, more usually, the farmhouse was sited near, but apart from the courtyard, having stables, cow house, shades [sheds] for the implements of husbandry, strawyard for feeding cattle, milkhouse, hog house etc. all built of stone and lime, covered with slate or tyle, conveniently arranged and of sufficient dimensions for the size of the farm.[84] (Plate 21)

The farm-workers' houses were generally improved after the farmhouses and steadings. Some at first formed the fourth side of the courtyards, but later were built in rows or semi-detached and were usually single storey cottages. Single farm-workers found accommodation in bothies, rooms located in separate buildings or in the steading.[85]

If the new farmhouses and steadings were beginning to appear in the last quarter of the eighteenth century as an integral part of the reshaped landscape, many of the present buildings date from the nineteenth century. As agricultural technology developed and powered machinery was introduced, modifications were made within the steadings to accommodate these changes.[86] In the crofting fringe, where the houses were built by the tenants, the traditional *black houses* continued to be built into the twentieth century but have gradually been replaced by modern houses although some of these thatched, double-walled drystone buildings still remain in use as byres and barns.

Roads

Roads were also an integral part of the reshaped landscape. The state of roads in Scotland in the eighteenth century is the subject of adverse comment in most of the contributions to the *Old Statistical Account*. The Statute Labour Acts were not being efficiently implemented[87] and minor roads leading to and from the farming communities were almost non-existent. The improving lairds, as heritors, were largely responsible for the carrying out of the provisions of the legislation and during the second half of the century the advantage of a proper road system led to the passing of numerous Turnpike Acts.[88] The conversion of statute labour to monetary payments in the latter part of the eighteenth century and in the early nineteenth century was partly responsible for the extension of the road network and the improved upkeep of road surfaces, but it was in the interests of laird and tenant alike to have better roads. As in all aspects of improvement, the state of the roads varied from parish to parish. Beyond the Lowlands, a network of military roads had been constructed by Wade and his successors and, after 1801, the Commissioner of Highland Roads and Bridges added to the network.[89]

The provision and improvement of roads played an essential part in the development of the reshaped landscape, for it enabled freer movement of farm produce and carriage of lime and dung. At the beginning of the improving period, such roads as existed were often impassable in winter. Most goods were carried on horseback, on horse-drawn slips or wheelless carts, or on human backs.[90]

To improve or replace the old, muddy tracks, a bottoming of large stones was laid, surfaced with gravel to a depth of four or five inches, but the large stones tended to work their way to the surface. Macadam solved this problem by laying roads consisting of 0.3m of stones of 2.5cms both as a foundation and as a surface.[91]

New lines of roads were constructed to avoid steep gradients and, by 1800, branch roads to the harbours at Inchyra, Errol and Powgavie had been constructed from the Perth to Dundee road.[92]

> Before 1790, a great part of the interior of the Carse of Gowrie was perfectly inaccessible to carts for almost half a year; so that they were obliged to deliver their produce on horseback. . . Now there is not a farm in the Carse but what is accessible in every part and at all times to carts.[93]

In the parish of Kilpatrick Fleming, Dumfriesshire, the tenants of the Springkell estate voluntarily subscribed two and a half per cent of their rents and the proprietor added one and a quarter per cent 'to be annually laid out in repairing roads within the estate'.[94] At Hoddam in the same county, lime, 'the only manure used for the improvement of waste lands, can now, by means of good roads, be without difficulty transported to a considerable distance at all seasons'.[95]

As agricultural improvements proceeded, roads were diverted round the walls of policies and former tracks running through open fields were replaced by new roads, characterised by sharp, regular angled bends, round the new enclosures and policies.[96] Streams and gorges were crossed by bridges and viaducts, and, on certain estates, tree-planting of road edges and steep banks added to the aesthetic character of the countryside (Plates 7 and 19).

By the early nineteenth century, the post roads were a width of 12 to 15m; the turnpike roads from 9 to 12m wide and metalled from 3.5 to 6m in the middle and there were feeder roads linking up the rural communities, eventually up to 7m in width.[97] By the 1840s, the authors of the *New Statistical Account* generally agree that a tolerable road system had been achieved over much of Scotland. The turnpike trusts and the statute labour system were finally effectively abolished in 1883 when County Road Boards became responsible for the road network.[98]

Conclusion

From the evidence available, there is little doubt that the agricultural landscape of Scotland was almost entirely reshaped during the improving period and little of the previous patterns remain. So thorough was the reshaping and reclamation in the Lowlands that fragments of wildscape remain only on the most intractable deep mosses. In the uplands too, the landscape was altered and enclosed fields replaced the patches of infield and outfield although ruins of fermtouns and traces of former cultivation remain. In the Highlands and Islands, the regular lines of crofts or isolated farms have almost everywhere replaced the clustered settlements: on farms which were cleared, there is often abundant evidence of former settlements and feal dykes.

The timing and form of the reshaping was neither simultaneous nor uniform. One Lowland laird made the point aptly in 1804:

> The fever of improvements, so common and malignant between 30 and 40 years ago, does not alwise appear in the same form, or produce entirely the same effects. Your friend Lord Hermand's fever is by all accounts abundantly high, yet very different from that of some of my neighbours, each of whom has his own system, or rather his own crotchets.[99]

The variations of field patterns, farm sizes, types of enclosure and farmsteads varied according to the ideas, contacts and sometimes idiosyncracies of the laird and his land surveyor within the context of environmental characteristics, financial and material resources and the dictates of economic conditions. Reshaping first proceeded round the Lowland lairds' mansions, on the home farm, on the other farms, but later on the uplands and in the Highlands and Islands.

Was this reshaping a form of evolution or revolution?[100] While there were enclosures on a limited scale on certain estates in the seventeenth century, the pace of reshaping gathered momentum in the eighteenth century, at first with partial consolidation without enclosure, but accelerated in the second half of the eighteenth century with the widespread adoption of the ideas of agricultural improvement. On some estates, the reshaping was carried out over a short period; on others, change was more gradual. But a relatively small number of commercial farmers replaced groups of peasant smallholders who became the agricultural workers on the reshaped units or moved to the new villages and expanding towns. In some areas, this took place relatively rapidly, while in other, but limited areas, the hamlet clusters survived into the twentieth century. The agricultural landscape was reshaped on geometrical lines and the settlement forms were also radically reshaped. Agricultural improvement has been suggested as a more appropriate term than Agricultural Revolution[101] but the changes made and the reshaping brought about were certainly radical and most of the new features have persisted to the present, if, in the last two decades, sizes of fields and farm units have been increased to meet contemporary needs.

Insufficient studies in depth have been made of Scottish estates to make a definitive statement on the timing and extent of the reshaping possible. Fairhurst asked whether the reshaping processes at Lix were typical of the southern Highlands and very properly stated that further studies were required to establish the pattern of reshaping in that area.[102] Whittington's patient analysis of the evolution of holdings at Pitkellony in Perthshire[103] and Dodgshon's studies of Roxburgh and Berwickshire[104] point the way forward. Much more detailed work remains to be done and the materials for these studies are now available with the assembling and cataloguing of estate plans and documents in the Scottish Record Office[105] and the lists of the National Register of Archives.

Geddes remarked forty years ago that 'the geographer's first task is to describe and analyse the scene and adequate synthesis must follow upon extended survey'.[106] Only patient study will provide solutions to the many problems remaining and furnish the basis for a definitive synthesis on the nature of the reshaping of the agricultural landscape.

Notes

1. Sinclair, Sir J. (ed.) (1791-9), *The statistical account of Scotland* (hereafter *OSA*) (Edinburgh). Vols. 1-21
2. The Ministers of the Respective Parishes (1845), *The new statistical account of Scotland* (hereafter *NSA*) (Edinburgh), Vols. 1-15
3. *NSA*, Vol. XI, p. 684
4. Colville, J. (ed.) (1904), *Letters of John Cockburn of Ormistoun to his gardner, 1727-1744* (Publications of the Scottish History Society (hereafter Pubs. SHS), *45*
5. Cregeen, E. R. (1964), *The Argyll estate instructions* (Pubs. SHS) (fourth series), *1*
6. Adams, I. H. (1968), 'The land surveyor and his influence on the Scottish rural landscape', *Scottish Geographical Magazine* (hereafter *SGM*), *84*, 248-55
7. Adams, I. H. (ed.) (1966, 1970, 1974), *Descriptive lists of plans in the Scottish Record Office* (Edinburgh), Vols. 1, 2 and 3
8. Scottish Record Office (hereafter SRO), RHP 3482
9. Storrie, M. C. (1961), 'A note on William Bald's plan of Ardnamurchan and Sunart, 1807', *Scottish Studies*, *5*, 112-17
10. Third, B. M. W. (1957), 'The significance of Scottish estate plans and associated documents', *Scottish Studies*, *1*, 45-8
11. SRO, RHP 1306
12. Moisley, H. A. (1961), 'North Uist in 1799', *SGM*, *77*, 89-92
13. Adams (1968), 'The land surveyor', 249
14. *OSA*, Vol. X, pp. 484-5
15. Whittington, G. (1973), 'Field systems of Scotland', pp. 566-7 in Baker, A. R. H. and Butlin, R. A. (eds.), *Studies of field systems in the British Isles* (Cambridge)
16. Adams, I. H. (ed.) (1971), *Directory of Scottish commonties* (Scottish Record Society), New Series, *2*, vii
17. Adams, I. H. (1971), 'Division of the commonty of Hassendean, 1761-1763', *The Stair Society*, Miscellany One, 171-92
18. Symon, J. (1959), *Scottish farming past and present* (Edinburgh and London), p. 116
19. Turnock, D. (1977), 'Stages of agricultural improvements in the Uplands in Scotland's Grampian Region', *Journal of Historical Geography*, *3*, 343
20. *Acts of Parliament of Scotland*, Vol. VII, p. 263 (1661, *c.* 284)
21. Bogle, J. (ed.) (1842), *The Coltness collections* (Maitland Club), *55*
22. *OSA*, Vol. X, p. 141
23. Fenton, A. (1963), 'The rural economy of East Lothian in the 17th and 18th centuries', *Transactions of the East Lothian Antiquarian and Field Naturalists' Society*, *9*, 1-23
24. Hamilton, H. (1946), *Life and labour on an Aberdeenshire estate 1735-1750* (Third Spalding Club), xi, xxvii
25. Third (1957), 'Significance of Scottish estate plans', 46
26. Geddes, A. (1938), 'The changing landscape of the Lothians, 1600-1800, as revealed by old estate plans', *SGM*, *54*, 130-3
27. Whittington (1973), 'Field systems', pp. 530-79
28. Dodgshon, R. A. (1972), 'The removal of runrig in Roxburgh and Berwickshire', *Scottish Studies*, *16*, 121-7

29. Storrie, M. A. (1965), 'Land holdings and settlement evolution in west highland Scotland', *Geografiske Annaler, 47B*, 138-61
30. Wight, A. (1778), *Present state of husbandry in Scotland, extracted from reports made to the Commissioners of the Annexed Estates* (Edinburgh), Vol. I, pp. 59-89
31. *NSA*, Vol. X, p. 292
32. Lebon, J. H. G. (1946), 'The process of enclosure in the western lowlands', *SGM, 62*, 100-10
33. Gailey, R. A. (1960), 'Settlement and population in Kintyre 1760-1800', *SGM, 76*, 99-107
34. Turnock, (1977), 'Stages of Agricultural Improvements', 337
35. Caird, J. B. (1972), 'The old statistical account of Scotland, with special reference to parishes of Kirkmichael and Moulin', *Scottish Field Studies Association Ltd*, Annual Report, 1971, p. 16
36. Turnock, D. (1975), 'Small farms in north Scotland: an exploration in historical geography', *SGM, 91*, 165
37. Parry, M. L. (1976), 'The abandonment of upland settlement in Southern Scotland', *SGM, 92*, 50-60
38. Fairhurst, H. (1968-9), 'The deserted settlement at Lix, west Perthshire', *Proceedings of the Society of Antiquaries of Scotland, 51*, 160-99
39. Robertson, I. M. L. (1967), 'Changing form and function of settlement in south-west Argyll', *SGM, 83*, 34
40. Whittington (1973), 'Field systems', 548-50
41. Smout, T. C. (1970), 'The landowner and the planned village', pp. 90-1 in Phillipson, N. T. and Mitchison, R. (eds.), *Scotland in the age of improvement* (Edinburgh); Caird, J. B. (1964), 'The making of the Scottish rural landscape', *SGM, 80*, 76 and 79
42. Whittington, G. (1968), 'Landscape changes in the Vale of Menteith', pp. 188-206 in Whittow, J. B. and Wood, P. D. (eds.), *Essays in Geography for Austin Miller* (Reading)
43. Kay, G. (1962), 'The landscape of improvement: a case study of agricultural change in north-east Scotland', *SGM, 78*, 104-6
44. Fraser, Col. (1837), 'Settlement of crofters on waste land on the estate of Castle Fraser, Aberdeenshire ', *Transactions of the Highland and Agricultural Society of Scotland* (second series), *5*, 387-90
45. Thomson, G. (1837), 'On the settlement of crofters', ibid., 379-83; Walton, K. (1963), 'Regional settlement', pp. 93-4 in O'Dell, A. C. and Mackintosh, J. (eds.), *The North East of Scotland* (Aberdeen)
46. Kay (1962), 'The landscape of improvement'
47. Turnock (1975), 'Small farms in north Scotland'
48. Ibid., 343-4
49. Ibid.
50. Tivy, J. (1965), 'Easter Ross, a residual crofting area', *Scottish Studies, 9*, 69
51. Rennie, R. (1803), 'Plan of an inland village', *Transactions of the Highland and Agricultural Society, II*, 250-69
52. Fairhurst, H. (1964), 'Surveys for the Sutherland Clearances', *Scottish Studies, 8*, 1-16
53. Wheeler, P. T. (1966), 'Land ownership and the crofting system in Sutherland since 1800', *Agricultural History Review, 14*, 54-5
54. Turnock, D. (1970), *Patterns of Highland development*, (London), pp. 33-5
55. Cregeen (1964), *The Argyll estate instructions,* xxxii
56. Ibid., 73
57. Ibid., 202
58. Blackadder, J. (1799), 'Survey and valuation of Lord MacDonald's estate', 131-3, *Bosville Macdonald Family Papers*, DDBM/27/3, Brynmor Jones Library, University of Hull
59. Bald, W. (1805), *The Island of Benbecula, the property of Ranald George McDonald, Esq. of Clanranald* (with table of contents corrected in 1829), SRO, RHP 1039
60. Caird, J. B. (1978), 'Land use in the Uists since 1800', *Proceedings of the Royal Society of Edinburgh* (forthcoming)
61. Caird, J. B. and Moisley, H. A. (1964), 'The Outer Hebrides', pp. 382-5 in Steers, J. A. (ed.), *Field studies in the British Isles* (London)
62. Caird, J. B. (1972), 'Changes in the Highlands and Islands of Scotland 1951-71', *Geoforum, 12*, 5-36

63. Sinclair, Sir J. (1813), *An account of the systems of husbandry adopted in the more improved districts of Scotland* (Edinburgh), Vol. I, p. 32

64. Wilson, J. (1812), *General view of the agriculture of Renfrewshire*, (Paisley), p. 91

65. Dodgshon, R. A. (1970), 'Agricultural change in Roxburgh and Berwickshire' (unpublished Phd thesis, University of Liverpool), p. 206

66. Wight (1778), *Present state of husbandry in Scotland*, p. 281

67. Sinclair (1813), *An account*, Vol. I, facing page 44

68. Loudon, J. C. (1831), *An encyclopaedia of agriculture,* (London), p. 689

69. Hamilton (1946), *Life and Labour*, pp. xxvi, xxvii

70. Ibid., p. xxvi

71. *OSA*, Vol. XI, p. 502

72. *OSA*, Vol. IX, p. 360

73. *OSA*, Vol. II, p. 192

74. *OSA*, Vol. V, p. 441

75. Maxwell, I. (1974), *Functional architecture: Hopetoun estate, West Lothian*, 2 vols. MSS. in Country Life Museum, National Museum of Antiquities, Edinburgh. Vol. 1, 3.2

76. Anderson, M. L. (ed. Taylor, C. J.) (1967), *A history of Scottish forestry*, Vol. II (London and Edinburgh), p. 303

77. *OSA*, Vol. III, p. 308

78. Brewster, D. (1830), *The Edinburgh encyclopaedia* (Edinburgh), Vol. I, p. 369

79. Anderson (1967), *A history of Scottish forestry*, p. 197

80. Loudon, J. (1803), *A treatise on the improvements proposed for Scone* MSS. Mansfield Estates Office, Scone Palace, 42

81. Anderson (1967), *A history of Scottish forestry*, p. 488

82. Hamilton, J. (Lord Belhaven) (1699), *The country-man's rudiments* (Edinburgh), pp. 29-33

83. Sinclair, Sir John (1825), *Analysis of the statistical account of Scotland* (Edinburgh), p. 253

84. Thomson, Rev. J. (1800), *General view of the agriculture of Fife* (Edinburgh), pp. 75-6

85. For two useful accounts of farms, steadings and cottages, see Dunbar, J. G. (1966), *The historic architecture of Scotland* (London), pp. 238-44 and Fenton, A. (1976), *Scottish country life* (Edinburgh), pp. 181-92

86. Walker, B. (1977), 'The influence of fixed farm machinery on farm building design in eastern Scotland in the late 18th and 19th centuries', *Scottish Archaeological Forum*, *8*, 52-74

87. Moir, D. G. (1957), 'The Statute Labour Roads', *SGM*, *73*, 175

88. Campbell, R. H. (1965), *Scotland since 1707* (Oxford), pp. 51-3, 84-8

89. Haldane, A. R. B. (1962), *New ways through the glens* (London)

90. Fenton (1976), *Scottish country life*, pp. 200-12

91. Sinclair (1813), *An account*, Vol. I, pp. 70-1

92. Robertson, J. (1799), *General view of the agriculture of the county of Perth*, (Perth), pp. 357-60

93. *OSA*, Vol. XIX, p. 552

94. Ibid., Vol. XIII, p. 264

95. Ibid., Vol. III, p. 353

96. Geddes (1938), 'The changing landscape of the Lothians', 141

97. Handley, J. (1963), *The agricultural revolution in Scotland* (Glasgow), p. 267

98. Campbell (1965), *Scotland since 1707*, p. 88

99. Horn, B. L. H. (ed.) (1966), *Letters of John Ramsay of Ochtertyre* (Pubs. SHS), fourth series, *3*, 121

100. Whittington, G. (1975), 'Was there a Scottish Agricultural Revolution?' *Area*, *7*, 204-6

101. Parry, M. L. (1976), 'A Scottish Agricultural Revolution', *Area*, *8*, 238-9

102. Fairhurst (1968-9), 'The deserted settlement at Lix', 192

103. Whittington (1973), 'Field systems'

104. Dodgshon (1972), 'The removal of runrig', 121-7

105. Adams (1966, 1970, 1974), *Descriptive lists of plans*; see also Adams, I. H. (1976), 'Sources for Scottish local history — 5 Estate plans', *The Local Historian*, *12.1*, 26-30, for a useful account of where estate plans are recorded and their availability.

106. Geddes (1938), 'The changing landscape of the Lothians', 130

10 THE MANSION AND POLICY

T. R. Slater

One of the characteristic features of Lowland Scotland's rural landscape from the mid-seventeenth century has been the tower house or mansion surrounded by walled gardens, tree-lined rectangular enclosures, or less formal policies. 'Policies' was the normal Scottish term for the gardens and parks surrounding the houses of the aristocracy and landed gentry. Though often used for grazing and some commercial timber production, their primary purpose was ornamental. The study of these mansions and policies has been much neglected, in contrast to their English counterparts, for which there is a substantial literature of specialised studies by social and economic historians, architects and geographers. That such neglect needs to be remedied is apparent after only the most cursory investigation of relevant sources, since Scottish parks differ significantly from their English equivalents in their history, design and economic and social effects. The aim of this chapter is to provide a general outline of the development of the policies of landed estates between 1600 and 1850.

Sources

Cartographic and literary sources which describe the general characteristics and distribution of Scotland's policies exist from the late sixteenth century onwards. The county and regional maps of Blaeu's *Atlas Novus*, published in 1654 (Plate 5), many of them based on Pont's surveys of half a century earlier, the detailed manuscript survey made by General Roy between 1747 and 1755 (Plate 6), and the first editions of the one-inch and six-inch Ordnance Survey maps provide distributional data for the whole country. In addition, most Lowland areas had been mapped by county cartographers before 1820, although the Scottish heritage of county surveys is by no means as rich as for English counties.[1]

Impressionistic descriptions of the principal mansions and their policies are to be found in the published tours of Scotland, primarily made by English visitors. Some of the more useful include Lowther's *Journall* of 1629;[2] tours by Macky and Defoe, both published in the 1720s;[3] the visits of Bishop Pococke in the 1750s, and the tours of Pennant (1769), Gilpin (1776) and Dorothy Wordsworth (1803).[4] Comparative descriptions are also to be found in some volumes of the *Old Statistical Account* and the *New Statistical Account*, the Board of Agriculture reports and mid-nineteenth-century topographical dictionaries.[5] To supplement these general surveys, county, area or family histories often provide much detailed information for individual estates, but there are few modern studies of this kind. Marshall's study of seventeenth-century Hamilton[6] is a notable exception, and similarly Lindsay and Cosh's analysis of eighteenth-century Inveraray,[7] whilst the early accessibility of the Clerk manuscripts have yielded a number of studies of the Penicuik estate.[8]

The wealth of information in private estate papers is, as yet, virtually untouched, although many published selections of documents are relevant to the study of Scotland's policies. There is only one substantial history of gardening in Scotland, by Cox,[9] who drew extensively upon the Buccleugh manuscripts, but this concerns itself only incidentally with the wider area of the policies. Some geographers have taken note of policies as one aspect of the changing landscape of eighteenth-century Scotland,[10] whilst Gilbert has provided a sound foundation for studies of seventeenth-century progress, by analysing the preceding period of medieval hunting preserves.[11] But in sum, the interpretation of this important aspect of change in the Scottish countryside has hardly begun, and this chapter can aim no further than to present a general framework on which subsequent investigations may be built.

The Country House

Improvement of an estate almost invariably began with the house, although frequently house and gardens were remodelled in concert. Between 1560 and 1640 the majority of the castles and towers of the landed aristocracy were added to, rebuilt *in situ*, or deserted in favour of a new dwelling elsewhere. The period is one in which defensive features are progressively abandoned in favour of more comfortable living conditions with larger rooms and windows and better services. Defence was not wholly forgotten in this 'baronial' period, however, as Sir Robert Kerr warned his son in 1632, 'the world may change agayn'. So houses remained 'strong in the out syde',[12] especially in less settled areas, as windowless ground storeys, stout doors and inaccessible sites testify.

When landowners removed to a new site, they sought shelter and protection from the elements. They did not seek prospects, since high ground was very often 'cold, wild ground', even in the Lowlands,[13] and it was to escape from cliff-top promontory, riverside rock or inaccessible island that these new houses were built. The failure to take advantage of local topography to enhance the prospect from the house and the exclusion of more distant prospects by new plantations were among the principal criticisms of English visitors. Few could understand why Lord Hamilton chose the Clyde meadows, close to the growing burgh of Hamilton, for the site of his new house in 1591, when the family's medieval castle at Cadzow was romantically situated high above the tributary Avon a mile away.

Some of these new houses were domestic and Jacobean in design. Houses such as Pinkie (Midlothian), built in 1613, and Winton (East Lothian), dating from 1620,[14] had abandoned defensive features, but the majority continued to display the decorative-defensive elements of the 'Baronial' style which were to enthuse nineteenth-century revivalists. These elements include Z-, T-, or L-shaped plans; towers and turrets, the latter often corbelled out between first and second floors; conical roofs; and tiny windows on the ground floor contrasting with larger openings on the upper floors, some of which, by 1600, had become wide oriel windows as, for example, at Huntly Castle (Aberdeenshire).[15]

A typical laird's tower was Coltness (Lanarkshire) where Thomas Stewart added to the 'old toure a large addition . . . of a good kitchen, celler, meat-room or low parlour, a large hall or dyning-room, with a small bed-chamber and closet over these, and above that two bed-chambers with closets'.[16] From the early years of the seventeenth century, too, date the visually dramatic castles such as Glamis (Angus) and Fochabers (Moray). They were enlarged to five or six storeys high and their towers and roofs are massed for effect rather than defence. Even in the 1720s, Macky was struck 'with awe and admiration, by the many turrets and gilded ballustrades' of Glamis, and considered it 'the highest I ever saw, consisting of a high tower in the middle, with two wings and a tower at each end'.[17]

Despite the considerable rebuilding taking place in Lowland Scotland through the first half of the seventeenth century, it was only from 1660 that a fully developed Renaissance classicism was established, and the nobility began to build true mansion houses. Often these classical mansions incorporated older tower houses, so that exterior regularity belies internal complexity. Sir William Bruce's reconstruction of the royal palace of Holyroodhouse (Edinburgh), begun in 1671, incorporated the early sixteenth-century tower, for example, whilst James Smith encased Dalkeith Palace (Midlothian) in a symmetrical mansion for the Duke of Buccleugh, a procedure also followed at Hatton (West Lothian)[18] (Plate 15). A few completely new houses were built, including Hamilton Palace (Lanarkshire), built to the designs of James Smith between 1684 and 1701, the first Duke of Queensberry's Drumlanrig Castle (Dumfriesshire), also designed by Smith,[19] and Sir William Bruce's own Kinross House (Kinross-shire), which was 'admyred by everie bodie' from its completion in 1690, and became the accepted yardstick of architectural fashion for several decades. It was important, too, in introducing to Scotland the concept of a unified plan for house and gardens.[20] By this time the Scottish nobility were taking note of English fashion and before embarking on major reconstructions of their dwellings either took advice from English architects or, more usually, inspected English mansions on their frequent journeys to Court and Parliament in London[21] (see Chapter 7). The lairds followed these fashions more circumspectly, but by 1720 the development of agriculture in Lowland areas, particularly around the larger towns, had advanced sufficiently to allow the lairds to improve their living standards.[22] Around Edinburgh, lawyers and merchants invested their profits in country estates and built small classical houses such as Prestonfield (1687) or Sir John Clerk's Mavisbank, built in the 1720s. In Perthshire, too, there were numerous houses 'of a modern fashion, three storie high. . .making a great dash to the countrey about,'[23] whilst even those lairds who could not contemplate a full rebuilding added wings of larger and more comfortable rooms to their towers.

Rebuilding and reconstruction were not confined to the house. Sometimes the domestic buildings, offices and stables also demanded early attention, as they were often insubstantial, thatched, and crowded close around the house. Sir Archibald Grant found 'granaries, stables and houses for all cattle, and of the vermine attending them, close adjoining' his house at Monymusk (Aberdeenshire) in 1716;[24] and the Duke of Hamilton began the late-seventeenth-century reconstruction of his palace with the offices of the 'Back Close'. New stables (with doors wide enough to take a coach), kitchens, bakehouse and other offices were all completed before work commenced on the house itself.[25]

For much of the eighteenth century, extension and rebuilding of houses large and small continued, but architectural styles varied from equivalent English designs much less distinctively, and prominent Scottish architects such as William Adam senior, Sir William Chambers and Robert Adam were as much in demand by English landowners as by their Scottish clientele. From the 1770s, the Scottish landscape proved an ideal setting for houses and mansions designed in the Picturesque Gothick style, and as landowners were prospering, many houses were rebuilt to castellated Gothick designs at this time. Examples include Robert Adam's Culzean Castle (Ayrshire), built during the last quarter of the century, James Playfair's Melville Castle (Midlothian), built in 1786 for Viscount Melville on the site of an earlier castle, and the very early and influential Inveraray Castle (Argyllshire) built for the Duke of Argyll between 1745 and 1761 to the designs of Robert Morris (Plate 16).[26] Sir William Scott's new home at Abbotsford (Roxburghshire), built between 1816 and 1823, was the harbinger of a change from eighteenth-century Gothick to the nineteenth-century revival of Scots Baronial, a revival which culminated in the rebuilding of Queen Victoria's Balmoral (Aberdeenshire) in the 1850s.

Throughout the period of rebuilding one factor remained constant: almost all houses, from the smallest to the grandest palace, remained obstinately in the valleys, ignoring extensive prospects from hillsides. Houses were rebuilt on the sites of their predecessors, or perhaps a hundred metres or so from an older building, but rarely were removed a kilometre or more to obtain a better prospect, as was often the case in England. Dorothy Wordsworth noted of Lord Breadalbane's Taymouth (Perthshire) that

> many workmen were employed in building a large mansion . . . close to the old house; the situation as we thought, very bad, considering that Lord Breadalbane had the command of all the ground at the foot of the lake, including hills both high and low. It is in a hollow, without prospect . . .

seeing nothing and adorning nothing.[27]

Even on those estates where a town was considered inconveniently close for eighteenth-century sensibilities, it was as often the town as the mansion that was removed to a satisfactory distance; thus successive Dukes of Hamilton spent much time and money in the early nineteenth century trying to ensure that the burgeoning town at the gates of Hamilton Palace did not intrude on their privacy and limited prospects.[28]

Gardens and Policies to 1760

Before the Restoration

Medieval deer parks, so often the precursors of English landscape parks, were not common in Scotland. Indeed few walled or hedged enclosures of any kind were to be seen in the rural landscape before the early seventeenth century. There were perhaps a score of royal parks, some of which — Stirling, Falkland, Linlithgow — were partly walled and survived into the early eighteenth century. The barons also possessed parks. About fifty are documented, the majority of which seem to have originated in the troubled years of the fourteenth and fifteenth centuries when royal control was weak.[29] Since deer parks were not common, by 1600 the term 'park' was not applied specifically to an enclosure for deer, but to any enclosure, whether it be for woods, pasture or, more rarely, for arable. The mansions of seventeenth- and eighteenth-century Scotland were thus surrounded by a large number of 'parks', each with its own distinctive appellation. The usual Scottish term for the ornamental gardens around a house and the associated enclosures of its mains farm was 'policies'. Only towards the end of the eighteenth century, when informal landscaping came into vogue, was the English usage of 'park' adopted, and then by no means universally.

The lack of timber in the country became the concern of government in the sixteenth century and a number of orders were made to encourage landowners to 'mak theme to have parkis with dere. . .and plant at the leist ane aker of wod'.[30] The enforcement of such regulations was difficult, but maps in the Blaeu atlas bear witness to the planting that was undoubtedly taking place (Plate 5). Almost every castle in the southern counties had its enclosure of wood nearby and these were to form the basis of many of the more extensive policies of the eighteenth century.

By the first half of the seventeenth century, the internal peace of James VI's reign had encouraged many lairds to add formal, walled gardens and deer parks to improve the environs of the house. Such improvements were particularly prominent about Edinburgh, where lawyers and members of the Privy Council established country houses within easy travelling distance of the city (Plate 5). But it was the nobility who took the lead in creating parks. The Earl of Lothian, for example, added a walled park, a large orchard and formal gardens to Ancram

House (Roxburghshire) in the 1630s,[31] while in the Moray Firth lowlands, the Marquis of Huntly 'gave himself whollie to policie, planting and building' in the 1620s when he enlarged and 'parked about' Gordon Castle (Moray).[32] Another well walled park was that built on the Lochtayside estates of Lord Breadalbane at Finlanrig in 1620.[33] Even in the remote fastnesses of Sutherland, Sir Robert Gordon was urging the youthful Earl of Sutherland 'to build a house in Dunrobin, for that is the. . .most pleasant habitation you hawe. Ther yow may easilie mak a fyne delicat park.'[34]

Such parks were often treeless, indeed Sir Robert Kerr specifically advised that the new park at Ancram should 'have noe trees nor bushes within'.[35] Where trees were planted, they tended to be 'firrs', a ubiquitous term usually signifying the native Scots pine. In 1541, the King's tenants in Fife were required to plant ash, elm and plane trees in hedged parks,[36] whilst alders were commonly used for wetter areas and sycamores were an early introduction (both plane and sycamore were probably introduced to Scotland before England). Birches were another commonly planted tree. Sir David Lindsay planted a thousand of them at Edzell (Kincardineshire) at the beginning of the seventeenth century,[37] while thorn and holly were already in use for hedgerows.

The orchards and 'yards', or walled gardens, supplied fruit and vegetables to the laird's household. The new Ancram House orchards were to contain apples, plums, pears and cherries acquired from former monastic orchards, as well as 'strauberryes, and roses and all flowers all over',[38] an indication that ornament was not neglected in early-seventeenth-century gardens. Other descriptions confirm this. Lowther's record of Sir James Pringle's seat at Gala (Selkirkshire) in 1629, for example, where

> he hath a very pretty park, with many natural walks in it, artificial ponds and arbours now a making, he hath neat gardens and orchards. . .he hath abundance of cherry trees . . . great store of sycamores, trees he calleth silk trees [white mulberry?], and fir trees',[39]

and Gordon's description of Dunrobin in 1620, 'where there be pleasant gardens planted with all kinds of froots, hearbs and floors'.[40] Perhaps the most comprehensive description of a Scottish garden before 1660 is that of Coltness (Lanarkshire), where, in 1654, the gardens were terraced before the house and there was a 'square parterre, or floor garden. . .cherry and nut gardens, and walnut and chestnut-trees' and a strawberry border.[41]

In Lowland Scotland, therefore, improvement of the immediate environs of the house was already under way by the 1630s. Parks for deer and for cattle were enclosed with hedges or stone walls; trees and small woods were planted for shelter, economy and decoration; well stocked orchards provided an improved diet, and sometimes a surplus for market;[42] and flowers and arbours within walled enclosures marked the beginnings of a concern with pleasure and re-creation.

The Formal Garden, 1660-1760

The Restoration saw a quickening of the pace of change. The strong influence of French culture and design in Scotland was considerably enhanced, whilst the influence of English fashions was transmitted by the nobles who travelled to the Court in London.[43] Both gardens and policies were subject to improvement, but continuity rather than change was the predominant theme. The gardens and park at Hamilton are among the most fully described in the 1660s. There was a statue garden with painted statues and a sundial (carved in 1648); a pond garden with large fishponds and fountains; a bowling green, laid out in 1666; extensive yards of some eight hectares with 'great abundance of as good wines [vines], peaches, apricoats, figs, walnuts, chaistins [chestnuts], philberts etc., in it as in any part of France. . . The wals are built of brick, which conduces much to the ripening of the fruits'; beyond were 'brave palissades of firs' and a vast park 'thought to be five miles about'.[44]

Many of these elements are repeated elsewhere. Painted or gilded statues are known at Newbattle Abbey (Midlothian), seat of the Marquis of Lothian, where they greatly impressed John Macky in the 1720s, and at the Earl of Strathmore's, Glamis (Angus), where the statue garden was planned in the 1680s, again to be described by Macky and, in great detail, by Daniel Defoe.[45] There was 'a fine dyal' at Glamis, and more than sixty dated seventeenth-century sundials are listed by Macgibbon and Ross.[46] Bowling greens became a fashionable addition from the 1660s and ponds and fountains were planned on an increasingly spectacular scale. The Duke of Queensberry's Drumlanrig Castle (Dumfriesshire) evoked comparison with Chatsworth in the minds of early-eighteenth-century visitors, but with its cascades, canals and fountains it was exceptional. Even so, by 1700, many estates could boast extensive formalised ponds, canals and basins, often with a central fountain. At the Marquis of Tweeddale's Yester (East Lothian), for example, there was 'a handsome Basin, with a jett d'eau in the middle of the parterre, with four good statues upon pedastals at each corner'.[47] The formalisation of the gardens followed the advice given by Reid in the first Scottish gardening book, that

all the buildings and plantings [should] ly so about the house, as that the house may be the centre; all the walks, trees and hedges running to the house. Therefore whatever you have on the one hand, make as much of the same forme and in the same place, on the other.[48] (Plate 15)

As the seventeenth century progressed, many of the nobility converted their walled gardens into grander parterres on the French model, with clipped evergreens, gravelled walks and 'labyrinths', designed to be viewed from the principal apartments of the mansion or from surrounding grass-covered slopes 'regularly disposed'. However, the majority of lairds followed the older tradition of small enclosed gardens around the house, though they were now laid out more formally. Seventeenth-century topiary work, in the Dutch manner, is preserved in the small garden of Barncluith (Lanarkshire), which includes two other common features: small brick or stone pavilions for summer entertainments, which were often built at the corners of walled gardens (Plate 15), and formal terracing of the gardens down the slope of a deeply incised stream.[49] The scale of the retaining walls at Barncluith is exceptional but extensive terraces were cut into rock at Drumlanrig and at Brechin (Angus), Culross (Fife), and Cockpen (Midlothian).[50]

In Scotland, by contrast with England, formal gardens in the immediate vicinity of the house continued to be maintained, improved and extended until the mid-eighteenth century and later. Indeed, some survived until formal gardening was revived in the mid-nineteenth century. The many new 'little commodious house[s]' of the lairds, built in the first half of the eighteenth century,[51] were adorned with walled gardens and regularly planted orchards. There is little evidence in the descriptions provided by Bishop Pococke in the mid-eighteenth century, or on Roy's military survey, of the adoption of informal landscape gardening of the kind so fashionable in England.[52]

Plantations and Policies

The encouragement of tree-planting began in the sixteenth century, but not until 1660 was the scale of planting sufficient to be remarked upon in travellers' descriptions. By then most large landowners shared the opinion of Sir John Clerk, that their estates could in 'no way be so much improven as by planting . . . to take off the dismal prospect of the moors'. The campaigns of John Evelyn to increase timber-planting in England also undoubtedly had an effect on those landowners who attended Parliament.[53] The planting of Scottish estates was rather different from the English pattern. Rides and avenues were more frequently planted to divide plantations of woodland, on the French model, rather than as lines of single trees, while the remaining policies were divided into rectangular pasture parks, each enclosed with its own shelter belts, hedges or walls, and usually divided from each other by tree-lined avenues. Such parks had both an aesthetic appeal of ordered formality in a largely treeless countryside, and also brought economic benefits to the estate by providing shelter and improved grazing for cattle. This was most significant in the vicinity of large cities where livestock production was increasingly market-oriented, and in Galloway and Dumfries, where droving to the London market was well developed by 1700. The policies often served also as an example to a conservative, and sometimes recalcitrant, tenantry of the benefits to be obtained from planting and enclosing. Even so, in the mid-eighteenth century, the parks and plantations of the larger estates were still small islands of enclosure in a broad sea of open runrig lands, muir and moss. Only in the Lothians, and in the Lowland south-west, could one expect to travel more than a mile or two with enclosures on either side.

Among seventeenth-century planters, the Marquis of Tweeddale was one of the more influential. Both Macky and Defoe were impressed by the sixty-year-old plantations of 'firr' at Yester (East Lothian). Macky described it as 'the best planted park I ever saw: the park walls are about eight miles in circumference and I dare venture to say there is a million full-grown trees in it'.[54] Beginning in 1702, the Earl of Haddington was similarly planting on a vast scale at Tynninghame (East Lothian) on the sand dunes around the house. The trees were protected with hedges of holly and the earl subsequently published a tract on planting to inspire his fellow nobles to similar efforts.[55] In the High-land margins the Duke of Argyll at Inveraray (Argyllshire), the Duke of Atholl at Dunkeld (Perthshire) and the Earl of Panmure were similarly regarded as leaders. The Duke of Atholl was influential in using larch for extensive commercial plantations, rather than as a specimen tree, while at Panmure (Angus) many thousands of trees were added to the policies between 1660 and 1680, some of them early introductions of exotic species.[56] In the north-east, Sir Archibald Grant, with extensive planting at Monymusk (Aberdeen) in the early eighteenth century, and the Earls of Fife and Findlater planting in the Moray Firth lowlands are regarded as the principal improvers (see Chapter 7).

Descriptions of early plantations are much less evocative than those of corresponding gardens. They consist mostly of brief notes on avenues and vistas. At Panmure, the approach to the house was along

> an avenue cut thro' the wood, of half a mile in length and 150 foot broad . . .and on each side of this avenue is a fine hedge which reaches the branches of the trees . . . From the gardens there are eight or nine visto's cut thro' the wood.[57]

In the best-designed examples such as Allaway (Fife), vistas focused on churches, mansions, hills, or carefully positioned statues or buildings as in English formal gardens. But Scots utility could also play a part, as at Penicuik where, in the 1740s, Sir John Clerk designed a hilltop Gothick tower which besides being 'an ornament to the country', was also to be 'beneficial to my family as a dovecoat'.[58]

Descriptions can be supplemented with early cartographic evidence for the eighteenth century. The Military Survey allows a national comparison to be made, while early estate plans often provide rich detail. A few early plans have been published, but they give little indication of the value of these sources.[59] A fine series of mid-eighteenth-century plans of the Gordon Castle estates of the Duke of Gordon (Moray) may be used to illustrate the landscape of a large park following more than a century of formal gardening (Figure 10.1). The complex of canals, ponds, orchards, grass platts, slopes, statuary and well clipped hedges that made up the formal gardens in front of the house are clearly revealed, whilst within the walled policies there are tree-lined avenues, pasture parks for deer, cattle, horses and swans, a dovecote, some arable land, and a plantation more recently divided with winding paths. Beyond the policies lay the open arable lands of Fochabers and Bellie and extensive early-eighteenth-century

Figure 10.1: The Changing Design of Gordon Castle Policies, Fochabers (Moray), 1760-1810

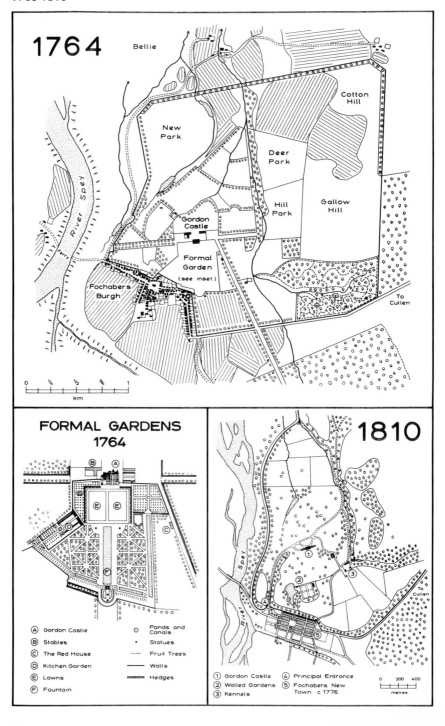

plantations.[60]

Enclosure, planting and associated agricultural improvements in the period before 1760 did not extend much beyond the policies and mains farm. Even within this limited area, improvement was gradual, small changes being made whenever sufficient capital was available from the increasingly commercially oriented estate. Such long-term changes over the lifetime, or sometimes over several generations, of improving landowners is exemplified in the much-studied improvement of Penicuik by Sir John Clerk, and of Monymusk by Sir Archibald Grant. Similar changes occur elsewhere. At Melville, near Dalkeith (Midlothian), Sir John Clerk's neighbour, Lord Ross, improved some 250 ha of his estate by enclosing parks, planting shelter belts around the margins of the enclosures, improving poorly drained land with extensive plantation and erecting new farm buildings, though he made only minor improvements to Melville Castle (Figure 10.2). The history of Melville clearly demonstrates the integration of mains and policies. Their contribution to the economy and ornament of the estate was planned in unison. Star-shaped vistas were cut in some of the larger plantations, with a classical temple in the midst of one; statuary was erected in appropriate places, and the principal avenue provided both a vista from the castle and access to most of the parks.[61]

The improvement of such medium-sized and smaller estates was devised, for the most part, by lairds themselves. The opinions of neighbours were sought; improvements elsewhere were viewed, including contemporary changes in England; one or more architects might be consulted and asked to draw up plans, but the improving laird usually took the initiative and provided many of the ideas for a design, whether it be for mansion, farmhouse, gardens or plantation.[62] The execution of the plans, however, was normally delegated to a trusted employee: the gardener or, on larger estates, the bailiff. The intimate relationship between laird and gardener is revealed in the published correspondence between John Cockburn of Ormistoun (East Lothian) and his gardener Charles Bell, between Sir Archibald Grant of Monymusk and his gardener Alexander Gordon, and between the Earl of Stair and his gardener Thomas McAlla. The landowners, away in London attending Parliament, were always anxious to know precisely how their plans were being executed and what problems were being encountered, and they received detailed accounts and plans from their employees.[63]

Even on the greatest estates improving nobles took a close personal interest in new designs, but here a greater expertise in fashionable design was deemed necessary if they were to attain the splendid effects seen on their travels to England and Continental Europe. Professional garden designers were therefore employed. Early historians of Scottish gardening, beginning with Loudon in the 1820s,[64] did not consider Scots gardeners sufficiently skilled in the period before 1760 and the grander designs have usually been attributed to the principal English gardeners, notably the partnership of London and Wise, and to Stephen Switzer. Recently, however, evidence has been accumulating for the existence of at least one Scottish designer of comparable standing, Alexander Edward. He

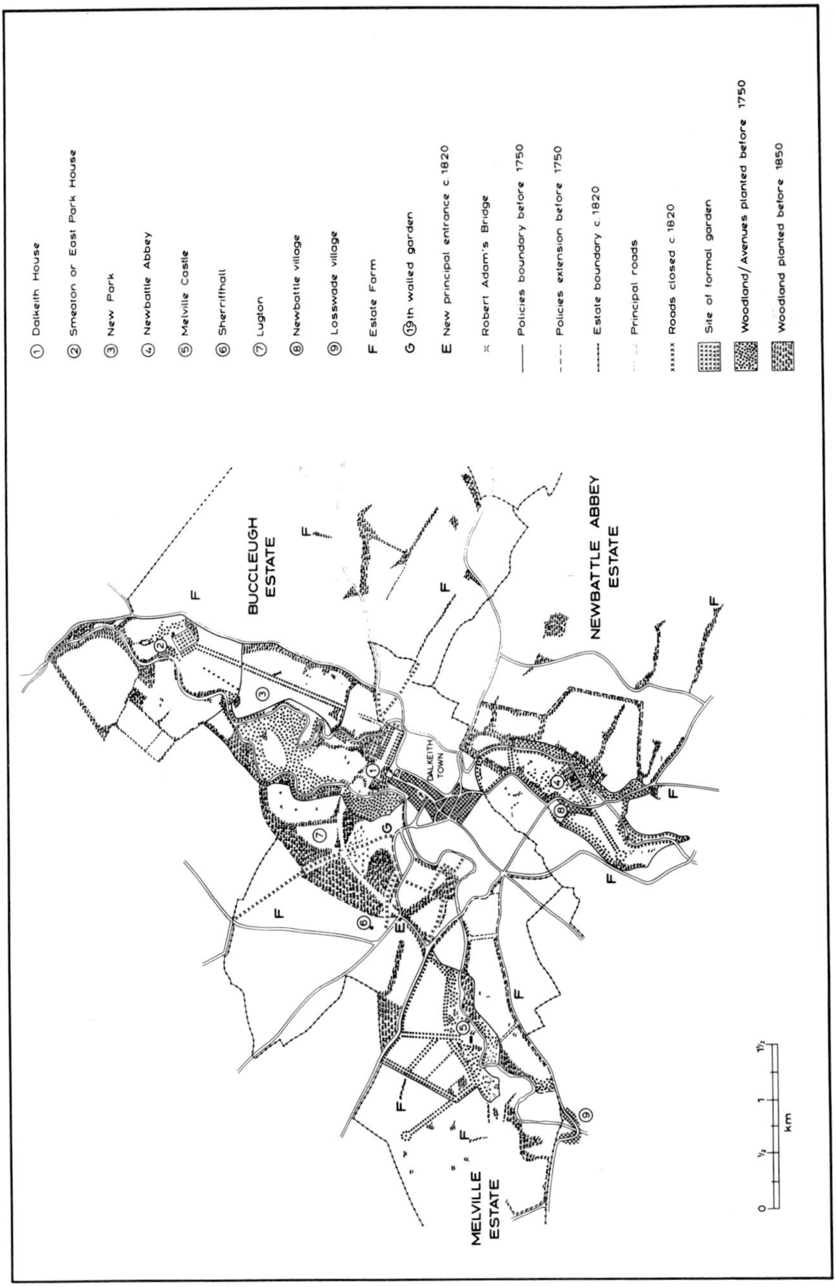

Figure 10.2: Policies about Dalkeith (Midlothian), 1750-1850

was originally a minister, but from the 1680s worked as an architect and gardener, often in association with Sir William Bruce. In 1701-2, Edward toured England, France and the Netherlands at the expense of a group of nobles 'for takeing draughts of the most curious and remarkable houses'.[65] He is known to have worked at Panmure and at Brechin Castle for the 4th Earl of Panmure, at Kinross with Sir William Bruce, at Hopetoun, again with Bruce, for the Earl of Hopetoun, at Allaway for the Earl of Mar, and in 1708 he drew up an extensive scheme for the remodelling of Hamilton Palace policies.[66]

The majority of owners engaged in extensive and long-term woodland planting, and managed their own tree nurseries to raise the necessary seedlings. These nurseries were a significant element in the overall design of the policies and often thousands of trees were raised each year. Neighbouring lairds and nobles maintained a close interest in each other's operations and often exchanged or sold plants.[67] Marriage links were another channel for the diffusion of new plants. The Duchess of Hamilton's daughter was Countess to the 4th Earl of Panmure so that some of the rare plants from the Panmure nurseries came to be planted at Hamilton. Commercial nurseries, notably in Edinburgh, supplied some estates with common trees, whilst rarer species were sent up from London when lairds were in the capital (see Chapter 7). Many planters propagated particular species and helped to disseminate them. Sir John Fergusson at Kilkerran (Ayrshire) planted silver firs extensively;[68] the laburnums at Panmure were famed in the late eighteenth century and at Dunkeld, the Duke of Atholl grew larch in plantation. Scots pine, ash, elm, sycamore, beech, lime, hornbeam, alder, birch, holly and walnut were generally favoured for lowland shelter belts and avenues,[69] whilst hedgerows were planted with thorns, as in England.

Policies and Plantations, 1760-1850

English landscape gardening began to affect Scottish policies only after 1760. From the beginning, the Picturesque style was more suited, and found more favour with estate owners, than the sweeping lawns, clumps of trees, timber belts, Classical temples and broad lakes with which Capability Brown and his imitators were adorning lowland England.[70] In Scotland, even in the Lowlands, deeply incised, fast-flowing streams, rock outcrops and maturing stands of coniferous trees set the scene for Gothick and Chinoiserie, rather than Classical, park buildings. The streams were utilised for water-powered industry and were too closely confined within steep banks to allow for the creation of lakes. In the Highland margins and straths, extensive natural lochs were often encompassed within prospects, but artificial lakes are not characteristic elements of late-eighteenth-century park scenery in Scotland.

Changes in design came slowly. They appeared first on the largest estates, and on some of the smaller policies around Edinburgh. One of the most notable early landscape designs was Arniston (Midlothian), the seat of Robert Dundas.

Pococke describes it in terms which leave no doubt that it was fully transformed into a landscape garden by 1760. In front of the house was 'a fine lawn adorned with single trees and clumps . . . [there] are beautiful winding walks round some uneven grounds over glyns beautified by the prospect of Chinese and other bridges that make it a most delightful place'.[71] Cox dates these changes to *c*. 1753, but provides no evidence as to who the designer might have been.[72] In Perthshire, the descriptions of the Duke of Atholl's Dunkeld and Blair Atholl also notice Chinese buildings and elements of a more naturalistic design, but even by the 1770s this had not progressed sufficiently to satisfy the picturesque sensibilities of William Gilpin. The River Tilt, 'a rapid and rocky stream', was within the policies of Blair Atholl, for example, and 'there the duke has conducted walks; but I cannot say much in praise either of the artifice with which they are conducted or of their simplicity'.[73] Dorothy Wordsworth could find little more to praise on her visit to Blair in 1803.

Lord Abercorn's Duddingstone House, on the outskirts of Edinburgh, was another landscape park subjected to sustained criticism, notably from Sir Walter Scott. His critique of Robert Robinson's design pointed to a brook which had been 'twisted into the links of a string of pork-sausages, flung over a stone embankment, and taught to stagnate in a lake'.[74] Loudon, disliked the 'tame, spiritless beauty' of the layout. The trees 'seem to grow by rule', and clumps reminded him of 'regularly tufted perukes'.[75]

Numerous English visitors to Scotland in the second half of the eighteenth century made it clear that landscaping was confined to small areas near great houses, and that even on many of the largest estates the mains farms and plantations retained their formality. On more conservative and generally smaller estates little was altered, except that the walled court before the house was replaced by a lawn and specimen trees. Walled gardens, avenues and rectangular shelter belts were retained or were still planted, whilst in many ways the estate landscape became even more formalised as enclosure and planting was extended to tenant farms (see Chapter 9).

From 1760, planting became an accepted means of improvement on most estates, but it was not until the early nineteenth century that many of the 'fields resembling parallelograms, divided like a chess-board by thin stripes of plantation'[76] were modified, and new planting produced a more natural effect where woods conformed to the contours of hill-slopes. Within the policies, informality was often obtained quite simply, though sometimes with the help of professional advice, by the judicious removal of hedges, by the thinning of selected trees from avenues and shelter belts, and by a little new planting within old enclosures. At Floors Castle (Roxburghshire) such modifications were undertaken in the 1790s to produce an enlarged stretch of natural parkland scenery.[77]

Among other common landscape improvements, winding walks were drawn through glens and incised valleys (Figures 10.1 and 10.2); walls and hedgerows were replaced with sunk fences to enlarge the very limited prospects from houses, and new walled kitchen and flower gardens were built away from the immediate vicinity of the house and often furnished with extensive greenhouses. The new kitchen gardens of some great estates were of truly noble proportions. At Blair Atholl in 1760, they were reported to be some 150 x 365 m with a central canal, a dovecote and a summer house,[78] while the largest of all was probably that at Dalkeith Palace, enclosing 6.7 ha and costing some £1,300 per annum to run in the early nineteenth century.[79] Kitchen gardens, having been banished from the vicinity of the house, were concealed from view in extensive shrubberies of evergreen and flowering trees and shrubs (Figures 10.1 and 10.2).

Very few estate accounts have been published, so it is difficult to make comparisons either of annual running costs or of the costs of improvements. Certainly, Dalkeith was exceptional. At Dunrobin (Sutherland), early-nineteenth-century expenditure on woods and nurseries varied from almost nothing to more than £750 per annum, while improvements to mansion and policies between 1810 and 1815 involved an average expenditure of over £1,800 a year.[80] On the smaller estates of the lairds, expenditure would not have approached these figures, but often a substantial proportion of the estate income was devoted to improvement, rationalisation and new planting. At Balbirnie House (Fife), the estate income rose from £1,722 in 1777 to £7,697 in 1813, as a result of coal-mining development and improved agricultural income. This was sufficient to finance one of the largest and earliest Greek Revival houses in Scotland and a landscape park designed by Robert Robinson,[81] and paid for the enclosure and improvement of the estate with 'belts of plantation and by placing clumps of trees on the higher grounds arranged and disposed in such a manner as to please the eye and to afford shelter to the adjacent fields'.[82]

The Landscape Designers

Few of the great English landscape gardeners are known to have worked in Scotland. Humphry Repton provided designs for Valleyfield (Perthshire) in 1804, though without visiting the estate. No other plans are attributed to either Repton or 'Capability' Brown. John Claudius Loudon, a native Scot, provided designs for a number of Scottish estates[83] and a group of landscape designers practising in the north of England also worked extensively in Scotland. Robert Robinson was one such person. He is a rather shadowy figure at present, but he had an architectural practice in Edinburgh and his brother, Thomas, was master gardener to George III at Kensington.[84] Robinson supplied J. C. Balfour with landscape designs for Balbirnie House in 1779; designed Duddingstone in the 1760s, for Lord Abercorn, and was employed at Paxton House (Berwickshire). He probably worked, too, at Hopetoun, Dalkeith and Dalhousie Castle.[85] Another landscaper, Thomas White the elder, who worked extensively in Northumberland and Durham, provided plans for Wemyss Castle (Fife), Duff House (Banffshire) and Bargany (Ayrshire) amongst others, while his son, Thomas, remodelled Robinson's landscape at Balbirnie between 1815 and 1819.[86]

A variety of other artists, including writers, architects and painters, provided landscape designs from time to time, as did landowners themselves. Pre-eminent amongst the writers was the lawyer, Lord Kames, who enjoyed a wide reputation in England as well as Scotland in matters of taste. His comments on landscape gardening are found in *Elements of Criticism*, published in 1760, and they were put into practice on his own estate at Blair Drummond (Perthshire). His letters to Mrs Montagu in 1766 make it clear that a 'winter garden' was being made whose 'variety of evergreens will afford shelter, verdure and dry-footing all the winter over'.[87] The other influential writer on landscape design was Sir Walter Scott. His strictures on the needless destruction and neglect of antiquities did much to develop antiquarian interests amongst landowners in the early nineteenth century,[88] so that restoration of medieval buildings and the building of revival Baronial castles began to recommend themselves. Similarly, essays in the *Quarterly Review* encouraged the less regular planting of woodland within policies. Many of these ideas were incorporated into Scott's own estate at Abbotsford (Roxburghshire).

Among architects, James Ramsay is known to have worked at Leith Head; Alexander Naysmyth is said to have been 'much employed. . .in improving the landscape appearance of estates, especially when seen from their mansion windows', while James Playfair provided a plan for Ardkinglas (Argyllshire) and perhaps for other estates also. Finally, James Naysmyth, the artist, is known to have worked at Loudon Castle (Ayrshire).[89] All these designers provided plans in the accepted landscape mode of their day.

Estate owners whose landscaping influenced a wider circle than their own policies included the Earl of Haddington, whose treatise on planting was widely read; Sir John Clerk, whose ideas found voice in an epic poem; Sir Henry Steuart, who wrote widely on trees and plantations, and whose estate at Allanton (Lanarkshire) was much admired by Scott; William Adam who, in 1834, published a description of the improvements carried out at Blair Adam (Kinross-shire) over the course of a century; and Sir Thomas Dick-Lauder, who edited an edition of Price's *On the Picturesque* in 1842, which contained extensive comments and additions of his own.[90]

The Estate Landscape

From 1760 it is increasingly difficult to separate changes in the landscapes of policies from changes in wider agricultural landscapes because the improvement of the former went hand in hand with the latter. In the great upland estates, plantations were both an ornament to the countryside and commercially managed. On lowland estates, the scale of farming operations was increasing, and as farms were enlarged by amalgamation, opportunities were taken to enlarge both the policies and the mains. At Melville (Midlothian), for example, Viscount Melville's new Gothick castle, designed by James Playfair, was surrounded by a more extensive, tree-studded lawn in the landscape mode and with walks through the woodlands clothing the Esk valley. The wider policies were doubled in size as five tenant farms were incorporated into the mains and new shelter belts added[91] (Figure 10.2). Similarly, at nearby Dalkeith, the already extensive policies of the Duke of Buccleugh were enlarged by the addition of one of the biggest tenant farms, Lugton, into the decorative parkland. This allowed the Duke to lay out a new entrance drive so that visitors could avoid the growing burgh. Robert Adam was called in to design the necessary new bridge over the North Esk, which formed an architectural centrepiece to the vista down-river from the house[92] (Figure 10.2).

Elsewhere, the many new, stone-built farms with their yards and byres associated with the enclosure and commercial rationalisation of an estate were sometimes designed as objects in vistas from the mansion and thus were subject to architectural elaboration. Other more utilitarian parts of the estate such as mills, road and river bridges and, later, railway bridges were similarly treated. A common effect of policy extension was the substantial modification of road networks, partly in response to economic needs for improved transport on the estate, and to market centres, and partly as a direct response to the enlargement of policies and an increasing desire for privacy on the part of landowners. Between Melville and Dalkeith, for example, the main road to Leith was re-aligned no less than three times in thirty years in the early nineteenth century as the conception of the two policies became successively grander in the minds of the two landowners.[93] (Figure 10.2).

That a desire for privacy was developing, and that the intrusion of the public into policies was a problem, is well illustrated by a letter from Lord Fife to his factor at Duff House (Banffshire), in 1765. The factor was requested to employ a park-keeper

> just to keep idle people and cattle from going through the park. . .the gates must be kept constantly lock'd. There is nothing makes the place so disagreeable to me as that constant crowd of idle people that are walking over my grounds when I am at home.[94]

The park-keepers lived in lodge cottages beside the newly locked gates set in high stone walls, and such cottages, usually well built and ornate, quickly became a characteristic feature of this later period of landscaping.

Another characteristic feature of the landscape phase is the construction of new drives within the policies. The entrance drive up to the house often swept in gentle curves round the park, both to show off the new landscape to best advantage and to give an impression that the park was much larger than might be supposed; a useful device for those landowners lacking the resources of the Duke of Buccleugh. Sometimes, with the use of carefully placed plantations, the whole estate could be designed to appear as part of the parkland, but such contrivance was more characteristic of the larger estates of the nobility than of the lairds. However, it could be done, as it was at Fintray House (Aberdeenshire), where 'the woods. . .extend above two miles in length, not in square plantations, but happily distributed in different figures adapted to the nature of the grounds, and interspersed with the fields of the personal farm of the worthy proprietor'.[95]

Rural Settlement

Model farms, 'Chinese' dairies, mills, Gothick lodge cottages and sham-castle dovecotes were all part of the great rebuilding on Scottish landed estates and their policies from the mid-eighteenth century; but perhaps the most significant addition to the rural landscape over much of Scotland was the planned village and regularly laid-out new town. Many of these villages and burghs formed integral parts of landowners' plans for the economic improvement of their estates and are described in a subsequent chapter. Others were quite clearly the consequence of new policy and planting and the desire of landowners for privacy.

In the 1820s, the ancient burgh of Cullen (Banffshire) was removed from the gates of the Earl of Seafield's Cullen House to a new site beside the fishing village of Sea-town. The economic basis of the new burgh was entirely based upon fishing, there being 'no manufacturers of any consequence, and but little trade'.[96] It added little to the income of the Seafield estate, but its removal increased the privacy and amenities of Cullen House, and its rectangular street grid gave an air of neatness to the estate improvements which had been proceeding since the 1790s.

Fochabers (Moray) is even more clearly the result of landscaping policies. Plans for remodelling the formal splendours of Gordon Castle were first mooted in the 1760s. The improving lord was Alexander, fourth Duke of Gordon, who inherited the Gordon estates as a minor in 1752. Following a 'Grand Tour' and upon attaining his majority, he entered at once upon a massive scheme of improvement that was to last almost to his death in 1827.[97] First, the already large baronial castle was extended between 1768 and 1774, 'in all the elegant magnificence of modern architecture' to the designs of John Baxter.[98] Then, while building work continued, the extensive formal gardens to the south of the castle were levelled, the canals filled in, new drives laid out, the park substantially extended eastwards and new plantations begun, both within the extended policies and beyond (Figure 10.1).

The town of Fochabers stood only a few hundred metres from the castle. In the 1660s it was little more than a cluster of half a dozen cottages, but by 1720 a flourishing burgh contained 'above 600 inhabitants. . .a grammar school, several good lodgins & inns' and a weekly market.[99] It expanded further in 1754 when it acquired a court-house and more than fifty new feus were sold off by the dowager Duchess.[100] The presence of this flourishing, noisy, irregularly built community so close to his dwelling annoyed both the Duke and his wife and strengthened his resolve to remove it. Thus, in 1775, following the example of other improving lairds in the north-east, he chose a site for a new, regularly planned burgh designed by Baxter to the south of the existing town.

Meanwhile, work continued in the policies. Clumps of trees were planted on the former arable lands, a sunk fence more than two kilometres in length divided the lawns about the house from the pasture lands, and a new walled kitchen garden was built and suitably screened from sight with shrubberies (Figure 10.1). Beyond the policies, the open fields of the town were enclosed and the main road to Cullen realigned in 1772.[101] Towards the end of 1775 all was ready for a start to be made upon the new town, and in January 1776 the Duke's solicitor began issuing new feus and buying up the old. Duke Alexander was quite specific that he was 'desirous to remove the present town or village of Fochabers upon account of inconvenient nearness to Gordon Castle'.[102] There was no particular encouragement in the new-town feus for manufacturers to establish themselves in the town and even for the old-town feuars the incentives to move seemed negligible.

The earliest feuars were almost wholly persons holding responsible positions in the Gordon household and although 'removal expenses' were paid to those willing to move, the money was often insufficient to cover the cost of a new dwelling. These houses had to conform to designs prepared by John Baxter, who also designed the principal buildings about the central square. The majority of the old town's inhabitants were unwilling to move and it was not until 1802 that the last tenement was purchased by the Duke, all vestiges of the settlement were cleared away, and plans for the policies were brought to fruition.[103]

Almost from the beginning the Duke's conception of the new settlement was of a village rather than a town, and certainly by the early nineteenth century it was little more than a rather grandiose estate village. As Lord Cockburn scathingly noted in his journal, it appeared to be 'a kennel for the retired lacqueys and ladies'-maids of the castle, and for the natural children and pensioned mistresses of the noble family, with a due proportion of factors, gamekeepers, and all the other adherents of such establishments'.[104]

Other towns where replanning can be linked specifically to the aesthetic considerations of park design and the desire for more privacy include Grantown-on-Spey (Moray), begun in 1766, where the landowner, Sir Ludovic Grant, made a much more strenuous effort to attract new industry and trade,[105] and Inveraray (Argyllshire), perhaps the most attractive of all the planned settlements, designed to enhance a vista from the castle (Plate 17). Its 'line of white buildings. . .is so little like an ordinary town, from the mixture of regularity and irregularity. . .with the expanse of water and pleasant mountains, the scattered boats and sloops' that 'it had a truly festive appearance' to Dorothy Wordsworth in 1803.[106] However, beyond the façade she found it to be 'but a doleful example of Scotch filth', despite the well built stone houses of the planned burgh. Finally, there is evidence that even in the early nineteenth century attitudes to towns adjacent to policies had not become entirely negative. William Young, the factor of the Sutherland estate, felt able to recommend the construction of a new port at Dunrobin in 1809, telling the Marchioness of Stafford that 'the policies of Dunrobin. . .would not be enjoyed the less, for their vicinity to a fine bustling Sea port Town'.[107] However, since the town remained unbuilt, the Marchioness presumably disagreed with this estimate.

Conclusions

While the overall distribution of policies within Scotland changed little over
the period from 1550 to 1850, there was a substantial increase in their number.
The Lowland south-west, the valleys of the Tweed Basin and most of the central
Lowland belt were already well populated with woods and parks in the last
decade of the sixteenth century; but by the early seventeenth century the first
policies were being established in the Highland margins and Moray Firth lowlands. Between 1660 and 1730, the number of policies also increased in the
Lowland zone, especially Fife, Ayrshire and the Lothians, where the 'abundance
of the houses of the nobility and gentry' and their policies about Edinburgh was
especially apparent to visitors, and in the north-east, which 'however remote
[was] full of nobility and gentry and their seats'.[108]

In the late eighteenth century, the number of policies continued to increase
steadily as those who had made profits in the law, trade and industry sought to
emulate their social superiors and obtain a country estate. Most regions shared
in this increase, but it was especially notable in the Tweed Basin and in the wider
environs of Glasgow, Aberdeen, Dundee and Edinburgh. In the central Lowlands,
though overall numbers continued to increase into the nineteenth century, many
long-established policies ceased to be occupied, either as a result of absorption
into the urban fabric of the larger cities with consequent development as institutions or for building, or because of the deterioration of their immediate environment from mining or industry.

The design of policy landscape changed only slowly, and throughout the
period 1600-1850 formal aspects of design were of continued significance. Most
of the larger policies were altered in part in the late eighteenth century in the
fashionable informal manner, but tree-lined avenues were spared, rectangular
plantations were softened only a little, many walled and terraced gardens survived,
mansions were added to and altered more often than they were new-built, and
parkland continued to be integrated with the mains farm pastures. This continued
importance of formal aspects of design was emphasised later by enclosure and
planting on the whole estate, and by the nineteenth-century revival of some
aspects of formal gardening.

The integration of agricultural improvement with landscape change within
the policies should be emphasised. Only in the late eighteenth century were
significant proportions of policies used exclusively for ornamental and recrea-
tional purposes. Landowners saw no dichotomy in the multiple use of their
policies for ornament, recreation and productive agriculture and sylviculture.
On many estates the policies and mains were used as an example to the tenantry
of particular improved techniques and operations. Agricultural improvement
was itself the basis upon which many of the alterations within the policies were
financed. Initially, profits were used to raise living standards; new rooms were
added to small and cramped houses and walled gardens for fruit and vegetables
were built. Later, attention moved outwards to the mains farm, where enclosure

and plantation were the principal changes in the landscape, while farming operations were geared to the market, in particular the profitable livestock market. In turn, profits from these improvements were applied to building a new mansion and laying out extensive formal gardens. Then, usually in the second half of the eighteenth century, agricultural improvement was extended to the remainder of the estate and profits were invested in refurbishing the house and extending and replanning policies in the landscape mode.

The evolution of the Scottish country house is now reasonably well charted and further research should aim to elucidate the detailed history of particular houses or the work of particular architects, but the understanding of the history of the policies of those country houses has barely begun. Little is known about the impressions Scottish landscape designers sought to create for their clients or about the aspirations of the landowners themselves. Certainly they were more conservative than their English counterparts. They were less concerned with antiquity, they were actively engaged in taming a barren, treeless and often rather forbidding landscape before the mid-eighteenth century, and they were less concerned therefore with the niceties of philosophical and moral debate about landscape design than with the necessity of ploughing, draining, planting and building. Most Scottish garden designers remain rather shadowy figures at present, and the uniquely Scottish aspects of policy landscape are but ill-appreciated and still less understood. Moreover, the nature of the interaction with English fashion and society in terms of landscape design is unknown. The sources and chronology of the introduction of new tree species is uncharted before the second half of the nineteenth century, and the true significance of particular 'improving' nobles and lairds cannot be appreciated until a wider corpus of detailed studies is available for comparison. When such research work has been undertaken, many of the tentative chronologies and ideas outlined here no doubt will be overtaken, but until that time they stand as a framework for future work.

Notes

1. Blaeu, J. (1654), *Atlas Novus V* (Amsterdam); British Museum (hereafter BM) Maps C9b, 'General Roy's survey of Scotland'; Royal Scottish Geographical Society (1973), *The early maps of Scotland to 1850*, 3rd edn (Edinburgh), pp. 37-53; Stone, J. C. (1970), 'The preparation of the Blaeu maps of Scotland: a further assessment', *Scottish Geographical Magazine* (hereafter *SGM*), *86*, 16-24; Thomson, J. (1831), *Atlas of Scotland*, BM Maps 36f 18

2. Lowther, C. (1894), *Our journall into Scotland in 1629* (Edinburgh)

3. Defoe, D. (1724), *A tour throughout the whole island of Great Britain* (London), letters X-XII; see volume 2 of 'Everyman edition' (1962) for subsequent page references; Macky, J. (1729), *A journey through Scotland*, 2nd edn (London)

4. Kemp, D. W. (ed.) (1887), *Tours in Scotland, 1747, 1750, 1760 by Richard Pococke* (Publications of Scottish History Society) (hereafter Pubs. SHS) 1; Pennant, T. (1774), *A tour in Scotland and a voyage to the Hebrides, 1772* (Chester); Gilpin, W. (1789), *Observations relative chiefly to Picturesque beauty made in the year 1776, on several parts*

of Great Britain, particularly the Highlands of Scotland, 2 vols. (London); Wordsworth, D. (1874), *Recollections of a tour made in Scotland AD 1803* (Edinburgh)

5. Sinclair, Sir J. (1791-9) *Statistical account of Scotland*, 21 vols. (Edinburgh) (hereafter *OSA*); the *OSA* is at present being re-issued, Grant, I. R. and Withrington, D. J. (1975-8) (Wakefield); – (1845), *The new statistical account of Scotland*, 15 vols. (Edinburgh); for the authors of the volumes in the two *General view of the agriculture of . . .* series (1793-1816) see Symon, J. A. (1959), *Scottish farming past and present* (Edinburgh), pp. 445-7; Lewis, S. (1846), *A topographical dictionary of Scotland*, 2 vols. (London)

6. Marshall, R. K. (1973), *The days of Duchess Anne* (London)

7. Lindsay, I. G. and Cosh, M. (1972), *Inveraray and the Dukes of Argyll* (Edinburgh)

8. Gray, J. M. (ed.) (1892), *Memoirs of the life of Sir John Clerk of Penicuik* (Pubs. SHS), *13*; Piggott, S. (1970), 'Sir John Clerk and "The country seat" ', pp. 110-16 in Colvin, H. and Harris, J. (eds.), *The country seat: studies in the history of the British country house presented to Sir John Summerson* (London); Spink, W. (1974), 'Sir John Clerk of Penicuik, landowner as designer', pp. 31-40 of Willis, P. (ed.) *Furor Hortensis* (Edinburgh)

9. Cox, E. H. M. (1935), *A history of gardening in Scotland* (London); see also Haldane, E. S. (1934), *Scots gardens in old times* (London); also Ch. 3 of Plant, M. (1952), *The domestic life of Scotland in the eighteenth century* (Edinburgh), pp. 61-74

10. Third, B. M. W. (1957), 'Estate plans and associated documents', *Scottish Studies*, *1*, 39-65; Millman, R. (1975), *The making of the Scottish landscape* (London), especially Chs. 5-7

11. Gilbert, J. M. (1975), 'Hunting reserves in medieval Scotland' (unpublished PhD thesis, University of Edinburgh)

12. Laing, D. (ed.) (1875), *Correspondence of 1st Earl of Ancram and his son the 3rd Earl of Lothian* (Roxburgh Club), *1*, 66

13. Gray (1892), *Memoirs*, p. 148

14. Summerson, Sir J. (1953), *Architecture in Britain, 1530-1830* (London), pp. 325-6; see also Dunbar, J. G. (1966), *The historic architecture of Scotland* (London), *passim*

15. Hill, O. (1943), *Scottish castles of the sixteenth and seventeenth century* (London), *passim*; Hay, G. (1969), *Architecture in Scotland* (Newcastle upon Tyne), pp. 58-65; Mathew, D. (1955), *Scotland under Charles I* (London), pp. 109-26

16. Quoted in Cox (1935), *History of gardening*, pp. 40-1 from 'Coltness collections' (Maitland Club) (1842)

17. Macky (1729), *Journey through Scotland,* p. 135

18. Richardson, J. S. (1950), *The abbey and palace of Holyroodhouse* (Edinburgh), pp. 14-17; Royal Commission on the Ancient and Historical Monuments of Scotland (hereafter RCAHMS) (1929), *Inventory of monuments and constructions in the counties of Midlothian and West Lothian* (Edinburgh), pp. 61-5; Findlay, J. R. (1875), *Hatton House* (Edinburgh), pp. 10-16; three other adaptations are described in Dunbar, J. G. (1975), 'The building activities of the Duke and Duchess of Lauderdale, 1670-82', *Archaeological Journal, 132*, 202-30

19. Marshall (1973), *The days of Duchess Anne*, pp. 189-208

20. Dunbar, J. G. (1970), 'Kinross house, Kinross-shire', pp. 64-9 in Colvin and Harris, *The country seat*

21. See the example of the Duke of Hamilton in Marshall (1973), *The days of Duchess Anne*, p. 191; and of Sir John Clerk in Spink (1974), 'Sir John Clerk', 31-2

22. Hamilton, H. (ed.) (1945), *Selections from the Monymusk papers, 1713-1755* (Pubs. SHS), 3rd series, *39*, provides one detailed case study; see also the general comments in Smout, T. C. (1969), *A history of the Scottish people 1560-1830* (London), pp. 265-77

23. Mitchell, Sir A. (ed.) (1906), *Geographical collections relating to Scotland made by Walter Macfarlane I* (Pubs. SHS), *51*, 122-3; for Mavisbank see Gray (1892), *Memoirs*, pp. 115-16, 154

24. Hamilton (1945), *Selections from the Monymusk papers*, p. 151

25. Marshall (1973), *The days of Duchess Anne*, pp. 191-3

26. Dunbar (1966), 'Kinross house', *passim*; Lindsay and Cosh (1972) *Inveraray, passim*

27. Wordsworth (1874), *Recollections*, pp. 93-4

28. Scottish Record Office (hereafter SRO), Hamilton MSS., RHP 11272, RHP 11275, 'plans of new roads and property purchased'

29. Gilbert (1975), 'Hunting reserves', pp. 258-73

30. Acts of Parliament of Scotland, *2*, 251, c.19 (1504), quoted in Dickinson, W. C., Donaldson, G. and Milne, I. A. (eds.) (1953), *Source book of Scottish history* (Edinburgh), Vol. 2, p. 227

31. Laing (1875), *Correspondence*, pp. 62-76

32. Mathew (1955), *Scotland under Charles I*, pp. 139-40, quoting from Fraser, Sir. W. (1892), *The Sutherland book*, 3 vols. (Edinburgh), p. 231

33. McArthur, M. M. (ed.) (1936), *Survey of Lochtayside, 1769* (Pubs. SHS), 3rd series, *27*, contains a description of the park; Walker, J. (1808), *An economical history of the Hebrides and Highlands of Scotland* (Edinburgh), p. 376, provides dating evidence.

34. Mathew (1955), *Scotland under Charles I*, p. 179, quoting from Fraser (1892), *The Sutherland book*, p. 363

35. Laing (1875), *Correspondence*, p. 70

36. Royal Rentals E.R., xvii, 719 (1541) quoted in Dickinson *et al* (1953), *Source book*, p. 229

37. Lindsay, A. W. E. (1849), *Lives of the Lindsays*, 3 vols. (London), quoted in Cox (1935), *History of Gardening*, p. 32

38. Laing (1875), *Correspondence*, pp. 70, 73-4

39. Lowther (1894), *Journall*, p. 114

40. Mathew (1955), *Scotland under Charles I*, p. 173

41. Cox (1935), *History of Gardening*, p. 41

42. Smout (1969), *History of the Scottish people*, pp. 127-9, and see also the specific evidence in Marshall (1973), *The days of Duchess Anne*, p. 59

43. Smout (1969) *History of the Scottish people, passim*

44. Crawford, D. (ed.) (1900), *Journals of Sir John Lauder, Lord Fountainhall 1665-1676* (Pubs SHS), *36*, 186; see also Marshall (1973), *The days of Duchess Anne*, pp. 50-61 for further evidence of the gardens.

45. Macky (1729), *Journey through Scotland*, pp. 52, 135; Defoe, D. (1724-26), *Tour*, pp. 388-9

46. Millar, A. H. (ed.) (1890), *Glamis book of record* (Pubs. SHS), *9*, 44; MacGibbon, D. and Ross, T. (1883-9), *The castellated and domestic architecture of Scotland from the twelfth to the eighteenth century*, 5 vols. (Edinburgh), *5*, 511-14

47. Macky (1729), *Journey through Scotland*, p. 32

48. Reid, J. (1683), *The Scots gard'ner* (Edinburgh), p. 3

49. The gardens at Barncluith are described by Scott, Sir W. (1828), 'On ornamental plantations and landscape gardening', *Quarterly Review*, *74*, 303-44; and are analysed in detail by Joass, J. J. (1896), 'On gardening: with descriptions of some formal gardens in Scotland', *The Studio*, *11*, 165-76; Maxwell, I. S. (1908), *Scottish gardens* (London), pp. 186-90, provides some additional information.

50. Macky (1729), *Journey through Scotland, passim*; Maxwell, I. S. (1908), *Scottish gardens*, pp. 147-8, 182-3; other descriptions of late-seventeenth-century gardens are found in early county histories such as Sibbald, Sir R. (1710), *The history of the sherriffdoms of Fife and Kinross* (Cupar, Fife), and Edward, R. (1793), *A description of the county of Angus, translated from the original Latin of Robert Edward (1678)* (Dundee)

51. Hamilton (1945), *Selections from the Monymusk papers*, p. 78; for the continuing formality of gardens see the evidence compiled by Plant (1952), *Domestic life of Scotland*, pp. 19-74

52. Kemp (1887), *Tours in Scotland, passim*

53. Gray (1892), *Memoirs*, p. 148; Evelyn, J. (1664), *Sylva, or a discourse of forest-trees* (London); for evidence of the influence of Evelyn's ideas in Scotland, see Hamilton (1945), *Selections from the Monymusk papers,* xlvix, 151

54. Macky (1729), *Journey through Scotland*, p. 31

55. Hamilton, T. (1761), *A treatise on the manner of raising forest trees* (Edinburgh); a modern reprint is also available, Anderson, M. L. (ed.) (1953) (London); for other descriptions of holly hedges see Maxwell (1908), *Scottish gardens*, pp. 92-3

56. SRO, Dalhousie MSS., GD 45/18/753, 'inventory of trees at Panmure in 1694'; see

also Walker (1808), *Economical history*, pp. 200-16

57. Macky (1729), *Journey through Scotland*, p. 99

58. Gray (1892), *Memoirs*, p. 224

59. See the plans in Spink (1974), 'Sir John Clerk', plates 8 and 9 (Penicuik); in Dunbar (1970), 'Kinross house', 66 (Kinross); and Dunbar (1975), 'Building activities', 202-31 (Thirlestone and Lethington)

60. SRO, Gordon Castle MSS., RHP 2381, RHP 2379, 'plans of the barony of Fochabers and the policies and gardens of Gordon Castle'

61. SRO, Melville Castle MSS., RHP 2087, RHP 2088, GD 51/11/54-101, 'plans of 1751 and 1764; estate letters'

62. See Gray (1892), *Memoirs*, *passim* for Sir John Clerk's initiatives at Penicuik, especially for his relationship with William Adam in the design of Mavisbank, 115; Dunbar (1975), 'Building activities', provides similar evidence for the Duke of Lauderdale.

63. Colville, J. (ed.) (1904), *Letters of John Cockburn of Ormiston to his gardener 1727-1744* (Pubs. SHS), *45*; Hamilton (1945), *Selections from the Monymusk papers*; Haldane (1934) *Scots gardens*, pp. 134-45; Dick-Lauder, Sir T. (ed.) (1842), *Sir Uvedale Price on the Picturesque* (Edinburgh), pp. 170-5; Maxwell, I. S. (1908), *Scottish gardens*, pp. 75-81

64. Loudon, J. C. (1828), *An encyclopaedia of gardening* (London), pp. 80-4, 1086-93; Cox (1935), *History of gardening, passim*

65. Walker, D. and Dunbar, J. G. (1971), 'Brechin castle, Angus', *Country Life* (12 and 17 August)

66. Ibid.; Dunbar (1970), 'Kinross house', 66-7 for Kinross; Marshall (1973), *The days of Duchess Anne*, pp. 206-7

67. Hamilton (1945), *Selections from the Monymusk papers*, p. 151; Marshall (1973), *The days of Duchess Anne*

68. Fergusson, J. (1949), *Lowland lairds* (London), Ch. 6

69. Walker (1808), *Economical history*, pp. 199-266 contains extensive comments on tree species; see also the trees noted in Scott-Moncrieff, R. (ed.) (1911), *The household book of Lady Grisell Baillie 1692-1733* (Pubs. SHS), 2nd series, *1*, 250-5

70. See the comments of Loudon (1828) *Encyclopaedia of Gardening*, pp. 80-4; Dick-Lauder (1842), *Sir Uvedale Price, passim*; Cox (1935), *History of gardening*, pp. 83-122

71. Kemp (1887), *Tours in Scotland*, p. 313

72. Cox (1935), *History of Gardening*, pp. 54-5; see also Omond, G. (1887), *The Arniston memoirs: three centuries of a Scottish house, 1571-1838* (Edinburgh), pp. 76-7

73. Gilpin (1789), *Observations*, p. 113

74. Scott (1828), 'On ornamental plantations', 316

75. Loudon (1828), *Encyclopaedia of gardening*, p. 82

76. Scott, Sir W. (1827), 'On planting waste lands', *Quarterly Review, 72*, pp. 558-600

77. Binney, M. (1978), 'Floors castle, Roxburghshire', *Country Life* (11 May)

78. Kemp (1887), *Tours in Scotland*, pp. 230-1

79. Cox (1935), *History of Gardening*, pp. 109-10

80. Adam, R. J. (1972), *Papers on Sutherland estate management, 1802-1816* (Pubs. SHS), 4th series, *8* and *9*, *8*, 248-9

81. Rowan, A. (1972), 'Balbirnie House, Fife, former home of J. C. Balfour', *Country Life* (29 June, 6 July)

82. *OSA*, Fife, quoted in Rowan, ibid.

83. Stroud, D. (1962), *Humphry Repton* (London); Loudon (1828), *Encyclopaedia of Gardening*, pp. 80-3

84. Lee, S. (ed.) (1909), *Dictionary of national biography* (London), Vol. 17, p. 55

85. Rowan (1972), 'Balbirnie house'; Loudon (1828), *Encyclopaedia of gardening*, pp. 80-3

86. Loudon (1828), *Encyclopaedia of gardening*

87. Woodhouslee, Lord (1808), *Memoirs of the life and writings of Lord Kames* (Edinburgh), pp. 33-44

88. Scott, Sir W. (1814), *The Border antiquities of England and Scotland* (London), p. 66

89. Loudon (1828), *Encyclopaedia of gardening*, pp. 80-4; McWilliam, C. (1970), 'James Playfair's designs for Ardkinglas', pp. 193-8 of Colvin and Harris, *The country seat*; Naysmyth, J. (1883), *An autobiography* (London), pp. 38-9

90. Hamilton (1761), *Treatise*; Piggott (1970), 'Sir John Clerk'; Steuart, Sir H. (1828), *The planters guide* (Edinburgh); Dick-Lauder (1842), *Sir Uvedale Price*; the latter quotes extensively from the Blair Adam book.

91. SRO, Melville Castle MSS., RHP 2095, RHP 10598, GD 51/11/101, 109, 'surveys and plans of Melville estate'

92. SRO, Buccleugh MSS., RHP 9528, RHP 9537, 'plans of new drive and roads at Lugton'; the bridge is illustrated in Cox (1935), *History of gardening*, p. 84

93. SRO, Buccleugh MSS., RHP 9530, 'plan of new roads'

94. Tayler, A. and H. (eds.) (1925), *Lord Fife and his factor* (London), p. 17

95. Keith, G. S. (1811), *General view of the agriculture of Aberdeen* (Aberdeen), p. 118

96. Parliamentary Papers (1832), 'Reports upon the boundaries of the several cities, burghs and towns in Scotland', p. 45

97. Shaw, L. (1882), *History of the province of Moray enlarged by J. F. S. Gordon*, 3 vols. (Glasgow), Vol. 1, pp. 58-9; Lee (1909), *Dictionary of national biography*, Vol. 8, pp. 167-8

98. Shaw (1882), *History of Moray*, pp. 68-71; SRO, Gordon Castle MSS., RHP 2389, RHP 2390, 'plans of Gordon castle'

99. Mitchell (1906), *Geographical collections*, p. 241

100. SRO, Gordon Castle MSS., GD 44/32/7; Shaw (1882), *History of Moray*, p. 52

101. SRO, Gordon Castle MSS., RHP 2312, RHP 2356, RHP 2381, 'plans of lands of Fochabers 1760-1780'

102. SRO, Gordon Castle MSS., GD 44/32/7, 'Commission from Duke of Gordon to James Ross, 1776'

103. Ibid., 'Sketch of tenements'; 'plan of houses'; GD 44/32/4, 'tenements purchased 1769-84'; GD 44/51/25, 'tenements purchased 1785-1802'; RHP 2359, 'plan of Fochabers c.1783'

104. Cockburn, Lord (1888), *Circuit Journeys* (Edinburgh), p. 154

105. Woolmer, H. (1970), 'Grantown-on-Spey: an eighteenth century new town', *Town planning review*, *41*, 237-50; Geddes, A. (1945), 'The foundation of Grantown-on-Spey', *SGM*, *61*, 19-22; Fraser, Sir W. (1883), *The chiefs of Grant*, 3 vols. (Edinburgh)

106. Wordsworth (1874), *Recollections*, p. 126; for a modern analysis see Lindsay and Cosh (1972), *Inveraray*

107. Adam (1972), *Papers on Sutherland*, *2*, 107

108. Defoe (1724-6), *Tour*, pp. 293, 402-3

11 THE PLANNED VILLAGES

D. G. Lockhart

Planned villages are one of the most important elements in the fabric of the Scottish countryside. These were settlements founded by landowners on their estates between *c.* 1735 and *c.* 1850 and were characterised by a regular layout of streets and building plots. Several factors explain their founding at this time, particularly natural increase in population and structural change in farming which created a surplus rural labour supply. In response, landowners built planned villages to rehouse some of this excess labour, subsidised local textile industries and built new harbours to provide employment for tradesmen and fishermen. Markets and fairs were established in all but the smallest villages, so that farmers and tradesmen had a convenient outlet for the sale of their produce. A number of villages which had specialised functions were also established, for instance, to house the work-force of remote rural textile mills, and in association with transport development such as canal and cargo ports. Villages were founded throughout the period in almost every county in Scotland, and it is not surprising that publications on this settlement type have been numerous.

Although several books written by economic historians such as Hamilton and Youngson[1] and by geographers, particularly O'Dell and Walton,[2] discuss planned villages, the bulk of published material occurs in articles in journals which range from general commentaries at the national level to detailed descriptions of particular villages. In one of the earliest papers, Houston pointed to the existence of about 150 villages scattered throughout Scotland and went on to outline their functions, distribution and period of founding.[3] In 1971, Smout published a more detailed analysis which expanded on themes discussed by Houston.[4] The origins and morphology of villages were considered and the distribution pattern was plotted on a map showing regions defined according to date of founding and economic activities. While both papers dealt exclusively with planned villages, other general papers such as those by Caird and by Storrie have set villages in the context of the wider farming changes of the period,[5] and Smout has also linked them to the varied investment activities of landowners.[6]

Studies of individual estates and villages include examples from many parts of Scotland. Grantown-on-Spey (Moray) is the subject of two articles, that by Geddes is largely concerned with early newspaper evidence, and that by Woolmer provides a wider account of the development of the village.[7] The founding of the neighbouring village of Tomintoul (Banffshire) has been studied by Gaffney, and changes on the Sutherland estates, including village planning, have been analysed by Adam.[8] A variety of other case studies have been published, such as Brydekirk (Dumfriesshire), Gatehouse-of-Fleet (Kirkcudbrightshire), Ormiston (East Lothian) and New Pitsligo (Aberdeenshire), while Turner's study of the occurrence of the place name 'Osnaburg' includes a section on Dairsie (Fife) which was formerly known as Osnaburgh.[9]

Most of these studies have relied heavily on secondary sources: local histories and the volumes of the *Old statistical account* and the *New statistical account*. Smout and Woolmer both consulted a limited selection of estate papers and government reports, but only Gaffney and Adam have made extensive use of contemporary estate records. Therefore, in spite of the number of previous publications, there are many research opportunities for scholars willing to examine new source materials, some of which have been suggested here. Newspapers, which are briefly alluded to by several authors, provide a wealth of information on attempts by landowners to attract settlers, to develop infant textile industries and to construct new harbours.[10] The register of deeds in sheriff-court records contains examples of building regulations which were registered to ensure preservation. Records of government departments and associated organisations deposited in the Scottish Record Office in Edinburgh are especially useful in studies of textile industries, harbour development and villages founded on estates which had been forfeited from their owners after the Jacobite Rebellion. Finally, estate management papers provide the most important source: plans, memoranda, account books, rentals and correspondence collectively give a detailed picture of the planning of villages as well as a record of the ambitions and motives of their founders.

The aim of this chapter is to examine the origins and distribution of villages, the planning methods used by landowners, and village morphology and field systems. The number of themes has been restricted to ensure treatment in depth and inevitably aspects of the subject which might have deserved consideration, such as the profits of planning and the structure of textile and fishing industries, have largely been omitted. Nevertheless, it is hoped that this chapter will encourage historical geographers and scholars in cognate disciplines to embark upon detailed regional research.

Origins and Distribution

The period leading up to the founding of the first planned villages is poorly documented. It is possible, however, to point to characteristics present in existing nucleated settlements and to the establishment of new organisations which help to explain the timing of the planned village movement. Landowners had acquired prior knowledge of the founding of new settlements because between the fifteenth and seventeenth centuries burghs of barony had been erected on many estates. Such burghs have characteristics in common with planned villages. Both were market centres and were inhabited by tradesmen, while some even had a planned layout of streets and building plots such as Rosehearty (Aberdeen-shire) where a large rectangular square was the main feature of the plan.

Agrarian change contributed to the founding of planned villages in two ways. First, the reorganisation of landholdings created new enclosed farms which were tenanted by progressive farmers instead of the part-time tenants who had been resident in the open-field farming townships. Planned villages encouraged the migration of surplus labour from estates where enclosure was taking place. Second, the diffusion of new farming techniques during the eighteenth century was assisted by the formation of agricultural societies. The membership consisted largely of landowners and it seems probable that such organisations would also have provided a forum for the discussion of village planning. Furthermore, landowners participated in organisations whose aim was to promote sectoral and regional economic growth. For example, the Board of Trustees for fisheries, manufactures and improvements in Scotland (founded in 1726) was largely concerned with expanding and improving the quality of textile production throughout Scotland. Subsidies and equipment were provided for village industry and the Board of Trustees also played a supporting role in attempts by the commissioners of the Forfeited Estates to expand indigenous manufacturing. Three organisations were involved in the Highland region: the commissioners of the Forfeited Estates set up in 1752, the Highland and Agricultural Society founded in 1784, and the British Fisheries Society begun in 1786. The commis-sioners and the British Fisheries Society established villages on their own lands while the Highland Society offered prizes for essays on the theme of planning a successful village and premiums to landowners who had founded planned villages.[11] The membership of these organisations included landowners who were among the earliest founders of planned villages on their own estates and who subsequently were able to offer advice on planning techniques to their neighbours (see Chapter 7). In this way, the idea of the planned village was diffused from a small number of innovation sources.

The distribution of planned villages is shown in Figure 11.1. There are several areas where villages are concentrated, namely the north-east Lowlands between the Laigh of Moray and Buchan, a broad belt stretching in a south-west direction from Angus to the Ayrshire coast, and in Dumfries and Galloway. Outwith these areas, villages are less common, for instance in the Lothians and Borders and throughout the Highlands and Western Isles. Planned villages were never founded in the Northern Isles although proposals to build villages were discussed at a meeting of landowners in Lerwick (Shetland) and building plots were briefly offered for sale at Longhope (Orkney).[12] The present distribution pattern is best explained in terms of the date of founding and their original functions. In certain instances regional variations are very marked. Most villages in Angus date from after 1820, are located close to existing towns and were peopled by weavers and labourers who were employed by local manufacturers. In contrast, the majority of villages in Moray were already established by 1820 and had markets and fairs and independent textile factories or were ports and

Figure 11.1: The Distribution of Planned Villages

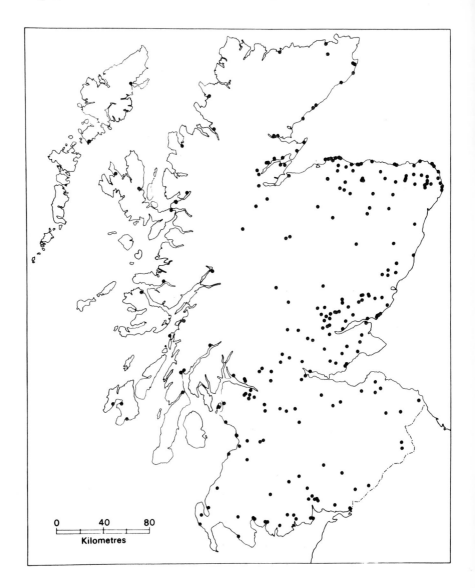

fishing settlements. Three phases may be identified between 1735 and 1850.

1735-1769

The earliest planned villages originated in the replanning of existing settlements such as Ormiston (East Lothian), begun in 1735 to replace a fermtoun, and Crieff and Callander (Perthshire), where new feus were sold from 1738 and 1740 respectively.[13] Although further planning was abruptly halted by the Jacobite Rebellion (1745), the two decades following the Rebellion were characterised by intensive village-founding, particularly in north-east Scotland. Elsewhere new villages were fewer in number, though the Highlands acquired several villages including Bowmore (Argyllshire) and Stornoway (Inverness-shire), which became models for later development in that region. The principal motives during this period were attempts to remedy unemployment in the Highlands and in neighbouring districts of upland Moray and Banffshire in order to prevent a further outbreak of civil disturbances. Attempts to introduce industry can be seen in the proposals of the Highland Plan, which involved the founding of four small textile villages in remote areas, the establishment of planned villages for disbanded servicemen on several of the forfeited estates, and the continued development of Crieff and Callander which were managed by the commissioners of the Forfeited Estates for more than thirty years. Private landowners associated with the Board of Trustees and the commissioners were among the earliest village planners. In this category were Alexander Fraser (Strichen, Aberdeenshire) and the Earl of Findlater (New Keith, Banffshire). New Keith (1750) grew rapidly from an initial plan which had envisaged only one street and a market-place on a moor near the kirktown. It became a model for other landowners who planned villages on their estates. In 1755, the Earl of Fife laid out Newmill (Banffshire) about 3 km north of Keith and in 1760 Sir Archibald Grant of Monymusk used the plan and charters of Keith to help in the planning of Archiestown (Moray). The friendship between Sir Archibald and Joseph Cumine of Auchry may account for the building of Cuminestown in Buchan which in turn led to Cumine planning New Byth (Aberdeenshire) on behalf of his neighbour William Urquhart. There followed a rapid diffusion of villages characterised by similar functions.

1770-1819

After 1770 the distribution of villages changed dramatically as new settlements were founded in areas which had little previous experience of planning. Villages continued to be founded in inland districts throughout the north-east in response to continuing estate improvement and also fishing villages were established along the shores of the Moray Firth, especially between Burghead and Lossiemouth (Moray), near Buckie (Banffshire) and Peterhead (Aberdeenshire). Developments were almost as numerous in other regions. In the western counties, the expansion of the cotton industry provided many opportunities to build villages adjacent to water mills and printfields, such as Houston (Renfrewshire), Balfron and Lennoxtown (Stirlingshire) and Catrine (Ayrshire). Some overspill of the cotton industry to areas beyond west central Scotland also occurred, particularly in the district around Perth, and in Dumfries and Galloway. Other planned villages in Galloway display a variety of different functions such as small ports, roadside settlements peopled by tradesmen and weavers who relied on passing trade and employment from the parent estate or neighbouring urban centre, and housing for estate workers.

A thin scattering of villages was founded in south-east and east central Scotland. Tradesmen villages with market functions occurred at Newcastleton and Morebattle (Roxburghshire) and at Westruther (Berwickshire). Prinlaws and Kennoway (Fife) had similar functions, while in the south of the county early evidence of urbanisation can be seen in the founding of Sinclairtown and the New Town of Kirkcaldy adjacent to existing settlements.

Finally, this period was important for the number of villages built in the Highlands. Along the western coast the dominant theme, especially during the 1780s, had become the development of the fishing industry. The British Fisheries Society and private landowners were both active in projects which, it was believed, would result in significant economic growth. Based in part on observing successful planning at Bowmore and Stornoway and favourable public opinion, the British Fisheries Society established Ullapool (Ross and Cromarty), Tobermory (Argyllshire) and Lochbay (Inverness-shire), while private enterprise during the early nineteenth century accounts for Poolewe (Ross and Cromarty), Plockton and Kyleakin (Inverness-shire). The eastern coastal strip also witnessed intensive effort. In Caithness and east Sutherland, villages were founded in conjunction with harbour development at Lybster and Sarclet (Caithness), the reorganisation of farms and the displacement of minor tenants by sheep walks, and the promotion of mining and fishing on the Marchioness of Sutherland's estates (Golspie, Brora, Portgower and Helmsdale (Plates 19 and 20), Sutherland). Completing the scene were a number of roadside and tradesmen settlements founded near Dingwall (Ross and Cromarty).

1820-1850

In many counties by 1820, villages had ceased to be founded, and the majority of those which were, were small. They comprised roadside settlements, railway villages, and fishing and cargo ports. The first two categories shared many common characteristics and occur widely in Angus and in adjacent parts of Kincardineshire and Perthshire, where their founding was linked to the transfer of coarse linen-weaving from Dundee to the towns and villages of Strathmore in which labour was cheaper and more plentiful. Landed proprietors seized the opportunity to divide small areas of waste land near existing towns into building plots for labourers and weavers, for instance Maryton and Padanaram between Kirriemuir and Forfar, and Lunanhead 1.5 km east of Forfar. The construction of a railway from Dundee to Newtyle to serve the expanding rural linen industry provided the impetus for a planned village near Newtyle station

(1833). As the railway network spread, further associated village planning occurred at Ardler (Perthshire) on the Newtyle to Coupar Angus railway and at Newton of Panbride near Carnoustie (Angus) on the Dundee and Arbroath railway.

Ports and fishing villages of various sizes continued to be founded throughout Scotland until about 1840. Port Allen on the River Tay had only a small pier and was built by John Allen of Errol to export potatoes and grain from his estate. In contrast, the new town of Branderburgh in Moray was a regular port of call for packet steamers on the Leith to Inverness route and also had a large home-based fishing fleet. Several small fishing ports were also built in Ross-shire (Balintraid, Rockfield), in Aberdeenshire (Burnhaven, Sandhaven) and in Ayrshire (Dunure), in part reflecting the policy of the Board of Fisheries to provide grant aid to landowners who built new harbours on their estates.

After 1850, the conditions which had made planned villages a profitable form of landed investment were steadily eroded. Industrialisation in the towns of central Scotland and better transport undermined local markets and the products of rural craftsmen by allowing more efficient distribution of mass-produced goods to the countryside, while on the coast, fish catches became increasingly concentrated on ports adjacent to railway services.

Planning a Village

Choosing the Site

Although the period and area of founding varied considerably, the planning stages were remarkably similar in most villages. The first stage began when a landowner took the decision to establish a village and selected a suitable site. Landowners were able to acquire information from landowning friends, factors and land surveyors, or could observe the progress of other planned villages. Occasionally, formal memoranda and drawings accompanied by an explanatory letter supplemented oral information sources. Selection of a site was made on two principal criteria: increasing the estate rental and accessibility. Profits could be maximised by choosing a site on poor quality soils. The site of Grantown-on-Spey (Moray), for instance, was described as a barren heath moor which had been barely capable of providing grazing for a score of sheep.[14] Similarly, during the 1820s, when Gilbert Meason of Lindertis founded Maryton and Padanaram (Angus), a neighbouring factor noted that there was a great demand for lots of 'very worthless land'.[15] Occasionally, a village was endowed with land which had been previously cultivated such as Rothes (Moray) which was situated adjacent to a 'fruitful field',[16] but in the majority of cases the provision of the village site was hardly a great sacrifice. Most typical was a site at the edge of a moor or low plateau, which had the advantage of peat fuel, materials for roofing the house and low initial value which could be improved by intensive ditching and manuring.

Although the agrarian endowment of the village site was often inferior, landowners took great care to ensure that the site was close to major routes travelled by merchants. The development of the turnpike network during the late eighteenth and early nineteenth centuries presented new opportunities for landowners to establish villages. Routes differed in detail from their predecessors, for example New Scone (Perthshire) was built along the Perth to Coupar Angus turnpike when it bypassed the old village.[17] A river bridge also acted as a focus for the roads on either bank and was a popular location for the founding of villages (Ballater, Aberdeenshire; Creebridge, Kirkcudbrightshire).

Despite substantial road improvements in the pre-railway period, water transport was preferred for the carriage of bulky goods. The Forth and Clyde Canal gave birth to Grangemouth (Stirlingshire) and the Crinan Canal helped foster the growth of Ardrishaig (Argyllshire).[18] Coastal trade was also a contributory factor in establishing harbours at fishing villages, such as that at Burghead (Moray) and Portpatrick (Wigtownshire) and other smaller Solway ports which had trading links with Cumberland and Northern Ireland. Another factor was the relationship with existing nucleated settlements. In every rural parish, the kirktown was the social and religious centre and a market-place, and as such it was also likely to be the focus of the road network, and planned villages were frequently built adjacent to kirktowns (Cuminestown, Aberdeenshire).[19] Villages which were not planned as market centres had greater freedom of location, such as residential villages which were often founded adjacent to existing planned villages (Woodside and Burrelton, Perthshire).[20] Other examples of places where several planned villages have merged to form a continuous built area include Kirkcaldy (Fife) and Carnoustie (Angus).

Feuing the Village

Having selected a site, the landowner sought the assistance of a land surveyor who was employed to measure and mark out streets and building plots on the site and to prepare a plan. Choosing a name for the village occurred about the same time as the preparation of the plan. Once the plan had been drawn, general regulations which governed the settling of the village were prepared. Conditions varied from place to place, but generally specified the dimensions of each building plot, the annual feu-duty, and housing and boundary regulations. The location of lands where villagers could dig peat, divots and moss were defined, and finally provision was made for heirs to succeed to land.[21]

Regulations were read on the day of the auction of land,[22] but before this could take place, public intimation was made several weeks in advance. Handbills and the services of criers at local markets were sometimes used to announce auctions,[23] though in practice newspaper advertising was most popular. A typical example of advertising is the notice for Tongland (Kirkcudbrightshire):

VILLAGE to be Built at TONGUELAND

MR MURRAY of Broughton having determined to have a VILLAGE upon the Clauchan of Tongueland, he has got a regular plan for the same, by which there is to be a square in the middle, and three principal streets; and most excellent water will be brought into the square for the benefit of the inhabitants, from a very fine spring in the neighbourhood.

The situation of the Village will command a most delightful view of the river, the town of Kirkcudbright, St Mary's Isle, and the Rosses.

It is little more than a mile from Kirkcudbright; the tide flows up the river, so that large ships can come up and discharge at the Village, where there is a safe well sheltered harbour; and upon the banks of the river are most convenient situations for warehouses, stores, Ec. and there is no doubt trade may be carried on to great advantage, as the Village will be free of those taxes and burdens, payable by the inhabitants to the burgh of Kirkcudbright.

Mr Murray will be willing to grant feu rights, on reasonable terms, for houses and yeards, to those who chuse to build; and he intends to inclose and subdivide the farm of Clauchan of Tongueland, so as to have it in his power to accommodate the inhabitants with suitable fields.

For further particulars apply to Mr Bushby at Tinwalddouns; Mr Buchanan at Kirkcudbright; or John Thompson at Boreland, the factor.[24]

Advertisements were almost always inserted in newspapers which circulated in the local area. In cases where a village was situated an equal distance from two publishing towns, notices were likely to be placed in both newspapers. A secondary function of the newspaper publisher was to print handbills which were exact copies of press advertisements. Handbills were distributed to parish clergy, posted on church doors and at market-places, or sent in response to inquiries concerning the village. Their circulation may have been quite extensive, since it is known that at least 2,000 copies of one New Pitsligo (Aberdeenshire) advertisement were printed.[25]

Between 40 and 50 per cent of villages were never advertised. Advertising implied a need to make the existence of a village well known, but in many instances this was not necessary. Large estates could plan villages to coincide with the internal reorganisation of landholdings, each new village being built only when a surplus of farm labour and tradesmen had accumulated. Similarly, a population was already available when an old settlement was replaced by a planned village and a simple transfer of population from one settlement to the other took place.

Many settlers negotiated the purchase of building plots individually, as a direct result of having been attracted by press advertisements. On the other hand, proprietors also relied on friends and relatives to provide introductions to persons who might be interested in removing to a new village.[26] In this respect, John Grant of Lurg who was a minor landowner in Speyside wrote to Sir Archibald Grant in 1760 pledging his support for Archiestown: 'I shall not only putt your Advertisements in proper hands, but exhert my Self as much as possible to promote your Undertaking, agreeable to your instructions & conditions.'[27]

Migration to the Village

Advertising and active recruitment policies attracted persons with widely different migration and occupational characteristics. A twofold division can be drawn according to the distance over which migration took place. The first category, which accounted for between 90 and 95 per cent of household heads, consisted largely of tradesmen, agricultural labourers and fishermen who migrated distances up to 40 km. The remainder, chiefly merchants and manufacturers, travelled distances greater than 40 km. Differences in occupational structure, area and period of founding are reflected in variations in aggregate migration distances. This can be illustrated by reference to tradesmen and textile-working villages in north-east Scotland. Villages in Moray, Banffshire and Aberdeenshire attracted long-distance as well as short-distance migrants, but migrants to villages in Angus and Perthshire were mostly drawn from the lower end of the short-distance range.

In the north, villages were widely spaced and resulted in higher mean distance values. Parts of this area, such as Speyside and Buchan, contained few major towns and developed small independent textile factories responsible for every stage of manufacturing from the preparation of flax to the sale of finished goods. Personnel engaged in textile manufacturing were consistently the longest-distance migrants, since local skilled labour was largely absent. In Archiestown, for example, the longest distances recorded were for the manager of the linen factory, his brother, and a foreman. Distance values for weavers were greater than for any other craft and with one exception the minimum distance was 22 km. This may be explained by the marked tendency to recruit from major manufacturing centres (Table 11.1). Lesser distances were recorded for tradesmen not directly employed in textiles, and for migrants to places without small factories and bleachfields.

The planned villages in Angus and Perthshire founded in the 1820s and 1830s present some contrasts. For example, the mean migration distance of Friockheim, a satellite of Arbroath, was only half that recorded in villages in Speyside and Strathisla in the 1760s, and of 40 household heads who are known to have migrated to Friockheim between 1807 and 1855, 32 travelled distances less than 20 km. Newtyle (Angus) also provides evidence of the nature of short-distance migration. Proximity to Dundee (16 km) accounts for the fact that 37 per cent of building plots sold between 1833 and 1850 were purchased by Dundee residents. Some plots were purchased individually, while others were bought by manufacturers who built cottages and sublet these to weavers. Plots were also purchased by tradesmen living in the area from Dunkeld

Table 11.1: Mean Migration Distance by Type of Employment (km)

Employment	Archiestown (1761-6)	North Morayshire Fishing Villages (1805-30)	Friockheim (1807-55)	Burrelton (1812-15)
Agricultural	2.4	13.3	7.0	6.4
Maritime	—	31.7	—	—
Crafts (textiles)	33.6	—	10.6	6.1
(other)	19.0	9.9	11.4	4.5
Manufacturers	48.0	—	–	—
Shops/inns	5.6	12.0	12.8	4.0
Transport	3.2	—	—	—
Professions	—	4.0	2.4	—
Not stated	—	11.2	—	—
Maximum distance	54.4	56.0	36.8	60.8
Mean distance	21.4	14.2	10.1	5.4

Note: The fishing villages are Burghead, Cummingstown and Hopeman
Sources: Lockhart (1974) and the references cited therein.

eastwards as far as Forfar, and finally the Dundee and Newtyle Railway Company which had bought land for a station and goods yard also built cottages to be let to tradesmen and advertised these in the Dundee newspapers.[28]

Friockheim and Newtyle grew into large villages, which in addition to housing textile workers also attracted a varied group of tradesmen. Twenty-three different occupations were given by migrants to Friockheim and at least twelve trades were practised in Newtyle during the 1840s. However, other planned villages, particularly those situated within a five-mile radius of manufacturing towns, contain a higher proportion of weavers and have extremely short migration distances. For example, slightly more than half the household heads who settled in Wolfhill were engaged in weaving and only six other occupations were identified.

Migration to villages which were designed to replace existing nucleated settlements was very localised. Between 1812 and 1815 Burrelton drew one-third of its population from the decaying village of Strelitz only 1 km away and the overall mean distance of migration was as little as 5.4 km (Table 11.1). In Moray, the inhabitants of New Duffus, apart from a few labourers from the estate, had been resident in the old village, and other direct transfers of population took place near Perth when New Scone replaced Old Scone during the last decade of the eighteenth century.

The findings that short-distance migration predominated are in accord with the observations of contemporary writers. Duncan Grant, who witnessed the founding of Grantown-on-Spey, for example, reasoned that the village would be peopled by 'the natives of the country, as strangers in tolerable circumstances will be averse to going there'.[29] Patrick Thomson, sheriff-substitute in Keith, fared little better when asked by Sir Archibald Grant to find settlers for Archiestown. His reply records that: 'I have done all I could to get some feuars for Archiestoun but I'm sorry, to no purpose.'[30] The unknown environment, lack of social contacts and doubts about employment prospects were sufficient reasons to discourage long-distance migration.

Building the Village

The stage was now set for building to begin. Many householders erected houses themselves or contracted with local masons to build for them. Occasionally, however, dwellings were built by the landowner for particular occupational groups, usually estate workers (Kenmore, Perthshire), mill-workers (Douglastown, Angus) or for fishermen (Cummingstown, Moray). Housing for estate workers was intended to enhance the appearance of the estate, while the provision of accommodation for mill-workers and fishermen could help to attract occupational groups with scarce skills but who neither had the ability, time nor capital to build for themselves. More commonly, a proprietor endowed the village with its public buildings: the church and the inn. The scene in large villages would have been characterised by considerable activity with a new house beginning to be built almost every week. However, the rapid growth of some places was in contrast to other settlements which made an unsatisfactory start. Robert Young, land steward on Sir William Gordon Cumming's estates in Moray, wrote to his employer during 1811 describing a disappointing auction at two new villages: 'I am Sorry to say that no Fishermen appeared at Covesea or Port Cumming upon the 26th Currt I only Set Ten Feus at the former place.'[31] Subsequently, settlers were obtained for both these villages, but complete failure was not unknown. One reason for failure was that a landowner could be confronted by a change in demand if a rival village on an adjoining estate eroded the supply of potential settlers. Another reason might have been a poor choice of site. It was unlikely, for instance, that anyone would have wished to settle in the proposed village of Rathven (Banffshire) which was 2 km inland from Buckie when this and other coastal villages were being expanded. Similarly, Macharmuir (Aberdeenshire), situated on the shallow River Ythan upstream from the existing port of Newburgh, could never have become a serious trading competitor.[32] Such mistakes, however, were relatively few in number and for every failure approximately ten successful villages were built.

Morphology

The morphology of planned villages was perhaps their most distinguishing feature. The main factor determining the character of every plan was the street network, since it formed a frame for the arrangement of building plots and access lanes. Four different street types can be identified: simple linear; complex grid forms; semi-circular and elliptical; and one-row settlements (Figure 11.2).

Figure 11.2: Planned Village Forms

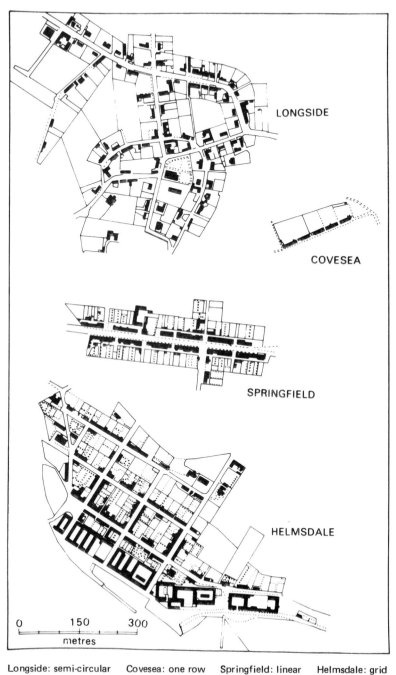

Longside: semi-circular   Covesea: one row   Springfield: linear   Helmsdale: grid

Street Plans

Simple linear forms occur in villages which have only one street. This type of development required a minimum of planning effort and houses were arranged at regular intervals along an existing roadway at Lybster (Caithness) and Springfield (Dumfriesshire) (Figure 11.2). The addition of a second street or a square produced a slightly more elaborate plan (Lumsden, Aberdeenshire; Auchenblae, (Kincardineshire. Transitional plans which incorporate elements of linear and grid types can also be found. Examples occur where the square was positioned at a central point at which the principal street was crossed by a lesser street such as Stuartfield (Aberdeenshire) and Laurieston (Stirlingshire).

Grid plans were either designed to maximise the density of building plots on a small restricted site (New Leeds, Aberdeenshire; Helmsdale, Sutherland) (Figure 11.2) (Plates 19 and 20), or were optimistically designed to allow for later growth and several streets and a square could form the basis for a large town (New Buckie, Banffshire). Elliptical plans are uncommon and the precise reasons for choosing this layout are not clear. Such plans may have been an adjustment to suit local topography such as the hilltop site occupied by St Fergus (Aberdeenshire), or were perhaps an attempt to introduce some variety into landscapes otherwise dominated by linear road and field patterns (Longside, Aberdeenshire). One-row settlements comprised mostly estate workers' cottages, housing adjacent to isolated textile mills and small fishing villages which usually lacked harbour facilities. Well preserved examples can be found at Baledgarno (Perthshire), Douglastown (Angus) and Covesea (Moray).

Houses and Building Plots

A network of lanes which ran parallel with and at right angles to the main streets provided the framework in many villages for the domestic building plots (Figure 11.2). Except for a few houses of fairly recent date, almost every house faced directly across a narrow pavement on to the street. Front gardens were absent in linear street villages, primarily as a means of saving land and also because of a belief among landowners that a front garden would attract dunghills and therefore become untidy. Each building plot or tenement was a rectangular-shaped piece of ground intended to be occupied by a house along its street edge. Land use in the remaining part of each lot comprised garden ground where vegetables and fruit were grown, a small byre or barn, and occasionally a weaver's workshop.

Regulations governing the type of house varied greatly. On the Strichen estate in Aberdeenshire (Strichen and New Leeds) the only requirement was the building of two stone chimneys on each house.[33] In the same district, the regulations at New Aberdour were even more liberal and 'industrious tradesmen and honest labourers' were invited to build using any materials. After twelve years they had the option of erecting a stone-walled house in order to qualify for permanent title deeds.[34] Gradually, however, more comprehensive regulations were introduced. A minimum house value ensured an improvement in building standards and slate roofs became compulsory almost everywhere during the early nineteenth century.[35]

Although relatively few original houses have survived in villages planned before 1800, it is probable that domestic architecture varied considerably. Householders with differing standards of living would have erected different styles of housing. Houses were also built to higher standards by masons either under contract to the landowner or for private sale. Single-storey dwellings predominated before 1850 and only after that date did two-storey structures become more common. In 1859, Strichen was said to have been largely re-built and in New Deer (Aberdeenshire) all the houses in Main Street date from about 1878 when new leasing arrangements were introduced.[36] Nevertheless, photographic evidence of the late Victorian period emphasises that one-storey cottages still predominated in the back streets and in remote villages, whilst the more prestigious buildings in large settlements were clustered around the square and along adjacent parts of the main street (Plate 18).

The shape of building plots and the location of housing in elliptical plan villages is more variable than that found in linear settlements. Owing to the curved nature of the streets, building plots tend to be wedge-shaped and differ in size throughout. House positioning was difficult since the dwelling could not fit the street edge of the plot, and instead was situated some distance back towards its centre. The garden was therefore divided and the symmetry of the plan could only be maintained by placing each house at an equal distance from the street. In one-row fishing villages, the absence of a formal garden is noticeable. Small patches of ground were cleared out of the area surrounding the cottages at Covesea while at Burnhaven (Aberdeenshire), plots were situated on an adjacent hill slope.

Village Fields

Planned villages in the period up to the First World War were surrounded by extensive areas of pasture and arable fields known as lotted lands. Large areas of which had been reclaimed from moor and bog. In remote areas and in districts where the textile industry, estate labouring and crafts failed to provide adequate sources of income, an element of small-scale agricultural production for domestic consumption was necessary. The villages of the Highlands, north-east counties and the Borders, therefore, were heavily involved in part-time agriculture and in Kingussie (Inverness-shire) the feuars were said to 'farm with great spirit and taste'.[37] In contrast, although maritime settlements also had lotted lands, periodic absence of the fishing fleet and the traditional reluctance of fishermen to engage in part-time farming tended to restrict the area under cultivation. Similarly, where full-time occupations were available, such as in the linen-weaving communities in Angus during the early nineteenth century and in cotton-mill settlements in west central Scotland, a field system was entirely absent.

Lotted lands included unimproved land, improved arable and grassland which were subdivided into individual lots each farmed by one tenant. Individuals might rent lots in all three land-use categories, though more often only arable and improvable lots were granted and grazing was restricted to lots in fallow. The extent of land rented by each householder varied greatly, though advertisements and conditions of settlement suggest that fairly uniform grants of land were made when villages were founded.[38] Differences in the size of holdings appear to have occurred at an early date, and manufacturers, merchants and innkeepers, realising that their skills put them in an advantageous position, frequently demanded or were offered greater amounts of land.[39] Gradually, amalgamation of lots took place as a result of illness and death which meant that wives and widows were unable to cultivate much of the ground and all or part of the holding would revert to the landowner for redistribution to other feuars. Exchange of lots and more extensive improvement of moor by some feuars also led to variations in the size of holdings.[40]

The distribution of lots throughout the village lands was complex. Rectangular fields, known as the back ground, were lotted out immediately beyond the building plots and it was normal practice when a village was laid out that the occupier of each building plot also tenanted the adjacent back ground. In small planned villages such as Cummingstown (Figure 11.3), lotted lands comprised only back ground, but where a larger population was accommodated in several streets, a simple relationship between building plot and lotted land tenancies was no longer feasible and a second or even a third series of lots lay some distance from the village. The occupancy patterns of these lots rarely reflected that of the inner lots or the ownership of building stances and it was quite common for adjoining lots to have been tenanted by the same person in order to reduce travelling time.[41]

After 1850 the structure of lotted lands gradually changed. Full-time occupations became more common, thus diminishing the opportunity to cultivate lotted lands. Lands were given up and leased to other villagers or to farmers in the district. By the third quarter of the century there emerged a small number of villagers who occupied quite substantial tracts of land measuring in some instances as much as 10 ha. Labourers continued to rent a few hectares, but it was among craftsmen and shopkeepers that decline was most noticeable and this continued down to the early years of the twentieth century.[42] Lotted lands survived longest in north-east Scotland — in 1911 18 villagers still farmed at Longside, whilst at Hopeman (Moray) and Macduff (Banffshire) they survived in modified form as late as the mid-1950s.[43]

Village Growth

A useful method of tracing village growth is to make a comparison between the original feuing plan and the first and second editions of the Ordnance Survey map. It was found that four out of every five villages have remained within the area defined in their initial feuing plans. In these, houses were gradually built, thus filling the available plots. The smallest villages at first

Figure 11.3: Plan of Cummingstown (Moray), 1809

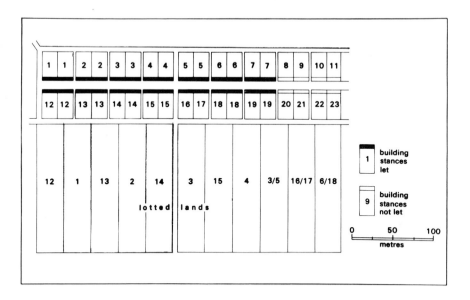

feuing frequently remained without further addition, and many large settlements such as Burghead had been laid out on a very optimistic scale so that subsequent growth was easily contained within the area of the initial plan. Those villages which were expanded at a later date appear to have been laid out with optional plans complete in their original form but readily adaptable should demand prove necessary. This type of plan can be seen in New Keith and Aberchirder (Banffshire) where the central street and a square were flanked by lanes capable of being widened for later street development.[44] Similarly the basic triangle of streets in Strichen was extended by the addition of another street parallel to its longest side.

Some original features were inevitably lost when a village was expanded, particularly the inner series of lotted lands which were acquired for feuing and as a result new lands were taken in from the waste. Nevertheless strong legal factors helped conserve the character of the original plan. Each building stance was indivisible and in most places regulations prohibited the obstruction of lanes, or the construction of back houses in the garden ground, and although the original dwellings have largely been replaced, the second generation of houses maintained the same alignment to the street thus preserving much of the original planned character, for example Strichen (Figure 11.4).

Figure 11.4: The Growth of Strichen (Aberdeenshire), 1763-1970

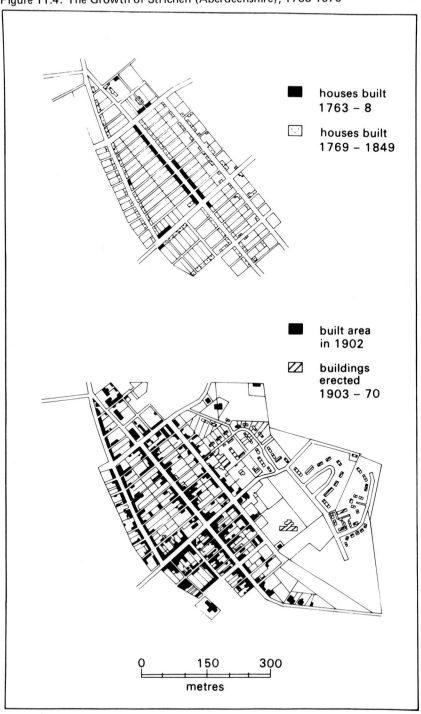

Conclusion

At the present time, villages planned between about 1735 and 1850 remain the most numerous type of nucleated settlement in rural districts in many parts of Scotland. Very few villages have failed to survive.[45] Some like Balfron (Stirling-shire) are admittedly undergoing rapid change as a result of redevelopment, while others have become the focus for new housing developments associated with growth industries such as whisky distilling and the servicing of offshore oil development (Bowmore, Argyllshire; Mintlaw, Aberdeenshire).

The author has used contemporary newspaper coverage for the whole of Scotland and work on estate papers in public repositories and in private owner-ship has been completed for the north-east counties. As this research has pro-ceeded it has been possible to identify many villages hitherto unrecognised. Nevertheless further investigation of primary sources is required, first to identify all villages, and second to answer questions about certain themes which are still inadequately understood. The latter would include problems such as the con-tinuity between burghs of barony and planned villages, the diffusion of ideas among landowners, migration patterns and the impact which investment in planned villages had upon the surrounding district.

There is also a need to extend the study beyond Scotland. Planned villages are not unique to Scotland – new villages were established throughout Western Europe. Lord Gardenstone, the founder of Laurencekirk (Kincardineshire), visited one near Geneva,[46] whilst contemporary propagandists such as George Dempster and James Anderson cited the growth of ports in England, the Netherlands and Italy as an inducement to establish planned fishing villages in Scotland.[47] However it is in Ireland, which shared common problems of agri-cultural improvement and the development of textile industries, that one might expect to find links. Certainly villages had been established by landowners earlier in Ireland than in Scotland. For example, publication of a pamphlet by Sir Richard Cox of Dunmanway (County Cork) which described planning on his estate, probably influenced several Scottish landowners.[48] A visit to Ireland may have provided Sir William Forbes of Pitsligo with ideas for planning New Pitsligo (Aberdeenshire) in 1787 and, at about the same time, his friend and business associate, James Hunter Blair of Dunskey, replanned Portpatrick (Wigtownshire) which had a regular ferry service to Donaghadee (County Down).[49] Furthermore, the advertising of several villages in Wigtownshire in the Belfast press during the eighteenth century seems to indicate that cross-channel economic ties and migration were commonplace.[50] The precise nature of the diffusion of ideas from Ireland therefore forms a further avenue for future research. Although important gaps in our knowledge still remain to be filled, it can be seen that the planned village is a major element in the enduring Scottish rural landscape and its distinctive morphology is visible across the length and breadth of the country.

Notes

1. Hamilton, H. (1963), *An economic history of Scotland in the eighteenth century* (Oxford), pp. 31-6; Youngson, A. J. (1973), *After the forty-five* (Edinburgh)

2. O'Dell, A. C. and Walton, K. (1962), *The Highlands and Islands of Scotland* (London and Edinburgh), pp. 154-7

3. Houston, J. M. (1948), 'Village planning in Scotland, 1745-1845', *Advancement of Science, 5*, 129-32

4. Smout, T. C. (1970), 'The landowner and the planned village in Scotland, 1730-1830', pp. 73-106 in Phillipson, N. T. and Mitchison, R. (eds.), *Scotland in the age of improvement* (Edinburgh)

5. Caird, J. B. (1964), 'The making of the Scottish rural landscape', *Scottish Geographical Magazine* (hereafter *SGM*), *80*, 72-80; Storrie, M. (1961), 'Islay: a Hebridean exception', *Geographical Review, 51*, 87-108; *idem* (1965), 'Landholdings and settlement evolution in West Highland Scotland', *Geografiske Annaler, 47B*, 138-61

6. Smout, T. C. (1964), 'Scottish landowners and economic growth, 1650-1850', *Scottish Journal of Political Economy, 11,* 218-34

7. Geddes, A. (1945), 'The foundation of Grantown-on-Spey, 1765', *SGM, 61*, 19-22; Woolmer, H. (1970), 'Grantown-on-Spey: an eighteenth-century new town', *Town Planning Review, 41*, 237-49; Gaffney, V. (1960), *The lordship of Strathavon: Tomintoul under the Gordons* (Third Spalding Club, Aberdeen), 34-61

8. Adam, R. J. (ed.) (1972), *Papers on Sutherland estate management 1802-1816* (Publications of the Scottish History Society (hereafter Pubs. SHS), 4th series, *8* and *9*

9. Wood, J. D. (1971), 'Regulating the settlers, and establishing industry: planning intentions for a nineteenth-century Scottish estate village', *Scottish Studies, 15*, 39-52; Butt, J. (1966), 'The industrial archaeology of Gatehouse-of-Fleet', *Industrial Archaeology, 3*, 127-37; Matthew, R. H. and Nuttgens, P. J. (1959), 'Two Scottish villages: a planning study', *Scottish Studies, 3*, 113-42; Milne, J. (1960), 'New Pitsligo seventy years ago', *Transactions Buchan Field Club, 17*, 53-73; Turner, W. H. K. (1966), 'Osnabrück and Osnaburg', *Osnabrucker Mitteilungen, 73*, 55-70

10. Lockhart, D. G. (1978), 'The planned villages of Aberdeenshire: the evidence from newspaper advertisements', SGM, *94*, 95-102; a useful finding list of newspaper files is Ferguson, J. P. S. (1956), *Scottish newspapers held in Scottish libraries* (Edinburgh)

11. *Edinburgh Evening Courant*, 20 February 1787; 30 June 1787; *Glasgow Mercury*, 5 March 1788; Royal Highland and Agricultural Society National Register of Archives, Scotland (hereafter NRA, Scot.), survey 0392, Sederunt Book, vol. 2, 24 July 1789, 1 August 1789, 4 December 1789

12. Gardie House MSS., NRA, Scot., survey 0450, Vetro lateral file, 'Date uncertain pre-1855', Questions for the consideration of the heritors of Shetland . . .; *Caledonian Mercury*, 24 March 1800

13. Colville, J. (ed.) (1904), *Letters of John Cockburn of Ormistoun to his gardener, 1727-1743* (Pubs. SHS), *45*; Drummond Castle Estates Office, Muthill: Perth Chartulary, Vol. 2, number 3; the foundation dates of other villages mentioned in this section are largely drawn from local newspapers

14. Scottish Record Office (hereafter SRO), Seafield Papers, GD 248/25/2/6/, Notes on the scheme propos'd for erecting the village of Grantstown

15. Sheffield City Libraries, Wharncliffe Muniments, Wh.M. 277, letter A. Dalgairns to Lord Wharncliffe: Ingliston, 3 January 1832

16. *Aberdeen Journal*, 12 December 1763

17. Estates Office, Scone Palace, Perth: Plan of the grounds about Scone House . . . By Andrew Coch, 1795

18. *New Statistical Account* (hereafter *NSA*), Vol. 7, South Knapdale, p. 270; ibid., Vol. 8, Falkirk, p. 24

19. *Aberdeen Journal*, 7 December 1761

20. Lockhart, D. G. (1974), 'The evolution of the planned villages of north-east Scotland: studies in settlement geography *c*. 1700-*c*. 1900' (unpublished PhD thesis, University of Dundee), Vol. 1, p. 105

21. See, for example, Aberdeen Sheriff Court (hereafter ASC), Commissary Clerk's deeds, Contract & agreement, Sir William Forbes and the feuars of New Pitsligo, dated 1 September 1796, registered 25 March 1805

22. See, for example, W. and J. Cook, Writers to the Signet, Edinburgh: Chartulary of the Brucklay Estates 1844, 12-18 Articles of Feu of New Aberdour dated 1797

23. Cramond, W. (1893), *The making of a Banffshire burgh* (Banff), p. 12; SRO, Dalguise Muniments, GD 38/2/57, letter Charles Duncan to Charles Stewart: Perth, 9 September 1813

24. *Dumfries Weekly Journal*, 24 December 1793

25. National Library of Scotland (hereafter NLS), Fettercairn Papers Acc 4796 box 37 (first deposit), Discd Accot Jas Chalmers & Coy advertisements anent New pitsligo £7. 7. 10., 11 July 1796

26. Grant of Monymusk Papers NRA, *Scot.*, survey 099, uniform box H, letter Joseph Cumine to Sir Archibald Grant: Auchry, 26 November 1765; ibid., uniform box G, bundle 29, another letter, 4 December 1765

27. Ibid., uniform box G, bundle 29, letter John Grant to Sir Archibald Grant: Lurg, 13 December 1760

28. *Dundee Advertiser*, 8 April 1836; 8 July 1836

29. SRO, Seafield Papers, GD 248/25/2/6

30. Grant of Monymusk Papers, uniform box C bundle 12, letter Patrick Thomson to Sir Archibald Grant: Keith, 12 April 1765

31. NLS, Gordon Cumming Papers, deposit 175, box 140, letter Robert Young to Sir William Gordon Cumming: Inchbroom, 31 March 1811

32. *Aberdeen Journal*, 7 March 1791; 13 May 1771; 1 July 1776

33. ASC, Register of Deeds, Articles relative to the feus in the village of Mormond, dated 2 June 1766, registered 8 June 1766; ibid., Articles of erection of the village of Leeds belonging to Strichen, dated 9 March 1798, registered 14 March 1798

34. Chartulary of the Brucklay Estates 1844

35. See for example, ASC, Register of Deeds, Rules and regulations for the erection and government of the village of Leith Lumsden, dated 7 December 1829, registered 12 December 1829

36. *Banffshire Journal*, 8 February 1859; Dingwall-Fordyce Papers, Brucklay estates office, Maud; Brucklay letter book No. 5 f.245, letter Charles Barclay to W. Dingwall Fordyce: Aberdour House, 21 March 1878

37. NSA, Vol. 14, Kingussie, p. 75

38. Sinclair, Sir J. (ed.) (1795), *The statistical account of Scotland*, Vol. 16, Castletown, p. 75

39. NLS, Gordon Cumming Papers, box 139, letter Donald Smith to Sir William Gordon Cumming: Gordonstoun, 29 November 1808

40. Signet Library, Edinburgh, Session Papers, vol. 651, number 177, Clinton *v*. Brown, Print for the Pursuer, 23 February 1874

41. Fettercairn estates office, Fettercairn: Plan of New Pitsligo village and lands adjacent as it presently is, (No surveyor) May 1803

42. Middlemuir farm office, Strichen: Tenants rental of New Pitsligo

43. Wink and Mackenzie, Solicitors, Elgin: Deed box 'Lt Col T. R. Gordon Duff – Hopeman estate'; Macduff Town Council (1966), *Macduff and its harbour* (Banff), p. 13

44. The relevant plans for New Keith and Aberchirder are listed in Lockhart (1974), 'Evolution of planned villages', Vol. 2, pp. 30, 39

45. Two villages in north-east Scotland: Barracks (Angus) and Strelitz (Perthshire) have disappeared: ibid., pp. 98-9, 130-2

46. Garden, F. (1791), *Travelling Memorandums* (Edinburgh), Vol. 1, pp. 234-7

47. Dempster, G. (1789), *A discourse containing a summary of the Directors of the Society for extending the Fisheries and improving the Sea Coasts of Great Britain . . .* (London), pp. 55-62; Anderson, J. (1785), *An account of the present state of the Hebrides and Western coasts of Scotland* (Edinburgh), pp. xxxiv-xxxviii

48. Lockhart, D. G. (1976), 'Select documents XXXIII: Dunmanway, County Cork, 1746-9', *Irish Historical Studies, 20*, 170-5

49. NLS, Fettercairn Papers, box 47 (second deposit), letters of Sir William Forbes

to James Hunter Blair, 1785, *passim*; NLS, Journal of Sir William Forbes, 6th Bart of Pitsligo, Tour to Continent 1792-93, MS. 1539, f.1; *Caledonian Mercury*, 9 November 1785; *Belfast News Letter*, 25 November 1757; 12 August 1791; 22 March 1808

   50. Lockhart, D. G. (1976), 'The advertising of towns and villages in the Belfast News Letter 1738-1825', *Ulster Folklife, 22*, 91-3

12 THE COMMERCIAL USE OF WOODLAND AND COPPICE MANAGEMENT

J. M. Lindsay

Scottish woodland history needs reinvigoration. It would be unfair to deny that some useful work has appeared in the last half century, but all too many authors have accepted myth and legend at face value, and reverently copied their predecessors' unverified claims and fictive episodes. There is a real need for critical reassessment, and above all for careful use of the large amount of primary manuscript material that has become accessible for study in the last few decades.

No topic shows the confused state of woodland history more than the treatment of commercial forestry (which is best defined in this context as the management or exploitation of woodland for profit). On the one hand, we have recent publications in which commercial activity is blamed for the wholesale destruction of the Highland woods.[1] On the other, we have the work of economic historians who assign commercial forestry the most negligible of roles in the Highland economy.[2]

Are we to suppose that there was really such a difference between the ecological and the economic impact of forestry? If we do not — and as we shall see later, there are good reasons why we should not — how are we to reconcile these assessments? Questions like these require answers, and ultimately the most reliable answers will be provided by the accumulation of case studies based on primary evidence. In the contribution that follows two case studies will be examined.

It is necessary to be selective, and attention will be concentrated on commercial forestry. This means that little reference will be made to purely decorative plantations, or to the areas of woodland (common in the Highlands) within which cutting by estate tenants was tolerated or encouraged. Within the sphere of commercial forestry we can usefully distinguish between semi-natural woodland and plantations.[3] These tended to be subject to different cutting regimes, although we should not draw too definite a line; planted and semi-natural woods were not invariably distinct physically or differently treated. In general (there were significant exceptions) the commercial value of plantations lay in the production of what was called 'measurable timber', timber large enough for use in the different forms of construction. This was also true of the semi-natural pinewoods that remained on a limited number of sites in the Highlands. On the other hand, the semi-natural deciduous woods that survived with varying degrees of success throughout Scotland were subjected to coppicing regimes which put more emphasis on tanbark and specialised

271

forms of small 'unmeasurable timber'. It is only relatively recently that the extent and significance of coppice in Scotland has been realised; it is this form of management which will be examined in the case studies that follow.

Interpretations of Woodland History

First of all, though, it is appropriate to look briefly at the ways in which emphasis in woodland history has evolved over the last few centuries.

Post-medieval Scotland was a relatively bare country, lacking both residual woodland and the hedgerow trees and planted clumps that formed a tolerable substitute in the critical eyes of English travellers. Native Scots lamented the shortage of trees, and visitors were not above making unkind comments.[4] As late as 1775 Samuel Johnson's mischievous remarks — he said, for example, that 'a tree might be a show in Scotland as a horse in Venice' — touched a spot sensitive enough to bring forth volumes of indignant refutation.[5]

The Highlands were better wooded than the south. An Act of the Scottish Parliament in 1609 stated that it had 'plesit God to discover certane wodis in the heylandis wlkis wodis by reasoun of the savagnes of the inhabitantis thairabout wer ather vnknawin or at the leist vnproffitable and vnused'.[6] The writings of John Spreull a century later echoed this optimism about Highland resources, and soon afterwards Defoe urged landowners in the Highlands to make use of their abundant timber.[7] We should be cautious about accepting these authors' assessments, though, for there is no evidence that either travelled extensively in the Highlands. Accounts of visits to the Highlands by Scots and Englishmen alike before 1700 indicate that the woods, impressive though they may have been by Lowland standards, were fragmented and frequently difficult to reach.[8] Certainly no part of Scotland was really well wooded when the Military Survey was produced around 1750 (Plate 6). If we measure woodland cover on the Survey we find that the figure tends to run around 2 or 3 per cent in Lowland areas and some parts of the Highlands, but rises to 7 per cent or more in other Highland districts. It may be noted in comparison that in 1965 Scotland had 8.5 per cent tree cover, still a poor figure in European terms.[9]

During the period we are studying it was natural for intelligent observers to compare visible poverty with past glories, and to seek reasons for the decline. Tacitus, Ptolemy, Dio Cassius and other classical authors had left descriptions which were copied and embellished by later historians to create the image of a former vast and almost unbroken forest.[10] It was also common knowledge that huge numbers of stumps and fallen trees, the relics of great ancient woods, were to be found in peat deposits. In William Aiton's *Treatise on moss-earth* (1811) we can see a representative example of the range of explanations put forward for the disappearance of the woods. Having 'proved' from place-names and classical authorities that there had been 'immense forests which in former ages covered and beautified Scotland', Aiton explained their demise as the work of the saw and axe. 'These instruments', he wrote, 'have been used partly to enlarge the scope of agricultural operations, partly to extirpate devouring animals, but chiefly to facilitate the operations of war.'[11] Huge tracts had been cleared by the Romans, the Danes, the English and by the Scots themselves in their internal disputes.

Picturesque tales of military destruction and wholesale clearance to destroy cover for wolves and outlaws are still part of the repertoire of explanations, but more recently commercial forestry has been assigned a major role in deforestation. Particularly significant in bringing about this change of emphasis were two papers on charcoal iron-smelting in Scotland read to learned societies in 1886 by Macadam and Kemp.[12] Their conclusions (Macadam's especially) have been taken and interpreted by popularisers such as the geologist H. M. Cadell in his *Story of the Forth* (1913) and the zoologist James Ritchie in *The influence of man on animal life in Scotland* (1921).[13] Ritchie's version in particular has been perpetuated and modified by later authors, notably F. Fraser Darling, to provide the basis of a new popular view.[14]

Summarised briefly, this interpretation retains the traditional elements but adds to the catalogue of destruction the damage caused by ironmasters and timber merchants, working separately or together in extensive Highland woods. Smelting is taken to be vitally important; according to Cadell, 'the ancient iron smelters are probably largely to blame for the wholesale destruction of the old Caledonian forests.'[15] English involvement is also cited as a major factor, and in Fraser Darling's view, 'the English have been the greatest agents of destruction in Scottish forests.'[16] The attack on the Highland woods is seen as accelerating after 1715, and particularly after 1745, reaching a peak around 1800. The woods which survived to that date, it is claimed, suffered further due to clearance to make way for sheep walks.[17]

There are many reasons for doubting this interpretation. Apart from anything else, we know from the Military Survey that even the Highlands were poorly wooded by 1750. If commercial activity reached its peak later than that, it can hardly be regarded as the prime destroyer of Scotland's woods. There is also remarkably little primary evidence to support the argument. This we might expect of the traditional explanations, which mainly concern periods remote enough to be poorly recorded, but some episodes can be checked and the evidence for 'devastation' is not convincing. Thus several authors have cited a formal request made in 1654 by General Monk to the Earl of Airth, calling on him to cut certain woods in Aberfoyle parish which sheltered rebels. There is primary evidence, though, that these same woods were cut as coppice commercially in the few years after 1678, and regularly thereafter. We must assume that they had not in fact been cut in 1654, or else that they had regenerated successfully; whichever was the case, there is no question of devastation.[18] In other instances genuine but trivial events seem to have been magnified. To take one example, the nineteenth-century tradition that the people of Glen Urquhart had curbed a forest fire around 1770 by cutting a firebreak 500 yards wide in its path may describe a real incident, but there can be little doubt that it has been greatly exaggerated in the retelling.[19]

Much the same is true of commercial activity, and the primary evidence available actually suggests that operations were on a small scale and made a relatively limited impact. This was the case even in the notorious smelting industry. The present author has reviewed the evidence in this field, and found that in only one decade after 1600 (1700-9) were there as many as four blast furnaces active in the Highlands. In most decades there were only one or two, and there were appreciable periods with none at all.[20] It is also apparent from careful evaluation of map evidence that various commercial activities were carried on for long periods, on certain sites at least, without disastrous effects on the neighbouring woodlands being recognisable.[21]

Apart from the problem of evidence, the popular interpretation is weak on other grounds. It tends to ignore the possibility of regeneration, treating tree cover as something which can never re-establish itself once removed. It also gives too little attention to grazing damage, trampling, clearance for cultivation, and the other unspectacular but persistent attritive forces associated with agricultural communities in Scotland during the prehistoric and historic periods.

For these reasons one must reject this interpretation; it has already been pointed out that it is not universally accepted, although it survives in popular texts and makes disturbing appearances in specialised work by botanists and ecologists. On the other hand, there is so much evidence of sustained commercial forestry that one should not, as some economic historians have done, dismiss it as a minor activity. Although one may be able to dismiss the more grotesque charges at this stage, a thorough reappraisal of commercial forestry is still necessary, for it is open to lesser accusations. It might, for instance, be argued that commercial use inflicted severe localised damage on the woods which were accessible, even though these woods might have been limited in extent when activity began.

Careful analysis of primary evidence is necessary to resolve the problems of commercial use, as emphasised earlier, but this has been remarkably rare so far. The most abundant recent research has been the work of botanists, foresters and ecologists, and has made little or no use of primary historical material. Pinewoods have received most attention; apart from the major works of Steven and Carlisle and McVean, there is the interesting work on the ecological evolution of the Wood of Rannoch by Malcolm and Hayes.[22] Tittensor has provided a useful historical ecology of the Loch Lomond oak woods, although it is marred by some gross historical errors.[23]

Forest historians and historical geographers have been much less productive. Anderson's major text, admirable as it is in conception, is far from ideal in its posthumously published form and very uncritical in its use of evidence.[24] In a brief but valuable paper of 1955, Edlin revived an awareness of the former importance of coppice in Scotland, and the present author has pursued points raised by this paper as well as examining different aspects of the role of commercial forestry and the place of woodland in Highland rural life.[25] The recent work of Dixon on the eighteenth-century management of the Strath Spey pinewoods may pave the way for the reassessment of the activities of timber merchants in that area, the focus of a great deal of wildly inaccurate writing in the past.[26] A lot nevertheless remains to be done.

Coppice in Scotland

In the period considered here, estate forestry was predominant in Scotland, and this tended to put emphasis on non-silvicultural factors. The needs of farming limited extension of the wooded area, and fashions in estate planning encouraged the creation of parkland, mixed woodland, or plantations on visually striking but difficult terrain of low value for timber production. There can be no doubt that such considerations were important to some major innovators in extensive planting, like the fourth Duke of Atholl, and small proprietors too were swayed by the vogue for the ornamental or picturesque.[27] Plantations tended to be small, mixed and attractively arranged rather than extensive, uniform and utilitarian.

In the absence of a strong utilitarian tradition, it is not surprising to find that the considerable expertise of the period was directed towards the cultivation of individual species rather than to the development of schemes for the systematic management of woodland for profit. This is evident, for example, in Justice's *Dissertation on the culture of forest trees* (1759), and elements of such an approach are still evident in later guides like Brown's *Forester* (1847).[28]

Coppicing was an exception. Whereas the planting, management and felling of high forest could be (and frequently was) irregular and selective, coppicing was widely recognised as a distinct management technique. Regular coppice management had several advantages in estate forestry. It brought in a sustained cash income in the short term, and it could be developed from existing semi-natural woodland. For the latter reason, and because it could be applied profitably to relatively small areas, it was within the means of 'gentlemen of but very moderate fortunes'.[29]

There are many forms of coppice management, all of which make use of the ability of trees to produce new growth from the bole, stub or stump left after felling (Plate 22). Almost all native British species (Scots pine is a notable exception) and many exotics will coppice with differing degrees of vigour. The attraction of this property to foresters is of course that trees will, with careful management, produce an indefinite series of crops of wood. Careful choice of species and cutting age produces material suitable for particular markets.[30]

The evidence available shows that in Scotland the commonest form by far was coppice-with-standards for tanbark. In such a system most of the trees were cut over regularly at or near the ground, leaving 'stools' from which the next crop grew, but a relative few were left for longer periods as 'standards' or 'maidens'. In this way the woods were made to produce some timber larger than the coppiced 'underwood' could provide. Most coppice seems to have been created by cutting over semi-natural woodland, much of which was probably scrubby and degraded after centuries of unenlightened use. Initially at least, species composition therefore reflected that of the original mixed woodland, but the bark of oak was the only one consistently required for tanning. It is not therefore surprising to find evidence that the more oak-rich woodland was selected for management, that mixed coppice was 'planted up' with oak, and even that oak woods were planted with the aim of cutting as coppice.

There is evidence of formal coppicing on monastic lands in Perthshire as early as the 1470s, and seventeenth-century contracts indicate quite a high level of management on some estates, but the widespread adoption of commercial coppicing was a later phenomenon.[31] Much remains to be done before we can make precise statements about the progress of adoption, but the peak of activity certainly came around 1800. Coppicing became a component part of the fashion for estate improvement, providing as it did a convenient way of turning untidy semi-natural woods to profitable use. At the same time coppice was remarkably valuable, a point emphasised by Robert Monteath in his *Forester's guide* (1820), which is perhaps the best contemporary text on coppice in Scotland.[32] Among contributing factors was the prolonged period of war after 1793, which boosted demand for timber and tanned leather, while the difficulties of overseas trade in wartime put additional emphasis on domestic resources. In the Glasgow district bark prices were around £5 or £6 per ton delivered in 1790 but as high as £17 in 1809, and prices up to £20 per ton were recorded.[33]

As semi-natural wood was a suitable basic stock, it is not surprising that coppicing developed most strongly on the south and west Highland margins, where semi-natural woodland with a major oak component was relatively abundant on the shores of freshwater and sea lochs, along the rivers, and on the intermediate slopes. Of 202 Edinburgh press advertisements of 1790-1814 collected by Anderson, no less than 118 related to Perthshire and Argyll and another twenty to Dunbartonshire and Stirlingshire, making 68 per cent in all. Only a few other counties accounted for five or more advertisements – East Lothian and Midlothian, Fife, Roxburghshire, Ayr, Wigtown and Kirkcudbright. The whole north Highland and north-east area produced only five.[34] We must be careful with this evidence – a survey of the Glasgow press might have produced a different pattern – but the importance of the Highland margins is emphasised continually by other forms of contemporary evidence.

An initial post-war slump was followed by a gradual decline after 1815. The attention of proprietors tended to shift to other forms of forestry and other uses of wooded land. Competition first from imported oak bark and later from other tanning agents undermined the tanbark trade, and the associated fall in prices must have done much to discourage proprietors from maintaining coppice.

By mid-century prices had fallen to 1790 levels, although on some estates at least the cost of production was much higher than it had been then. Coppice management lingered on into the 1870s, especially in the south Highland counties, but seems to have been almost extinct in Scotland by 1900.[35]

One more introductory point should be made. When coppice was ready (bark between 20 and 24 years old was usually thought best for tannin production) it was cut and stripped; the operation normally took place between the beginning of May and early or mid-July.[36] When this had been done the coppice consisted of an area of bare stumps, a sight which caused unwarranted distress among observers ignorant of the nature of coppice. The success of the next crop depended largely on the degree to which the vulnerable shoots springing from these stools were protected from grazing animals in the following few years. Even brief forays by grazing animals were known to cause damage which during the period of peak prices could be valued in hundreds of pounds. On the other hand, grazing land was vital in many coppice districts, and every acre enclosed as coppice might represent a loss of winter pasture. Proprietors were confronted by the need to balance the conflicting requirements of coppice and livestock; reactions to this fundamental problem varied greatly.[37]

Kincardine Wood

The first case study concerns Kincardine Wood in south Perthshire, between Auchterarder and the northern edge of the Ochils. It is a compact and fairly small wood (less than 200 ha) lying between 60 and 120 m O.D. (Figure 12.1). During the period of coppice management birch, ash, elm, alder, willow and hazel were recorded as well as oak; there is little doubt that the wood was natural in origin, although trees were planted at least as early as 1709.[38] Kincardine was possessed by the Grahams of Montrose from the fourteenth century, but Duncan Campbell of Glenure acquired the wood in 1771, and it changed hands again in 1798. Documentary evidence is extant for the Montrose and Glenure periods.[39]

Under the Montrose regime cuttings of the wood were sold by contract. In the earlier contracts the wood was cut in a few large annual sections or 'haggs', then left until ready for cutting again; the first recorded cutting lasted for only six years and the next for twelve. From 1705 onward, though, haggs were reduced to a size which spread cutting through the whole rotation, and thereafter years in which there was no cutting were very rare (Figure 12.1). Rotation length ranged from 24 to 27 years until 1736, after which the wood was divided into four sections sold in succession for cutting in seven or eight years, giving a total rotation length of 28 to 32 years.[40] In Scotland as a whole rotation periods between 19 and 25 years were more common.[41]

There was no basic change in the method of sale during the rest of the Montrose period. Indeed, one Andrew Carrick and later his son Robert were the only purchasers of the wood after 1736, taking a series of short tacks that ended with Robert's death 44 years later; his last contract was actually with Campbell

Figure 12.1: Kincardine Wood: Area, Cutting Regime and Income

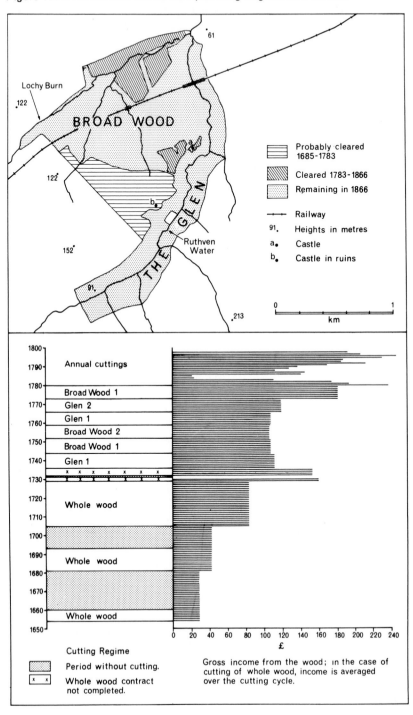

of Glenure.[42] As Figure 12.1 suggests, a new system emerged in the 1780s after a few years of uncertainty. Under their contracts the Carricks had paid fixed sums annually and were obliged to cut more or less equal haggs every year. In the 1780s, though, bark prices were beginning to rise; in such circumstances medium- or long-term contracts did not suit proprietors, and there was also an advantage in adjusting the amount cut each year according to the state of the market.

This may help to explain why the estate began to cut and sell the produce on its own account at that time, meanwhile altering the size of haggs in accordance with anticipated demand and other considerations. It is also worth noting that Robert Carrick's treatment of the wood in his final years was thought to be poor; this may have encouraged the new proprietor to bring management of the wood under his own control.[43] The new system took some time to become established. The mean gross annual income between 1780 and 1798 was only £157, whereas Carrick had been paying £180 annually, and it was not until 1792 that annual gross income began to exceed £180 regularly.[44]

Among the most important aspects of coppice management were the measures taken to prevent damage caused by grazing animals. From 1653 onward contracts made provision for enclosing the newly cut haggs. At least as early as 1682 there was a turf perimeter dyke and some stone walling, and substantial sums were spent on the building of stone walls between 1703 and 1723.[45] By mid-century there was a perimeter wall as well as strong turf dykes dividing the wood into groups of haggs; the estate maintained these and the purchaser erected temporary palings around individual haggs after cutting.[46] Enclosure for at least seven years as protection against grazing damage was the rule after 1705, and possibly earlier.[47] There was not a consensus among Scottish foresters about the age at which animals could safely be admitted, but in practice protection for more than six years seems to have been rather uncommon.

One of the main purposes of subdividing the wood within the perimeter wall was to allow safe use of as much wood pasture as possible. Apart from its intrinsic value, wood pasture was valuable in an arable district like that around Kincardine because the wood dykes, while designed to exclude animals, also served very well to contain them while the crops grew and ripened in the unenclosed countryside. All of the early contracts allowed the purchaser to use some or all of the wood pasture in haggs old enough to be thought safe from damage and, apart from one short period, this continued until the end of Carrick's tenure. Entries for grassmail in the estate accounts after 1780 indicate that the factor continued to make the wood grass available.[48]

Nevertheless the pasture of Kincardine was not proportionately very valuable. It was reckoned in the 1750s to provide less than 9 per cent of the value of the wood over the cutting cycle.[49] The proportion was presumably even smaller in 1781, when the estate factor observed that the spread of enclosure locally was reducing the special value of wood pasture and making it more difficult to find takers for the grazing.[50]

Other practices that were potentially more harmful survived into the 1730s. The early contracts allowed purchasers to cultivate within the wood, presumably where gaps existed among the stools, and after 1705 they were also allowed to cut grass for fodder 'behind the axe', i.e. in haggs cut recently enough still to be enclosed. It was realised that this was dangerous, particularly to young growth, and the contracts incorporated a number of safeguards.[51] In 1737, though, Andrew Carrick was induced to quit the pasture and tillage rights granted by his 1736 contract because of abuse of the souming arrangements.[52] The right to use pasture before the axe, i.e. in open haggs, was restored in 1740, but tillage in the wood ceased permanently and grass-cutting behind the axe made only rare appearances in later records.[53]

The most difficult aspect of management to assess is routine maintenance; little information has survived. Relevant entries in the Montrose accounts refer almost exclusively to the upkeep of the walls, and apart from sporadic references to brushwood clearance and ditching the accounts for the Glenure period are not much more helpful. The factor's letters are a little more informative. They describe a plan for the alteration of the cutting rota and reduction of the rotation to 25 years, and refer to the intention of planting up the Broad Wood with a few thousand nursery-grown seedlings as well as acorns from the wood itself.[54] It must be said that the accounts contain no reference to any outlay for this purpose.

Management at Kincardine was certainly not perfect. The overseers of the wood were not always vigilant enough to prevent theft and damage, and the walls were sometimes allowed to deteriorate until they presented little obstacle to determined 'dyke-loupers' and other animals that 'fell in to' the haggs.[55] The adjustments of the 1730s and a period of what Campbell of Glenure called 'total confusion' in the early 1780s indicate more serious crises.[56] All in all, though, management shows both remarkable continuity over a long period and an application of sound principles. The wood was cut regularly and at a reasonable age; the haggs were protected for longer than was normal, and certain unsatisfactory aspects of management were recognised and eliminated during the period.

It is obviously of interest to see how the wood fared during the period, and Figure 12.1 summarises change in area during the period as indicated by Adair's 1/126,720 map of Strath Earn (c. 1683), Stobie's 1/63,360 county map of 1783, and the first edition of the Ordnance Survey 1/10,560 map (1866).[57] The Military Survey represents the district too poorly to be of use in this context. Adair's rather stylised small-scale map is the least reliable of the three, but shows the old Kincardine Castle lying within the wood. If this was correct, the wood presumably extended farther west in the 1680s than it did later. Stobie's map shows the wood very much as it survives today, and the 1866 map indicates only a relatively few changes that had probably taken place since 1783, including some clearance around the new castle and the creation of a number of fields in the north part of the Broad Wood.

Measurements made on this basis suggest that the wood may have been as large as 180 ha in the 1680s, 160 ha in 1783 and 140 ha in 1866. This indicates a reduction by about 22 per cent over about 180 years, but two things must be said in qualification. First, only the location of the castle on Adair's map points to a greater extent in the 1680s, and none of the documentary evidence relating to the following century makes reference to reduction in area. Second, the changes that can be identified with reasonable certainty before 1866 are sharply delimited. This indicates deliberate clearance, and while the poorer parts of the wood may have been selected, there is no indication here of the gradual shrinking of the wood that might be expected if coppice management had been inadequate.

The Barcaldine Estate

The woods of Barcaldine in Argyllshire were very different. They extended irregularly down Glen Creran and Glen Ure almost to the mouth of Loch Creran (Figure 12.2). The estate lay mainly south of the Creran and was divided into two sections (Barcaldine and Glenure) by the small estate of Druimvick. Species composition was typical of south-west Highland semi-natural woodland. In 1807 the Barcaldine woods were estimated to be two-thirds birch, a quarter oak, and the rest ash with a little elm; estimates of bark and timber yield suggest that oak was even less prominent in the eastern (Glenure) section.[58] It is difficult to assess the total extent of woodland, but it is likely that there were between 400 and 600 ha of compact woodland at that time.

From the late sixteenth century until 1842 the lands were possessed by the line of Campbells that also acquired Kincardine in 1771, but division into two parts complicates interpretation of the estate's woodland history, especially as they were held by different members of the family between 1740 and 1775. The Barcaldine Muniments contain adequate documentation about forestry only for the period 1770-1830.[59]

It is hard to tell when true coppicing began. Although Clydeside merchants were buying oak timber at least as early as 1688, definite evidence of coppicing is not available before the middle of the next century.[60] Major cuttings started in 1781, 1808 and 1828, the intervals therefore being 27 and 20 years.[61] The cutting ages of individual woods on the estate varied quite a lot, but in general illustrate a similar trend of reduction in rotation length. The wood of Craig, for example, was cut in 1754 (it was then in other hands) and again in 1782; the oak wood of Craig was next cut in 1808-10 and again in 1830, the intervals being 28, 26-8 and 20-2 years.[62]

The cutting of the Barcaldine woods was always concentrated within a few years of the rotation, rather than being evenly spread as at Kincardine, and this increased the flexibility indicated by the variation in cutting interval. Proprietors were better able to seize a chance to sell if they were not tied to rigid rotational timetables. In January 1775 we find Glenure's son urging his father to clinch a bargain that year 'before the American disturbances are made up & before they

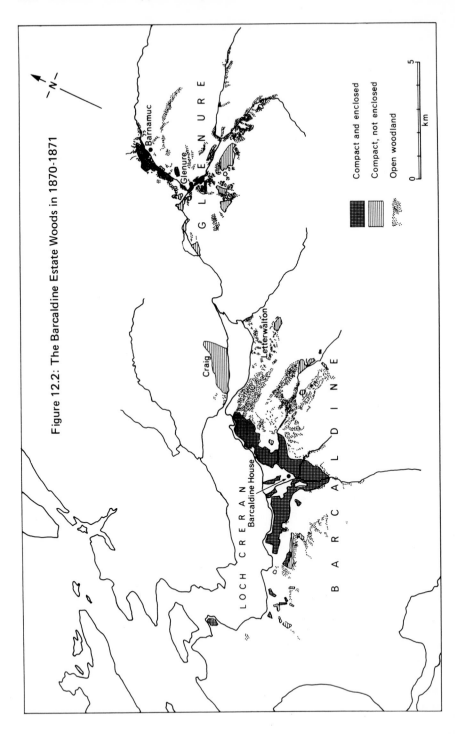

Figure 12.2: The Barcaldine Estate Woods in 1870-1871

[the potential customers] have settled with the Duke about his woods'.[63] Proprietors might of course have to be flexible, willing or not, and Glenure did not actually manage to sell the woods in question until 1780.[64] The shortening of the rotation was in line with a national trend; in some parts of Perthshire rotations as short as sixteen years were recorded in the mid-nineteenth century.[65]

Barcaldine also differed from Kincardine in having one major customer with specialised requirements. Lorn Furnace at Taynuilt on Loch Etive had a major impact on the woodland economy of the district after 1752, and was certainly the main purchaser of the coppices of Barcaldine between 1780 and 1815.[66] The wood was bought on contracts like those of Kincardine during the Montrose period, but after 1815 the estate began to cut and sell the produce directly, and it is not clear whether the furnace continued to be a major customer.[67]

The contracts gave the furnace company both timber for smelting charcoal (coalwood) and oak bark, which the company shipped mainly to the Clyde.[68] A system developed which accentuated the selective emphasis on oak inherent in tanbark coppicing. Woods in which oak was dominant were cut, stripped and coaled in early summer as was usual, and to ensure a consistent supply of charcoal for the furnace the remaining 'black wood' with little or no oak (also called 'barren timber' or 'winter wood') was cut and coaled in the winter half of the year. An obvious consequence was that oak and black wood came to be treated differently and sold separately, a marked feature of management on the Barcaldine estate after 1800 in particular.[69]

Whereas Kincardine Wood was recorded in estate rentals as a distinct holding unit, the Barcaldine woods (the policies excepted) were scattered through the agricultural area. Most were indeed parts of the limited stock of low-lying wintering ground, and long-term enclosure could not be achieved without granting tenants substantial rent rebates (abatement) or reducing the number of holdings. Both actions entailed losses of revenue which it could not be certain would be offset by improvement in the value of the protected coppice.

It is not therefore surprising to find that enclosure was fairly limited on the Barcaldine estate. By the 1780s at least temporary fences were being put up around the newly cut haggs (there is no evidence as to the period of protection), but they were designed in a way that favoured oak in particular.[70] Thus the fence put up at Craig after the wood was cut in 1782 enclosed about 90 per cent of the oak and ash (by estimated value), but only 75 per cent of the black wood.[71] When the estate finally committed itself to stone walls on a large scale soon after 1800, the same principle was followed. As a valuator called in from Perthshire said in 1801, 'As to Birch, Aller, Hasle, &c, they are not worth the grass lost for their preservation & the expence of inclosing.'[72] Even the smaller oak woods were excluded when the stone walls were laid out.[73]

During the majority of Sir Duncan Campbell after 1807, attention to coppice and particularly black wood seems to have diminished. Sir Duncan retained a coppice regime until the estate was sold, but his interest was primarily in plantation and the improvement of the policies.[74] In addition, he brought about changes in land use which are likely to have been detrimental to coppice. The estate had carried stocks of sheep since the 1760s, but in the early nineteenth century the number of animals on the Barcaldine and Glenure lands rose considerably, reaching 5,000 and more in the 1830s.[75] Ornamental deer were introduced, and in 1814 it was found that deer had caused damage to oak coppice which it was estimated would reduce its value by several hundred pounds unless prompt remedial action was taken.[76]

Barcaldine therefore presents a picture of a much less regular and careful coppice regime than was found at Kincardine. It is also apparent that after 1800 management became more selective and the relative importance of coppice declined, while the danger of certain types of grazing damage intensified. Did the relatively low standard of management have detectable effects on the extent of woodland?

This question is not easily answered. Map coverage of the district is very poor and the estate records provide no information about the area of woodland at different dates. On the other hand, they do include estimates of bark and charcoal yield that can be used to assess changes in productivity. The pattern is rather complex and has been discussed in detail elsewhere, but it can be summarised here.[77] Most of the bark was produced by the Barcaldine section of the estate, and estimates of the bark yield of that section show a substantial fall between 1777 and 1807. Because hagg boundaries shifted frequently, it is possible to trace only a few of the individual woods in the Barcaldine and Glenure sections through the two rotations after 1777, but where this is possible there is evidence of sustained or increased production, in contrast to the overall decline in the Barcaldine figure. Management is known to have changed in ways which may account for part of this apparent decline. Thus a large number of standards were cut in the 1781-9 felling and they do not seem to have been fully replaced in later rotations; there is also some evidence of coppiced woodland around the policies being converted to high forest after 1800 and thus removed from the productive coppice stock.[78] If we add to these structural factors the evidence that productivity was sustained in identifiable woods, it is appropriate to be cautious about attributing the overall decline to the kind of deterioration that might be expected to accompany poor management.

There was also a decline in the yield of charcoal and timber, and part of this was undoubtedly associated with the reduction in the quantity of oak cut as coppice, however caused, which lowered bark yield. Charcoal and timber were also obtained from black wood, however, and we have already seen that black wood tended to be deprived of adequate management. When the Ordnance Survey produced the first 1/10,560 maps of the district in 1870-1 there was a sharp contrast between the compact enclosed woods and the scatterings of trees outside (Figure 12.2). It is evident that in some cases decline had taken place during the preceding hundred years. Thus the woods of Letterwalton, which were reckoned in 1777 to contain between 300 and 350 dozens of charcoal consisting of black wood, survived in 1870-1 only as a thin scattering of trees. In contrast, the woods of Barnamuc and Glenure were a little larger in 1771 (between 350 and 420 dozens of charcoal and a little oak bark), but in 1870-1 there remained not only scattered trees but a few enclosures and a number of compact clumps.[79]

On one hand, we have indications that oak yields were sustained or augmented under coppice management; on the other, we have the evidence that black wood was reduced in area during a period in which it was cut as coppice. The kind of management employed at Barcaldine was largely a matter of conservation, protecting existing stocks against grazing damage, casual cutting, muirburn and other hazards. Black wood was cut as coppice, but management of it seems to have been rudimentary in general and enclosure in particular was limited or non-existent. Coppice treatment seems at best to have provided a respite from the steady attrition associated with grazing pressure and the other harmful factors; at worst it left stools in a condition that was especially vulnerable to these hazards, and it may thus have contributed to an acceleration of an existing process of gradual decline.

It might therefore be suggested that coppice management, as distinct from simple coppice-cutting, provided adequate protection while it was maintained, even in the imperfect form employed in the Barcaldine oak woods. Where management was not employed, or where it was abandoned by ceasing to protect newly cut coppice stools from damage, these stools were endangered. By the 1820s, according to Monteath, such abandonment had been encouraged throughout Argyllshire by the spread of sheep husbandry.[80] At Barcaldine some of the oak at least continued to be coppiced in the 1840s, but when the estate came up for sale again in 1886 coppice management was so much a thing of the past that the sale plans commended the woods only for their aesthetic appeal and their value as shelter for deer.[81]

Conclusion

In both cases coppice made a modest but not negligible contribution to the local economy. It can be calculated, for example, that in the thirty years up to 1799 both Kincardine and the larger but less well stocked woods of Barcaldine produced gross incomes between £4,000 and £5,000, and prices of coppice produce did not reach their peak until after 1800.[82] On the other hand, the two examples show substantial differences in the forms taken by tanbark coppice management, although both were for some time under the same control. Neither should be labelled as typical, but the Barcaldine woods were probably more representative in being scattered among agricultural holdings, managed well for only a relatively short time, and divided into 'oak' and 'black wood' which were differently treated.

Neither case provides conclusive evidence that this form of commercial forestry had a significant cost in terms of destruction of woodland. Obviously more work remains to be done, but these examples indicate that coppice management, even at a fairly low standard, was not associated with rapid destruction of the woods involved. If coppicing was carried on without elementary measures to protect the growing stock, though, it does seem to have left wood vulnerable to damage by grazing and other agencies.

There is a need for further use of primary sources to investigate the form and significance of coppicing. Both examples fall within the major belt of coppicing activity that ran along the southern and south-western margins of the Highlands. Examples that throw light on the situation in central and southern Scotland or the northern and eastern Highlands would be most valuable, and this study indicates that attention should be given particularly to the difference between management and exploitation of woodland as coppice.

Coppicing was clearly only one of several forms of forestry employed during the period. Throughout the Highlands were relict pinewoods of different sizes, almost all of which were utilised to some degree in the eighteenth and nineteenth centuries. Throughout the whole of Scotland the same period saw a great wave of planting for both decorative and utilitarian motives. The development and spread of plantation is a topic that has so far remained almost untouched by serious research; only when much more is known of this process will we be anywhere near a real understanding of the role of forestry in the development of the Scottish countryside.

Notes

1. See, for example, Darling, F. F. and Boyd, J. M. (1964), *The Highlands and islands* (London), pp. 54-9

2. Gray, M. (1957), *The Highland economy, 1750-1850* (Edinburgh); Youngson, A. J. (1973), *After the forty-five: the economic impact on the Scottish Highlands* (Edinburgh)

3. A. G. Tansley's term 'semi-natural' will be used throughout to describe woodland which is basically self-sown but has been subject to the impact of human communities, their land use, and their livestock for long enough to have become substantially different from its primary state

4. See Mackintosh, W. (1729), *An essay on ways and means for inclosing, fallowing, planting &c Scotland . . .* (Edinburgh), pp. 23-4

5. Johnson, S. (1775), *A journey to the western islands of Scotland* (Dublin), p. 13. For the most notable show of displeasure see McNicol, D. (1779), *Remarks on Dr Samuel Johnson's journey to the Hebrides* (London)

6. Thomson, T. and Innes, C. (eds.) (1814-75), *The acts of the parliament of Scotland* (Edinburgh), Vol. 4, p. 408

7. Spreull, J. (1705), *An accompt current betwixt Scotland and England balanced* (Edinburgh), pp. 1-4; Defoe, D. (1724-7), *A tour through the whole island of Great Britain* (London), Vol. 3, pp. 208-9

8. See the texts preserved in Mitchell, A. (ed.) (1907), *Geographical collections relating to Scotland made by Walter Macfarlane* (Publications of the Scottish History Society), *52*. See also Brown, P. H. (ed.) (1892), *Tours in Scotland, 1677 and 1681, by Thomas Kirk and Ralph Thoresby* (Edinburgh), pp. 29, 35

9. The percentages are based on measurements of sections of the survey representing

about 600 km^2 each; obviously certain parts of the Highlands had higher proportions on a localised scale. See Locke, G. M. L. (1970), *Census of woodlands 1965-67* (London), pp. 31-2

10. For a brief critique see Fairhurst, H. (1939), 'The natural vegetation of Scotland; its character and development', *Scottish Geographical Magazine* (hereafter *SGM*), *55*, 208-9

11. Aiton, W. (1811), *A treatise on the origin, qualities, and cultivation of moss-earth* (Ayr), pp. 55-9, 71-8

12. MacAdam W. I. (1886-7), 'Notes on the ancient iron industry of Scotland', *Proceedings of the Society of Antiquaries of Scotland, 21*, 89-131; Kemp, D. W. (1887), 'An unwritten chapter in the early history of the iron industry in Scotland; smelting in Sutherland and the north of Scotland', *Transactions of the Royal Scottish Society of Arts, 11*, 286-303

13. Cadell, H. M. (1913), *The story of the Forth* (Glasgow); Ritchie, J. (1921), *The influence of man on animal life in Scotland* (Cambridge)

14. See particularly Darling, F. F. (1949), 'History of the Scottish forests', *SGM, 65*, 132-7; Darling and Boyd (1964), *The Highlands and islands*, pp. 54-9

15. Cadell (1913), *Story of the Forth*, p. 150

16. Darling (1949), 'History of the Scottish forests', 133

17. Ibid., 134

18. The order has been reproduced several times. It is found for example in Anderson, M. L. (1967), *A history of Scottish forestry* (Edinburgh), Vol. 1, p. 348; for a review of the evidence see Lindsay, J. M. (1974), 'The use of woodland in Argyllshire and Perthshire between 1650 and 1850' (unpublished PhD thesis, University of Edinburgh), pp. 490-1

19. Nairne, D. (1890-1), 'Notes on Highland woods, ancient and modern', *Transactions of the Gaelic Society of Inverness, 17*, 193

20. Lindsay, J. M. (1977a), 'The iron industry in the Highlands; charcoal blast furnaces', *Scottish Historical Review, 56*, 49-63

21. Lindsay, J. M. (1976), 'The commercial use of Highland woodland, 1750-1870: a reconsideration', *SGM, 92*, 30-40

22. Steven, H. M. and Carlisle, A. (1959), *The native pinewoods of Scotland* (Edinburgh); McVean, D. N. (1963), 'Ecology of Scots pine in the Scottish Highlands', *Journal of Ecology, 51*, 671-86; Malcolm, D. C. (1957), 'Site degradation in stands of natural pine in Scotland', *Bulletin of the Forestry Department, University of Edinburgh, 4*; Hayes, A. J. (1967), 'Observations on the palaeo-oecology of the Black Wood of Rannoch', *Scottish Forestry* (hereafter *Scot. For.*), *21*, 153-62

23. Tittensor, R. M. (1970), 'History of the Loch Lomond oakwoods', *Scot. For., 24*, 100-18

24. Anderson (1967), *History of Scottish forestry*

25. Edlin, H. L. (1955), 'Coppice-with-standards and the oak tanning bark trade in the Scottish Highlands', *Scot. For., 9*, 145-8; Lindsay (1974), 'Woodland in Argyllshire'; Lindsay, J. M. (1975a), 'The history of oak coppice in Scotland', *Scot. For., 29*, 87-93; Lindsay, J. M. (1975b), 'Some aspects of the timber supply in the Highlands, 1700-1850', *Scottish Studies, 19*, 39-53; Lindsay, J. M. (1975c), 'Charcoal iron smelting and its fuel supply; the example of Lorn furnace, Argyllshire, 1753-1876', *Journal of Historical Geography, 1*, 283-98; Lindsay (1976), 'Highland woodland'; Lindsay, J. M. (1977b), 'Forestry and agriculture in the Scottish Highlands, 1700-1850; a problem in estate management', *Agricultural History Review, 25*, 23-36

26. Dixon, G. A. (1976), 'Forestry in Strathspey in the 1760s', *Scot. For., 30*, 38-60

27. See, for example, MacCulloch, J. (1823), *A description of the scenery of Dunkeld and of Blair in Atholl* (London), pp. 14-60

28. Anderson, M. L. (ed.) (1959), 'A dissertation on the culture of forest trees by James Justice', *Bulletin of the Forestry Department, University of Edinburgh, 6*; Brown, J. (1847), *The forester* (London)

29. Anderson (1959) 'Dissertation', 25

30. Rackham, O. (1976), *Trees and woodland in the British landscape* (London), pp. 66-102 has a good introduction to British coppicing, but little to say specifically

about Scotland.

31. Lindsay (1975a), 'History of oak coppice', 87-8

32. Monteath, R. (1824), *The forester's guide and profitable planter* 2nd edn (Edinburgh), pp. 27-8

33. Lindsay (1974), 'Woodland in Argyllshire', p. 404

34. Anderson (1967), *History of Scottish forestry*, Vol. 2, pp. 85-93

35. Lindsay (1974), 'Woodland in Argyllshire', p. 88

36. Ibid., pp. 447-8

37. Lindsay (1977b), 'Forestry and agriculture', discusses this problem more fully

38. The management of Kincardine Wood is described in more detail in Lindsay (1974), 'Woodland in Argyllshire', pp. 465-536. The Montrose Muniments in the Scottish Record Office (hereafter SRO) provide the first evidence of planting; see GD 220/6(47), ff. 43-4, Kincardine and Braco account, 1709.

39. The Montrose Muniments (SRO, GD 220) are still partly sorted. A box labelled 'wood contracts' (hereafter WC) houses many items without individual reference numbers; SRO, Barcaldine Muniments (GD 170)

40. SRO, GD 220 WC, Memorandum for those who are to visit the wood of Kincardine 1736

41. Lindsay (1974), 'Woodland in Argyllshire', pp. 353-5

42. SRO, GD 220 WC, contracts, Montrose commissioners and Andrew Carrick 1736, 1743; GD 220/6(50), Kincardine and Braco account 1759; GD 170/431(18) scroll tack, Campbell of Glenure and Robert Carrick 1772

43. SRO, GD 170/1825 (1, 2, 5) factor's letters to Alexander Campbell yr of Barcaldine, 1780-1

44. Derived from accounts in GD 170/407(2), Kincardine Wood documents 1780-3, and GD 170/475, Kincardine Wood documents 1780-98

45. SRO, GD 220 WC, contract, Montrose and Stirling 1653, tack of forestership 1682, GD 220/6(46), Kincardine and Braco accounts 1703-8, GD 220/6(47), Kincardine and Braco accounts 1709-23

46. Lindsay (1974), 'Woodland in Argyllshire', pp. 479-80

47. SRO, GD 220 WC, contract, Montrose and Sheddan 1704, contract, Montrose commrs and Andrew Carrick 1736; GD 170/431(18), scroll tack, Campbell of Glenure and Robert Carrick 1772, GD 170/1825(5), factor's letter to Alexander Campbell yr of Barcaldine 1781

48. SRO, GD 170/407(2), statements of account 1780-3, GD 170/475 accounts 1784-96

49. SRO, GD 220/6(70), 231 estimate of value of the woods c. 1752

50. SRO, GD 170/1825(5), factor's letter to Alexander Campbell yr of Barcaldine 1781

51. SRO, GD 220 WC, contract, Montrose and Stirling 1653, Montrose and Stewart 1680, Montrose and Sheddan 1704, articles of roup 1729, contract, commrs and Fentons 1732, commrs and Andrew Carrick 1736

52. SRO, GD 220 WC agreement, Montrose and Carrick 1737

53. SRO, GD 220 WC contract, commrs and Carrick 1743, GD 220/6(49) Kincardine accounts for 1741-2

54. SRO, GD 170/1825(12, 13) factor's letters to Alexander Campbell yr of Barcaldine 1783

55. SRO, GD 220 WC, report on dykes of Kincardine 1749, GD 170/1825(2) factor's letter to Alexander Campbell yr of Barcaldine 1780

56. SRO, GD 170/1643(32), Duncan Campbell of Glenure to Alexander Campbell yr of Barcaldine 1783

57. Adair, J. (c. 1683), *The mappe of Straithern, Stormont & Cars of Gaurie . . .*, National Library of Scotland (hereafter NLS) Map Room, Case 8A.2.2; Stobie, J. (1783), *The counties of Perth and Clackmannan* (London); Ordnance Survey, 1/10560 first edition, Perthshire, sheet 118

58. SRO, GD 170/438, estimate of Glenure's woods by Duncan McIntyre 1777, GD 170/587(1), estimate by James Campbell 1807

59. SRO, Barcaldine Muniments (GD 170)

60. SRO, GD 170/231, agreement about wood of Condolich 1688

61. SRO, GD 170/438, contract, Glenure and Lorn Furnace Company 1780, GD 170/587(3), memorandum concerning woods on Barcaldine estate, n.d.

62. SRO, GD 170/438, contract, Duncan McLaughland and Nathaniel Taylor 1754; GD 170/1256(2), George Knott to Campbell of Glenure 1781; GD 170/587(1), contract, Barcaldine and Lorn Furnace Company 1808; GD 170/2241(1), Thomas Benson to Duncan Campbell 1830

63. SRO, GD 170/1062(52), Alexander Campbell to Duncan Campbell of Glenure 1775

64. SRO, GD 170/438 contract, Glenure and Lorn Furnace Company 1780

65. Lindsay (1974), 'Woodland in Argyllshire', pp. 370-1

66. Lindsay (1975c) 'Charcoal iron smelting', 289-93

67. The change of approach can be seen by comparing the contents of SRO, GD 170/587(1), forestry papers 1800-19, and GD 170/587(2), forestry papers 1820-87

68. Lindsay (1975c), 'Charcoal iron smelting', 290

69. See, for example, the case of Craig wood. SRO, GD 170/587(1), articles of roup, barren wood of Craig 1803, contract, Barcaldine and Lorn Furnace Company 1808

70. SRO, GD 170/438, contract, Glenure and Lorn Furnace Company 1780

71. SRO, GD 170/587(1), estimate of Barcaldine woods, James Campbell and J. Sinclair 1802

72. SRO, GD 170/587(1), letter, James Inches to J. Campbell 1801

73. See SRO, GD 170/587(1), J. Sinclair's offer to enclose the oak clumps of Acha with brushwood paling 1814

74. Fraser, A. C. (1936), *The book of Barcaldine* (London), p. 112; SRO GD 170/2412, letters from Dickson & Turnbull, Perth 1820-33

75. Compare SRO, GD 170/411(2), inventory of Glenure's small cattle, December 1764, and GD 170/553(2), list of Barcaldine's sheep, July 1822

76. SRO, GD 170/587(1), report on condition of Barcaldine's woods by J. Campbell 1814

77. Lindsay, J. M. (1977c), *Land use history and tenure of Glasdrum National Nature Reserve*, Nature Conservancy Council, South-west Region (Scotland) (Balloch), pp. 18-21

78. Ibid., p. 20

79. Ibid., pp. 20-1

80. Monteath, R. (1827), *Miscellaneous reports on woods and plantations* (Dundee), p. 53

81. SRO, RHP 3308, RHP 3314, sale plans 1886

82. For Kincardine there are Carrick's contracts of 1766 and 1772; see SRO, GD 220/6(50), Kincardine account for 1766, and GD 170/431(18) scroll tack, Campbell of Glenure and Robert Carrick 1772, as well as the accounts contained in GD 170/407(2) and GD 170/475. For Barcaldine there is the material in SRO, GD 170/438, including the contract of 1780 and detail of a number of small sales of semi-natural and planted timber.

13 THE NEW RURAL INDUSTRIES: WATER POWER AND TEXTILES

J. P. Shaw

During the period 1730-1830 revolutionary changes in agriculture left Scotland with a smaller farming population: this, with an outward-looking landed class, greater social mobility and an all-pervasive 'spirit of industry' created conditions favourable to the establishment of rural industries.

While few of these industries were, strictly speaking, new to Scotland, the diffusion which they achieved and the scale of investment which they attracted were quite unprecedented. For the most part these industries exploited the country's mineral or organic resources. Coal- and lead-mining had been carried on since the thirteenth and sixteenth centuries respectively, and were already moving on to a large-scale commercial footing by the mid-seventeenth century. Between 1730 and 1830, both industries grew substantially in scale of production and extent of exploitation, leaving their mark on the coalfields of central Scotland and on isolated pockets of lead-bearing land from Strontian in Argyll to Blackcraig in Kirkcudbrightshire. Quarrying, an industry of indeterminate age, expanded to meet the demands of new enclosures, farms, villages and industrial buildings, and of a general move from organic to inorganic building materials. In south-east Scotland there had been a lime-burning industry since at least the sixteenth century, but only after 1730 did improvements in building technique and the widespread use of lime as a fertiliser lead to the construction of lime kilns wherever limestone and fuel could be obtained.

Of the industries based on organic raw materials, grain-milling was probably the oldest, and while the decay of thirlage, among other changes, reduced the number of grain mills from about 5,000 in 1730 to about 3,000 in 1830, those of the latter date were generally better equipped and of greater capacity than those of 1730. For an improving landowner a good 'set' of mills for meal, barley and flour was an essential addition to his estate. Prior to 1730, brewing had been little more than a domestic pursuit, except in the burghs, but thereafter commercial breweries, utilising locally grown barley, were set up in planned villages such as Ormiston (East Lothian), Cromarty (Ross and Cromarty) and Gatehouse of Fleet (Kirkcudbrightshire). During the 1820s distilling, which had already established itself in the Lowlands, developed into an important rural industry in the Highlands, particularly in the Grampians. Fisheries received assistance from landowners in the north-east and from the state in the northern and western Highlands, while saw-milling, established at a few Highland localities in the seventeenth century, increased in scale not only in the Highlands but also on those Lowland estates where plantations had matured by 1830. A by-product of the timber trade, bark, was used by tanneries set up to exploit Scotland's cattle production.

For all their new-found prosperity, none of these industries compared with textile manufacturing. Scottish wool and woollen cloth had dominated her exports for several centuries, and despite the failure of seventeenth-century ventures into fine woollen manufacture, the traditional coarse cloth industry was still active. The linen industry, though small compared to wool, had a firm basis and vied with its bigger rival for the favours of the Scots Parliament in the years immediately before Union. During the period 1730-1830 an enormous increase in employment, investment and output enabled wool, linen and, later, cotton to maintain and, indeed, increase the textile industry's lead over other sectors of the economy. The success of the textile industry was due, in part, to the application of water-power, and while almost every rural industry used it to some extent, more water-mills were employed in textile manufacture than in any other activity, grain-milling and threshing excepted. In view of the contribution made by textiles to the economy, and of water-power to the textile industry, an analysis of textile mill development offers the most useful line of inquiry into the role of industry in the new rural order.

Sources

Of the available contemporary publications, the most useful are the *Statistical Accounts*, which give detailed national coverage for the 1790s and the 1830s or 1840s.[1] For an earlier period Loch's *Tour* (1778) furnishes useful information on the woollen industry, whilst the county *Agricultural Reports* help bridge the gap between *Statistical Accounts*.[2] Parliamentary papers provide information on spinning mills, while gazetteers, directories and travelogues contain useful supporting material. Finally, there are numerous published maps, notably town plans, county maps and the Ordnance Survey series (1846 *et seq*.).

Of the unpublished sources, the most important group is the Records of the Board of Trustees, particularly their minute books and their lint mill survey of 1772.[3] A second group, Gifts and Deposits, contains much relevant information, scattered among some 300 collections;[4] the records of the Forfeited Estates Commission and sequestration papers also merit consultation.[5] All four groups are located at the Scottish Record Office.

Legal papers, housed at the Signet Library, Edinburgh, often provide histories of individual mills; an index of cases is kept at the Scottish Record Office. Lastly, two important manuscript collections, 'Accessions' and 'Manuscripts', are to be found at the National Library of Scotland.[6]

Secondary Sources

While the existing literature is rather sparse, some useful ground work has been carried out by economic historians, industrial archaeologists and local historians. Among economic historians, Gulvin has written on the woollen industry,[7] and McClain, Durie and Gauldie on various aspects of the linen industry.[8] Others, notably Butt, Donnachie and Hume, have been active both as economic historians and industrial archaeologists.[9] Local histories vary much in emphasis; of the vast number published, the most important are Hall's on Galashiels, Buchan's on Peebles-shire, Gibson's on Clackmannanshire, Cameron's on Campsie, Morgan's on Newhills and Macdonald's on Blairgowrie.[10] Anders Jespersen's early study of the River Eden[11] defies classification but comes closest to industrial archaeology. One rare example of an industrial history is Warden's *Linen Trade*,[12] which despite its age remains the most comprehensive work on the industry. Among historical geographers only Turner, in his work on east central Scotland, has considered the textile industry.[13]

From the foregoing summary it is obvious that there is no shortage of relevant information. However, its scattered occurrence, the restricted spatial, thematic or academic interests of authors and the sheer scale of the subject make for great difficulties in obtaining a comprehensive view. This chapter seeks a balanced view by first examining the development of all types of textile mills over the whole of Scotland, in terms of the roles played by landowners, merchant manufacturers and tenants. It then proceeds to consider distribution, chronology and finally impact on the landscape and economy of Scotland.

Technical Progress, 1730-1830

By 1730 Scotland had a well established textile industry based on coarse woollen and linen cloth. In terms of its technology, however, the industry was still a primitive one in which only one process, fulling, utilised water-power.[14] In contrast, the century after 1730 saw the mechanisation of almost every process in textile manufacture, and the introduction of a new raw material, cotton.

Only a limited range of power sources was available during the period: animal power was restricted in scale and necessitated the upkeep of cattle or horses; wind power was expensive to install and could only be used intermittently. Neither was used to any great extent. The steam-engine, so often associated with the textile industry, was not adapted for rotary motion until 1781 and was so unreliable as to be still a rarity in the 1800s.[15] Even in the early nineteenth century, when steam-power helped create an urban textile industry, water-power remained the cheaper alternative and continued to be applied in new rural mills. In the majority of cases, therefore, and right up to the 1830s, water-power dominated the Scottish textile industry, giving it a strongly rural bias. This rural bias in turn influenced the type of developers involved in mill-building.

The Role of the Landowner

During the century 1730-1830 Scottish agriculture underwent radical changes: runrig disappeared, land was enclosed and commercial farmers replaced smaller tenants and cottars. On the worst estates the choice for those displaced was between migration and starvation. Elsewhere, however, the landowner, moved by a spirit of paternalism or more probably by a wish to maximise his rental, sought to create alternative employment, even to the extent of increasing his estate's population beyond that of pre-enclosure times.

In creating employment, the landowner had four principal options. Some former tenants and cottars could be re-absorbed into agriculture as farm servants or in cultivating wastes; others could be employed in food-processing activities such as brewing and distilling. In certain areas the landowner could try to re-employ them in fisheries, but the greatest potential lay in the fourth option, textiles, which could create domestic employment in spinning and weaving or in mill-based employment in a variety of processes.

Incentives to Investment

In establishing or accepting textile mills on his estate a landowner stood to gain in several ways. The tenant or owner of a mill paid rent or feu duty and additional rent could be derived from workers' housing. A mill provided direct employment, for three or four people in the case of a lint or waulk mill and for several hundred in a large bleachfield, printfield or spinning mill. It also generated other employment: carding or waulk mills, by performing the most arduous processes, stimulated wool-spinning and weaving. Rent from these workers' houses, and from those of associated tradesmen, further enhanced the estate's value.

The agricultural sector also benefited by supplying flax or wool to lint or carding mills and food to workers. Enhanced local markets for agricultural produce brought increased farm rents. A manufacturing population also provided work for estate grain mills, many of them newly renovated. Furthermore, tenants who were no longer bound by thirlage to use the estate mill might have disposed of their grain unmilled; the local market for meal, which the presence of textile workers created, prevented this from happening and augmented mill rents.

Disincentives to Investment

As the scale of textile mills increased, so also did the range of processes performed by them, and with control passing increasingly to merchants and manufacturers, the benefits to the landowner were correspondingly reduced. High mill wages drew labour from a still only partly mechanised agriculture, while from pastoral estates, with few job opportunities, people left in great numbers for the spinning mills of the central Lowlands.

Although spinning mills created extra work for weavers, they gradually destroyed the hand-spinning industry. In Collace parish, Perthshire, yarn from Dundee mills kept 100 looms at work in the 1830s, but many of these were operated by women, forced out of their previous occupation in spinning.[16] When, in turn, power-loom weaving was adopted, a great number of weavers, many of them working on mill-spun yarn, were reduced to poverty.

The benefits to agriculture also declined. Home-grown flax had never satisfied the market and once mill-spinning developed, manufacturers tended to import all their flax, thus contributing to the decline of flax-growing in Scotland. In the west the substitution of cotton extinguished it almost completely.

Level of Involvement

Besides actually building a textile mill, the landowner could participate in the development of one at various other levels. Where a large capital outlay was required, a landowner possessing land, water-power and a potential labour force might go into partnership with other parties. In 1792 Peter Speirs, owner of Culcreuch estate, Stirlingshire, entered into partnership with another landowner and five Glasgow merchants to establish a cotton mill on the estate. Enclosure, among other things, had caused a drop in population, but by building the mill and a new village for the work-force, he succeeded in reversing the trend.[17] Similarly, Lord Milton was a partner with other landowners and manufacturers in the Haddington Tarred Wool Company, and in Saltoun bleachfield with the British Linen Company.[18] Where mercantile and manufacturing capital could not be found, the 'other parties' with whom the landowner might join could be his fellow landowners, as in the firm of John Mitchell & Co., owners of Catfirth bleachfield, Shetland.[19] The role of a landowner as partner can be difficult to define, as successful merchant families often became landowners. William McDougall, a partner in a Renfrewshire cotton mill, was one such, while Peter Speirs, referred to above, was the second son of Alexander Speirs, 'the mercantile god of Glasgow'.[20]

At a lower level of involvement, a landowner could provide capital or credit for a project undertaken by others. In Strathspey the Duke of Gordon was said to afford 'various conveniences to the Kingussie company', owners of a wool-carding mill.[21] At Midcalder, Midlothian, financial aid was offered to anyone wishing to convert a grain mill for spinning.[22] Even without investing capital a landowner could attract textile mills to his estate by advertising sites or simply accepting offers for their use. Lord Gardenstone is often credited with laying out the bleachfields at Laurencekirk, but in reality he did no more than provide a site.[23] During the cotton mania of the early 1790s many unlikely sites were advertised as suitable locations for cotton mills.

Finally, a landowner might totally prohibit mill development because of the possible detriment, aesthetic or economic, to his estate. In the Hawick area several falls which were suitable for woollen mills were withheld from use 'owing to a whim of the late Duke of Buccleuch'.[24] In the parish of Mains and Strath-martine it was said in the *New Statistical Account* that 'the bleaching business is now in such a flourishing state that new works would be erected if they were not opposed by the neighbouring proprietors as a public nuisance.'[25]

Generally speaking, the later the period and the larger the proposed development, the greater was the chance of a new mill being refused. For the landowner of the 1750s, with few other sources of income, it was expedient to encourage, for example, a tenant farmer to build a lint mill and thereby enhance the value of the estate; however, his early-nineteenth-century counterpart, already wearied of industry and with wider financial interests, tended to look less favourably on, for example, a proposal by merchant manufacturers to feu land for a large spinning mill over which he had no control.

Types of Mill Built by Landowners

For the most part, landowners provided finance for those types of mill which required only a small capital outlay and which fitted into a broader policy of estate improvement. Most were eligible for grants from the Board of Trustees.[26] From an early stage landowners became involved in building lint mills. Some, such as Hope of Rankeilour and Lord Belhaven, were connected with the Board of Trustees, but the majority were enlightened landowners interested in improving their estates. Besides well known improvers such as Grant of Monymusk and Sinclair of Ulbster, many lesser-known figures, such as Brisbane of Brisbane and Campbell of Duntroon, also built mills.[27] The landowner's interest in lint mills reached a peak in the 1780s; thereafter initiative passed to tenants and artisans.

Investment in the woollen industry was also forthcoming. The capital required to build, or renovate, a waulk mill was moderately small and skills and technology well established. Loch, touring Scotland in the late 1770s, saw waulk mills built by Lord Lauderdale at Lauder, Lord Hopetoun at Moffat and the Duke of Buccleuch at Dalkeith.[28] At Ednam, Roxburghshire, James Dickson built a 'neat village', established a woollen manufactory with its own waulk mill, and imported skilled workers from Yorkshire.[29] At Inveraray the Duke of Argyll, using overseers from west central Scotland, tried to achieve similar results, but with less success.[30]

When it came to heavier investment and greater risks the landowner was less active. At a time when most had little capital to spare, a bleachfield, costing anything from a few hundred to a few thousand pounds, was generally too large to take on. However, there were exceptions. In Fife, Adam of Blairadam, having founded the village of Maryburgh, 'endeavoured to advance the system of population and the happy beneficial effects of industry. . . He erected all the mills, machinery and different vats for the manufacture of bleaching, and a lint mill.'[31] In 1781, on a visit to Grantown on Spey, Wight noted that Grant of Grant had 'erected a house and machinery for a bleachfield'.[32] Lord Findlater spent £628 on a bleachfield at Cullen and Sir William Forbes laid out £1,000 on one at New Pitsligo.[33] Neither field enjoyed much success. Although landowners showed considerable interest in bleachfields during the 1780s, this all but disappeared in the 1790s.

By the 1790s landowners had also lost interest in other types of mill. Wool-carding mills, introduced *c.* 1785, were almost invariably the work of manu-facturers or small artisans, while involvement in spinning mills usually went no further than joining a partnership. Even Archibald Speirs, who built a cotton mill on his Renfrewshire estate, was the son of a Glasgow merchant.[34]

A few exceptions occurred in connection with wool-spinning mills. In 1796 Urquhart of Braelanguell built a spinning mill beside the Cromarty Firth 'with a view. . .to provide employment for and to ameliorate the condition of the people, many of whom are yearly emigrating'.[35] Major Dirom built a woollen mill at his village of Brydekirk, Dunfriesshire,[36] while at Innerleithen, Peebles-shire, a Mr Brodie built a four-story mill with a separate waulk mill. Brodie was hardly typical of Scottish landowners, having started as a local blacksmith and having made his fortune in London before buying land in his native county. The mill at Innerleithen was built more out of philanthropy than for sound economic reasons and within a few years it was in financial difficulties, a state typical of landowner-built spinning mills.[37]

The Role of Merchants and Manufacturers

Despite the activity of Scottish merchants and manufacturers in the late seven-teenth century, the Scottish economy languished during the early post-Union years. When, after 1730, it did finally pick up again, textiles played a leading role.

Merchants and manufacturers had good reason to invest in the textile industry. The manufacture of coarse cloth was already well established and Scottish merchants were trading in whatever cloth came on to the market. The quality controls and incentives to production instigated by the Board of Trustees improved the quality and marketability of Scottish cloth, while British colonies offered a ready market.[38]

Types of Mill Built by Merchants and Manufacturers

Prior to 1780, mercantile capital in textile manufacture was largely directed towards fulling and bleaching, the respective finishing processes in woollen and linen textiles. Small-scale bleaching by private individuals produced poor results, but a merchant or manufacturer having a bleachfield equipped with water-powered wash mills, beetles and rubbing boards could give the cloth a good finish and thereby enhance its value. A merchant, by buying cloth at one stage earlier in its manufacture (i.e. prior to bleaching) could obtain a better hold over cloth coming on to the market; conversely, a manufacturer already employ-ing weavers could also buy unbleached cloth from other weavers before selling both types, bleached, to a cloth merchant. In practice, the merchant and the manufacturer were often one and the same person. Control over bleaching also implied control over the profits accruing from it. Even merchant manufacturers sometimes preferred to share costs among themselves, or with other groups, so great was the cost and risk involved. The Board of Trustees, or the landowner on whose land the field was to be sited, might contribute towards construction costs, but running costs had to be borne unaided.

The most famous company to establish a bleachfield was undoubtedly the British Linen Company, established in 1745 to trade in linen. The principal partners were two merchants, William Tod and Ebenezer McCulloch, and Lord Milton who, besides owning lands in Mid- and East Lothian, held the office of Lord Justice Clerk. Finding the best Scottish bleachfields already overworked and all fields too expensive, the company chose to start its own field on Lord Milton's Saltoun estate, East Lothian.[39] Other companies included Leys, Still & Co. (at Gordon's Mills (Aberdeen), established *pre*-1755), the Melrose Linen Company (at Melrose, established 1753) and J. MacWhirter & Co. (at Dumfries, established *pre*-1766). Arbroath bleachfield (Wallace, Gardine & Co.) was established in 1746 by three local merchants, and Bervie (R. Ochterlony & Co.) by manufacturers in Montrose, *c.* 1750.[40] Of the individual merchants who established bleachfields, the best known is William Sandeman, a Perth manufacturer, who invested £3,500 between 1752 and 1762 on establishing Luncarty field, Perthshire.[41]

In the woollen industry there was a similar investment in finishing. The Haddington Tarred Wool Company, already referred to in connection with Lord Milton, also included local clothiers. A waulk mill, to the best English design, was built for them in 1750 by Andrew Meikle.[42] At Camlachie, near Glasgow, a group of Glasgow merchants started a woollen manufactory with a similar waulk mill at about the same time.[43] By the 1770s the waulkers of the Borders, by assuming control of weaving and marketing, were taking on the status of merchant manufacturers. At Melrose, John Lyell, who had built his own waulk mill, was described as a merchant, manufacturer and clothier; at Yetholm, Andrew Kerr, farmer, manufacturer and clothier, had 'a good waulk mill and houses of his own property sufficient to carry on his work to a large extent' and in the village of Dryburgh, Alexander Hopkirk, 'a noted clothier', had 'a good waulk mill and well employed'.[44]

In contrast to their active role in finishing processes, merchants and manufacturers were seldom involved in the primary stages of manufacture, such as flax-scutching. Those who were, such as the Fochabers manufacturer who built the lint mill at Gollachie (Banffshire), tended to use imported flax.[45] Attempts by the Board of Trustees to create flax merchants in the form of 'lint boors' achieved little success.

During the third quarter of the eighteenth century water-power was extended to other processes. Plash mills, designed to wash linen yarn prior to weaving, appeared in the east of Scotland but remained uncommon until the mechanisation of spinning.[46] Thread-twisting by water-power was adopted at a few sites in both east and west, including Dalquhurn, Dunbartonshire, a former bleachfield, where eight thread mills were installed by 1765.[47] Other mills beat the dry thread to give a smooth, shiny finish. All three types of mill attracted attention from merchants and manufacturers.

In the 1780s and 1790s, water-powered spinning mills for cotton, flax and wool gave merchants and manufacturers an opportunity to centralise yarn-spinning, which had formerly been carried out domestically or in small work-shops. Furthermore, this capital-intensive form of production offered better profits than manual spinning. There is a significant amount of evidence to suggest that merchants and manufacturers who were already manufacturing, finishing or marketing textiles extended their interests into mill-spinning once the necessary technology became available. Besides controlling the physical infrastructure of the industry, these merchants and manufacturers had access to the capital or credit required to establish a spinning mill.

Robert Dunmore of Ballindalloch, who established a cotton mill on his Stirlingshire estate, already had a printfield there and a cotton-importing busi-ness. By taking in James and Archibald Buchanan as partners, he was able to exploit their knowledge of both cotton manufacture and the textile industry in general: the Buchanans had imported and distributed yarn from England and had set up the Adelphi cotton works at Deanston (Perthshire) in 1785. Dunmore also had connections with cotton mills at Spinningdale (Sutherland), and Duntocher (Dunbartonshire).[48] New Lanark, the largest mill complex in Scotland, was founded in 1785 by a manufacturer in the linen trade, David Dale, in association with Richard Arkwright. Dale was also involved with cotton mills at Blantyre, Catrine and Newton Stewart.[49] Gordon, Barron & Co., the mercantile partnership which built Woodside cotton mill (Aberdeen) in 1785, had already ventured into textile-finishing by establishing a bleachfield and printfield at Woodside some years beforehand.

A similar involvement was to be found in flax-spinning. Scottish-grown flax had never eliminated the need for imports; those merchants who already controlled flax imports, or manufacturers controlling hand-spinning or weaving, could profit further by building mills and thereby assuming or tightening control over spinning. As with cotton, economies of scale and savings on labour made mill-spinning more profitable than manual. Baxters, who founded the Glamis (Angus) mill in 1806, and Archibald Neilson, who co-founded the Kirkland (Fife) mill c. 1790,[50] were already established as linen merchants, while Mark Stark already ran bleachfields in the near vicinity.[51] The majority of bleach-fields established during the 1790s and the early nineteenth century were, like that at Grandholm, associated with spinning mills.

In the woollen industry, a substantial proportion of carding mills and the majority of spinning mills were built by clothiers and waulker-manufacturers. In 1791, John Archibald, manufacturer at Tullibody, and John Wilson at Alloa petitioned the Board of Trustees for assistance in buying scribbling and carding machinery. Although Archibald did not take up the Board's offered grant, he submitted a second petition with his brother, William, in 1799, claiming to have built a waulk mill and asking assistance to install preparing and carding machinery.

This may well have been the mill which John, William and a third brother, Robert, established at Menstrie *c*. 1800.[52] These three, with their descendants, went on to found or enlarge five other Clackmannanshire mills: Craigfoot and Midtown in Tillicoultry, Strude in Alva and two mills at Keillarsbrae, Alloa.[53]

In the Borders, small waulker-manufacturers, renting mills individually or collectively, gradually assumed the role of large-scale spinning mill-owners. In the Nether, Mid and Upper waulk mills of Galashiels, preparing and carding machinery was installed in 1805, 1794 and 1802 respectively. At each of these, and at a fourth mill, Weirhaugh, founded in 1797, four waulker-manufacturers shared the costs. Two other mills, Wilderhaugh Burn and Ladhope, founded in 1793 and 1786 respectively, were the work of individuals and, in the case of the latter mill, used an existing waulk mill. A further five mills were built in Galashiels by this first group of mill-spinners and their descendants.[54]

The Role of Tenants and Artisans

The third group of mill-builders comprised farm and mill tenants and those employed in various trades; of these latter some, such as weavers, flax-hecklers and small-scale waulk-millers, were already employed in the textile industry, but a few others, such as masons, joiners and millwrights, became involved through their construction skills. Neither tenants nor artisans had very great assets or access to credit. Unlike the landowners, they had no command of labour, land or water-power and, unlike the merchant manufacturer, they had little knowledge of trade or control over other stages in marketing or production. Given these restraints, tenants and artisans concentrated on small-scale mills, closely related to rural pursuits such as farming and hand-loom weaving.

Types of Mill Built by Tenants and Artisans

From the 1760s onwards, tenants were building lint mills in Perthshire, Angus and Lanarkshire, where flax cultivation was already well established, while in Aberdeenshire flax-hecklers figured prominently. The late eighteenth century saw an extension of their activities over a much wider area, and the participation of masons, joiners and millwrights; only in areas marginal to flax cultivation was the initiative still confined to landowners. Between 1800 and 1830 most of the new lint mills were built by tenants and artisans in areas where flax cultivation had sufficient impetus to continue into the nineteenth century, and where mill-spinning had failed to take root.

Besides the waulker-manufacturer, many small-scale waulkers, with little control over other processes, took to building waulk and carding mills during the early nineteenth century. Dyers built waulk mills at Dalry (Ayrshire), near Dumfries and at Killin (Perthshire). Carding machinery was added to waulk mills at Plaidy (Aberdeenshire), and Moulin (Perthshire), and to corn mills at Newmil of Arnbeg (Stirlingshire), and Dunphail (Nairn).[55] Occasionally disused lint mills were refitted as waulk or carding mills.[56]

In the few cases where tenants and artisans took on larger ventures they generally failed. In 1821, at the age of 21, James Smith, son of a millwright and a weaver by trade, built a flax-spinning mill near Dundee. Unable to pay the building contractors, Smith was forced into bankruptcy only a year after construction had commenced.[57] David Grimond, whose family had operated a lint mill near Blairgowrie, had more success. He built his first four-framed flax-spinning mill on the site of the lint mill in 1814 and later established a second mill adjacent to it.[58] During the 1790s a group of Kirkcudbrightshire farmers planned to build a cotton mill, but it is doubtful whether it ever came to fruition.[59] Generally speaking, textile trade workers had to be content with working for, or holding a minor share in, these larger ventures. Both tenants and artisans were at the mercy of landowners when it came to obtaining leases of land and water-power. Occasionally tenants and artisans built mills near to, and dependent on, other well established textile mills. In Perthshire, farmers and millers established farina mills to supply starch to bleachfields. In Stirlingshire and the Vale of Leven small mills prepared dyestuffs for printfields, while in Angus a few of the plash mills serving spinning mills were independently owned.

The Board of Trustees for Manufactures

From its inception in 1727 until the 1830s, the Board of Trustees played a secondary, but by no means passive, role in the development of textile mills. Its contribution took four forms: control of standards, technical research, industrial training and construction grants.

Undoubtedly the linen industry benefited from the quality controls instigated by the Board. By locating stamp masters throughout Scotland they ensured that only cloth of a certain quality could be marketed, thus enhancing the sales and reputation of Scottish linen. At the opposite end of production, they confiscated, or sent to oil mills, any flax seed found unsuitable for propagation.[60]

In the technical field the Board not only gave awards for improvements in machinery, but also instigated and applied its own research. The research into, and the construction of, the first lint mill were largely their work.[61] On the same site at Bonnington, near Edinburgh, the Board later financed the construction of experimental plash and thread mills.[62] Occasionally Andrew or Robert Meikle was employed to assess the usefulness of new machines or to provide on-site technical assistance; on one occasion they themselves received a premium for bleaching machinery.[63]

Associated with technical research was the diffusion of skills. Instruction in flax-dressing was provided at Hospital Mill, Fife, where the Board paid wages to both instructor and trainees; once qualified, ex-trainees were paid salaries to cover their expenses in establishing and running lint mills.[64] The 'art of bleaching' was taught at the British Linen Company's Saltoun field, East Lothian. The Board paid an annual fee to the company and a wage to each of the apprentices during the rigorous three-year training. On completion of their training, the latter received a £50 premium towards the cost of establishing, or becoming a partner in, a bleachfield.[65] In later years, the Board paid experienced millwrights, bleachers and flax-dressers to take apprentices of its own choosing.[66]

The Board's most valuable contribution was of the fourth type, financial aid. Sums ranging from £10 to £2,000 were paid out to cover the cost of buildings, site work and machinery, initially only on lint mills and bleachfields, later on waulk mills, plash mills and thread mills, and eventually on wool-carding and spinning mills. Although the sums involved were generally small, they could be crucial to the smaller mills, especially if they helped to attract additional financial aid from landowners. Few mills gained more than one or two premiums. As a matter of policy the Board favoured small, dispersed mills using Scottish raw materials; in the case of flax and cotton mills, both large-scale units dependent upon imports, assistance was limited respectively to the earliest mills or not given at all.

Distribution and Chronology

Before going on to consider individual types of mill, something should be said of the general factors affecting distribution. The most obvious consideration was the provision of running water in sufficient volume, and with a large enough fall, to power a mill. For the smaller mill this requirement was only a minor constraint on distribution, as sufficiently large streams could be found over much of Scotland, but the heavier demands of large mills tended to confine them to the middle reaches of rivers, above the flood plain and below upland reaches. Related to the provision of water-power was the need for clear water in bleaching and printing. The availability of raw materials could also influence distributions. Home-grown wool or flax attracted mills to sources or to marketing centres, although, conversely, the provision of mills might encourage sheep husbandry or flax cultivation in areas where little had existed before. Mills depending on imported raw materials tended to gravitate towards ports of entry, though this tendency was tempered by the need for water-power; thus Greenock, an obvious port of entry, failed to participate in the development of cotton mills until an artificial water-course was created, while Dundee, well placed for importing flax, had to await the perfection of steam-power to drive its flax-spinning mills. Those mills which utilised raw materials which were already partly manufactured, notably bleachfield and printfield mills, favoured areas in which the textile industry was already well established. Similarly, the presence of suitable skills in, say, fine linen-weaving attracted cotton-spinning mills, as was certainly the case in west central Scotland. The influence of markets on mill distribution is difficult to assess in that goods may have been destined for the immediate area, elsewhere in Scotland, England, the Continent or the North American colonies. The early development of the linen trade in the Edinburgh area reflects its favourable location in relation to Scottish, English and European markets while the later success of west central Scotland may have owed something to its accessibility to colonial markets. Improvements in internal communications (still a little-researched subject) could have, at the same time, encouraged dispersal and nucleation through providing better access to markets: rural manufacturing areas might have become more viable through cheaper, quicker transport media, but the same media could have, for example, extended the range over which an already well sited and therefore successful bleachfield could take in and return cloth.

Finally, distribution was influenced by the presence or absence of the initiative to build a mill. From the geographer's point of view it is all too easy to ignore or play down the importance of individual or collective decision-making, especially as it is unquantifiable, often irrational and not always conducive to the creation of a clear spatial pattern. Nevertheless, the presence of mercantile interests or the attitude of a particular landowner was quite as potent as any other factor in determining the distribution of water-powered textile mills. Thus the enthusiasm of merchants or landowners could lead to the development of mills in areas poor in water-power and distant from raw materials, markets and established skills, while the outright opposition of landowners or a dearth of mercantile initiative could prevent mills from establishing in areas otherwise well endowed.

Lint Mills

From their introduction in 1728, lint mills were slow to develop until the 1760s, when building accelerated; by 1772 nearly 350 had been built, although only 246 of these were still operating.[67] Between 1780 and 1794 there was a 50 per cent increase in the cumulative total of mills, from 364 to 538. Prior to the 1790s their range had steadily widened: at an early stage they had become well established in central and eastern districts, and had extended into the south-west, the north-east and the central Highlands during the last quarter of the century.

After the 1790s mill-building eased off until, by 1825, it had all but ceased; contemporary evidence suggests that a contraction in range and a decline in total numbers working also took place.[68] Most of the surviving mills were on marginal lands in Highland Perthshire, the Kirkintilloch-Bathgate area, north Ayrshire and Galloway.

In all, more than 700 lint mills were built between 1728 and 1830, covering the whole of Scotland except the north and west Highlands and Islands, with the strongest concentration in a belt running from Ayrshire to Kincardineshire[69] (Figure 13.1).

Bleachfields

In Scotland, both the Dutch and Irish methods of bleaching were introduced

Figure 13.1: Lint Mills in Scotland, 1730-1830

c. 1730, but only the latter employed water-power. Of the 100 or so fields established between 1730 and 1765, perhaps three-quarters were water-powered; by the 1760s only a few fields still used the Dutch method exclusively, and almost all of the further 100 established between 1765 and 1790 used the Irish method. While most of the early fields had been in central Scotland, those built after 1765 had a much wider distribution, with significant numbers in the north-east, the south-west and as far afield as Shetland.

After 1790 bleachfields suffered a decline in numbers and a contraction in range. The 50 or so fields established between 1790 and 1830, with those surviving from earlier periods, concentrated on bleaching yarn from water-, and latterly steam-powered mills; hence the strong nucleation in west central Scotland, notably on the Cart and Levern, and in eastern Scotland, on the Dighty, the

Leven and in the Perth area. As technical progress was slow, and water was still required for other purposes, steam-power was not usually applied until a later date. In all, about 200 water-powered bleachfields were laid out between 1730 and 1830.

Plash, Yarn Beating and Thread Mills

Plash mills, for washing linen yarn, first appeared in Angus during the 1740s, although the majority post-dated the mechanisation of flax spinning, c. 1790. The heaviest concentration was on the Dighty, a river with only one plash mill in 1760, but seventeen by 1790;[70] its overall range coincided with that of flax-spinning mills. Available evidence suggests a total of about 50 mills.

From their introduction in the 1750s, beating mills, which gave yarn or thread a smooth finish, never became very common. Perhaps twenty or so mills were built, almost all of them in eastern Scotland.

Although a great many thread mills were in use in the Paisley area during the late eighteenth century, most were driven by hand. Authenticated water-powered sites, mostly in eastern, north-eastern and west central Scotland, total about twenty.[71]

Figure 13.2: Water-powered Carding and Spinning Mills in Central Scotland, 1778-1830

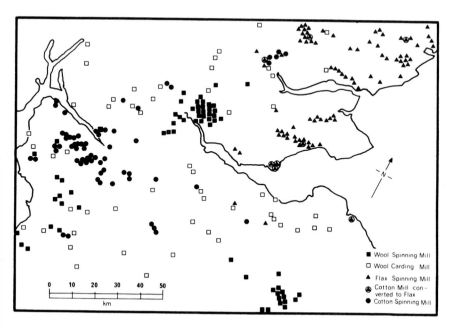

■ Wool Spinning Mill
□ Wool Carding Mill
▲ Flax Spinning Mill
⊛ Cotton Mill con-
verted to Flax
● Cotton Spinning Mill

Flax Spinning Mills

From the establishment of the first mill in 1787, flax-spinning by water-power was concentrated in east central Scotland (Figure 13.2). Most of the flax was imported from the Baltic ports and therefore favoured sites accessible from east coast ports, which had well established trading links and existing manufacturing interests. Furthermore, the Kendrew and Porthouse machine, on which flax was dry-spun, was best adapted to the coarse yarn produced in eastern Scotland. Indeed, mill-spinning of linen yarn was not perfected until the introduction of wet spinning in the 1820s.[72] In the west of Scotland, cotton-spinning had already taken over from linen.

Of the 100 or more mills traced, about 45 were built before 1800, several of them in small buildings with as few as one spinning frame.[73] Many of these suffered an early demise as the difficulties of dry spinning became apparent. Although the majority were situated in Fife, Angus and eastern Perthshire, a few were built as far south as the Lothians and as far north as Aberdeen.

Between 1800 and 1820 enthusiasm waned, with only half as many mills built as had been between 1787 and 1800. Competition from steam was limited: in 1819 there were still only six steam-powered mills in Dundee.[74]

The introduction of wet spinning in the 1820s brought a revival in interest, with 40 or so additional mills built during that decade. While the concentration of mills in Dundee, Arbroath and Kirkcaldy favoured steam, water-mills with good access to ports and adequate water-power found a new lease of life. On the Ericht in Perthshire, the Leven and Eden in Fife and the Esk in Angus, new water-powered mills were built and existing ones extended. On the other hand, many of the spinning mills which had been established on the Dighty were converted to wash yarn for the steam-powered mills of Dundee. As late as 1838 flax-spinning mills still derived 30 per cent of their power from water.[75]

Waulk Mills

Although more than 300 waulk mills had been built throughout Scotland by 1730, it is doubtful whether, in the depressed conditions of the early eighteenth century, more than two-thirds of that number were still operating. From mid-century, however, mill-building recommenced, notably in the southern central Lowlands and the Borders. By the 1770s numbers may well have reached 300 again. Building gained further impetus in the late eighteenth and early nineteenth centuries from the mechanisation of carding and spinning, machinery for all three often occupying the same building. During this period the distribution of waulk mills, while covering most of Scotland, favoured areas such as the Borders, Galloway, Ayrshire, Clackmannanshire, the north-east, Strathtay and Strathspey, where neither cotton nor flax mills had taken root (Figure 13.3). Including those installed in integrated mills, about 500 waulk mills were in use between 1730 and 1830.

Figure 13.3: Woollen Mills in Scotland 1730-1830

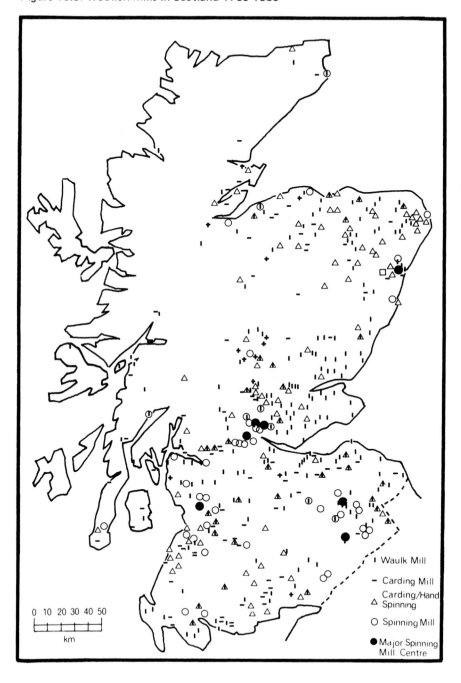

Waulk Mill

- Carding Mill

△ Carding/Hand Spinning

O Spinning Mill

● Major Spinning Mill Centre

0 10 20 30 40 50

km

Carding Mills

From its introduction to Scotland in the 1780s, the carding machine became well established in traditional, well organised wool manufacturing areas such as the Borders, Aberdeenshire, Clackmannanshire and Ayrshire (Figure 13.2). By the 1830s, however, the revival of the woollen industry and the extension of sheep-farming over most upland areas had helped widen its range to cover almost every marginal area from Lewis to Galloway. Although carding mills performed one of the most arduous processes in wool manufacture, they still allowed, or even encouraged, spinning to be performed on the more labour-intensive spinning wheel or jenny. This factor, the small scale of production, and relatively low construction costs favoured their development in areas where landowners and tenants or artisans were still active, although carding machinery was also installed in spinning mills. Broadly speaking, the distribution of carding mills was similar to that of the waulk mill, though with only about 250 sites, its density was much less (Figure 13.3).

Wool Spinning Mills

Water-powered spinning reached Scotland in the early 1810s. The Borders took an early lead which they still held at the end of the period: Galashiels had ten mills in 1830 and Hawick eight in 1825.[76] Second only to the Borders was Clackmannanshire, where Alva and Tillicoultry were the main centres. Elsewhere, in Aberdeenshire, Galloway, Ayrshire and west Perthshire, spinning mills were common, though not so numerous nor so nucleated. Outwith these areas lay a scattering of mills, some only short-lived or using hand-operated jennies and thereby more correctly regarded as carding mills. Broadly speaking, spinning mills flourished most in those areas where clothiers and waulker-manufacturers were already well established (Figures 13.2, 13.3).

Competition from steam was less marked than in linen- or cotton-spinning mills, and water-powered mills were still being built in the 1850s.[77] In 1838 Scottish wool-spinning mills still derived about 70 per cent of their power from water.[78] Most mills had been established on rivers with large upland catchment areas and little competition from other users; many of them had only poor access to coal. Furthermore, the local availability of raw materials and skilled labour militated against a move to urban centres. In all, about 100 water-powered wool-spinning mills were built.

Cotton Spinning Mills

The first Scottish cotton mill was built in 1778 at Penicuik, Midlothian.[79] By the mid-1790s the enthusiasm for cotton had produced a rash of mills over much of Scotland, including Galloway, the Perth area (Plate 23) and the east coast counties as far north as Sutherland. However, it was on the Glasgow area, with its established fine weaving industry, its accessibility to imported raw materials and its existing mercantile and manufacturing interests, that the industry had become centred (Figure 13.2).

From an early date the outlying mills began to close down: in the east, Brechin and Kirkland mills took to flax-spinning, while in Dumfries and Galloway a few became woollen mills. Near to Glasgow, mills with adequate water-power survived beyond the early nineteenth century, as did a few exceptionally well endowed mills, notably Woodside in Aberdeenshire, Stanley and Deanston in Perthshire and Catrine in Ayrshire, outwith the area.

Steam-power, first applied to cotton-spinning in the 1790s, accentuated the nucleation of the industry in Glasgow and Paisley. Nevertheless, water-power continued to play an important role, with new water-mills still being built, and existing ones refitted, in Renfrewshire during the 1820s, using mules in place of the less efficient water frame. In 1838 cotton-spinning mills still derived about 30 per cent of their power from water.[80] The total number of mills built was slightly in excess of 100.

Printfields

Textile printing, usually on cotton, became water-powered with the introduction of copper rollers in the 1790s,[81] though for some time thereafter flat plates, operated manually, continued to be used at certain fields. With few exceptions, such as Linlithgow and Keir, printfields were situated in the Glasgow area, notably on the Glazert and Leven, both of which had good falls of clear water. In all there were probably no more than 25 water-powered printfields in Scotland.

Mordant and Dyestuff Mills

Dyestuff mills, while not actually manufacturing textiles, were closely related to the industry, both functionally and spatially. In all, about 25 mills were employed for these purposes. A wide variety of dyes was produced, using logwood, cudbear, madder and indigo mostly. Alum, an important mordant, was crushed by water power at Hurlet in Renfrewshire and at Lennoxtown in Stirlingshire.

Weaving Mills

According to tradition, the first power-looms were introduced to Scotland at Milntown printfield, Dunbartonshire, in the early 1800s,[82] although several earlier attempts had been made with mixed success. By 1814 some 1,500 were operating in the cotton industry, and the machinery had been adapted for use with linen and wool.[83] For various reasons, the majority of power-loom factories were steam-powered: by the early nineteenth century most water-powered spinning mills were using the available power to its full potential, leaving little to spare for weaving; steam-power had become a viable alternative and the move to urban centres was already well under way. Despite this, some water-powered looms were installed at Scottish mills, although they were outnumbered by steam-powered looms and, in 1830, hand-looms still outnumbered all power-looms. In all, about 50 water-powered mills had power looms by 1830.

Altogether approximately 2,000 water-powered textile mills operated in Scotland between 1730 and 1830, over an area from Shetland and Lewis in the north to Berwickshire and Galloway in the south.[84]

Impact on the Economy and Landscape of Rural Scotland

In the period 1730-1830 the application of water-power to the textile industry was on such a scale as to make a significant contribution to the making of the Scottish countryside. Broadly speaking, this contribution falls into two categories: the indirect impact on employment, living standards and agriculture, and the direct impact in terms of industrialisation, urbanisation and the physical fabric of the built environment.

Indirect Impact

At a time of extensive reorganisation in agriculture, and prior to the development of urban-based industry, the employment generated by textile mills provided a safety net which prevented emigration from assuming a scale even greater than it did. In addition to the employment generated by the mills themselves, the gradual mechanisation of the textile industry, by increasing output, enhanced employment potential in those processes which were still performed manually. In the long term, however, technical progress reduced total employment and restricted the spatial extent of the industry, though not to the same degree as steam-power was later to do. Bleachfields, lint mills and waulk mills helped to introduce the textile industry to new areas, but spinning and, later, weaving mills performed processes which were already well established and which generated more employment over a wider area when performed by hand.

The improvements which textile mills brought to living standards were important in stimulating demand in other sectors of the economy. Some types of mill, notably bleachfields and lint mills, could provide seasonal work; while by offering ample scope for child labour, spinning mills encouraged population growth. On the other hand, spinning mills and weaving mills seriously damaged the living standards of those manual workers whom they replaced.

The impact on agriculture was also double-edged. On the one hand, the need to feed textile workers and provide raw materials in the form of wool and flax stimulated agriculture and helped integrate it into the money economy. One could even argue that without this market, 'improved' agriculture might have failed, or at least been delayed. On the other hand, competition for labour forced up farm wages, though this also had the effect of encouraging a more efficient, capital-intensive farming, employing machinery such as the threshing mill and the improved plough.

Direct Impact

The more direct impact of textile mills on the landscape is still apparent today

(Plate 23). While many of the mills were abandoned long ago, some were later applied to other purposes and a few continued to be in use for their original purpose. Less transient are the houses or entire communities once occupied by, or otherwise relating to, textile mill-workers.

In some cases the arrival of textile mills contributed to the success of newly established planned villages. Renton, Dunbartonshire, established by Mrs Smollet of Bonhill, became an extensive village housing printfield workers. Houston, Johnstone and Newton Ralston, all established in Renfrewshire in the 1780s, benefited from the influx of cotton mill-workers, as did Newton Stewart and Gatehouse of Fleet in Kirkcudbrightshire. Grantown in Inverness-shire, New Pitsligo in Aberdeenshire and Ormiston in East Lothian all derived support from the presence of bleachfields, while numerous other communities, such as Monymusk, Aberdeenshire, gained from the presence of lint mills. George Dempster's village of Letham, Angus, had at various times a lint mill, plash mills, a thread mill and two spinning mills. Woollen mills gave a boost to planned villages such as Brydekirk and New Langholm in Dumfries-shire, Kingussie in Inverness-shire and Inveraray in Argyll. At Penicuik, Midlothian, a new suburb, Kirkhill, was appended to the existing planned village to house cotton mill-workers.

Long-established communities also benefited. Innerleithen, Peebles-shire, had been a 'tiny sequestered hamlet, comprising only a few thatched houses, a mill and a church'.[85] Woollen mills turned it into a prosperous manufacturing village. At Rattray, Perthshire, a new village was laid out between the old one and the River Ericht.

A third group of communities owed not only its growth but its very existence to water-powered textile mills. From the cotton industry one might cite the examples of New Lanark, Catrine, Deanston, Fintry and Stanley. The best example in the woollen industry is probably Walkerburn and in the linen industry Douglastown. In addition there were, and still are, numerous groups of workers' houses which have long outlived the textile mills for which they were built, while in districts near to former cotton- or flax-spinning mills, such as south-west Stirlingshire, Renfrewshire, Fife and Angus, one can still find numerous houses once occupied by weavers working on mill-spun yarn.

Conclusion

Of all the rural industries which grew up in Scotland between 1730 and 1830, textiles were by far the most successful. More sites were occupied, a wider area benefited and a greater contribution was made to the economy and to the landscape of Scotland through textiles than through any other industry except agriculture. Without adopting a technological determinist stance, it is clear that this pre-eminence was achieved through the harnessing of water-power to almost every stage in textile manufacture over an area which extended from Shetland

and Lewis in the north to Berwickshire and Galloway in the south. Within that area all but the most sparsely populated districts participated in this process of mechanisation.

The establishment of any rural industry was in the improving landowner's interest. Why, then, did textiles achieve such pre-eminence? The answer probably lies in the community of interests which existed not only within the landowning class but also between landowners, farmers, artisans, merchants, manufacturers and the state. The landowner's interest lay in the incentive which it gave to agricultural improvement, in the broader economic base which it gave to his estate, and in the enhanced estate value which accrued directly or indirectly from the presence of the textile industry. From the farmer's point of view it offered a local market for produce at a time when yields were rising and rents were being paid in cash rather than in kind. For workers already engaged in textile manufacture it provided employment, as it did also for millwrights, masons and joiners once the industry was put on to a water-powered footing. The state had, in the Board of Trustees, an agency whose prime function was the development of the textile industry; among its trustees were some of the best known Improvers of the age. For the most part, merchants and manu-facturers stood to gain through the exploitation of developing home and overseas markets, through income from textile manufacture and from the sale of imports purchased or bargained for with the help of exported textile products.

Equally important to the inclination to develop the rural textile industry was having the means to do so; here again the complementary roles of a wide range of interests contributed to the success of the industry. Landowners could provide sites endowed with almost inexhaustible, if not always steady, supplies of energy in the form of water-power, and sometimes the necessary buildings on these sites. Farmers could provide raw materials in the form of flax or wool, artisans could build the mills and textile trade workers could contribute estab-lished or newly acquired skills. Small-scale tenants, cottars and labourers, dis-placed from the land by Improvements, provided a pool of labour which could be drawn upon for unskilled or semi-skilled work. The Board of Trustees im-proved standards, technology and skills and gave grants towards the construction and renovation of mills. Lastly, merchants and manufacturers provided marketing facilities, commercial knowledge and capital, especially for larger projects.

While diverse interests and means converged on the same aim — the develop-ment of the textile industry — they did not necessarily act in concert, nor did they always exert the same level of influence. From 1730 until about 1760 landowners and, to a lesser extent, the Board of Trustees were the most im-portant agents in the development of the industry. Distributions of textile mills tended to reflect the attitudes of landowners and the preferences of the Board of Trustees for certain areas. Between 1760 and 1790, while the landowner continued to exert the greatest influence in more marginal areas, his role within established manufacturing areas began to pass to tenants and artisans in the case of mills requiring a small capital outlay and to merchants and manufacturers where a more substantial investment was required. From the late eighteenth century to the 1830s the development of machinery for carding and spinning brought a slight revival in landowner interest, but by far the greatest influence now lay with merchants and manufacturers, who were better placed to exploit the new technology than any other group. Eventually even the Board of Trustees had to acknowledge their ascendancy.

These changes in relative status had important repercussions. Whereas the landowner had been interested primarily in the enhancement of his estate, the motivation of the merchant or manufacturer was the achievement of maximum production and profitability; the locations chosen for textile mills came to be not so much those best suited to a particular estate but rather those which offered the lowest production costs. While the landowner was predisposed to build mills which processed local produce, the merchant or manufacturer concentrated on whatever commodity promised to give the best return. Thus, when a fashion grew for cotton, rather than linen cloth, the merchant manufacturer found it quite natural to move from a partially home-grown raw material to one which was wholly imported, and as distance from raw materials only increased costs, mills began to concentrate near ports: Glasgow for cotton and Dundee for flax.

In contrast to the landowner, the merchant manufacturer sought to minimise labour intensity, reducing costs wherever possible by substituting machinery for workers. The application of machinery to spinning, and eventually to weaving, was therefore an obvious move and one which, from the manufacturer's point of view, had the additional attraction of centralising production and thereby offering economies of scale. On the other hand, it brought about a rapid decline in hand-spinning, once a major source of rural employment, and while increased output from spinning mills brought unprecedented prosperity to weavers, this only attracted more and more people to the trade so that by the late 1830s a glut of labour, aggravated by the beginnings of mechanisation, enabled manufacturers to cut the wages of hand-loom weavers, reducing many of them to a state of desperate poverty.

The new types of mill developed by merchants and manufacturers also brought a change in the nature of employment. Lint mills, bleachfields and even wool-carding mills were seldom used to capacity, and being seasonal in their operation were still compatible with agriculture. On the other hand, the need to maximise productivity led manufacturers to work spinning mills day and night, all the year round, at least when the market demanded it. This emphasis on output, with ever-larger units of production and an ever-widening range of machinery, led to increased power requirements. Many streams suited to small-scale or seasonal production proved totally inadequate for the larger mills, while some larger rivers with variable flow could not maintain a consistently high horse-power potential. The unsuitability of so many streams was further aggravated by the work of improving landowners in draining lochs, marshes and upland catchment areas, thereby increasing the speed of run-off.

Meanwhile the steam-engine was emerging as a viable alternative to the water-wheel, and despite the high cost of transporting coal, several rural mills were given auxiliary steam-power.

By the 1820s conditions were right for a move to urban locations. The textile industry was controlled by merchant manufacturers with no vested interests in maintaining rural employment; energy requirements were growing beyond the capabilities of most streams; and improvements in communications and technology were reducing the cost of steam-power. Thus urban centres which had access to raw materials by sea, to coal by canal or sea also, which had good access to markets, and which could house a highly centralised labour force began to develop and during the 1820s the urban textile industry grew at a remarkable rate. The water-powered textile industry was essentially rural and dispersed. The steam-powered industry was centralised and urban; the decline of the rural industry was inevitable.

Notes

1. Sinclair, J. (ed.) (1791-9), *The statistical account of Scotland*, 21 vols. (Edinburgh) (hereafter *OSA*); (1845) *New statistical account of Scotland*, 15 vols. (Edinburgh) (hereafter *NSA*)

2. Loch, D. (1778), *A tour through most of the trading towns and villages of Scotland* (Edinburgh); for a complete list of Agricultural Reports see Symon, J. A. (1959), *Scottish farming past and present* (Edinburgh)

3. *Scottish Record Office* (hereafter SRO), NG1/1/1-32; NG1/19/1

4. SRO, GD series

5. SRO, E 700 series; records of the Forfeited Estates Commission; SRO, CS 96, Sequestrations

6. *National Library of Scotland* (hereafter NLS), Acc. series, NLS, MSS. series

7. Gulvin, C. (1973), *The tweedmakers* (Newton Abbot)

8. McClain, N. E. (1970), 'Scottish lint mills, 1729-70', *Textile History I*; Durie, A. J. (1973), 'The Scottish linen industry, 1707-1775, with particular reference to the early history of the British Linen Company' (unpublished PhD thesis, University of Edinburgh); Gauldie, E. E. (1966), 'Scottish bleachfields, 1718-1862' (unpublished BPhil thesis, University of St Andrews)

9. Butt, J. (1967), *The industrial archaeology of Scotland* (Newton Abbot); *idem* (1966), 'The industrial archaeology of Gatehouse of Fleet', *Industrial Archaeology*, 127-37; Donnachie, I. L. (1971), *The industrial archaeology of Galloway* (Newton Abbot); Hume, J. R. (1976-7), *The industrial archaeology of Scotland*, 2 vols. (London)

10. Hall, R. (1898), *The history of Galashiels* (Galashiels), pp. 390-407; Buchan, J. W. (1925), *The history of Peebles-shire*, 3 vols. (Glasgow) pp. 217-24; Gibson, W. (1883), *Reminiscences of Dollar, Tillicoultry and other districts adjoining the Ochils* (Edinburgh), pp. 171-91; Cameron, J. (1892), *Parish of Campsie* (Kirkintilloch), pp. 6-33, 47-51; Morgan, P. (1886), *Annals of Woodside and Newhills* (Aberdeen), pp. 19-35, 57-75; Macdonald, J. A. R. (1899), *History of Blairgowrie* (Blairgowrie), pp. 167-71

11. Jespersen, A. (1963-4), 'Watermills on the River Eden', *Proceedings of the Society of Antiquaries of Scotland*, *47*, 237-44. A much more detailed version is kept at the Country Life section of the National Museum of Antiquities, Edinburgh

12. Warden, A. J. (1864), *The linen trade, ancient and modern* (London), *passim*

13. Turner, W. H. K. (1958), 'The significance of water power in industrial location: some Perthshire examples', *Scottish Geographical Magazine*, *74*, 98-115 (hereafter *SGM*); *idem* (1957), 'The textile industry of Perth and district', *Trans. of Inst. Br.*

Geogr., *23*, 123-40; *idem* (1953), 'Some eighteenth century developments in the textile region of east central Scotland', *SGM, 69*, 10-21

14. Fulling mills are referred to in Scotland as tuke mills, wash mills and, most commonly, waulk mills

15. Robinson, E. and Musson, A. E. (1969), *James Watt and the steam engine* (London), pp. 89-95; Lord, J. (1966), *Capital and steam power, 1750-1800* (London), pp. 172-3, Table IV; Hills, R. L. (1970), *Power in the industrial revolution* (Manchester), p. 159, Table 8

16. *NSA*, Vol. 10, Collace, Perthshire, pp. 215-16

17. Devine, T. M. (1972), 'Glasgow merchants and colonial trade, 1770-1815' (unpublished PhD thesis, 2 vols., University of Strathclyde), pp. 375-8

18. NLS, Acc. 2933, Box 354, contract of co-partnery, Tarred Wool Co., 1750; Durie, 'Scottish linen industry', p. 204

19. SRO, NG1/1/19, 22 January 1772; Petition, gentlemen of Zetland

20. Devine (1972), 'Glasgow merchants', pp. 380-3

21. Robertson, J. (1808), *General view of the agriculture of Inverness-shire* (London), p. 314

22. *Caledonian Mercury*, 28 February 1793

23. Gauldie (1966), 'Scottish bleachfields', pp. 250-3

24. Wilson, R. (1825), *The history of Hawick* (Hawick), p. 287

25. *NSA*, Vol. 11, Mains & Strathmartine, Angus, p. 65

26. See Chapter 11

27. SRO, NG1/1/2, 17 January 1730, Hospital Mill, lint mill funds; SRO, NG1/19/1, Grangehaugh Mill, lint mill survey, 1772; SRO, NG1/1/26, 23 July 1788, Haugh of Stainland, petition; Hamilton, H. (ed.) (1945), 'Monymusk papers, 1713-1775', *Publications of the Scottish History Society* (hereafter Pubs. SHS); SRO, NG1/1/22, 19 January 1780, Gogo Water mill, petition; SRO, NG1/1/20, 10 March 1773, Kilmartin, petition

28. Loch (1778), *Tour*, pp. 44, 42, 5

29. *OSA*, Vol. 11, Ednam, Roxburghshire, p. 303; Burleigh, J. (1912), *Ednam and its indwellers* (Glasgow), p. 198

30. Lindsay, I. G. and Cosh, M. (1973), *Inveraray and the Dukes of Argyll* (Edinburgh), pp. 273-5

31. Anonymous (1834), *Blair Adam*, 6 vols., Vol. 1, p. 96

32. Wight, A. (1781), *Present state of husbandry in Scotland*, 4th survey, p. 385

33. SRO, NG1/1/12, 10 August 1753, certificate of expenditure, Cullen bleachfield; *OSA*, Vol. 5, Pitsligo, Aberdeenshire, p. 96

34. Devine (1972), 'Glasgow merchants', p. 383

35. SRO, NG1/1/29, 8 June 1796, petition

36. Singer, W. (1812), *General view of the agriculture of the county of Dumfries* (Edinburgh), pp. 62-3

37. *OSA*, Vol. 19, Innerleithen, Peebles-shire, p. 598; Buchan (1925), *History of Peebles-shire*, Vol. 2, pp. 217-18

38. Gulvin (1973), *The tweedmakers*, pp. 11-37; Durie (1973), 'Scottish linen industry', p. 10

39. NLS, Acc. 2933/350. Minute of the proprietors of the British Linen Company, 7 September 1747

40. SRO, NG1/1/12, 17 January 1755, premium, Wallace, Gardyne & Co.; NG1/1/18, 1 February 1756, premium, Leys, Still & Co.; SRO, NG1/1/12, 7 December 1754, petition, Melrose Linen Co.; SRO, NG1/1/8, 19 December 1746, petition, Wallace, Gardyne and Gardner, merchants of Arbroath; SRO, NG1/1/10, 12 January 1750, petition R. Ouchterlany & Co.

41. SRO, NG1/1/11, 3 January 1752, petition; NLS, Acc. 2933/330, money expended on Luncarty bleachfield

42. NLS, Acc. 2933/354, Contract of co-partnery, 1750. SRO, NG1/1/10, 8 June 1750, petition; NG1/1/11, 3 January 1752, expenses etc. Tarred Wool Company

43. SRO, NG1/1/12, 13 December 1754, petition

44. Loch (1778), *Tour*, pp. 45, 48, 46

45. *OSA*, Vol. 13, Rathven, Banffshire, p. 425

46. NLS, Acc 2933/330, Proposals for encouraging the linen manufacture, 1760

47. SRO, E. 728/18/2, petition, 1765

48. Devine (1972), 'Glasgow merchants', Vol. 2, pp. 375-8

49. *OSA*, Vol. 15, Lanark, Lanarkshire, p. 34; *NSA*, Vol. 6, Blantyre, Lanarkshire, p. 322, *OSA*, Vol. 20, Sorn, Ayrshire, p. 176; *Caledonian Mercury*, 31 January 1793

50. Gauldie, E. E. (1969), *The Dundee textile industry 1790-1885* (Pubs. SHS), 4th series, *6*, xix-xx

51. Morgan (1886), *Annals*, p. 58; *OSA*, Vol. 13, Dunfermline, Fife, p. 433; SRO, NG1/1/18, 8 December 1767, Bleachfield premiums

52. SRO, NG1/1/28, 30 November 1791, petition; SRO, NG1/1/30, 11 December 1799, petition; Gibson (1883), *Reminiscences*, p. 177

53. Ibid., pp. 177-81

54. Hall, (1898), *History of Galashiels*, pp. 390-405

55. SRO, NG1/1/30, 5 June 1799, petition, Berryscar (Dumfriesshire); SRO, NG1/1/34. 15 June 1819, petition, Dalry (Ayrshire); SRO, NG1/1/31, 8 July 1808, petition, Killin (Perthshire); SRO, NG1/1/31, 6 July 1803, premiums; SRO, NG1/1/32, 10 July 1811, premium, Arnbeg (Stirlingshire); Dick-Lauder, T. (1830), *An account of the great floods of August 1829, in the province of Moray and adjoining districts* (Edinburgh), p. 73

56. See, for example, NG1/1/33, 5 July 1815, Lint mill of Islay

57. SRO, CS96/419, sequestration, Rose mill of Strathmartin (Angus)

58. SRO, NG1/1/31, 6 July 1803, premium, Lint mill of Lornty (Perthshire); Macdonald (1899), *History of Blairgowrie*, p. 168

59. Donnachie (1971), *Industrial archaeology of Galloway*, pp. 94-5

60. SRO, NG1/1/30, 23 November 1799, Minutes

61. SRO, NG1/1/1, 1 September 1727; 26 April 1728; 18 July 1728; SRO, NG1/1/2, 19 September 1729; 28 November 1729; 12 December 1729; 10 March 1730, Minutes *re* introduction of flax-breaking and scutching machinery

62. SRO, NG1/1/9, 18 January 1748, petition; NLS, Acc. 2933/330, 23 January 1759, Notes concerning the yarn mill at Bonny mills

63. SRO, NG1/1/10, 23 June 1749, work at Bonnington mills (Midlothian); SRO, NG1/1/12, 15 December 1753; 13 December 1754, Garvaldfoot manufactory; SRO, NG1/1/13, 4 November 1755, award

64. SRO, NG1/1/4, 3 December 1736, proposals for raising and heckling of lint

65. SRO, NG1/1/11, 23 November 1750, proposals for promoting and cheapening linen

66. SRO, NG1/1/16, 22 January 1762, Minutes: committee for new schemes and new regulations; SRO, NG1/1/18, 18 March 1765; SRO, NG1/1/25, 19 December 1785; SRO, NG1/1/26, 30 July 1788; SRO, NG1/1/28, 15 January 1794; SRO, NG1/1/32, 9 July 1806, Progress of apprenticeship schemes

67. SRO, NG1/19/1. One of the mills in the survey was enumerated twice. See also McClain, N. E. (1970), 'Scottish lint mills, 1729-70', *Textile History, I*

68. See, for example *NSA*, Vol. 2, Edrom, Berwickshire, p. 271; Vol. 9, Abdrie, Fife, p. 49; Vol. 11, Inverkeilor, Angus, p. 241; Vol. 12, Old Deer, Aberdeenshire, p. 158; Vol. 13, Boindie, Banffshire, p. 238

69. Almost all of the information on distribution, numbers and chronology is based on Shaw, J. P., 'The development of water power in the Scottish economy, 1550-1850' (unpublished PhD thesis (forthcoming), University of Edinburgh)

70. *OSA*, Vol. 5, Mains of Fintry, Angus, p. 218

71. Shaw (forthcoming), 'Development of water power'

72. Gauldie (1969), *Dundee textile industry*, pp. xxii-xxiii

73. See, for example, Newbiggin, Angus, *NSA*, Vol. 11, p. 407

74. Warden (1864), *The linen trade*, p. 592

75. Factory Returns, *Parliamentary Papers*, 1839, p. 42

76. Hall (1898), *History of Galashiels*, pp. 390-405; Wilson (1825), *The history of Hawick*, p. 267

77. Buchan (1925), *History of Peebles-shire*, Vol. 2, p. 220, Tweedholm mill, Walkerburn

78. Factory Returns, *Parliamentary Papers*, 1893, p. 42

79. SRO, NG1/1/22, 8 July, petition

80. Factory Returns, *Parliamentary Papers*, 1839, p. 42

81. Clow, A. and Clow, N. L. (1952), *The chemical revolution* (London), p. 227; *OSA*, Vol. 3, Bonhill, Dunbartonshire, p. 442

82. Sinclair, J. (1814), 'View of the present state of the cotton manufacture in Scotland', *Scots Magazine, 76*, 905

83. Ibid., 905-6

84. Shaw (forthcoming), 'Development of water power'

85. Wilson, J. M. (ed.) (n.d.), *The imperial gazetteer of Scotland*, 2 vols. (London, Edinburgh and Dublin)

NOTES ON CONTRIBUTORS

Ian H. Adams, MA, PhD	Lecturer in Geography, University of Edinburgh
James B. Caird, MA, DU	Professor of Geography, University of Dundee
Robert A. Dodgshon, BA, PhD	Lecturer in Geography, University of Aberystwyth
Alexander Fenton, MA	Keeper, National Museum of the Antiquities of Scotland, Edinburgh
James M. Lindsay, MA, PhD	Lecturer in Geography, Polytechnic of North London
Douglas G. Lockhart, MA, PhD	Lecturer in Geography, University of Keele
Loretta Timperley, MA, PhD	Formerly Research Officer, Scottish Record Office
Martin L. Parry, BA, MSc, PhD	Lecturer in Geography, University of Birmingham
John P. Shaw, MA	Assistant Keeper of Technology, Glasgow Museums and Art Galleries
Terence R. Slater, BA	Lecturer in Geography, University of Birmingham
Ian Whyte, MA, PhD	Lecturer in Geography, University of Lancaster
Graeme Whittington, BA, PhD	Senior Lecturer in Geography, University of St Andrews